BEYOND
ANNE FRANK

BEYOND
ANNE FRANK

HIDDEN CHILDREN AND POSTWAR FAMILIES IN HOLLAND

DIANE L. WOLF

UNIVERSITY OF CALIFORNIA PRESS   BERKELEY   LOS ANGELES   LONDON

University of California Press, one of the most distinguished university presses in the United States, enriches lives around the world by advancing scholarship in the humanities, social sciences, and natural sciences. Its activities are supported by the UC Press Foundation and by philanthropic contributions from individuals and institutions. For more information, visit www.ucpress.edu.

University of California Press
Berkeley and Los Angeles, California

University of California Press, Ltd.
London, England

Library of Congress Cataloging-in-Publication Data

Wolf, Diane L.
    Beyond Anne Frank : hidden children and postwar families in Holland / Diane L. Wolf.
        p.   cm.
    Includes bibliographical references and index.
    ISBN-13: 978-0-520-22617-3 (cloth : alk. paper)
    ISBN-10: 0-520-22617-8 (cloth : alk. paper)
    ISBN-13: 978-0-520-24810-6 (pbk. : alk. paper)
    ISBN-10: 0-520-24810-4 (pbk. : alk. paper)
    1. Jews—Persecutions—Netherlands.   2. Hidden children (Holocaust)—Netherlands.   3. Holocaust, Jewish (1939–1945)—Netherlands.   4. Holocaust survivors—Netherlands.   5. Netherlands—Ethnic relations.   I. Title.
    DS135.N4W58   2007
    940.53′1808209492—dc22

                                                      2006016446

Manufactured in the United States of America
15   14   13   12   11   10   09   08   07   06
10 9 8 7 6 5 4 3 2 1

This book is printed on New Leaf EcoBook 50, a 100% recycled fiber of which 50% is de-inked post-consumer waste, processed chlorine-free. EcoBook 50 is acid-free and meets the minimum requirements of ANSI/ASTM D5634–01 (*Permanence of Paper*).

For my parents
In beloved memory

Contents

Acknowledgments

My deepest debt is to the former hidden children I interviewed who welcomed me into their homes with warmth and hospitality and entrusted to me painful memories of their past. Each story is different and precious; I only hope that I have done them justice. Many former hidden children helped facilitate my research, for which I am thankful: Jeannette Ringold, Max Arpels-Lezer, Carla and Ed Lessing, Michele and Josef Bar Pereg, Mirjam and the late David Geismar, Rozette Kats, and Mieke Bonn. I also wish to acknowledge that several people I interviewed for this book have died; I hope that in some small way their memory can live on through this text.

When I gave my farewell speech in a central Javanese village where I had lived and done research in the early 1980s, I began by invoking the Javanese tradition of apologizing a thousandfold *(minta seribu ma'af)* for any wrongdoings. Beginning with such an apology is in order here as well, for although I have tried to approach this topic and those I interviewed with humility and respect, undoubtedly I have made errors of omission and of commission. I apologize to one and all for any missteps.

My friend Keebet van Benda-Beckman inadvertently set me on this research road one day in fall 1992 in Wageningen by telling me about Dutch state involvement in Jewish family reunification after the war. Since our friendship includes a shared interest in Indonesia, perhaps it is appropriate that it has resulted in a book on the mother country.

I am very grateful to the Lucius Littauer Foundation, the Memorial Foundation for Jewish Culture, and the UC Berkeley Center for European Studies for grants that allowed me to pursue this research. After I was turned down for a faculty research grant at UC Davis for two consecutive years, Dean Steven Sheffrin generously granted me some research monies. I am also grateful for the UC Davis Publishing Award, which helped underwrite the inclusion of more photographs in the book.

I was aided by a great number of people in the Netherlands, and I thank them for their generosity and time. I am grateful to Professor Lodewijk Brunt; Rabbi Edward van Voolen, the director of the Jewish Museum in Amsterdam; Professor Ido de Haan; Professor Selma Leydesdorff; Professor Ido Abram; Mr. Hans Vuijsje, the librarian at ICODO; Elma Verhey; Peter Romijn; Rabbi Abram Soetendorp; Trix van der Schalk; Hans and Marjoline Karel; Dr. Regina van Gelderen; Dr. Marita Keilson-Lauritz; and Dr. Hans Keilson. A special thank-you to Dr. Bloeme Evers-Emden, who has written several books on hidden children and was a hidden child herself. In light of the usual way academics guard and mark their territory, her encouragement is deeply appreciated.

Friends such as Amrita Chhachhi, Rutie Waterman, Ruth Pearson, Marion Mineur, Ratna Saptari, and Ben White made our year in The Hague special. Through my association with the San Francisco Jewish Film Festival, I met Frans Weisz, whose films about the postwar families of former hidden children *(Qui Vive; Leedvermaak)* are brilliant in the way they portray complicated and multilayered family dynamics. Connecting with people like him and his wife, Regina, has been one of the unexpected windfalls of this project. I would also like to thank those in Israel, who supported my research there: Elisheva van der Hal and Mrs. José

Benaroch, both of ELAH; Rob Coopman; and Professor Joel Fishman. My apologies to anyone I have omitted.

Many friends and colleagues have directed me to important sources; my thanks to them all: Chaya Brasz, Lyn Lofland, Yen Le Espiritu, Ruth Jaeger, Laura Mason, Nancy Facher, Tai Katzenstein, Mary Jackman, Joan Meyers, Kathie Friedman, Judy Gerson, Maya Kronfeld, Bluma Goldstein, Marion Mineur, Hans Schulze, Fred Block, and Chana Kronfeld. My colleagues in the Department of Sociology have been extremely supportive of this project, even though it strays considerably from the field for which I was initially hired. I feel lucky to be in a department where international and qualitative work is valued.

To my wonderful research assistants over the years, some of whom did hours and hours of transcription, bibliographic work, or manuscript preparation—Yuval Sharon, Colleen Karpeles, Diana Carriaga, Carolina Apesoa-Varano, Jonathan Mermis-Cava, Naomi Rothman, Jane Le, and Colby Chlebowski—a mammoth thank-you for superb work!

I am very grateful to the two outside reviewers for their very useful insights and comments. In addition, Professor Dan Michman in Israel and Professor Ido de Haan in the Netherlands were kind enough to correct my errors and clarify my questions about my historical chapters. Any remaining errors are mine alone. I wholeheartedly thank them for their time, energy, and helpful comments.

I have often quipped that the women in my family are either crazy, or they're therapists. (This, of course, renders my status fairly problematic.) The great advantage of being related to therapists is getting a free professional analysis of those in the first category. It meant a lot to me to be able to discuss my work with my relative and surrogate mother, psychologist Hilde Burton. I was educated on the theory of attachment by another therapist, my sister-in-law and friend, Ruth Jaeger. Psychologist and sister-in-spirit Laura Mason guided me on issues of attachment in the book, just as she does in real life; her positive comments in the margins of the manuscript kept me going during the final revisions. Therapist and former hidden child Carla Lessing was extremely helpful with comments on chapter 9, as was then shrinkette, now psychologist Dr. Tai Katzenstein. Dutch psychotherapist Leidie Neijmeijer helped me to understand more clearly a number of issues that came up in the interviews. My colleague and sociological landsman Jeffrey Prager, also a trained analyst, made important suggestions, for which I am grateful. Thus, this book has been on a number of couches, so to speak, and I thank all those above for their time, insights, and encouragement.

It has been wonderful once again to work with Naomi Schneider, who has supported this book from the beginning and has kept me from becoming discouraged. She has gone above and beyond the call of duty by reading and commenting on each chapter as I wrote it. At UC Press, Justin Hunter managed all kinds of responsibilities with great efficiency and patience. I have fully enjoyed working with project editor Dore Brown due to her sensitivity to the material and her attention to detail. Mimi Kusch's keen editorial eye improved the manuscript. Jeannette Ringold translated and corrected the Dutch in this book and answered numerous questions quickly by email; it was a linguistic treat to work with her.

Because the interviews for this book were often raw, terribly painful, and very intense, there were some trying moments during the analysis and writing when I could not continue working. I am grateful to Jill Rosenthal for her empathetic responses when I called her about a particularly upsetting case, and to Donna Jaffe, who was kind enough to listen to my outpourings while we awaited our boys at the bus stop. My gratitude to Lida Lahidji for her friendship and her creative work. My thanks to Richie Holland for keeping our house clean, avoiding my study, and making me laugh.

My dearest friend, Chana Kronfeld, has been a source of inspiration, solidarity, wisdom, and important talks over sushi after the gym. Once again, mingling work with our friendship has been a *mechiah.*

My life partner and valentine, Frank Hirtz, has been patient and loving throughout, watching the home fires when I left for two-week stints to do the interviewing. He is my anchor and my safe harbor; I cannot thank him enough. Our son, Max, has been growing up alongside this book, at times resentful that my attention was not fully focused on him (at age 6 or so, he proclaimed, "All you care about is Starbucks and hidden children!"). I appreciate his big heart and his humor and only hope that I can keep mine as he moves into adolescence. I am blessed to have these two guys as my family, along with a fruitcake of a boxer, Shayne P.

In John Berger's most recent work of fiction, *Here Is Where We Meet*, the protagonist (also named John) runs into his mother, who had died fifteen years earlier, in a park in Lisbon. She takes his arm and advises him: "The thing you should know is this: the dead don't stay where they are buried" (3). How true. This book is dedicated to my late parents, because even though they died about three decades ago, they are always there somehow. I know that many of those I interviewed fully understand what it means to live alongside one's ghosts.

Introduction

I don't remember my mother. She was about 28. And one day she went walking in the street in Amsterdam, with my aunt, in 1942. Everybody said to her—and to them—"Don't walk in the street, because it's dangerous for Jewish people to walk in the street." And she said, "Well, then I'll dye my hair red instead of black." So she did! But they were picked up by the Nazis, both of them. And we never saw them again.

Thus began my first interview for this project, with Max L., in Amsterdam. The only child born to a middle-class nonobservant Jewish family in 1936, he has no recollection of his mother, who was deported to a concentration camp when he was 6 years old. (See figure 1.) After that, he was shuffled between various households—his uncle's, his grandparents', some family friends'—and even placed in an orphanage, a setting that frightened him. He remembers all these settings but not his mother; he has clearly repressed all memory of her. Sometime in 1942, when it was no longer safe for Jews to be in Holland, Max's grandfather retrieved him from the orphanage and took him by train to Friesland. At the train station at Leeuwarden, he gave Max to a stranger who was waiting for them. *My grandfather said to me, "You have to go with that gentleman, and he'll take care of you." My grandfather popped in the train, and he was gone. And . . . then you can feel your heart pounding. "What's going to happen to me?" and . . . well, the man, he took me by the hand and, he was talking to me, but I couldn't understand him because he spoke Frisian, not Dutch. When I came into his house, my foster mother, she came toward me, and she hugged me, and she said things like, "Oh, my poor child! You must be cold, because you don't have woolen stockings! Well, I will see to it that you get everything you need and . . ." Well, she was very kind.*

Max was welcomed into the man's family, which consisted of his very maternal wife and one other foster child; the couple could not have children of their own. (See figure 2.) As Max adapted to village life in Friesland, he learned the language, excelled in school, and grew to love his foster parents, as they did him. Max knew he was different—he was a dark-haired boy among blonds—and he knew his name was not Frisian, since people often commented that Max was a dog's name, not a person's. But he did not know he was Jewish. He played constantly with his friends, and like most village boys, accompanied his family to church on Sundays.

After the war, in 1945, someone began to visit occasionally whom Max described as a *dikke vette man* (a fat man; *dikke* and *vette* both mean "fat") and whom his foster parents referred to as his *vader* (father). He had no idea who this man was or what the term *vader* meant. Max himself used Frisian terms—*Mem* and *Heit*—to address his foster mother and father, who he believed were his real parents. He did not interact with the man, nor did the man talk with him.

His father paid these visits because he wanted Max back. His foster parents wanted to keep him. A great deal of correspondence flew back and forth, and Max's foster parents bought some time by convincing his father that it was not appropriate for him to take Max until he could provide him with a mother. Consequently, Max's father married a non-Jewish woman whom Max was to call "Tante Jo" (Aunt Jo, pronounced *Yo*). When they came to visit, Max paid no attention to them. When they tried to take him home with them to Amsterdam, he ran away, screaming and crying. They left without him. In 1948, when Max was 12, his foster father finally took him by train to Amsterdam; they met his father and stepmother at a train station, where Max was turned over. Tante Jo took one look at Max, his homespun country haircut and clothes, and laughed at him, causing immediate humiliation, a feeling that she inflicted on Max for years to come. He went home with them but immediately ran away to Friesland, something he continued to do his first year home. After that, Max stayed with his foster parents every summer during school vacation.

The separation from his "parents" and home in Friesland caused Max considerable stress and trauma—he began to wet his bed and started to lose some hair. He describes himself as being a timid, shy, and nervous child; he could never disagree or say no. Like most hidden children, he had realized that being agreeable was a key strategy in adapting to a foster family. At home in Amsterdam, he was withdrawn and rarely talked, a sharp contrast to his behavior when he lived in rural Friesland. He always thought of Friesland as home, as a refuge from his father and stepmother. It is also likely that the early trauma of losing his mother was replayed during this round of separation from foster parents to whom he was attached. Indeed, that early loss may have intensified his attempt to hold on to the only parents he knew.

When Max first arrived, his father and stepmother made an initial and short-lived attempt to be nice to him. Yet relations quickly soured, first between his father and stepmother and then between Max and both his parents. His father constantly lectured him about his schoolwork, his grades, his bed-wetting, and many other things. His stepmother insisted on being called "Mommy" instead of "Tante Jo" and began to punish him, often with beatings. *I had to call her "Mommy" after some months, and by that time, I hated her guts already. She started spanking me and slapping me, whenever I did something she didn't like, whatever I had done. When I wet my bed, I got punished.* Because Max's father was away on business most weeknights, his stepmother was the primary parent. Max found her to be kind and gentle at times and at others ferociously cruel.

Max was confused by his multiple parents and continued to distinguish between his biological father and his "real parents" in Friesland.

What I thought in those years was, "There's always for me a possibility to escape. To escape from my stepmother, to escape from my father. . . . And my real home is there, in Friesland. This Amsterdam is a temporary situation." When I ran away and came to Friesland, I was overwhelmed with a warm blanket of love and remembrance. I remember everything; every stone of the building in the house we lived in. Every stone in the cobblestone street I lived on. I saw my friends; I got seven or eight friends.

When he was around 13, one afternoon when his stepmother was out Max received a phone call from a Mr. Polak from the Joodse Gemeente (Jewish Community). Max's parents had been members of the Orthodox synagogue before the war; the man must have known about Max from records there or from the government's postwar organization. He asked if Max was going to have a bar mitzvah. Max, who knew nothing about Judaism, asked where he could get one. The caller realized that Max was ignorant about his Jewish background, and they made a date to meet, on an afternoon when Max's stepmother would be out. It was during that pivotal meeting that Max learned he was Jewish, that he had a Jewish mother who was dead, and that his stepmother was not his mother at all. That evening, he blew up at his stepmother, crying and yelling that she was not his mother. During this part of our interview, Max sobbed as he tried to tell the story. After he had stopped yelling at his stepmother, they talked, and she explained that his father had thought it best not to speak about his deceased mother. Through this dialogue, they seemed to reach a better understanding, and she even hugged and kissed him goodnight, "like a real mother."

But that improvement was not to last. When Max was 14, his stepmother punished him for altering his report card by throwing him through a glass door. Neighbors took him to the doctor to be stitched up. His stepmother apologized that evening. Later that night she invited him into her bed and forced him to touch her breasts and vagina. Thus began a four-year sexual relationship in which this kind of forced contact almost always followed beatings.

Max left home for the army at age 18 and later married and had two children. He always felt that his foster parents, the ones who had hidden him during the war, were his true parents and family. They had equally strong feelings for him, and it was no surprise when they left Max and their other foster son their property, money, and belongings.

Max's story, unfortunately not unique in its brutality, illuminates the focus of this book—the complexity of hidden children's experiences as they took on and confronted multiple parents, multiple families, and multiple identities, all the while dealing with emotional connections and separations. His story also demonstrates why it was only after the war that his troubles began.

At the age of 40, Max had a life-changing experience. His business failed, and as part of an application for financial help from the state to Holocaust victims, he received state-provided therapy. Although he did not qualify for financial help, therapy proved to be liberating when, for the first time, he talked about the incest imposed by his stepmother and realized that he had been victimized: *I am a victim. Not of the war, but . . . of what happened after the war. I am a postwar Holocaust victim.*

Max began to socialize with Jewish friends and to take part in Jewish social activities. He was asked to serve as an administrator for some Jewish clubs. Through these leadership roles, he began to feel that he wasn't a worthless person after all. Although Max identifies as Jewish, he is clearly more at home in a church than in a synagogue, where he doesn't recognize any of the songs.

·   ·   ·   ·   ·

This book is based on interviews with almost seventy people who, like Max, were hidden as children in Holland during World War II.[1] With a focus on family configurations and relationships, these histories demonstrate that we can only understand the effects of the Shoah by examining wartime and especially *postwar* contexts. Max's complicated family history alone defies facile sociological categorization. Max had three mothers and two fathers and lived in three different families before the age of twelve. He has repressed all memories of his biological mother; his foster mother was loving, and his stepmother was abusive; he loved his foster father and felt completely detached from his biological father. His sense of family derives from his life with his foster parents during and after the war. At the age of 6 Max had connected to them, and it was in their home that he experienced unconditional love and acceptance. It is, of course, highly likely that Max had experienced unconditional love from and attachment to his biological mother, but he has no memories of that. Indeed, that he was able to connect to his foster parents when he was 6 suggests that he had experienced a strong attachment earlier in life.

Max experienced firsthand the ramifications of the Nazi Occupation after his mother was deported, when he was shuffled from house to house and then placed in an orphanage. And in 1948, three years after the war's official end, he experienced the full ramifications of the Occupation and the war when his father forced him to come "home" to Amsterdam. The symptoms he describes—bed-wetting and hair loss—all point to the trauma of separation. In his Amsterdam home, he not only felt abandoned but was physically and sexually abused. While these violations were not common among hidden children after the war, they did occur with stepparents in a few instances.

Scholarship and popular literature about the Holocaust tend to focus on the systematic annihilation of European Jewry through deportation to concentration camps.[2] In light of the devastation suffered by the European Jewish population, such attention is clearly warranted. Because so few couples and families survived concentration camps intact, the theme of family loss rather than family life is prevalent.[3]

This book contributes a different perspective to that literature—that of family dynamics before, during, and especially after World War II as experienced by Jewish hidden children.[4] It also highlights a history that is not only different from, but often diametrically opposed to, that experienced by most European Jewry. For Jews who remained in Europe during the war, 1945 meant liberation from Nazi oppression, marking an end to the worst years of their lives. For many hidden children, however, the war years were passable, ranging from a marginal to a rather pleasant existence, depending on the hiding family. But an unexpected finding of this research was that for many hidden children, if not for most, the year 1945 marked what they see as the *beginning* of their problems rather than as their liberation. The other surprising, almost counterintuitive, finding was that those who were reunited with their parent(s) after the war echoed those who were orphaned in the refrain I so often heard: "My war began after the war."

The image of the hidden child has been shaped by Anne Frank, whose life ended in a brutal death. Her story continues to be discussed and analyzed, in psychological, spiritual, and sexual terms.[5] Scores of books have been written about her (Rittner 1998; Enzer and Solotaroff-Enzer 2000; Graver 1995; van Galen Last and Wolfswinkel 1996; van der Rol and Verhoeven 1993, to cite but a few), as well as literary analyses of her writing as a woman and as a resistor (Brenner 1997; de Costa 1998; Ezrahi 1980; and Lagerway 1996), again, to cite but a few. Her story continues to be dramatized—a recent film made for television stars Ben Kingsley as Otto Frank, and another movie about her is currently being made. Her globalized story has endeared her to many a teenage girl, and she is often used as the symbol of and poster girl for the Holocaust. Indeed, as the new millennium neared, Anne Frank was elected "person of the century" by a popular U.S. magazine poll. In the fall of 2004, she was ranked among the top candidates in a Dutch television channel's attempt to determine history's greatest Dutch person by popular vote. This touched off a public debate in which members of Parliament pushed to grant her citizenship posthumously, since she died stateless (Nazi Germany had revoked the citizenship of the German Jews) and, because she lacked a residency permit from the Netherlands, had never been Dutch.[6] Anne Frank's house is the most visited site in the Netherlands, with approximately one million mostly foreign visitors exploring the house annually since 1998. Like Yad Vashem, the Holocaust memorial in Israel where every foreign dignitary is taken, the Anne Frank House has become what Pierre Nora has termed a *lieu de mémoire,* a site of remembrance that is created by an interaction between history and memory (1992: 19). It is one of those Holocaust shrines to which a visit is imperative, if only to acknowledge the Holocaust; even Yasser Arafat felt compelled to visit the Anne Frank House.

Anne Frank may well be the best-recognized icon of the Holocaust. What is less well recognized is that her situation during the war was anomalous. Hiding together as a family was rare for one important reason—it was dangerous. During my three years of seeking hidden children to interview, I encountered only one person who had hidden with his entire family intact and a few more who had spent some or all of their time hiding with one parent. Few Dutch Gentile families would agree to take in an entire family because hiding adults seemed more difficult and risky. More often than not, children were sent individually to different homes, while parents often would hide together. Hiding separately also ensured that even if one family member was betrayed and caught, the others would survive. The relative wealth and foresight of Otto Frank allowed the Frank family to stay together and to do so above Otto's business, again, a highly unusual situation. Unfortunately, this seeming advantage turned out to be fatal for most of the Frank family.[7]

My initial interest in the topic of hidden Jewish children in Holland was kindled in 1992 when I was living in Holland and doing research at the University of Wageningen. A Dutch friend, a fellow Indonesianist, told me about the "Jewish war orphan" situation. The Dutch state had been involved with the question of hidden Jewish children and family reunification after the war. In the Netherlands, a new law about parental guardianship had been proposed by members of the Resistance and put into effect right after the war. It stated that if parents did not return to claim their children after a short absence, they would lose their right of guardianship over their children.

Although most Jewish parents who returned to claim their children after the war got them back directly from the foster parents, some did not, especially when the foster parents desired to keep the child (Verhey 2001). Many returning parents had to prove to state authorities that they were "fit parents." They had to present their case to a state committee headed by a very conservative Protestant who had religious motives for not returning Jewish children to Jewish families. The special circumstances of the Shoah and the decimation of the Netherlands' Jewish community were not seen by the state as a reason to make these "special cases" or to treat Jewish families with care. A few parents were found by state authorities to be "unfit" and were not allowed to have their children back; they were denied all contact and knowledge of their children's whereabouts. While in some cases family reunifications took place decades later, many are still searching, either for their parent(s) or for child(ren) (Verhey 1991 and 2001).

This committee was most influential in the cases of Jewish children whose parents did not survive the war. The relatives trying to claim these Jewish children had to go through this committee, and the courts as well, as they sought guardianship. In some instances, the children were returned to Jewish kin, and in others, they were kept by their Christian foster parents. In a few well-known cases, the children were kidnapped, some by their foster families, some by their Jewish families (Fishman 1978a). In no other European country was the state so involved in Jewish family reunification after the war, and nowhere else was it made so difficult for Jewish parents and kin to reclaim their children. Intrigued by this history, which countered every image I had held of Holland and its Jews during World War II, I slowly turned it into a research project.

Although initially I intended to investigate only the "Jewish war orphans," two compelling reasons changed and broadened my focus. First, once I was in the Netherlands, it became clear that I would be limiting my study to a small number of people. Second, my discussions with Jewish community leaders, academics, and some former hidden children convinced me that nonorphaned hidden children also had important war and family histories. Therefore, in order to analyze differences in the postwar reconstructions of family life, I expanded my focus to include all postwar family configurations among hidden children. I have divided them into three general categories: (1) those who had both parents return after the war, (2) those who had one parent return, and (3) those who were orphaned. The last category includes some hidden children whose cases were brought to the state committee and fought over in the Dutch courts after the war.

For those who were not orphaned, family life rarely returned to "normal" after the war. If biological parents returned, they were often strangers to their own children, and most children never reconnected emotionally with their parents. Some children, such as Max, viewed their foster parents as their true parents, having experienced a nicer family life with them. Some children were confronted with the loss of a beloved parent and sometimes with a new stepparent, which usually intensified feelings of dislocation, of not belonging, and of being unwanted. In other words, although surviving the war was a tremendous feat in itself, creating and re-creating a family in a post-Shoah context often incurred extraordinary emotional costs.

This book, then, will peer beyond the story of Anne Frank's truncated existence and illuminate the history and memory of the hiding experience for Jewish children in the Netherlands. I will put this experience into context by examining former hidden children's memories of the dynamics in hiding families and in their prewar families, if they remember. Just as important, if not more so, I will analyze the process of family reconstruction *after* the Shoah among those who were hidden. The experiences of hidden children represent a very particular war history, vastly different from what we usually read about survivors in the Holocaust literature. Through a focus on these differences and their ramifications on postwar family dynamics, this book unearths and articulates what has been, until now, a relatively hidden history and memory.

In late September 2005 the Dutch railway system formally apologized for its role in transporting, without any resistance from employees, over one hundred thousand Jews, about 75 percent of Holland's Jewish population, from Holland to a transit camp, from which they were deported to concentration camps. This apology is important since it demonstrates that the Netherlands is attempting to get beyond its dominant feelings of being victimized by the Germans while facing its collaboration during the war. That it took over sixty years suggests how difficult this process has been and perhaps how resistant many are to confronting the past. It also illustrates that the Nazi Occupation and the war are still very much alive for its survivors and for the state. This book revisits that past and focuses on the less well-known aspects of Holland and its relationship to the Jews.

1 The History and Memory of Hidden Children

The history and memory of hidden children create a very different legacy of the Shoah, one that has remained relatively unearthed. It is, in great part, a hidden history and part of a recently created collective memory of Jewish life. The purpose of this book is to use a sociological lens in the study of hidden children, in relation to their multiple families before, during, and after hiding, and in doing so, to analyze their shifting identities and family dynamics. Because of the particular nature of their survival and their postwar experiences, the sociology of hidden children reveals a vastly different trajectory than that of concentration camp survivors.

Most Holocaust research, memoirs, and testimonies, such as the fifty thousand gathered by Steven Spielberg's Shoah Visual History Project, focus primarily on the experience of individuals, usually concentration camp survivors, during the war years. While the main purpose of these various efforts is to document the Holocaust, they are missing an impor-

tant piece of its legacy, namely, how this event formed and perhaps de-
formed lives in its aftermath. As one former hidden child stated to me,
"I've been waiting for fifty years for someone to ask me about this. No
one ever did—they only wanted to hear about the war." Therefore, this
book focuses more on the post-Holocaust era and asks, How did the
trauma of war and genocide affect those who lived through it? How are
lives reshaped and families reconstituted in a postgenocidal setting? An
analysis of *post-Holocaust lives* will provide some insights and answers to
these questions.

This hidden history will unsettle a number of assumptions and popular conceptions of the Shoah as well. First, it will shatter a commonly accepted notion that the majority of the Dutch population was deeply involved in resisting the Nazis and in aiding their Jewish population.
Indeed, that notion is actually the inverse of what occurred. Second,
an examination of the laws and practices of the Dutch state after World
War II when a small number of Dutch Jewish survivors returned from
camps and emerged from hiding will demonstrate insensitivity at best,
and anti-Semitism at worst. Unfortunately, more evidence supports the
latter than the former. Third, this book will portray a very different reaction to the war's end among hidden children compared with that of concentration camp survivors, since many hidden children feel that their
problems really began when the war ended. Liberation and family reunification were far from a panacea for many of these Jewish children. Finally, this study will portray problematic and sometimes tragic postwar
family dynamics among surviving Dutch Jews, dispelling myths about
the strength and closeness of Jewish families. Indeed, my findings suggest that Jewish children who were orphaned and remained with their
Christian hiding families after the war seem to have done just as well as
and perhaps somewhat better psychologically as a group than those in
fully reconstituted Jewish families.

.   .   .   .   .

Haunting, argues sociologist Avery Gordon, "is a constituent element of
modern social life. It is neither pre-modern superstition nor individual
psychosis; it is a generalizable social phenomenon of great import." To

study social life, Gordon asserts, one must "confront the ghostly aspects of it" (1997: 7). "There is often a seething presence, acting on and often meddling with taken-for-granted realities. The ghost is just the sign, or the empirical evidence if you like, that tells you a haunting is taking place. . . . Investigating it can lead to that dense site where history and subjectivity make social life" (8).

To study and fully understand social life, therefore, "we must learn how to identify hauntings and reckon with ghosts, and must learn how to make contact with what is without doubt often painful, difficult, and unsettling" (23). Many of us live with ghosts, but the path of reconciling with them has been particularly troubling and haunting for hidden children. Given the violence of the twentieth century, detailed case studies of how biography and history interacted for hidden children can add an unsettling dimension to our understanding of childhood and family during and after genocide.

THE HIDING EXPERIENCE

To understand the distinctiveness of hidden children's lives and how their stories change our notions of the Holocaust, we must first examine the parameters of their experiences. There were two possibilities for hidden children in the Netherlands: either they were kept clandestinely in a non-Jewish household, or they were allowed to integrate into the family's life and circulate, spending their war years "passing" as non-Jews.[1] Elsewhere, in countries such as France, Belgium, and Italy, a third possibility existed—hiding the children in convents, monasteries, and other Catholic institutions. This third option was depicted in Louis Malle's autobiographical film *Au Revoir Les Enfants* (1987) and in the memoir of the eminent historian Saul Friedlander (1975). A fourth and unexpected option was recently revealed—a mosque in Paris hid Jewish children as well.[2] One of my interviewees spent the war passing as a non-Jew in a Salvation Army children's home, but hiding in such an institution appears to have been a rare occurrence in the Netherlands (Kestenberg 1996). Most of those I interviewed, however, did spend their war years passing as non-Jews in other settings. They underwent massive identity makeovers in their moves from their natal Jewish families to their life-saving Dutch Gentile families, in which their names, places of origin, histories, and religion were radically revised. Those who were hidden as infants or toddlers did not even realize that they were undergoing a transformation. As chapter 4 will elaborate, young children simply adapted to their new names, new parents, new siblings, new relatives, new beds, new friends, new villages, new churches, new practices, and new rules.

Jews who experienced the Shoah directly are generally called "survivors." Their children are known as the "second generation," or "children of survivors." It is generally assumed that children of survivors did not experience the Shoah directly and have no direct memory of it. Rather, they develop a "post-memory" transmitted by their parents (Hirsch 1997). Copious literature on children of survivors argues that they inherit certain kinds of psychological burdens and problems as a direct result of their parents' experiences (Hoffman 2004; Hass 1990; Wardi 1992; Epstein 1979). A second generation of Holocaust survivors is active worldwide, with their own organizations, groups, writings, and conferences.

Hidden children are an unusual group in that they are clearly survivors, and for those whose parent(s) returned, they are also children of survivors. They inhabit two distinct positions as both first and second generation and as both survivors and children of survivors who experienced the Shoah directly and indirectly—a situation that cannot help but intensify its effects. Since so few children and intact families survived concentration camps, such double positioning is rare among Jewish Holocaust survivors. This means that many are burdened both by their own traumatic histories and by those of their parents.

Hidden children constitute a very special group among Holocaust survivors for other reasons as well. With very few exceptions, until the early 1990s, the focus of the scholarly and popular literature on Jewish Holocaust survivors was almost solely limited to those who had been in concentration camps. That focus can be easily justified in light of the proportion of Jews who were in camps compared with those who were in hiding; additionally, concentration camp life was always more life-threatening on a daily basis compared with being in hiding. This is not to say that hidden children were not traumatized or that their lives were not threatened or that they were not starved during the Hunger Winter of 1945, when food was scarce; it is only to say that overall the hourly and daily brutality suffered by those in concentration camps was considerably greater.

The same might be said of those ten thousand Jewish children from Germany and Austria who were sent by their parents to safety on the Kindertransport to England. Recently brought into public consciousness through the film and book *Into the Arms of Strangers* (Harris and Oppenheimer 2000), children on the Kindertransport also left parents behind, most of whom did not survive the Shoah. The similarities between hidden children and those on the Kindertransport include such experiences as parting from parents who were trying to save them by sending them away, living in a new family, and for some, reuniting with parents after years of no communication.[3] For others, it meant coping with their parents' deaths. In all cases, the *Kinder* were thrust into a new culture and language, and when they were reunited with parents, many had forgotten their native tongue except for the words *Mutti* and *Papa* ("mommy" and "dad").

In contrast to the children of the Kindertransport, however, many of the hidden children were able to remain "at home" in the Netherlands, although for those, like Max, who went from Amsterdam to Friesland, their new home was often quite different culturally and linguistically. Some moved from urban areas to farms, and all moved from a Jewish home, however it was defined, to a non-Jewish one. But more important, all hidden children had to bury their Jewish identities and backgrounds, something not required of those who were sent to England. Furthermore, the identities of hidden children were changed to help conceal their Jewish background. While children sent to England on the Kindertransport may have had to give up some Jewish practices or perhaps even their Jewish identities if they ended up in Gentile homes, they did not have to change or hide their identities in order to survive.

Hidden children were in constant danger of being found out. Many had to change hiding families when the police were on their trail. Those on the Kindertransport did not have to live with such fears, although the *Kinder* in England faced the same dangers from bombings as everyone else. When we consider the experiences of children in concentration camps, we find more similarities than differences between the lives of hidden children and those of the children in the Kindertransport. All the same, hiding "at home" was quite a different existence than that led by Jewish children sent to safety in England.

As mentioned above, one of the unexpected findings of my research for this book is that the war's end in 1945 was very problematic for many hidden children, even (and perhaps especially) for those whose parents were still alive. Dutch-born child psychiatrist and former hidden child Robert Krell writes, "[Unlike concentration camp survivors] we were not displaced persons. We were in place, but family and community were gone" (2001: 4). If parents survived, there were problems, and if they did not, there were different problems. For many hidden children, Krell noted at a recent conference, "liberation was not liberating," but the antithesis.[4] What this book underscores is that for many, if not most, of those I interviewed, the end of the war signified the beginning of new and sometimes insurmountable difficulties. Family dynamics tended to be troubled as parents returned to claim children who had grown accustomed to another family and other parents. Most hidden children, whether or not they were orphaned, had to make another transition into a different setting. Only a very small minority of hidden children had a relatively smooth transition into postwar family life, and those were the ones who stayed with their non-Jewish foster families. Thus, contrary to what we might imagine, the survival and return of biological parents usually did not guarantee a "happy ending" for hidden children.

Until recently, former hidden children remained in hiding about their past as Holocaust survivors. There are many reasons for their silence. Once family life was resumed after the war, many parents did not want to hear about their children's wartime experiences and thought them best ignored. As we will explore later in the book, many hidden children were never asked a single question by their parents about their experiences in hiding, and orphans had no one to ask them. Others had their stories dismissed by parents who either felt guilty or could not tolerate hearing about their children's problems (or positive interactions with another family) during the war. Some parents simply silenced their children by claiming that their own experiences had been far worse. And some dismissed their children's attempts to discuss the past by stating that young children do not have memories and therefore cannot truly recall such things. In other words, most parents created a hierarchy of suffering after the war in which children had no place.

No one else wanted to know about their wartime travails either. Neither schoolmates nor teachers wanted to hear about their experiences; no one asked questions, and the message transmitted was to move on. This dynamic is not specific to the Netherlands, however. Historian Deborah Dwork (1991) points out that in all of Europe after the war, the sensibilities of Jewish survivors were dismissed and ignored; adults and children alike were "left to deal with their difficulties alone."[5] Dutch Gentiles were not interested in hearing about Jewish suffering since they too felt victimized by the war. Furthermore, they did not want to confront their own collaborative and highly passive behaviors that had led to the decimation of the Dutch Jewish population. Direct and indirect messages, then, contributed to hidden children's tendencies to keep their identities and histories hidden, a lesson they had learned quickly during the war. Having buried their identities and their pasts while in hiding, hidden children simply continued to use many of the skills they had learned in hiding and buried their more recent past after the war as well. Thus, most hidden children had no opportunity to process their wartime experiences and carried the additional burden either of their parents' experiences, as the second generation, or of being orphaned.

In the 1980s in the United States and Europe, Jewish concentration camp survivors began to be acknowledged and encouraged to tell their histories. Monuments, museums, and films such as the popularized TV miniseries *The Holocaust*, Claude Lanzmann's documentary *Shoah*, and other popular movies such as *Sophie's Choice* and *Schindler's List* brought attention to their suffering. The memory of those who did not survive was also honored through memorials and Holocaust museums. Hidden children, however, were not seen as survivors and hesitated to apply this label to themselves. According to several interviewees, they have been told by camp survivors that they were not really survivors, because they "had it easy during the war." This suggests not only a hierarchy of suffering but also that hidden children have no right to claim survivor status.[6]

For hidden children, it was only in the early 1990s, at the first international hidden child conferences, that they named their common history, spoke about its long-term effects, and acquired a group identity as hidden children and survivors of the Holocaust. We can better understand the liberation many former hidden children experienced at the first conference when they "came out"—wording they used deliberately to echo gays who at long last reveal their hidden sexual preferences—and then felt empowered to claim publicly their status as survivors, alongside those who had endured concentration camps. Thus, for many hidden children I interviewed, it was either May 1991, when the New York conference of hidden children was convened, or 1992, when the conference in Amsterdam was held, that marked their liberation, rather than May 1945. At these meetings, they gained clear and new identities shared with hundreds of other Jews in Holland and abroad, both as hidden children and as Holocaust survivors. As they began to voice their experiences, they created a new collective memory by resurrecting a history previously kept hidden by hundreds of individuals.

THE LITERATURE ON HIDDEN CHILDREN

Relatively little scholarly work exists on the topic of hidden children, as might be expected, in light of how long this history has been concealed.[7] Historian Deborah Dwork's *Children with a Star: Jewish Youth in Nazi Europe* (1991) analyzes all the possible outcomes for European Jewish youth. She includes a chapter on how hiding was organized and another on the hiding experience, as well as chapters on transit camps, ghettos, concentration camps, and the postwar period. Although her superb scholarship covers all European children, not just youth from the Netherlands, the Dutch are well represented in her writings. Bob Moore's exemplary book *Victims and Survivors* (1997) focuses on the persecution of the Jews in the Netherlands, including issues of hiding, betrayal, and postwar survival, of both adults and children.

Most of the academic research published on hidden children, in the Netherlands specifically, focuses on the particular and unique issue of

Dutch Jewish orphans, from historical, psychological, and journalistic perspectives. It unearths the workings of the state-appointed Voogdij-commissie voor Oorlogspleegkinderen, or Guardian Commission for War Foster Children (hereafter the OPK), which made recommendations about the futures of children with one or no surviving parents. Historians Joel Fishman (1973 and 1978a), Chaya Brasz (1995), Deborah Dwork (1991), and Jacob Presser (1988) have focused on the "Jewish war orphans" in the Netherlands and the tugs-of-war that ensued between either Jewish parents and hiding families, on the one hand, or between Jewish relatives of an orphaned child and the hiding families, on the other.[8] And Dutch historians Ido de Haan (1997) and Dienke Hondius (2003) have focused on the anti-Semitic atmosphere in the Netherlands after the war, an important theme in this study of postwar family life.[9]

However, the history of the state's often inappropriate intervention into Jewish family reunification only became part of the public discourse recently with Dutch journalist Elma Verhey's 1991 book *Om het joodse kind* (About the Jewish Child). Verhey documented cases in which the whereabouts of Jewish children were kept from their parents or other kin for reasons that appeared questionable, if not clearly anti-Semitic. Verhey's popular and very accessible book suddenly clarified for some former hidden children, who suffered from deep and long-lasting rejection as a result of being "abandoned" by their biological parent(s), that their parents' actions were dictated not by a personal decision but by a legal one in which they had absolutely no voice, no power, and no recourse (Verhey 2001). Since their savings, their apartments, their furniture, and all their belongings had been stolen and appropriated by the Dutch or German state, Jewish parents could not fight these legal decisions. In other words, for those who were not reunited with their biological parents after the war, even if those parents were still alive, Verhey's book suddenly transformed a personal, psychological wound into a social and collective experience, forty-five years after the fact.

Her more recent book, *Kind van de rekening: Het rechtsberstel van de joodse oorlogswezen, 1944–2004* (Footing the Bill: Redress for Jewish Orphans, 1944–2004), has caused another major upheaval. In it Verhey documents the problematic conditions in Jewish orphanages after the war and argues that Jewish agencies owe the orphans the money they originally received from the orphans' inheritances. This ongoing and very contentious issue has led to at least one lawsuit.

Former hidden child and child psychologist Bloeme Evers-Emden has done research and written books (not yet translated from Dutch) focusing on the foster parents who hid Jewish children (1994), the hidden children (Evers-Emden and Flim 1995), the Jewish parents who sent their children into hiding (1996), and the foster siblings of hidden children (1999). The most relevant book for our purposes is the second one, parts of which will be mentioned in my analysis. This book, *Ondergedoken geweest: een afgesloten verleden?* (Hidden During the War: A Closed-off Past?), is based on written responses to a survey administered to three hundred former hidden children who attended one of the international hidden child conferences.[10]

Psychiatrist and psychoanalyst Hans Keilson's 1992 *Sequential Traumatization in Children* (first published in 1979 in German) focuses on attachment and trauma among two hundred Jewish orphans whom he studied in orphanages for an organization called L'Ezrat ha-Yeled (Hebrew for "to the aid of the children") and followed up on years later in the 1960s. His sample is drawn exclusively from child survivors of concentration camps or of the hiding experience whom he treated.[11] About cumulative traumatization he wrote that "the extent and intensity of these disturbances exceeded anything previously experienced in the practice of child psychiatry" (1992: 1). Keilson argued that while legislation in the Netherlands gave priority to those who experienced severe traumatization in the concentration camps, his data suggest that persecution created other, less obvious and no less serious, forms of trauma (43). Through his research, Keilson publicly acknowledged the suffering of hidden children in particular, which was extremely important for them as a group politically. Because of Keilson's research, the diagnosis of post-traumatic stress disorder (PTSD) has been used to refer to the traumas experienced by child survivors and is acknowledged by the state and its social service agencies.[12]

While Keilson's sample consisted solely of orphans, mine is broader, including all postwar family configurations in which hidden children lived. In this way I hope to illuminate the differences and the similarities in the traumas experienced by both orphans and nonorphans after the war. Indeed, owing to the nature of my sample, this book will allow a unique comparison of these two groups. Thus, we will see that trauma was not limited to orphans but was far more extensive than Keilson's research suggests. In other words, not being orphaned did not decrease one's chance of experiencing sequential trauma. Given the nature of Keilson's approach, however, I doubt that he would find these conclusions surprising.

In this book, I confront numerous possibilities for linking with sociological literature on topics as diverse as emotions, childhood, family, religion, collective memory, war, and genocide. In the end, I touch on all these areas to some degree, either directly or indirectly, weaving together these relevant themes. My particular focus is on the child's prewar family life, the separation created by being ejected from the family of origin into a strange family, and what it meant to adapt to a new family (or families). In addition, I explore what it meant when a parent or parents returned, leading to yet another separation and ejection from a family into what was once again a strange family, even if it consisted of biological parents.

The challenge of doing this research is to bring a more sociological perspective to these very personal stories, emotions and all. I have attempted to do that in several ways. First, my focus is always on the relationship between the child and the family, in an attempt to get some sense of family relationships, at least from one perspective. I view these dynamics as ongoing processes that occur within and are often determined or constrained by the broader structures of society and the state, whether in war or peacetime. In this book, the microrelationships are depicted and analyzed within the confines and dictates of broader forces, both ideological and legal. Thus, these children and their families, regardless of whether they are biological or foster, cannot be divorced from such factors as Dutch state policies, Nazi laws and policies, the position of Dutch Jews in the Netherlands, the queen's wartime government-in-exile, and the like.

My previous research has also focused on the interactive relationships between young people and their families within broader structural transformations such as industrialization in Java, Indonesia (1992), or immigration from Asia to the United States (1997). In this book, the structural transformations covered are massive and global, those of war and peace. Many studies of families explore the individual actions and reactions of young people as they venture outside the family and then back in. In this case, the focus is on children and young people who sometimes tack back and forth within and between multiple families, a movement that created a more complex and confusing social milieu for them in postwar and postgenocide society.

CHILDREN, FAMILIES, AND THE SHOAH

While the best-known scholars of the Holocaust tend to focus more on the macro level, it has been women scholars, usually feminists, who have analyzed the Holocaust in terms of women, gender, children, and/or family life (Kaplan 1998; Dwork 1991; Hirsch 1997; Koonz 1987; Tec 2003; Ofer and Weitzman 1998). Those studies have illuminated the effects of the Nazis on German non-Jewish (Koonz 1987) and Jewish (Kaplan 1998; Ofer and Weitzman 1998) women as well as on Jewish children and families (Dwork 1991; Koonz 1987; Ofer and Weitzman 1998). However, since most Jewish families dissipated through emigration, deportation, or death, family studies of Jews and the Holocaust tend not to have a wartime and postwar focus.

Although sociologists are fond of large-scale transformations such as revolutions and war, the families living through such events have not been a major, or even minor, focus of study as of yet.[13] We can sometimes get a glimpse of families through research on gender and structural change. Thus, there is little, if any, family sociology with which this case study can be compared. However, there are several comparable empirical cases. The way Jewish families were torn apart during the Shoah might be compared to what families endured under the Khmer Rouge in Cambodia (Him 2000) or during genocides elsewhere. In several other instances the state intervened and made radical decisions for children and families—for example, with the Stolen Generation, the Aboriginal children who were kidnapped by the Australian government and placed in white homes or institutions (Manne 1998; Read 1998). The children of the disappeared in Argentina—those suspected of leftist activities—were often secretly adopted by military families and are still being sought by their grandmothers (Ardith 1999; Oren 2001). In El Salvador in the early 1980s, the army kidnapped hundreds of children, who were either placed in orphanages or adopted. In 1992 surviving parents formed an organization, Search for the Missing Children, and to date, they have located 310 out of 765 of the documented children who disappeared (Barnert 2006). Another related case is that of about one thousand babies of Yemenite immigrants to Israel who disappeared from the hospitals in transit camps (Greenberg 1997; Weiss 2001). The babies' graves were found empty, and it is still not clear whether these children were adopted or whether they ended up in criminal hands.

There are parallels between all these cases and the experiences of hidden children, whose fate was decided by a state heavily influenced by Christian notions. Although these cases are not pursued in the book, all of them reflect the commonality of the state's hegemonic power to force a particular racial-ethnic conformity while denying difference and minority rights.

The family is the social institution in which we first develop our social and cultural identities. Hidden children were part of multiple families with vastly different religious orientations, often different class locations, and different geographical locations (urban versus rural). A focus on the nexus between hidden children and their families—prewar natal family, hiding family, and postwar family—presents a view of shifting identities, complicated relationships, and questions about the meaning of "family." Hidden children's memories of these families, then, can result in contradictory and confusing multiple identities. Although this book focuses on what took place within these multiple families, it will also consider how the social environment (e.g., families, the state, hidden children organizations) affected hidden children's abilities to understand and claim their histories and identities.

The family, argues sociologist Eviatar Zerubavel, represents what he terms a "remembrance environment"—one of the many spaces that lie somewhere "between the personal and the universal."[14] The memories we share with others in these environments, Zerubavel asserts, constitute the sociology of memory (1996: 284). However, since I did not interview all family members, in this case "family memory" does not represent the families' experiences. Clearly, biological parents would have a very different view of family relationships, as would foster parents and foster siblings (see Evers Emden 1994 and 1999). What I have attempted here is to reconstruct family relationships through the eyes of a child as she or he experienced the war and the years after. This reconstruction encompasses family relationships after the war, as natal families, if the members survived, were reconstructed, and includes family life up to the present. There is no question that this perspective is greatly shaped by the age, gender, and the birth order of the child, and therefore it may differ dramatically from that of an adult or even an older or younger sibling.

It is not unusual for Holocaust survivors to portray prewar life in general and prewar family life specifically as idyllic, something historian Leo Spitzer refers to as "nostalgic memory" (1998: 153). Sidra Ezrahi explains that in such narratives, childhood is presented as a kind of "nature reserve," as a "paradise lost" (1997: 368). The survivors' need to uphold this kind of memory is completely understandable in light of how many of their families were murdered. At the same time, with deep respect for those who were killed, it is also important to overcome the tendency to be nostalgic and to focus on the realities of prewar family life.

In my research, I make no assumptions about family consensus or cohesion. Families are more often than not the locus of conflict and tension, even if (some might add, especially if) they survived the Shoah intact. Y. Michal Bodemann's 2005 book on one postwar Jewish family in Germany is an intimate portrait of such constant conflict. The majority of those I interviewed were very straightforward about conflicts within their hiding families, but also within their postwar reconstructed biological families. Indeed, I was surprised at how honest and direct many were concerning tensions in their prewar family life, presenting quite the opposite of nostalgic memory. However, it should be said that it was my perception that those whose parent(s) survived were more able to be honest. Orphans, if they could remember their parents at all, were never critical of them.

Analyzing the relationships between a child and her foster parents or her biological parents turned my attention to the psychology literature on parent-child attachment. This literature on the mother-child relationship in the first few years of a child's life focuses on how safe and secure the child feels with the mother. Feeling this security or attachment is different from feeling love or empathy. The kind of relationship the child has formed with his mother—secure, insecure, ambivalent, or avoidant—is thought to have significant implications for his personality and long-term development (Karen 1994).

My research is more focused on the sociology of attachment and how children connected with their different sets of parents—if at all. Although I am not measuring or categorizing the children's personalities, I am examining longer-term outcomes in light of their ability to create a coherent and satisfying adult life. Thus, I will refer to children's "connection" rather than their attachment to their parents, and the different degrees of connection they recalled. By *connection,* I am referring to a feeling of empathy, affection, and love. In psychologists' terms, a child might feel empathy from or for a parent but may not be securely attached, in that he or she doesn't feel safe with the parent. Clearly, I did not attempt to measure these feelings retrospectively.

This research on hidden children connects with the sociology of childhood as well by acknowledging children's agency as social actors. This is not to suggest that children had choices; certainly Jewish children during the Occupation did not. However, their memories and experiences are relevant to our understanding of the effects of war and genocide on everyday life and on emotional development. My interviews refute any notion that children cannot remember. Indeed, they can and do, from about age 5 on, although some can recall certain experiences even before the age of 5. Almost everyone I interviewed can still easily recall their feelings as children living with a family or families, and the radical changes they confronted after the war.

Some of the narratives exhibit what philosopher Mikhail Bakhtin calls "polyphony"—several different voices working together without harmonizing inherent tensions or contradictions (1991). For example, when those I interviewed spoke, a modified and sometimes thoughtful adult perspective was apparent, reflecting decades of experience, history, knowledge, and retrospection. Often, when they spoke about seeing their child or grandchild at the same age as they were when they went into hiding, or when they thought about their parents' predicament when they became parents of young children, their voices were reflective, as an adult voice would be. Indeed, this more reflective adult recounting of the past, aided by hindsight, constitutes most narratives.

At the same time, we will often hear the child's voice from the same person, particularly when she is speaking of certain memories, such as fears during hiding, likes, dislikes, or feelings of unfairness. Those feelings tend not to be as filtered by an adult perspective; parts of the narratives sound young, and the language may differ from that used by the adult voice, for example, "He always favored my sister" or "She liked him better." It is usually quite clear from the narrative which voice is speaking. Although I do not engage in a textual analysis of this dialogic tension, it is useful to keep these differences in mind. I want to clarify that in pointing out the existence of polyphony, I am not judging or valuing any one voice above another. They all exist in the same person, but the more childlike voice usually gets muted in adults. Owing to the sensitive and traumatic nature of hidden children's histories, some of these younger voices become more audible in the narratives.

Because of my interest in their experiences, many of the questions I asked of former hidden children and much of the information I sought were of an emotional nature. I sought feelings, and memories of their feelings, rather than facts (e.g., exact dates), since speaking of dramatic events such as separations from parents is likely to conjure up those emotions one felt as a child. I seek patterns in these emotions in order to link war and genocide with the emotional lives of children and families. Additionally, I am interested in the relational aspects of these emotions, not solely in the individual psyche. Although I consider some concepts that are central to the field of psychology, such as attachment, I do so in a more sociological manner.

This book can be seen as part of an increasing social scientific focus on children and childhood, particularly on children and the violence of war. In wars children, one of the most vulnerable groups in society, are caught in webs of politics beyond their control and often their comprehension. War also intrudes on and reshapes the course of childhood for those caught in its midst (Him 2000; see also the film *The Lost Boys of Sudan*). Although my focus is on children's memories of their families, it is also true that the experiences of these children and their families took place within a highly politicized environment. The cultural politics of childhood refers to the public nature of childhood and the inability of families to protect children from the "outrageous slings and arrows of the world's political and economic fortunes" (Scheper-Hughes and Sargent 1998: 1). Hidden children were caught up in anti-Semitic policies and laws that were mostly beyond their comprehension. Because their parents were incapable of protecting them, this job was left to strangers, some of whom were kind, some of whom were not. And after the war, the lives of many hidden children, particularly those who were orphaned, became highly politicized because of state interventions. Their experiences as hidden children and the effects of the war on their childhoods are part of a broader political culture and of cultural politics. This book, then, illuminates how escaping genocide was and to some extent still is seen through the eyes of the youngest and most vulnerable members of society, as well as how it affected them.

One motivation for using the term *genocide* in this book is to take the Holocaust out of its academic ghetto and to stimulate thinking about it in more comparative terms. Thus, although my use of the term *genocide,* or *Nazi genocide,* may be problematic for some historians of the Shoah who find it too limiting (D. Michman 2003), my reasons stem from a desire to consider what we can learn about genocide from the Shoah, and vice versa. A comparative approach to genocide that includes the Shoah challenges those scholars who claim that the Holocaust is unique and cannot be compared with other mass murders. My reasoning is that although all genocides have features not reproduced elsewhere, they also share some features. In addition, a comparative approach rejects any attempt to impose a hierarchy of genocides, which might suggest that the Holocaust was not only unique but also that it was worse than other genocides.

Our understanding of Jewish children's lives under Nazism tends to be reflected in Roman Vishniac–like images of small children with large, dark eyes, begging for food in a ghetto, Jewish stars prominent on their clothing, or the well-known photo of a Jewish boy in a cap and winter coat, walking by some Nazi soldiers with his hands up, like a criminal, his eyes fearful. We know that 1 million Jewish children in Europe did not survive World War II and that they were starved and gassed, their bodies burned and buried. Precisely because Binjamin Wilkomirski seemed to represent those children whose voices were never heard and whose lives were brutally and prematurely snuffed out, his 1996 memoir *Fragments* gained tremendous international attention. His descriptions of concentration camp life and death through the eyes of a rare child survivor captivated a global audience and won many awards—until it became clear that he had fabricated the entire book. But before his own story unraveled, the way his book swept up readers in many countries spoke to this lacuna in the literature about the experiences of children during the Shoah.

In their ethnographic volumes, anthropologist Veena Das and psychiatrist Arthur Kleinman advocate for an understanding of suffering and violence through a focus on subjectivities, defined as "the felt interior experience of the person that includes his or her positions in a field of relational power." Such an approach would attend to the way in which daily life and practices are transformed in reaction to engagement with violence (1997: 2). Indeed, rendering suffering meaningful remains "a formidable task for social anthropology and sociology" (Das 1997: 563). They argue for analyzing the interactions between social suffering and institutional, political, and economic power, acknowledging that pain, trauma, and suffering are not simply health problems but also social, political, and cultural issues (Kleinman, Das, and Lock 1997: ix).

Highlighting hidden children's experiences and emotions within their multiple families and linking them to broader social and political structures guide this study of state-inflicted violence done to children. As we will see, these children's memories of the Shoah differ considerably from our understanding of the Holocaust and from what usually constitutes Holocaust memory.

INDIVIDUAL MEMORY, FAMILY MEMORY, HOLOCAUST MEMORY

Holocaust memory in particular has been a central focus of scholarly research (e.g., Hartman 1994; Milton and Nowinski 1991; Young 1993 and

2000; Linenthal 1995; Friedlander 1993; among many others), which may be better understood in light of the central role that remembering injustice plays in Judaism. According to Jewish law, a witness must report any unjust event he or she has seen, thereby making "more witnesses by informing others of events" (Young 1988: 18). Yerushalmi notes that the command "to remember" *(zakhor)* is used 169 times in the Hebrew Bible (1996: 5). Rituals concerning remembering and retelling a history of oppression, injustice, and resistance, such as those found in the Passover seder, provide a cultural basis for Holocaust testimonials and for Jewish collective memory of the Holocaust. Indeed, the way Jews think about and use testimonials shares tenets with Latin American *testimonios* (Menchu 1984)—including that of exposing an injustice to begin righting the wrong.

The injunction to tell has led to a deluge of Holocaust memoirs and autobiographies, prominent among them the internationally renowned historian Saul Friedlander's 1975 *When Memory Comes* (see also Delbo 1995).[15] The need to remember has generated multiple oral history projects for Shoah survivors all over the United States, the best known being Steven Spielberg's Shoah Visual History Project, which has gathered over fifty thousand Holocaust testimonials worldwide (Greenspan 1998; Langer 1991). Owing to questions of reliability, historians have been disinclined to use these testimonials as historical evidence and would be even more disinclined to use the testimony of those who were children at the time of the war. Still, such oral histories have gained stature in popular culture for providing "a degree of authenticity absent from documentary records" (Gray and Oliver 2001: 13).

Scholars writing about the Holocaust have focused on how people remember, what they remember, and if they remember.[16] Primo Levi argued that with the passing of time, memories go through a sieve, with the most painful ones fading away (1986: 136). Others do not believe that the worst memories necessarily fade away over time (Delbo 1995). Contrary to Primo Levi, Pamela Ballinger, an anthropologist who focuses on memory and identity, asserts that it is not an inability to remember so much as *an inability to forget* that affects those who have survived trauma (1998: 117). Indeed, Lawrence Langer, scholar of Holocaust memory, asserts that survivors' memories do not need to be reawakened, since they were never dormant to begin with (1991: xv).[17]

The concept of memory is crucial not only in this aspect of Jewish history but also in a broad range of scholarship. Memory, argues anthropologist Michael Kenny, is "a key to personal, social and cultural identity" (1999: 420), a theme that is of prominent contemporary relevance both inside and outside the academy. As a result, the field of memory studies now boasts a rich and textured interdisciplinary literature that is flourishing in fields such as sociology, psychology, and anthropology (Olick and Robbins 1998: 106).

As sociologist Jeffrey Prager argues, memory is not simply or solely an individual experience. Rather, it is "produced by an individual, but it is always produced in relation to the larger interpersonal and cultural world in which that individual lives. . . . Memory is *embedded;* that is, the rememberer remembers in a contemporary world, peopled by others who collectively contribute to the construction of memory and help determine the importance that the past holds for an individual in the present" (1998: 70–71). Sociologists approach the self as a socially constructed entity that is embedded in a particular sociohistorical and cultural context. The self constructed in contemporary postmodern Western society is quite different from the self constructed there before industrialization or in contemporary rural Southeast Asia. Similarly, memory is located in particular sociohistorical and cultural contexts that allow or even encourage us to remember or *not* to remember certain types of experiences. In this manner, Prager argues, memory is "intersubjectively constituted. While memory is produced by an individual, what is remembered is always influenced by the cultural world in which the individual is embedded" (89).[18]

What are the ramifications of Prager's approach for this book? First, it establishes memory as relational and social rather than as the product of an isolated individual. Memories are created with respect to and in relation to others. Second, it helps put in context why and how hidden children learned to repress their memories of hiding after the war. Third, it helps explain how and why groups of former hidden children in the early 1990s were able to "come out" with their particular history and claim their identity and memory. It was, after all, an era of honoring Holocaust survivors, when the second and third generations wanted to hear from them. The environment was one in which the notion of a "survivor" was popularized far beyond the war, and a culture of victimization had been emerging. Thus, the historical and sociocultural context made it safe and possible for hidden children to reveal their memories. Finally, the social and relational aspects of creating memory are relevant for understanding the general social consensus around repressing these memories and then, as a group, around excavating and reclaiming them.

This sociological approach to memory is also relevant to the concept of collective memory, something that plays a large role in the construction of contemporary Jewish identity.[19] In modern and postmodern times, the Holocaust has been a primary example of, and in some cases a model for, the concept of collective memory.[20] It is generally accepted that the Shoah plays a crucial role in Jewish collective memory and, therefore, in the constitution of contemporary Jewish identity. Indeed, scholars note the increasing prominence of the Shoah as the basis, and sometimes the sole basis, of contemporary Jewish identity (Novick 1999; Stier 2003). Goldberg refers to this as the *Holocaust cult,* which, he says, has become the "civil religion" of U.S. Jews and of Israel (1995).

Younger Jewish people who may not know much about Judaism or Jewish history usually know about the Shoah. Courses on the Holocaust are always the most popular of all Jewish Studies offerings, and during Jewish Culture week at my campus, the evening on the Holocaust is always the most well attended. Some argue that placing an emphasis on the Shoah connects younger Jews to a sense of victimhood as part of their ethnic identity. The "post-memory" they have been taught admonishes them to "never forget," but this focus on Jewish death is not necessarily balanced with knowledge about Jewish life (Stier 2003).

COLLECTIVE MEMORY

Maurice Halbwachs, French philosopher, sociologist, and colleague of Emile Durkheim who was sent to (and died in) a concentration camp because of his socialist politics, created the concept of collective memory

(1992). His definition of collective memory refuted Freud's notion of the individual's unconscious as a "repository for all past experiences" (Olick and Robbins 1998: 109). Halbwachs argued that individuals bear not only their own autobiographical memory but also a collective memory that is passed along intergenerationally. Every group develops its own particular memory of the past, and that memory creates its unique identity as a group (Halbwachs 1992: 46–49, 86; Zerubavel 1995). His notion of collective memory sets it apart from individual memory, but he believed that it is collective memory that gives us our identity and meaning (Olick and Robbins 1998: 111).

Although scholars have been critical of its underlying assumptions (Olick and Robbins 1998; Zerubavel 1995), the concept of collective memory is still very much alive and part of contemporary sociological and historical discourse.[21] As a way to circumvent using the monolithic and somewhat mystical concept of collective memory, scholars have focused on more specific types of memory—for example, official memory, vernacular memory, public memory, popular memory, local memory, family memory, historical memory, and cultural memory, among others (Olick and Robbins 1998: 112). Indeed, rather than presume a collective mind that operates seemingly without power relations or any relations at all, it is important to discern the interactive relationship between individual memory and collective memory.[22]

Some scholars have turned to social or cultural memory instead of or as a refinement of collective memory. In their eloquent book on how trauma and traumatic loss affect and are affected by cultural memory and the Holocaust, Epstein and Lefkovitz assert that cultural memory refers to "ethnic group consciousness of the past and provides the philosophical and historical foundations for ethnic, religious, and racial identities. . . . It recasts the meaning of history and makes history a critical fact of life" (2001: 1). Their definition is quite similar to that of Marita Sturken, who analyzed "the politics of remembering" in relation to the Vietnam War and the AIDs epidemic (1997).

Both social memory and cultural memory are relevant to this book, but I will be analyzing them as part of collective memory. It was their religious and cultural backgrounds as Jews that endangered hidden children in the first place, whether or not they knew anything about Judaism. However, the Occupation, war, and hiding experience also encompassed a social aspect—being part of Dutch families within Dutch society. Thus, I would expect the experience of Jews who hid as children in France, for example, to resemble or even to replicate certain aspects of hiding in the Netherlands, while differing in ways related to French family life and society. Hidden children's memories are built on their grounded experiences as social actors who interacted within different family and broader social environments.

Hidden children and other Holocaust survivors have suffered, as individuals and as a group, what sociologist Jeffrey Alexander calls "cultural trauma" (2004). In a recent volume on cultural trauma and collective identity, Alexander defines cultural trauma as occurring "when members of a collectivity feel they have been subjected to a horrendous event that leaves indelible marks upon their group consciousness, marking their memories forever and changing their future identity in fundamental and irrevocable ways" (2004: 1). This definition clearly fits the effects of the Shoah on the Jews, as it does those of slavery on African Americans (Eyerman 2004).

Although I will be using the term *trauma* when analyzing the various separations experienced by hidden children, I am not grounding this study in a conceptual framework of trauma, either individual or group. Like memory, trauma has attracted considerable interdisciplinary interest among those in both the humanities and the social sciences. Yet using trauma as a framework superimposes and presumes its dominance over and above all other emotions and behaviors. Although hidden children obviously experienced their share of trauma, I do not want to privilege trauma above other kinds of emotions and prefer to explore the full gamut of reactions.

Thus, in this book I will approach memory from an individual and relational perspective, in regard to the hidden children's multiple families. This group's collective memory only just developed in the early 1990s and has become valuable to individual hidden children, both as social and emotional support and as a political tool. Later in this book I will demonstrate how the creation of a collective memory has become an important healing force for many hidden children. For now let us turn to a detailed discussion of research methodology.

RESEARCH DESIGN AND SAMPLE

I began conducting interviews as part of my research while living in the Netherlands for one year, in 1998. I deliberately began this project slowly and judiciously. Although I had already reviewed the English-language literature on this topic before arriving, I needed access to Dutch-language sources. In addition, I spoke with various Dutch academics and Jewish professional and lay leaders so that I could be sure that the kind of study I was proposing had not already been done. As mentioned earlier, although initially I wanted to focus my research solely on those who were orphaned after the war and whose fate was decided by the state-appointed committee on Jewish war orphans, I quickly modified that restriction after some meetings in 1998. I expanded my design to include anyone who was in hiding as a child, regardless of familial configuration after the war. Age 18 was my cutoff, which corresponds to Dutch legal notions of what constitutes a minor. Thus, a few respondents went into hiding as minors but were legally adults at the war's end.

Opening up my sample to anyone who had been hidden led to forming three main categories of postwar family outcomes—both parents returning, one parent returning, and no parents returning—and at least five subcategories. If both parents returned, the complete nuclear family of origin was reunited. If one parent returned, he or she either remained widowed or remarried. In the case of one widower, as we saw from Max L.'s story in the introduction, he remarried before he claimed his son, since a father and son were not considered a proper family. Widows, however, were usually able to claim their children and remarry if they wished, although Elma Verhey has documented cases in which returning Jewish widows were not allowed to reclaim their children (1991).

If no parents returned, the child may have stayed with the foster family, gone to live with kin, or been sent to a Jewish orphanage. From the orphanages, some children were eventually sent to Israel. I needed to interview a sufficient number of people to discern patterns in any one category or subcategory. Clearly, there is no "right" number for such research, but I sought to interview approximately seventy people, more than necessary for my purposes. When I went to Israel I oversampled. I already had enough interviews, but I wanted to ascertain the effects of being sent to Israel as a young orphan. Unfortunately, very few people I interviewed in Israel had had that experience.

My respondents lived in Holland (forty-one), Israel (eleven), and the United States (eighteen); I interviewed thirty-one men and thirty-nine women. Four additional interviews could not be used for various reasons.[23] It is difficult to know why more women than men volunteered to be interviewed without knowing the demographics of the entire population of former hidden children.[24]

I conducted the interviews between 1998 and 2001, during three different stays in the Netherlands. In both the Netherlands and the United States, I asked to publish a description of my project and my request for volunteers in the newsletters of various associations for hidden children and child survivors of the Holocaust. Sometimes those involved in such associations sent out emails to their lists with my request. In all such cases, the volunteers responded to someone in the organization, who then sent me all the names and numbers. One of my interviewees placed an ad for me in the Dutch Jewish liberal newspaper the *Nieuw Israelitisch Weekblad (NIW)* seeking volunteers, and the San Francisco *Jewish Bulletin* published my letter seeking volunteers.

In Israel, I had to rely more on personal networking, a situation that ended up creating an unexpected challenge. Generally I did not feel it was appropriate to approach people directly, since survivors of the Shoah may be sensitive to being sought out as Jews. Several social workers connected to survivor associations asked people they knew to volunteer, and one Dutch Jewish academic asked a number of hidden children to take part in the research as well. It proved difficult to find volunteers—most of those asked did not want to grant an interview. That may be due in part to an ideology in Israel that historically has posited Shoah victims as passive Jews of the *Galut* (Diaspora) who almost deserved their treatment; in other words, until recently, to be a survivor in Israel was shameful (Segev 2000). In the end, I was able to scrape together eleven interviews, but only after several people helped me out.

Here it should be said that in the survivor and hidden children associations in the Netherlands as well, only a minority volunteered to be interviewed. I heard from others that those unwilling to be interviewed either did not want to discuss their pasts or, because of the Spielberg project, did not want to be interviewed again. I asked one volunteer's husband if he would grant me an interview because I knew from his wife that he had a fascinating history, but he declined, saying he was unable to discuss it. A number of potential respondents told me that their story was not special or unusual in any way and would not be of interest to me; if I ended up interviewing them, I was always struck by how remarkable their histories were.

The problematic aspects of this sampling technique are well known and not specific to this book; these aspects merit discussion if only to clarify the limits of any generalizations made about these interviews. First, because I was seeking interviewees through associations connected with hidden children or child survivors of the Holocaust, the great majority of my sample is limited to those who currently identify with their past in some manner. In other words, the people involved in such associations tend to identify as Jewish and as former hidden children. Most characterize themselves as Jewish culturally and lead a fairly nonobservant Jewish life. My advertisement in the Dutch Jewish newspaper reaped a surprising number of calls from volunteers whose only Jewish activity is reading the weekly Jewish newspaper. Many in this group had never been interviewed and would not join an association focused on their war past. They might think about their past, perhaps even daily, but either did not feel the need to join a group or were averse to being part of such an organization. Yet, despite their lack of institutional affiliations, I still found these interviewees to be deeply connected to their histories.

I interviewed two people whom I knew through friends in The Hague. Neither of these men belongs to a hidden children's association, nor would they read the Jewish newspaper, yet in different ways they both identified as Jews. One former hidden child living in the United States connected me with her cousin in Israel when I traveled there; another in the States gave me the phone number of a friend in Holland who had been in the same orphanage as he. This person also does not engage in any Jewish activities. The kinds of people who are missing from my study are those who do not even know they were hidden children. This would be the case for what is presumed to be a small number of people who stayed with their foster families and whose foster families never revealed their pasts to them (Verhey 1991). I am also missing a large number of those who live secular lives, are not connected with any organization related to their wartime experiences, *and* do not read a weekly Jewish newspaper.

Does this constrict my findings significantly? I do not believe this mode of sampling constitutes a particular problem beyond the usual limitations of anything short of random sampling. Indeed, I oversampled in this study to avoid any problems associated with sampling limitations. I continued to interview volunteers despite reaching a saturation point where patterns were clearly being repeated. While it is possible that such patterns may not occur among those who are completely disassociated from any aspect of organized Jewish life, I am convinced that these are general patterns, in light of how many secular Jews I interviewed.

I conducted almost all my interviews in English, with a smattering of Dutch, Yiddish, and/or Hebrew words, languages in which I have some competence but not fluency. Three interviewees did not feel comfortable enough in English, so my Dutch teacher served as interpreter during those sessions. Working with an interpreter proved to be difficult and did not reap rich interviews. In such situations I was unable to make the kinds of personal connections I often made otherwise that could lead to more intense interactions.

I did not interview the living parents of those who went into hiding, nor did I interview those who hid Jewish children during the war, a focus that has been covered by others, such as Evers-Emden. My goal was not to seek some definable, recognizable "Truth" about these interactions. Since any two people in a family have different perspectives, particularly if there are age and gender differences, finding this so-called Truth would be impossible. I was not concerned with the veracity of dates or lengths of time, which children cannot usually estimate accurately. Instead, I sought the "partial truths" about these relationships from the perspective of the hidden child, who has now filtered these memories through a good fifty-five years of experience and perhaps some revisionism. My focus is on the narratives of those who were dependent and vulnerable during the process of hiding and reconstituting family relationships and on how these former hidden children viewed family dynamics.

Of course it is very possible that former hidden children have forgotten some important events or dynamics, while embellishing others. Yet they also have the advantage of being able to reflect on these relationships as adults, most of whom have become parents and have children and grandchildren themselves. Often repressed memories resurfaced when their own children, or more frequently, their grandchildren reached the age at which they went into hiding. At this point in their lives, they were less occupied with the details of work and everyday needs, since most were retired. For that reason and others, which will be explored later, many hidden children could only begin to discuss their pasts now, fifty-five years later.

METHODOLOGY AND THE RESEARCH PROCESS

In my research for this book I combined the methods of historical sociology with fieldwork, both qualitative approaches. My two historical chapters, chapters 2 and 3, are based on secondary sources. However, my analysis of narratives based on intensive interviews provides the core material of the book. In an effort to demystify research and to make it as transparent as possible to interested readers and students, I will detail this process here.

After making contact and setting a date with those who volunteered to be interviewed, I went to their homes to conduct the interviews. I was always treated hospitably. Good coffee and sweets are very much part of Dutch culture; when working in the Netherlands I was often greeted with cake and a cup of strong coffee when I sat down to begin. The efficiency of the Dutch rail system facilitated travel to all parts of Holland, although most Dutch respondents lived in Amsterdam. In the United

States, I interviewed sixteen people on the East Coast. Trains, buses, and car rides with some generous interviewees got me to Long Island, Connecticut, and New Jersey, and some very hospitable research subjects put me up overnight a few times. My few West Coast interviews were conducted near my home. Finally, in Israel I traveled widely by car to interview volunteers. Many people wanted to know my connection to this research topic before the interview began. It seemed that for most interviewees, my being Jewish was important and a sufficient explanation of my motives. The fact that my background is not Dutch Jewish but German Jewish did not seem problematic, even though German Jews are not viewed favorably in Holland among Jews of Eastern European descent. Also, my position as a professor did not hurt, I am sure. Very few of those interviewed asked me anything further about my family background, but whenever I was asked, I responded. Those questions, however, tended to come from the few I befriended after our interview and have seen socially.

My parents were born in Germany in the 1920s to solid petit-bourgeois Jewish families, and both their fathers served Germany in World War I. My mother, like Anne Frank, was born in Frankfurt am Main, just a few years before Anne Frank was born, to a similarly well-off family. They wore similar clothing, as seen in the picture of my mother that I always called her "Anne Frank photo." Both my parents fled Nazi Germany with their parents in the 1930s. My father and his widowed mother went straight to San Francisco, where a bachelor uncle sponsored them. My mother and her parents lived in Milan for a few years before leaving for San Francisco, also sponsored by a bachelor uncle, after an Italian friend warned my grandfather that Mussolini might not re-

Inge Scheuer, the author's mother, in Frankfurt am Main, ca. 1930.

main tolerant of the Jews in Italy. Like many other German Jews, relatives from both sides of my family fled to the Netherlands and were eventually able to emigrate to the United States, albeit quite late.

My parents were not *survivors*, even though they would be categorized as such by the U.S. Holocaust Memorial Museum; I reserve that term for Jews who lived in Europe during the war. However, they were refugees and had to register as aliens during World War II, since the State Department did not seem to distinguish between German Jews and German non-Jews. I grew up with some consciousness of the past but more with a sense of being different from my Jewish friends whose parents were born in the United States. By my mid-teens, I was deeply interested in the Holocaust and in family history, and I began my search in the small towns of my ancestry in Hessen and the Odenwald in Germany. My connection to and interest in this past and in trying to understand what my family experienced is still quite strong and made this research topic a very natural choice.[25]

Interviewing

Each person was first given an informed consent form and asked to sign it. The consent followed a format that is most relevant for experiments in medical science, outlining the possible costs and benefits of participating in the research. Nonetheless I had to use it, since it is legislated by the U.S. government. In one instance, a therapist was reading the informed consent sheet before our interview began when she suddenly exclaimed, "This is bullshit!" She had just read the section on "risks," which in her view understated the possible detrimental effects of participating in the interview. It read: "I do not feel that there is any medical risk involved in being part of this study, although it is likely to stir up certain emotions related to these memories." As a therapist as well as a former hidden child, she was amply aware of the potential aftereffects of dredging up traumatic memories. Indeed, she later explained that she had scheduled our interview on a Sunday rather than on a weeknight so that she would have some time to recover before going to work the next day.

I began the interview with great trepidation, fearful that she would interrupt and tell me how ridiculous or wrongheaded my questions were. Luckily, she did not, and we had an intense and insightful interview. We eventually became friends, and I later told her how much she had scared me with her forthrightness, and we were able to laugh about it. Indeed, having one's subjects "talk back" is one possible detrimental outcome when researchers are studying laterally (that is, studying those in the researcher's socioeconomic class) or up (studying those in a higher socioeconomic class). With her guidance, I amended the "risks" portion of the consent form by adding "although it is likely to stir up certain emotions related to these memories *and to the past*" and added another sentence: "In that sense, it could be upsetting for some."

Although I did not conceive this project within the framework of feminist theory or gender research, it is still no doubt affected by my approach as a feminist scholar. Thus, a focus on the young and vulnerable as well as a look inside families, where cooperation and cohesion are not assumed, reflect my general outlook as a critical and feminist sociologist. Although I was not doing research on gender issues per se, inevitably they have come up in the analysis, and perhaps it was my feminist eye that noted the distinctions in the first place. My interview style reflects a more feminist approach, although clearly feminists do not have a monopoly on such methods. I attempted to engage with my research subjects empathetically and sensitively, focusing on the particulars of each case, while asking certain similar questions of all respondents. The interviews often felt more like guided therapy sessions as I gently probed into deep and usually painful memories. No doubt I benefited from having had years of therapy myself as I took on the role of the one who asks and empathizes rather than the one who does the talking and in the process often gets upset.

I often felt that my own autobiography enhanced my ability to empathize with certain feelings that subjects expressed in interviews. I came into adulthood already orphaned, without the safety net of a large family. Rather, my fragmented family included my two elderly grandmothers and a brother with whom I was not close at that time. I know what it is like to feel alone, to have questions that no one but one's dead parents might be able to answer, and to envy others whose parents are alive and involved in their children's and grandchildren's lives. I felt this loss keenly when I had my own child, and my heart still wrenches when my son cries because he does not have any grandparents to dote on him, as do his friends. I also understand how difficult it is to experience not only sorrow about one's loss but also anger at those who are gone. Indeed, my autobiography has affected my choice of research topic, since I too have spent decades struggling with the challenge of creating a meaningful life and family after my natal family imploded.

My son was 4 when I began this research—a fair, blue-eyed, blond-haired Jewish boy who likely could have "passed" as a non-Jew at an earlier, more dangerous, time. I could not help but imagine the agony and vulnerability parents must have felt when they entrusted their child to a stranger and then again when they returned to claim a child who no longer knew them. But that's where the similarities end—in no way am I attempting to equate my imaginings with their experiences, since I did not live through persecution, separation from family, war, genocide, hunger, or poverty.

It is impossible to know whether my own story and the empathy it incurred truly affected the outcome of my research. All I can say is that generally I enjoyed a good rapport with those I interviewed, who seemed to respond positively to my approach. Some were complimentary and mentioned a previous researcher whom they had found cold, distant, and somewhat arrogant. Many were relieved to be talking about this part of their history, since previous interviews (such as the Spielberg project) had focused more on the war period. However, I am not claiming moral superiority in my positioning or arguing that only someone with the same position as her subjects can understand her respondents. It is simply that my particular vulnerabilities sometimes converged with those of my research subjects, and as a result I responded in a highly empathetic manner, whether verbally or nonverbally, consciously or unconsciously.

The first ten or so interviews were devastating for me. I often joined the interviewee in his or her tears and left their house in a state of numbness. I was glad to be alone and silent as I boarded a train home to The

Hague after those initial interviews. The pain suffered by these hidden children mostly after the war was beyond my imagination; I could not fathom a more tragic story, and then I would hear one the next day. It was overwhelming, exhausting, and at times unbearable, but after a while, it became easier, as I developed some distance. I certainly never became detached; instead, I attempted to conduct a kind of "compassionate sociology."

I interviewed two people who were emotionally frail and most probably were clinically diagnosed cases. One switched moods in a mercurial manner within seconds, from a kind of "high," which included singing, to deep lows of anger and crying; the other had suffered from depression for years and had been hospitalized for it. In both cases, I refrained from the prodding questions I would normally have formulated to follow up on the person's history. I shortened the interviews and asked both women several times whether they had someone they could call if they were upset after the interview; both claimed to have someone with whom they could talk.

Sex with Soup

My student research assistants in Davis and Berkeley transcribed the interviews. After the first twenty or so, I began to write down foreign words (either Dutch, Hebrew, German, or Yiddish) during the interview to accompany the tape to avoid what often resulted when American students tried to decipher foreign words. Two copies of the manuscript were mailed to each person so that she or he could correct one, send it back, and keep the other. In this way, interviewees were given a chance to read their narrative and to change or delete anything they did not want included. Very few sent back corrected transcripts, and among those few, little was changed or deleted; mostly spelling errors were corrected. One interviewee sent an angry letter about an error in her transcript that made her feel that it was "out of Kafka." It read:

Respondent: "We had sex with soup . . ."

　　　DW: "Uh-huh, sex with soup."

This respondent was so incensed by these lines that she withdrew her interview from my study. After listening to the original tape several times (because, like my student transcriber, I too heard "sex with soup"), I realized she was saying "sacks with soup," referring to packets of instant soup they had after the war. However, in her accented English, it came out more like "secks with soup." My letter of apology did not result in a change of mind, and her interview is not included.

I can well imagine that others might have reacted to this error differently, perhaps with more humor, but this interaction illustrates some of the many feelings—anger, resentment, sorrow—that can easily be provoked among those who have been deeply wounded. This person included in her letter that many others she knew also found many mistakes in their interviews. However, the entire purpose of sending two copies to each person was precisely to correct such mistakes! It was frustrating to hear that some people were complaining about my work in a situation they could correct.

I know that some interviewees will dislike the way they are portrayed in this book, most likely because they will feel that their story is being slighted, and that I gave more attention and space to someone else's. And I know that many, if not most, will not be shy in letting me know what they think. It is necessary to acknowledge that many people in my study have experienced significant trauma in their lives, which remains part of their psychological makeup. Deep feelings of deprivation that stem from their wartime experiences can be easily ignited, making them feel victimized once again. The last thing I want to do is to ignore the depth and importance of individual narratives or in any way to reproduce their postwar experience of having their particular traumas, tragedies, and triumphs downplayed. Indeed, I wish to honor each story and state how privileged I felt being able to meet these former hidden children. Yet this is a sociological analysis rather than a compilation of life histories and thus requires condensing individual stories and seeking general patterns. In addition, some interviews were richer than others, and those narratives may be easier to use more generously.

One great advantage and, as it turns out, great joy of studying laterally has been that I have been able to discuss my ideas and findings with some of my research subjects as colleagues—two therapists in particular—which has only deepened my understanding. This is a new experience for me, and a very satisfying one. I have maintained social ties with a small number of respondents, and I have communicated with everyone on occasion about the progress of this book. Because I am analyzing narratives and histories, these social connections do not bias my research.

In letting my research subjects decide what if any part of their narrative they wished to change, I was giving them the power not only to shape but to reshape their responses and the way they portrayed themselves. Ultimately, I am the one who analyzed the data and wrote the book. On the consent form, I asked each person whether they wanted their first name used in the book. In three cases where respondents wanted their names and identities changed so that they would not be recognized, I have sent parts of the book that are about them for their approval. Otherwise, those interviewed have not played any role in the way I have written about them.

I was able to present my research findings at the annual Conference of Jewish Child Survivors of the Holocaust in Amsterdam in August 2005. About forty people attended my talk, six of whom were in my study. Although I have given many talks during my twenty years of professional life, this particular presentation took me longer to shape, and I was atypically nervous about it a full week before my presentation. As I explained to my audience, it's rare for a sociologist to share her research results with those she studied. After all, when presenting to any other audience, it is clear who the "expert" on the topic is, but in this case, it was my audience who constituted the experts, experts who might "talk back" and be critical. Added to that, the Dutch are known to be very straightforward and honest in a manner that can be disarming to an American.

Judging by the forty-five minutes of discussion that followed my talk, I believe it went well. I was relieved when one of my subjects, the therapist who had been very direct with me when I gave her a consent form before our interview some years earlier, gave me a "thumbs-up" when I concluded. And a number of former hidden children reacted with moving comments and questions. Some expressed their pleasure at finally being seen and taken seriously as hidden children.

In terms of reciprocity, however, as with most research, I believe the payoff was unequal in the researcher's favor. I am aware that several former hidden children felt a sense of accomplishment at having done an interview with me because they were finally able to talk about their pasts. Some clearly appreciated the focus on and attention to their particular story, and I was thrilled when one therapist thanked me for a comment I made, which she considered an important insight. However, I do not assume that everyone felt similarly.

In a moving letter, one woman wrote the following to me after receiving copies of her interview:

> Reading this back, I realize how tremendously difficult your job is. So many not really relevant stories. . . . And I am not capable of sorting it out before telling it. I discovered, by reading this text, that this is a perfect image of my problem, for which I'm now in therapy: I just cannot think sharply enough to speak more simply. You must believe that reading this is very helpful for me, even though it must be difficult for you. That's part of the reason why I could not do this [the interview] earlier. I really am grateful to you, thank you.

LIVED EXPERIENCES

My family and I lived in The Hague for all of 1998, when my husband taught at the Institute of Social Studies (ISS) and I began this research. Our son, Max, was $3\frac{1}{2}$ when we arrived, and when he turned 4 that summer, he moved from a childcare setting to what we would call a nursery school within the larger public school in our neighborhood. The Dutch believe that this move at an early age helps socialize young children and assimilates them into the school system before they begin studying.

We met with his teacher at the Zonnenbloem School early on, a young woman freshly out of training beginning her first job. I had asked to meet with her to discuss Max's American background, his Dutch-language proficiency, and the subject of Christmas, since, as I explained to her, he is Jewish. We entered the classroom after school one day in September, and she began the conversation by offering that she knew something

about Jews because she had read a book about them. "You believe in Jesus Christ, right?" she asked. I hesitated and stated that Jews believe that
he existed but not that he was the son of God. "You drink goat's milk
when you eat meat, right?" she then asked. I was nonplussed but managed to say that religious Jews never mix milk with meat but that I had
never heard of the goat's milk part. I asked what the class would do for
Christmas, and she reassured me that there would be nothing religious,
so I left feeling reassured. However, the ignorance displayed by this educated young person who was also a teacher troubled me, to say the least.

Dutch slowly became my son's primary language, the one he played
and sang in, and he began to make mistakes in English grammar. As
Christmas (and our departure) neared, my son came home speaking
about *het kleine kindje Jezus* (the little baby Jesus), and I began to wonder
about the supposed nonreligious nature of the classroom teaching. I discovered that there was a manger in his classroom and that the New Testament story of Jesus was being taught to the children. I moved into high
gear, preparing Hanukkah decorations for his class, something I would
normally not do. I prepared cutouts of dreidels, a menorah, a Star of
David, and a list of these items for the teacher, encouraging her to have
my son explain them all to the class, since we were celebrating Hanukkah every night that particular week. As I cut out a Star of David, my son
said, "that's the *Ster van Bethlehem!*" (star of Bethlehem). I was appalled.
Though I had sent in the cutouts and the list with a letter to the teacher,
she never used any of it. Her explanation was: "We don't have time because we're preparing for Christmas."

I may have overestimated Dutch tolerance for diversity and inappro-
priately assumed that the teacher would embrace multiculturalism, as I
would expect her to do in the United States. And certainly, there were
other non-Christian children in that class besides my son. I felt very un-
easy, as though there was a strange undertone to all this. Perhaps mine is
an isolated story about one unusually ignorant young teacher; however,
I think not. I could not wait to fly back to California, where I felt at home
and where my son would forget about the little baby Jesus.

When we left the Netherlands in December 1998, I told my husband
that I would probably have felt more at ease had we spent the year in

Germany, since postwar generations there have done so much memory work and are not defensive, and certainly not smug. Just as an ethnographer's experiences with a culture are all part of the ethnographic process, I began to realize that these feelings of unease were part of my lived experience and also constituted an important aspect of my research (Gubrium and Holstein 1997).

Fast-forward seven years and six thousand miles to Berkeley, California, on November 21, 2004, to a late-afternoon talk by Philo Bregstein, co-author of the book *Remembering Jewish Amsterdam* (2004) and a filmmaker on the same topic. He was speaking about "the Jews of prewar Amsterdam," at an event co-sponsored by the Netherlands America University League of California (NAULCAL) and the contemporary Jewish Museum. The presentation took place in the Life Sciences Building at the University of California, Berkeley. About twenty to twenty-five people were in attendance, some of whom looked quite Jewish to me. At the beginning, an older slim, tall Dutch woman stood at the front of the room and spoke but did not welcome or even greet those present, most of whom were not part of NAULCAL. She started talking about the next event, a *kerstwijding*, which was a Christmas celebration, at a local church. She slightly berated the audience about how this event has not been well attended in the recent past, how people in attendance had put very little money in the collection box, and how these behaviors do not sufficiently show appreciation to the many people from NAULCAL who volunteered their entire day to prepare for the event. She droned on about the Christmas event, stating that "you don't need to be religious" to go and that "singing the songs feels very spiritual nonetheless."

She went on to discuss other events, but I could scarcely listen. Her announcement was shockingly surreal and made me wonder if I was in the right place. Here we were, a small, mostly Jewish crowd, gathered to hear about prewar Dutch Jewish life, which had been all but decimated owing in some part to the collaboration and inaction of the Dutch non-Jewish population. The generous interpretation is that either she had no idea that most of her audience was Jewish and/or she did not realize that Jews do not celebrate Christmas. The less generous interpretation is that by stating that one need not be religious to attend this church event she was completely erasing the identity and existence of most of her audience and the entire reason for their presence there that day. In this case, the perpetrator was not a young woman like my son's teacher, who may really not have known the history, but a much older person who had lived through the war.

A Dutch Jewish friend of mine who was there, a former hidden child who was interviewed for this book, was very upset by the announcement and spoke with another Dutch Jewish acquaintance in attendance, who was furious about the remarks. We all agreed that the announcement was shocking in its cluelessness. I am quite sure that had we discussed our feelings with this woman after the talk, rather than apologizing, she would have denied any wrongdoing and would likely have interpreted our reactions as "overly sensitive." Indeed, underlying her announcement and attitude was not only blatant tactlessness, but also either complete ignorance or a strain of latent anti-Semitism.

These incidences suggest tremendous ignorance as well as what appear to be somewhat smug assumptions. Both examples reflect an us-them approach that ignores anyone but the "us" and to some extent sees Jews as the Other, if they're seen at all. Although this book is more about what occurred within Dutch families after the war than it is about contemporary Dutch society, these themes are very present in parts of this book, especially when we consider the historical and postwar relationship between the Netherlands and Dutch Jews. I do not dwell on my experiences in this book, yet as lived experience, they constitute part of my knowledge and informed my understanding of the narratives I was privileged to hear.

As this book went into production, in February 2006, a *New York Times* article announced that the Dutch government finally had returned more than two hundred old-master paintings to the heir of Goudstikker, a Dutch Jewish art collector and dealer who in 1940 had sold his collection to Herman Göring and his dealer, Alois Miedl, a German businessman. Goudstikker then fled Holland and died in an accident on the boat taking him to safety. Since the end of the war, postwar Dutch governments had staved off claims by Goudstikker's heirs by arguing that the 1940 sale to Göring and his dealer was "voluntary." Goudstikker's heir was persistent, and eventually the Dutch government formed a commission to investigate these claims. In February 2006, the commission decided that the sale of Goudstikker's art to Göring and his dealer Meidl was "involuntary." The commission also recommended that Goudstikker's heir not be asked to pay for the returned art.

Medy van der Laan, the Dutch deputy culture minister, announced that the government felt that returning the paintings was "the morally correct action" and also that this restitution of Goudstikker's property was "a blood-letting for some of our museums" (Riding 2006). Just when I think I no longer can be affected by revelations about the Dutch government, I am proven wrong. The extreme insensitivity of a high government official's reaction in light of this case in particular and of the Jews in the Netherlands in general is truly astounding. I believe that it reflects a very particular attitude toward Jews that goes far beyond one young schoolteacher in The Hague.

A MAP OF THE BOOK

This book follows the chronology of events in the lives of hidden children and addresses the variety of post-Shoah family structures. In chapter 2 I delineate the relationship between the Dutch state and its Jewish population in modern history, with particular attention to the years 1940 to 1945. Chapter 3 examines how the postwar Netherlands absorbed its surviving Jewish population and how the state dealt with Jewish property and with Jewish children who had been orphaned by the war. Chapter 4 focuses on how children experienced the Nazi Occupation and their move into hiding, elucidating the experience of leaving parents and entering a new family, as well as the range of hiding experiences. While some hidden children lived in abysmal conditions, the majority did not, and some even had very positive experiences.

To facilitate an analysis of how the return of a parent or parents, compared with the return of no parents, affected hidden children and their respective family lives, the next several chapters are organized by the type of postwar family structure discussed. Thus, chapter 5 examines those families that remained intact, demonstrating that despite their relative "luck" and their enviable postwar context, children in such family structures often tended to experience unhappiness and a problematic family life. In chapter 6 I focus on families in which one parent returned, often leading to the addition of a stepparent. In some cases, stepparents were physically and sexually abusive to former hidden children, as we saw with Max L. in the introduction.

Chapter 7 focuses on orphans who either stayed in their foster/hiding family or joined either the family of a Jewish relative or another Jewish family who were not kin. A few people in my sample were fought over by their foster families and kin after the war, and some of these contentious cases ended up in the courts. An age-based analysis will be threaded throughout these empirical chapters to allow an understanding of how a child's age at hiding affected her or his postwar adjustments to family life. Chapter 8 deals specifically with those orphaned by the war who were placed in orphanages.

Finally, chapter 9 concerns the later lives of former hidden children as they married, created families, and entered professions. This chapter asks, How did hidden children fare as adults? After examining general patterns, I then turn to the development of a collective memory and identity among hidden children in the 1990s. The book concludes by elucidating what this hidden and haunted history contributes to our understanding of childhood, family, memory, and the Shoah, followed by an attempt to bring in a comparative perspective by discussing other relevant cases of war, genocide, and crimes against humanity.

CONCLUSIONS

Most scholarly work focused on Jewish Holocaust survivors has been done by psychologists who have tended to analyze their adaptation and the long-term clinical effects of the trauma they suffered (Kestenberg 1995). In most studies, the term *survivor* tends to be synonymous with those who were in concentration camps.[26] In light of the abundance of historical and psychological works on the Holocaust, sociologist Zygmunt Bauman (1989) pondered why there are massive "sociological silences" about one of the most defining events of the twentieth century.

This book, then, is part of a broader endeavor to create a sociology of the Holocaust and of post-Holocaust Jewish life (Gerson and Wolf, forthcoming; Lentin 2000; Wolf 2002), not only asking what sociology can offer to an analysis of the Holocaust, but, just as important, asking how the patterns, practices, and effects of the Holocaust can enrich the sociological endeavor.

This research focuses on a particular group of war survivors who have been missing from the limelight of Holocaust research. In addition to bringing in these overlooked survivors, this book deepens our understanding of the Shoah by focusing on its aftermath and not solely on its duration. In that manner, it contributes to a politics of memory in Jewish Studies as well.

A focus on post-Shoah life allows us to go beyond a view of European Jewry solely as victims, complicating the story considerably (Wolf 2002). This is not an attempt by any means to deny victimhood to European Jewry; rather, through its focus on childhood, family relations, and dynamics, this book highlights post-Shoah Jewish family life, in all its contradictions and complexities. Indeed, it may very well challenge myths about Jewish families, since in many cases, warmth, love, and connection were not in abundance in post-Holocaust Jewish family life. This research also challenges simplistic notions of the historical bourgeois family by demonstrating that what we think of as the "postmodern family" is actually not so new.

By analyzing some cases of Jewish war orphans whose fate was decided by the state, I cast an eye on state-family relations by examining how family is defined and how the state intervenes in dubious ways in family life. By looking at these orphans' fates, I highlight the cultural and historical specificities of "the best interests of the child," a contentious and highly fluid concept at best. At the same time, the Dutch state is implicated not only in the case of Jewish foster children but also in terms of postwar attitudes, policies, and practices.

This focus on children and families during and after genocide brings together the sociology of emotions with the sociology of war, interwoven with an examination of state-society ideologies and actions. In this way, the interactions of the micro-, meso-, and macrolevels are all addressed so as to better understand their sometimes deadly dynamics. My findings are not meant to bolster Holocaust studies alone; rather, they should help us to think comparatively about the effects of state, regional, and global politics on those who are vulnerable, marginal, and invisible, and whose haunting presence—and absence—deserves more attention.

2 Before and During the War

THE NETHERLANDS AND THE JEWS

The Jews have had a long historical presence in the Netherlands. Individual Ashkenazic Jews lived in several cities in the Netherlands during the Middle Ages, but the last ones left in the mid-sixteenth century. Portuguese Marranos—Sephardic Jews who were forced to convert to Christianity but who practiced Judaism in secret—and their descendants began living in the Netherlands in the late sixteenth century and practiced their Judaism openly without penalty, renewing Jewish life in this area. Eventually, the Dutch Jewish community received official recognition. Indeed, the famous Jewish philosopher and ethicist Spinoza was born in Amsterdam in 1632 to parents who had fled Portugal. Ashkenazic Jews started to arrive in the wake of the Portuguese Jews, and in 1635, they started their own community.[1]

After the mid-seventeenth-century Cossack massacres, there was an influx of Ashkenazic Jews from Poland and, after an invasion of Lithuania by the Swedes, from Lithuania as well. Jews "enjoyed tolerance and security of life and property" in the Netherlands (J. Michman 1990: 1045). In 1795, after French republican troops occupied the country, the Batavian Republic was founded, and in 1796, the Jews were granted full civil rights (van Galen Last and Wolfswinkel 1996). Compared with other European countries at that time, the Netherlands was seen by Jews as a relatively safe place to settle.

This popular image of Dutch historical tolerance toward the Jewish population continues today with Anne Frank, Holland's "unofficial patron saint" (Miller 1990: 96), dominating contemporary global images of the Netherlands during World War II. Our understanding of Anne Frank's story is emblematic of the image of staunch Dutch resistance to the Nazis. This image is corroborated to some extent by the number of Dutch non-Jews honored at the international Holocaust memorial, Yad Vashem, for their role in saving Jews; all those honored were nominated by surviving Jews.[2] Indeed, the Netherlands has one of the highest numbers of "Righteous Among the Nations" honored at Yad Vashem—4,716—ranking second only after Poland, with 5,941.[3] However, the Netherlands is quite competitive with Poland on another, less well-known, list. This list orders the proportion of each country's Jewish population killed during World War II (see table 1). Indeed, weighing in at more than 70 percent, and listed right before Poland, the Netherlands is the only Western European country whose rates of Jewish deportation and murder resemble those of an Eastern European country.

What exactly does this mean in human terms? It means that although Holland's prewar Jewish population was less than half that of France's, more Dutch than French Jews were deported and killed, in both absolute and relative terms. Twenty-five thousand more Dutch Jews were killed than French Jews—a full one-third more. Of course, we must note that some of the Jews in Holland were German Jewish refugees, and some of those in France were Polish Jewish refugees. Nonetheless, that does not change the numbers. In statistical terms, the odds of a Jew being deported from France and murdered compared with her odds of being deported from Holland were about 1:3.[4] These statistics are inverted when we examine postwar Jewish populations. Fully three-fourths of the Jewish population in France survived the war, compared with only one-

Table 1   Jewish Populations and Death Rates in Selected European Countries

Country	Prewar Jewish population	Number of deaths during World War II	Percentage of Jewish population killed
Italy	43,118[a]	9,000	20
France	310,000	75,000	24
Belgium	90,000	24,000	26
Luxembourg	3,000	<1,000	<33
The Netherlands	140,000	>100,000	>70
Poland	3,300,000	3,000,000	90

SOURCE: Hilberg 1985: 64.

[a]In 1941 there were 39,444 Italian citizens of Jewish descent and 3,674 Jews from other countries.

quarter in Holland. In other words, contrary to popular notions of virulent French anti-Semitism and a strong Dutch Resistance movement, Jews were actually safer in France than in the Netherlands during the war.

The Nazis found relatively little resistance to their occupation in the Netherlands; rather, they enjoyed acquiescence and cooperation from the Dutch state and its institutions, including the civil service and, for the most part, the police (Meershoek 1998). Indeed, Holland did quite well on the Nazi report card of good behavior: even Eichmann is reported to have said that "it was a pleasure to work with them" (cited in Blom 1989).

The history of acquiescence during the Nazi Occupation in the Netherlands, especially regarding the fate of the Dutch Jews, challenges popular assumptions about the tolerant if not supportive relationship between the Dutch state and its Jews. Despite images to the contrary, historians confirm that those who helped to save Jews during the Occupation in the Netherlands consisted of a small minority. By the time the Resistance was well organized, most Dutch Jews had already been deported to camps, and it was too late to help them. The majority of Dutch non-Jews apparently either did not care or were not unhappy about the fate of their Jewish compatriots. In fact, the number of Dutch collaborators with the Nazis exceeded the number of those in the Resistance. Relative to the population, the Netherlands had the highest number of Waffen-SS volunteers in Western Europe (Gerstenfeld 2001).

While a generous explanation might attribute Dutch passivity during the Occupation to fear of Nazi retribution, this cannot explain the cold and discriminatory reaction of the Dutch state and its non-Jewish population to surviving Dutch Jews *after* the war. The relatively few Dutch Jews who survived the Shoah were grudgingly received with minimal effort by the state to welcome or reintegrate them into Dutch society. Indeed, if anything, Jews experienced a complete lack of understanding, sympathy, and sensitivity from the state about their plight and the decimation of their community.

This chapter will delineate the relationship between the Netherlands and its Jewish citizens up until 1945, with particular attention paid to the German Occupation. The postwar context is the topic of the next chapter. The history of the Occupation has filled numerous books and articles. This chapter, however, is limited to certain highlights and questions that bear on the environments in which Jewish children were hidden, and from which they and their families emerged. But key to this discussion is an attempt to understand how and why the machinery of genocide found a comfortable home in the Netherlands. This exploration simultaneously defrocks an image that conflates "the Dutch" with "the Resistance" and lays bare a less well-known and less noble past. Gerstenfeld claims that compared with other European countries, the Netherlands suffers the greatest gap between its image and its reality (2001: 10). Based on secondary research, this chapter and the next will address that very gap.[5]

THE ROLE OF HISTORIOGRAPHY

Before delving into a description of Jewish life in the Netherlands, it is worthwhile to ponder why this brief depiction of the Netherlands and its behavior toward its Jewish population during and after the Nazi Occupation might be so surprising to some. Part of the answer lies in the historiography of Dutch Jewry—the ways in which history has or, in this case, has not been written, who has written it, and what was included or excluded. Indeed, historians of the Shoah have tended to ignore the Netherlands, devoting their attention to Germany and Eastern Europe. Relative to other European countries, there is very little written in English about the Netherlands and the Nazi Occupation, compared with, for example, what is written about Denmark or France.

When people have asked me about my research as I was writing this book, the usual initial response to my description of what happened to Dutch Jews has been surprise, since most people assume that the Dutch were, as one American Jewish woman stated to me, "the good ones." Surprise is usually followed by an admission that the person does not know anything about what happened in Holland during the war. The latter response is completely understandable, given that so little has been written in English about Holland and its Jews during the war. However, the surprise stems from a widely held assumption that Dutch Jews fared well because they were taken care of by the rest of the Dutch population. Some Dutch Jews joke bitterly and say that people abroad think that all Dutch Jews were saved except for Anne Frank.[6]

Indeed, it seems as if the Dutch postwar image of a nation of resistors became globalized through the Anne Frank story. Her diary has sold 25 to 30 million copies and has been translated into sixty languages, even though its initial printing in Holland drew little interest and was discontinued (Covington 2001: 74). This narrative was built on the relatively positive attitude of the Dutch state to the Jews for centuries, with no history of pogroms or blood libels. It is also possible that the strong and supportive reactions of the Dutch state and people to Israel after the 1967 and 1973 wars contributed to the narrative about the positive and helpful Dutch attitude toward Jews, at least in Israel. Simon Kuper (2003), a writer with a British, Dutch, and Jewish background and whose book focuses on Ajax, the so-called Jewish soccer team during World War II in Holland, finds that Israelis are inculcated with a great admiration for the Dutch and wholeheartedly believe that the Dutch were and still are good to the Jews (196–200).

Several historians have attended to the question of Dutch historiography with great acumen and in considerable depth (D. Michman 2001; Moore 1997; de Haan 1998 and 2001). Dan Michman, an Israeli historian of the Holocaust and the Netherlands, found that the historiography of the Occupation, the Netherlands, and its Jews has been divided between those who do and those who do not read Dutch.[7] Since until recently most scholarship on the Netherlands and its Jews was written in Dutch, most non-Dutch historians of the Holocaust either left the Netherlands out of their scholarship or relied on limited, and at times faulty, materials.

In the most comprehensive and well-known histories of the Holocaust and the Jews, such as those by Lucy Dawidowicz or Martin Gilbert, among many others, the Dutch case is missing. While Gilbert mentions Dutch Jews in a few places in his book, Holland does not appear once in Dawidowicz's text, but only in an appendix, and there in statistical form only (D. Michman 2001: 377–78). Dan Michman asserts that Raul Hilberg ignored a fair amount of data on the Netherlands so that Holland would fit into his framework. He also ignored Dutch-language scholarship on the topic. Michman found that the little Hilberg wrote on the Netherlands is not substantiated by the kinds of sources that normally typify his careful work. Zygmunt Bauman mentions Holland only once in his book (as does Daniel Goldhagen, but Michman points out that Goldhagen's reference is not to the country but to the scholar Dorothy Holland [2001: 379]). "The almost entire absence of the Netherlands in all these accounts is no accident," Michman argues (385).

As British historian and Dutch specialist Bob Moore points out, most Dutch scholarship was unknown internationally. Owing to a language barrier until recently, this has kept most scholarly research about that period limited to an internal discussion in Dutch among Dutch academics and Israeli academics with a Dutch background and was typified as a national discussion turned inward (1997: 14). The historiography of the persecution of the Jews in the Netherlands was viewed as a domestic issue rather than being linked to broader political or structural phenomena (1). Previous generations of Dutch historians did not publish in English-language journals or in other languages more accessible to the international community. For the most part, they did not participate in international conferences and did not engage in global academic debates in Shoah-related scholarship. Rather, they were more introverted and to some extent provincial. That dynamic has shifted with a generation or two of Dutch historians who publish in English, work in comparative frameworks, and are more engaged in international conferences and debates (de Haan 2001; Hondius 2003; Flim 2004). Additionally, Moore joins historians such as Joel Fishman (an American who lives in Israel) and Deborah Dwork as foreigners who have focused on the Netherlands and who read Dutch-language materials. Clearly, however, their group constitutes a very small number of outsiders looking in. Dutch historian Ido de Haan notes another division in the historiography of Dutch Jewry, especially about the experience of Jews during the Nazi Occupation, between Jewish and non-Jewish scholars. He argues that the persecution of the Jews in the Netherlands was seen as Jewish history, rather than as Dutch history:

> The memory of the persecution, as it was shaped in historical studies, was as divided as the experience, not because the experiences were different, but because the dividing line between Jews and non-Jews was still very much in place. Non-Jewish scholars did not write about the persecution of the Jews because it was considered "Jewish history" and Jewish scholars tended to write about the history of Jewish persecution as something that bore no relation to Dutch society. (2001: 411)

Joel Fishman pushes this argument even further: "Historians and political scientists . . . have ignored Dutch Jewry and its painful experience of reintegration" (1993: 99). Fishman argues that while the government can be criticized for its policies and (in)actions, historians and political scientists are complicit in that they have tended to ignore this less-than-noble past, particularly when writing for an international audience. These scholars, Fishman argues, have propagated the "myth of the Netherlands," a myth of a country with "an advanced policy toward all minorities," a myth that builds on the Anne Frank story (100). With the 2004 murder of film director Theo van Gogh in Amsterdam, followed by a strong outpouring of anti-Muslim sentiment and attacks, this myth of Dutch tolerance is once again being challenged.

Historian Werner Warmbrunn's 1963 book (in English) on the Dutch under German occupation is a good example of Fishman's and de Haan's points. Warmbrunn writes about "the Dutch" as though they are a category apart from Jews. There is no mention of Dutch anti-Semitism or of collaboration, only of Jewish "victimization," and that is presented in a passive manner that avoids any attribution. Political scientist Arend Lijphart's 1976 book on democracy and pluralism in Holland celebrates the Dutch political system as a model of tolerance and moderation in which there is universal justice and there are no disenfranchised minorities deprived of civil liberties (Fishman 1993: 100).

Fishman's 1993 essay on three then-recent studies of postwar Jewish life in the Netherlands points to gendered differences in research. He focuses on Chaya Brasz, a Dutch historian now living in Israel, on Dienke Hondius, a Dutch historian in Holland, and on Dutch journalist Elma Verhey. All three have written what could be considered critical examinations of postwar life for Jews in the Netherlands. The gender of these three writers may be important in that as women, and thus as those who have experienced marginalization, they are focusing on other marginalized groups. The exception to Fishman's findings, however, are Bob Moore (1977) and Ido de Haan (1997), both male historians whose writings are very critical indeed.

My reading of the English-language scholarship (and a smattering of Dutch-language materials) suggests that de Haan's argument concerning the divide between Jewish history and so-called Dutch history still remains intact to some extent, although a major generational shift has occurred recently, blurring these previous divisions. With those observations in mind, I will now turn to the position of the Jews in the Netherlands.

THE DUTCH JEWS, 1900–1939

It seems to be the general consensus among some historians that Dutch Jews in the 1930s were well integrated into Dutch society (Mason 1984: 315) and enjoyed a "relatively favorable" position in prewar Netherlands (Blom 1989: 388). Yet this premise is questioned by other historians

(Leydesdorff 1994; Moore 1997; D. Michman 1984; Hondius 2003; Boas 1967). What they all agree on is that a relatively low level of overt anti-Semitism existed in prewar Holland.

Who were the Jews in prewar Holland? Where did they live, what did they do, and what was their relationship to non-Jewish society? Early-twentieth-century Dutch Jewry from either Sephardic or Ashkenazic descent formed a relatively poor and urban group (Moore 1997). On the whole, most Dutch Jews were not religious but had a strong cultural connection to their Jewishness. The working-class Jews of the late nineteenth century were drawn to and involved in socialism, which, along with urbanization, tended to weaken religious observance. In 1930 the Dutch census reported 111,917 Jews, 95 percent of whom were Ashkenazic. The Jews in the Netherlands constituted only 1.41 percent of the total population at that time. Amsterdam Jews referred to Amsterdam as *mokum*, a word derived from the Hebrew word for place, *makom*. Indeed, *mokum* was home for the majority of Dutch Jews. Fifty-nine percent of the Jewish population lived in Amsterdam, and most others lived in the two next-largest cities—Rotterdam and The Hague. In all, 80 percent of the Jewish population lived in the seven largest cities in the Netherlands, while 10 percent lived in smaller towns, and only 10 percent in rural areas (Moore 1997: 25). The eminent Dutch-Israeli historian Jozeph Michman describes the interwar years as a period that witnessed the rebirth of Jewish literature, journalism, organizations, and social life as well as a small but growing Zionism movement among the young (2001: 214).

In her work on the Jewish proletariat in Amsterdam, Dutch historian Selma Leydesdorff (1994) argues that there was a kind of "Jewish economy"—specific sectors with high concentrations of Jews, with other sectors closed to Jews. Thus, as elsewhere in Europe, Jews were clustered in particular niches in the labor market. In 1930s Holland, these niches were diamonds, clothing, food, and retail. In fact, a 1936 study of and report on Jews in the Netherlands found 45 percent in "retail," which most likely meant selling at the marketplace or in shops.

Although there was a small number of well-off Jewish bankers and diamond dealers, in addition to a group of middle-class merchants and well-off professionals, the majority of Jews were in lower-middle-class or working-class occupations. Many were peddlers and market hawkers and were very poor (Moore 1997: 26; Bregstein and Bloemgarten 2004). Leydesdorff explains that certain occupations, such as working in Bijenkorf, a large department store, were culturally very acceptable and desirable at that time. The diamond workers' trade union and other unions were crucial for some of these families, since they raised their standard of living. Working in larger or smaller shops was acceptable but slightly less desirable. Although Leydesdorff uses the term *proletariat* to denote the culture of poor Jews, she explains that it was really more of a lumpenproletariat made up of Jews who eked out their living from day to day, for example, by peddling their wares. A report on Amsterdam Jews in 1937 found that 50 percent were very poor and about 70 percent were clearly at the poverty level (Moore 1997: 27).[8] Indeed, Leydesdorff's 1994 research warns against romanticizing about the past, because for most Dutch Jews, it was extremely difficult to survive.

Although a specifically Jewish workers' movement never developed in the Netherlands, an Amsterdam Jewish socialist workers' culture did. When people I interviewed said their parents were not religious, but were simply "Amsterdam Jews," they were referring to this cultural context, which was quite separate and different from the non-Jewish one. Although poor Jews who sold at the open market spoke Dutch rather than Yiddish, it was a Dutch mixed with Yiddish and impossible for an outsider to understand (Leydesdorff 2002: 229).

To understand how so many Jews could be deported to camps during the war from a large city such as Amsterdam, we must address the extent to which Jews and non-Jews interacted in pre-1940s Holland. And to do that we must understand the basic social structure of Dutch society. In the late 1880s, the Calvinists and Roman Catholics became coalition partners to protect their interests "against the demands of the 'liberal' state" (Moore 1997: 23). They realized that being socially organized could lead to political representation of their own interests. This process of "pillarization," or *verzuiling*—perhaps better understood as segmentation— refers to groups *(zuilen)* that united people on the basis of religious affiliation, cutting across class lines. The four main *zuilen* were (1) the Roman

Catholics and (2) the Calvinists, both stemming from the pre-nineteenth-century period, and (3) the socialists, consisting mostly of social democrats. The fourth, weaker, "pillar" was the liberal or neutral one. Most of Dutch society was part of one of these four *zuilen*, although many segments of society, such as urban male youth, large segments of business owners, and the cultural elite were not.

> Characterised as *burgerlijk-verzuild* (bourgeois-pillarised), this form of societal organisation was more or less unique to the Netherlands. . . . These four "pillars" . . . were bound together by a common adherence to what might essentially be termed bourgeois precepts and beliefs, namely capitalist production, parliamentary democracy, order and authority, national interests and a set of rules for civility and proper conduct. (Moore 1997: 23)

While the four main *zuilen* cooperated with each other, smaller minority groups were excluded from such interaction and from participation in mainstream Dutch society. These minority groups, however, mimicked some of the institutions and structures of the main *zuilen*. Moore asserts that the Jewish community was too fragmented to reproduce these organizational structures and did not create *zuilen*, or anything like them, to protect its interests. However, in their social and political activities Jews were associated only with the socialist and liberal pillars.

Although the Jews in prewar Holland did not have one particular interest in common, such as religious belief, they remained linked by a sense of an ethnic culture, at the very least. The divisions between Ashkenazic and Sephardic Jews, however, were substantial. Furthermore, strong class divisions existed. The commercial and financial bourgeoisie were assimilating into liberal institutions, while workers were turning to socialism. Thus, religious affiliation that was weak, if it existed at all, could not overcome the much stronger class and ethnic divisions to create and support a unified set of Jewish interests. Moore adds that fear of anti-Semitism may have prevented some Jews from attempting to organize politically. In addition, the preexistence of synagogues and Jewish schools may have provided some Jews with a sense of having a protective organization, however weak it might have been.

In the 1930s, Moore explains, the two most significant trends among Dutch Jews were acculturation and secularization, which meant that these Jews observed only the major holidays, if they observed any at all. In Bregstein and Bloemgarten's interviews, in which they asked questions of respondents about prewar Jewish Amsterdam, some Jews recounted their families' strong cultural identities despite their lack of religious observance. For example, in these types of households, families would observe three Jewish customs—circumcision, a Jewish wedding, and a Jewish funeral—in addition to adhering to the Jewish workweek, that is, resting on Saturday but working on Sunday (2004: 32).

This is not to say that the Jews simply melted into mainstream Dutch society and became indistinguishable from non-Jews. By 1941 less than 1 percent of Amsterdam Jews (500 out of a population of 79,400) had been baptized, only about 17 percent of Jewish marriages were "mixed marriages," that is, to a Catholic or Protestant partner, and about 92 percent of Jewish weddings were officiated in synagogues. Thus, despite the trends of assimilation and secularization, Jews were still operating within certain traditional parameters at higher rates than they were in almost all other Western and Central European countries. Indeed, the conversion rate was much lower in the Netherlands than it was among Jews in neighboring Germany.

Although there were certain sites of assimilation, such as unions and financial institutions (Moore 1997: 162), Jews were perceived by other sectors of Dutch society as a separate group, and on the whole, there was not much interaction between Jews and non-Jews. A number of historians have argued that Dutch Jews were assimilated into Dutch society and treated as equal under the law. However, as Dienke Hondius's 2003 research makes very clear, Dutch mainstream society was always very aware of who was Jewish, even if the Jews were highly assimilated. This scenario is somewhat comparable to the process of Jewish assimilation into North American society in the 1930s. Despite changing their names and dropping many Jewish religious and cultural practices, they were still viewed as Jews first by mainstream Anglo society.

After Hitler's ascendancy to power in 1933, there was an influx into the Netherlands of German Jewish refugees who either were seeking a new home or were simply on the way to another destination, such as the United States. Anne Frank's family, which left Frankfurt am Main in search of a safer place to settle, was part of that wave of refugees. The geographical proximity of the Netherlands to Germany made it particularly appealing to those who lived in western Germany, and many thought that the Dutch language would not be difficult to master, since it was close to German (D. Michman 1978). Preexisting economic ties were also an attraction for German Jews. Moore (1986) mentions another attraction for German Jews: Holland's neutrality during World War I meant that a historically based animosity toward Germans did not exist there, as it did in Belgium and France.

Dutch Jews may have shown solidarity toward these newly arriving German Jews, but they did not necessarily like them. Many German Jews seemed arrogant, and some did not hide their contempt for the Dutch Jews. Moore notes that some German Jews praised everything German, while treating Dutch Jews as inferior (1997: 31). It is also likely that these attitudes held by German Jews reflected class differences, since German Jews with resources were more likely to flee, and, as noted, a high proportion of Dutch Jews were poor. However, Dan Michman points out that the antagonism toward German Jews was felt most strongly by the Dutch bourgeois Jews, who felt that their "Dutchness" was being endangered. With the influx of refugees, local Dutch Jews were associated with "foreign Jews," which challenged their sense of citizenship and loyalty (1981).

The Dutch government was concerned about the rising tide of refugees and sought to stem it by closing the border. The Anschluss (the political union of Germany and Austria) and then Kristallnacht in November 1938 made many German Jews even more desperate to flee. At that point, the Dutch government closed the border but allowed 7,000 refugees in, with the understanding that they would be living in refugee camps. It also bears noting that a number of German Jewish children entered Holland without their parents and were put into orphanages or into foster Jewish homes rather than camps (Moore 1997: 34). One of the government's main arguments for not allowing in more German Jews was that it wanted to contain the number of Jews in Holland so as to not contribute to a rise in anti-Semitism (Hondius 2003: 13). This policy decision and its rationale likely reflected state anti-Semitism more than the state's fear of anti-Semitism. Indeed, many Dutch Gentile families resented the German Jews, who could afford to rent more expensive apartments in Amsterdam than they could.

The Dutch state was not prepared to help these Jewish refugees. It viewed the problem as a private matter for the international Jewish and Dutch Jewish communities to solve, not a public matter of state interest or obligation (Hondius 2003; D. Michman 1978). This view is consistent with the ways in which the *zuilen* operated—taking care of their own with specific social welfare agencies. Although some feel that this was not simply a Jewish problem but a European and international one with which the state should have helped, this pattern continued well into and after the war and will be relevant to our discussion about postwar Jewish children.

One result of this influx of German Jewish refugees was that the Dutch Jewish community was asked to pay for a central refugee camp in Westerbork, "an isolated and bleak spot . . . not far from the German border" (Moore 1997: 34). The government specified that conditions in Westerbork were not to be more comfortable or attractive than the housing of the very poor local population (Hondius 2003: 14), again using the argument that this was the best way to avoid inciting anti-Semitic sentiment. Housed in barrack blocks in a cold and isolated area, far from urban life, German Jews did not find this arrangement very dignified or appealing. Moore points out that the Dutch government wanted to avoid appearing to do more for the refugees than they would do for unemployed Dutch citizens. Furthermore, he suspects that the conditions at Westerbork were created to be less than welcoming in order to encourage the German Jews to emigrate elsewhere. Indeed, of the 34,000 refugees who entered Holland from 1939 to 1940, only about half remained when the Germans invaded in 1940.

THE 1940S: OCCUPATION

In 1940–41, the Jewish population in the Netherlands totaled 140,000 "full" Jews (those with two Jewish parents), constituting 1.6 percent of the total population of 8.9 million.[9] Fifty-three percent of the total Jewish population—75,000—lived in Amsterdam at that time (J. Michman 1990: 1045). Of the 140,000 "full" Jews, about 15,000 (11 percent) were German Jews, and about 7,000 (5 percent) were categorized as "Others," most likely Eastern European Jews. An additional 19,500 (12 percent) were born of mixed marriages, or what the Nazis considered a special category, *Mischlinge* (Moore 1997: 65). Of the 140,000 "full" Jews, almost 90 percent identified as Jewish. Twelve thousand of them (9 percent) had no religious affiliation, whereas 700 (0.5 percent) were Roman Catholics, and 1,200 (0.9 percent) were Protestants.

On the night of May 10, 1940, the Nazis invaded the Netherlands. The Dutch army surrendered on May 14. Queen Wilhelmina fled to London, where a government-in-exile was created. Many Jews panicked and attempted to leave on boats for England, but most of these boats were turned back. Dutch Jewish historian Jacob Presser estimated that only a "few hundred" with resources were able to escape by sea to Great Britain, including seventy-five German and Austrian Jewish children who had been part of several Kindertransports and were living in a Jewish orphanage in Amsterdam (cited in Moore 1997: 46). In a panic, German Jewish refugee Gerhard Durlacher and his parents drove to a harbor to flee Holland, but they were turned back and told to go home. He describes what it felt like to be trapped and hunted as a Jew under Nazi Occupation in the Netherlands, trying not to be caught: "Benumbed like rabbits caught in a strong beam of light, we waited and waited. Escape appeared to be fraught with danger. . . . The days were covered in a veil of fear" (1991: 33). Eventually he and his family were caught and sent to Auschwitz via Westerbork.

In the first days after Dutch capitulation to the Nazis, Jews committed suicide at a rate that is thought to be higher than that in other countries (L. de Jong 1990: 23). It is estimated that at least 700 Dutch Jews attempted suicide in 1940 (Ultee, van Tubergen, and Luijkx 2001). The Nazis' strategy in the Netherlands was similar to what had been used in Norway: they viewed the Dutch as another Aryan population that might be persuaded to join the cause of National Socialism. Therefore, they did not think that a large and strong military presence was needed. After an initial period of military rule, the Nazis appointed Arthur Seyss-Inquart, an Austrian officer, as *Reichskommissar* (Reich commissioner) to lead a civil administration. Seyss-Inquart had gained notoriety because of his role in the Anschluss in Austria. Moore (1997) and Dan Michman (1993) argue that, in fact, the creation of a civil administration allowed the SS and the Nazi Party much more influence in running the country. For that reason the position of the SS and the Gestapo was stronger in the Netherlands than it was in France or Belgium, where the military remained in charge. The administrative regime in the Netherlands, Michman argues, resembles the Polish model more than the French or Belgian one (D. Michman 1993: 374–75, 377). Five thousand German police were stationed in the Netherlands, compared to less than three thousand in the more populated France (Moore 1997: 193).

Initially, it was relatively quiet under the new regime, assuaging some fears, although rumors swirled fast and furious, keeping the Jewish population on edge. In late June, the Ministry of Labor stated that all unemployed Dutch males had to register for labor in Germany, where they would find good wages and benefits. A few days later, a more threatening edict stated that not registering would result in a loss of benefits to the unemployed male and his family. Shortly thereafter, edicts were issued that slowly and bureaucratically identified, isolated, and eventually removed the Jews from the country (Moore 1997: 53). The very first piece of legislation stated that by July 15, all Jews and anti-German Dutch were to be fired from the Dutch civilian air-raid protection services. This announcement came in letter form, along with a warning threatening further action if these orders were not followed (53).

September 1940 brought the banning of all Jewish newspapers. Later, after the Joodse Raad (Jewish Council) was established by Nazi edict, their newspaper, *Het Joodse Weekblad* (the Jewish Weekly Newspaper), was allowed to be printed. Simultaneously, the Nazi regime ordered all Dutch civil servants to fill out a form declaring whether they were Jewish or married to a Jewish woman. Although this process of Aryanizing the civil service did cause a "stir" among the Dutch population, as Jozeph Michman points out, "few civil servants failed to comply with it" (1990: 1047). By November 4, all Jewish civil servants had been suspended, although their salary and then some retirement pay continued for a short period. Again, there was widespread cooperation from the Dutch bureaucracy—no non-Jewish civil servants quit or tried to organize resistance to these orders. At the end of November, the occupying government informed all government departments, local authorities, and educational institutions that all their Jewish staff was to be fired (Moore 1997: 57). Some students protested and went on strike, and the universities strongly protested. Some academics wrote or spoke out in protest of their colleagues' dismissal. Most of the student leaders were arrested, and one law professor was detained. As a result of the protests, the Germans closed down many Dutch universities (57).

Bob Moore describes in more detail what happened in some cases. The Jews who worked for the Amsterdam telephone company were not even allowed to enter the building to bid farewell to their colleagues. The president of the Dutch Supreme Court, Lodewijk Visser, was Jewish and had been suspended and subsequently dismissed by the German occupying government. Moore points out, however, that there was collusion on the part of the Dutch government: "When debating the issue, his former colleagues voted in favour of his dismissal by a majority of 12 to 5. A good deal of justified criticism has been levelled at the High Court, not only because of its behaviour towards its former president, but also because no word of protest came from this body which was charged with upholding the very principles of Dutch law against which the 'aryanisation' of the civil service so grossly offended" (1997: 58).

Following their established pattern, the Nazi administration continued to deliver law after law that identified and then fully isolated the Jewish population, bit by bit. However, the most serious laws, those with lethal consequences, came in 1941. Some months earlier, all Jewish businesses had been registered. But in January 1941, another decree stated that all Jews, as defined by having one Jewish grandparent, had to report in person for registration. As Jozeph Michman reports, 140,245 "full" Jews registered, along with 19,561 *Mischlinge* (1990: 1047).

Why might have over 140,000 Jews registered willingly? How can we explain this orderly conduct and the lack of any substantial resistance to registration? One explanation is that the Dutch population was accustomed to registration, along with other similar types of bureaucratic practices.[10] Such registrations had been introduced in the Netherlands by the French during Napoleonic occupation and were not a new effort. Indeed, the Germans thought the Dutch organization of the census office was "exemplary" (Presser 1988: 37). As Moore points out, however, this registration, while innocent enough in peacetime, turned lethal in wartime. In effect, after the Final Solution was developed, this registration became the collective death warrant of the Jewish community under the Nazi Occupation, and paradoxically, the Jews had co-signed it (1997: 196). However, it should be noted that when the Jews registered in early 1941, their act spelled deportation but not yet certain death.

This is in no way to suggest that the blame lies with the victims. A number of scholars have underscored the accommodation of the Dutch civil service to the increasingly offensive laws introduced by the occupying regime. That no high administrator or police chief wavered in his support of Nazi edicts, uttered a protest, or resigned, set the tone and the stage for all lower bureaucrats, and to some extent for the Dutch population, to follow suit and to accommodate the racial laws of the Nazi administration.

One Dutch bureaucrat, Jacob Lentz, was the head of the state population registries and had been acknowledged and decorated by the Crown for his work in standardizing and compiling the registers in the mid-1930s. Before the Occupation, Lentz ambitiously had proposed creating identity cards with photographs. The Dutch government rejected his idea in favor of a much simpler ration card. One of the state's main reasons for rejecting Lentz's proposal was that "the introduction of a compulsory identity card, with the implication that every citizen was a potential criminal, was contrary to Dutch tradition" (Moore 1997: 196).

The arrival of new bosses—the Nazis—gave Lentz a new venue for his proposal and his ambitions, both of which had been shelved. Indeed, the Nazis welcomed his enthusiastic approach to creating a method that would help them divide and control the population. Lentz went above and beyond the call of duty and created an ID card that required two photos, two sets of fingerprints, a stamp, two signatures of the bearer, one signature and the initials of the officials, all on watermarked paper, using special ink. His ID card was difficult to replicate or forge, a problem not faced by the Belgian or French Underground. Indeed, the "apparent inviolability of the identity card system" was "undoubtedly a factor unique to the Netherlands in relation to other German occupied territories, and provided a major hindrance for any type of illegal work" (Moore 1997: 197). Lentz's foolproof identity card met with the approval of the Germans, who thought that his creation was even more secure than the *Kennkarte* (identity card) they had issued in Germany in the 1930s. Presser quotes a letter from Lentz, who was pleased with the Germans' response to his work, to German authorities in 1942: "Our slogan: 'To record is to serve'" (Presser 1988: 38). The cards were fully introduced by the end of 1941 (Moore 1997: 197).

Moore notes that Lentz worked especially hard on improving registration information on Jewish citizens in the Netherlands, whose cards were issued with a "J" stamped on them. Lentz went so far as to compile a list of what he thought were typically Jewish family names and then seek out citizens by the same names who had not registered as Jews. Apparently, Moore explains, this bureaucratic ingenuity met a roadblock when Lentz presented his system to Generalkommissar Wimmer, who found his own family name on the list (de Jong, L., cited in Moore 1997: 198)! Moore believes that Lentz was most likely pro-German, largely because of the German interest in efficiency: "His aim and motivation was bureaucratic perfection, apparently without concern for the practical effects of his work" (198). Although he apparently had "no love for the Jews," neither was he a Nazi. Indeed, he seems to have been a typical Dutch citizen who had anti-Semitic prejudices and also happened to be a bureaucrat who was given the chance to serve to his utmost: "If nothing else, here was a case where the traditional Dutch civil service ethos of obedience and order had shown itself capable of implication in the most heinous crimes when all moral and legal controls were removed." After the war, Lentz was sentenced to only three years of prison, despite the likelihood that his efforts had led to the killing of thousands of Jews and non-Jews by the Germans (Moore 1997: 199).

Dutch civil servants not only stamped the "J" on Jewish ID cards, but they also provided the Nazis with a map of Amsterdam, designating

Jewish areas. Between 1940 and 1942 the Office of the National Inspectorate of Registers produced detailed documentation of houses and streets occupied by Jews, with maps indicating Jews by dots ("one dot = 10 Jews"), according to Hondius (2003: 26). Dutch civil servants confiscated Jewish radios and bicycles. They also sent unemployed Jews to labor camps, even though some were unemployed because of Nazi regulations against Jewish employees. Because Dutch civil servants carried out their jobs so well, far fewer German police were needed in Amsterdam, even at the height of the raids, compared with Belgium and France, where the police force was less cooperative (Moore 1997: 204–6).

The Germans had reorganized the Dutch police so that they could distinguish between units that were not ideologically committed to National Socialist goals and those that were. Indeed, although there was some resistance among Amsterdam police to carrying out anti-Jewish measures, in the end, under the command of S. Tulp, a tough retired lieutenant colonel who was known for his rigid enforcement of "law and order" in the Dutch East Indies, where "racial discrimination was an administrative principle and reprisals against specific ethnic groups were common practice" (Meershoek 1998: 287), they obeyed orders. The more ideologically driven police were employed to carry out the bulk of the raids against Jewish citizens. More than half of the Schalkhaarders, as they were called, worked in Amsterdam (Moore 1997: 199). The Germans also created a Voluntary Auxiliary Police—Vrijwillige Politie—that was made up solely of Dutch SS and NSBers (members of the Dutch National Socialist Party). These two thousand volunteers were trained by the Germans and then used in their hometowns under the command of the local police chief. Their sole concern was the pursuit of Jews. These units of virulent "fanatical Jew hunters" had "no moral qualms" and were known for their use of brutal and illegal methods (van Galen Last and Wolfswinkel 1996: 71; Moore 1997: 199). Members of the regular Dutch police force were involved in the deportations for one month in the summer of 1942, after which they were replaced by the two ideologically committed forces merged into one: Schalkhaarders en Vrijwillige Politie.

Some of theVrijwillige Politie kept diaries and recorded their daily "catch"; a successful evening meant they "bagged several hundreds of them in the past few weeks" (Presser 1988: 354). Although initially they were paid seven and a half guilders a head for each Jew found, the price went as high as forty guilders in 1944 as Jews became scarcer. Moore recounts that a group of thirty-five men who succeeded in finding and arresting 3,400 Jews during a six-month period in 1943 would have reaped seven hundred and fifty guilders each, a very handsome sum at that time (Moore 1997: 207). The organization was disbanded in 1944 when there was no more work for them; the Jewish population of the Netherlands had been almost completely decimated. This volunteer force had been responsible for the arrest, deportation, and death of about six thousand Jews (209).

Unfortunately, it is crucial to add that a small number of Jews aided the Nazi effort by identifying and cornering Jews who were subsequently arrested (Moore 1997). One German Jew tracked down about twenty-five Jews in return for his and his family's exemption from being deported. Some Jews, when caught, tried to save themselves by becoming informants. Ans van Dijk, a Jewish Dutch woman who was active in the Resistance, was caught and then worked for the Germans by helping them find hidden Jews and, once they were in jail, by extracting information about others in hiding. She was responsible for the arrest of about one hundred Jews (Moore 1997: 209; Presser 1988: 355). Jozeph Michman points to another case of a Jewish economist who helped the Germans arrest 118 Jews, 70 of whom were killed (1990: 1054). However, these numbers do not compare to the number of Jews betrayed by non-Jewish Dutch citizens.

Several of my interviewees described how they were caught by the Dutch police or the Germans. Former Amsterdam mayor Ed van Thijn's account of being a child in hiding captures both his experience of being betrayed and his fear, and is quite similar to many of the stories I heard. Van Thijn was hiding on a farm in a closet behind a linen closet. Tipped off that there was a Jew in hiding, the German and Dutch police raided the farm and searched for hours without finding him. Van Thijn describes wetting his pants from fear. The following morning, the police returned and "headed straight for the closet. That's how I know we were betrayed. I never tried to find out who was responsible. What can you do? Shoot the person?" The closet was locked, and van Thijn's hiding father claimed that his wife was out and that he did not know where she kept the key. "We'll shoot it open!" threatened the police officer. "I heard that and started shrieking like a stuck pig. Then the farmer gave them the key. Seconds later I was looking down the barrel of a gun" (van Thijn 2001: 271). One of my respondents, Bloeme, also described knowing she had been betrayed because the police knew exactly where she was hiding.

In February 1941 the number of raids increased—Amsterdam Jews were rounded up, beaten, robbed, and taken away in large numbers (Presser 1988: 33). During 1941 German Occupation authorities arrested hundreds of Jewish men aged 20 to 35; this activity quickly evolved into massive raids in which hundreds were killed or taken away and killed later in camps. The roundups occurred in waves and in different parts of the country; they were not linear or relentless at that point. All Jews had to register their assets with Lippmann, Rosenthal, and Company, formerly a Jewish-owned bank taken over by the Germans. All checks, cash, stocks, and shares had to be declared and given to this bank; later this edict was to extend to all land and property owned by Jews (Moore 1997: 83).

Laws were handed down that stripped Jews of citizenship, jobs, education, and culture. By early summer 1941, Jews were no longer allowed in swimming pools or the North Sea; they could not enter public parks or rent hotel rooms. By mid-summer, zoos, cafés, restaurants, hotels, trains, theaters, cinemas, sports arenas, art exhibitions, concerts, public libraries, and museums were added to the list of sites declared off-limits to Jews (Presser 1988: 33). These humiliating constraints were often difficult for children on summer vacations to comprehend. It also left very little for them to do during what normally would have been an active holiday spent outdoors. In the meantime, their parents had no jobs and little money, and had been rendered stateless.

DEPORTATIONS

In early 1941 the Nazi administration in charge of the Netherlands demanded that a Jewish council be set up. Abraham Asscher, a wealthy diamond merchant, and Professor David Cohen, both members of a Jewish Coordinating Committee, set up only a few months before, created and led the infamous Jewish Council, hereafter called the Joodse Raad (Judenrat in German). In 1933 Cohen and Asscher had created and run the Comité voor Joodse Vluchtelingen, the Committee for Jewish Refugees (CJV), to help care for Jewish refugees who had arrived in the Netherlands without funds (Moore 1997: 29). Most of these same refugees did not have the resources to plan their migration to a third country. The organization raised funds from the Jewish community but did not attempt to settle the refugees in the Netherlands; instead, it encouraged and aided them in seeking somewhere else to go.

One major criticism of Asscher and Cohen and the CJV was that not only did they put Dutch state interests first—to eliminate the Jewish refugee problem as quietly as possible—but they also complied with state interests without making any other demands. Through its existence and activities, the CJV took care of a public issue in a private manner. Some argue that the CJV laid the groundwork for the Joodse Raad, particularly in its acquiescence to state rules, laws, policies, and ideologies, as well as in its role as self-appointed messenger between the state and its Jewish population. Historian Louis de Jong views their deferential and compliant attitude as a link between their behavior in CJV and what came later in the Joodse Raad (Moore 1997: 35; de Jong 1990). However, it should also be said that creating a committee such as the CJV reflects the Dutch pattern of social work within the different *zuilen*.

De Jong is direct in his strong criticism of the Joodse Raad. His views are very clear when he writes that although the Joodse Raad stated their intention not to carry out any activities that were "'contrary to Jewish honor,' the path of collaboration is a most slippery one and after some time, a different principle came to dominate the proceedings and the activities of the Council. This was a most human, but given the circumstances, a most fatal principle: self preservation" (1990: 11–12).

In his book *Holocaust Historiography*, however, Dan Michman points out that understanding and analyzing the role of the Jewish councils in Europe is a much more complex process. There are two basic schools of academic thought concerning the Jewish councils—one that sees them as instruments doing the Nazis' biddings and the other that stresses the councils' positive organizational role for the Jewish community (2003: 159–60). Through in-depth case studies, Michman demonstrates the complicated relationships among the Nazis that lurk behind the establishment of these councils. In the Dutch case, the establishment of the Joodse Raad replicated the Polish model and "clearly reflected power struggles within the Nazi administration" since the *Reichskommissar* in Holland, Seyss-Inquart, had wanted an organizational structure that would have given him more control and power (D. Michman 2003: 169).

In November 1941 all German Jews outside Germany were stripped of their nationality and rendered stateless. The next month in the Netherlands, all non-Dutch Jews were told to report for voluntary emigration, catalyzing another round of suicides (Presser 1988: 93). De Jong argues that by March 1942, the leaders of the Joodse Raad knew that the voluntary emigration for German Jews meant deportation to labor camps in the East but did not warn them or encourage them to go into hiding. De Jong believes that members of the Joodse Raad, and surely many other Dutch Jews as well, believed—or wanted to believe—that only the German Jews would be deported.

In January 1942 large-scale deportation of Dutch Jews to Dutch work camps began and continued throughout the year (Presser 1988: 94). The Joodse Raad not only helped select who was to be deported but advised deportees to obey orders and to cooperate, all in their own interest; otherwise, harsher measures would follow. De Jong notes that the Nazis were able to deport all "full" Jews within fourteen months, with the exception of those in hiding who were not caught. De Jong states that "there was no resistance on the part of the Jewish Council," strongly insinuating their culpability in this smooth operation (de Jong 1990: 14). Dan Michman (1993), however, believes that even if Cohen or Asscher had refused to draw up lists or had resigned, the outcome would have been the same; the Germans would simply have brought in new Jewish leaders. He views the local strength of the SS as much more crucial to the fate of the Dutch Jews than the individual leaders of the Joodse Raad. However, this may be a difficult conclusion to draw retrospectively. Without any Jewish cooperation, the Nazis in the Netherlands might have had a harder time creating lists of deportees, at least initially, which would have bought some time for Jews to escape and for the Underground to organize (Presser 1988: 271). At the same time, neither was there any resistance on the part of the German Jews who were working under the Nazis, controlling the Jewish prisoners at Westerbork (14). Indeed, after the war, the tension between surviving Dutch Jews and German Jews continued, since some Dutch Jews felt that German Jewish cooperation with the German administration had abetted rather than hindered the destruction of Dutch Jewry (Hondius 2003).

No matter how much opinions differ about its role, the fact remains that the Joodse Raad helped deport thousands of Jews. Presser argues that the lists of those to be shipped off started with the Jewish poor and working class. Wealthier Jews had the resources to find doctors who would give them a certificate claiming an exemption from deportation, at least temporarily (Presser 1988: 108).

In a rather gruesome chapter of this history, the Germans had the Joodse Raad create a list of several hundred "indispensable Jews" who would be exempt from deportation. The heads of the Joodse Raad did everything possible to save themselves and their families by keeping their names on the list. As the Germans tightened the noose by decreasing the number allowed on the list over time, Cohen and Asscher had to decide which Jews previously counted as indispensable would now become dispensable. Although their desire to save themselves and their families is understandable, this is a particularly distasteful and dishonorable part of Jewish history in the Netherlands. In the end, on September 29, 1943, the final roundup of all the Jews with exemptions occurred right before Rosh Hashanah, the Jewish New Year. Presser caustically remarks that the Germans "dragged the most 'indispensable of all indispensables' from their houses"; neither the Asscher nor the Cohen family was exempt this time. Cohen stated that he was relieved when he was finally sent on the train to Westerbork, no longer having to send others (Presser 1988: 213). His relief notwithstanding, between July 1942 and September 1943, over 100,000 Jews were deported from the Netherlands.

Even if we accept that the Joodse Raad cooperated with the Nazis, why didn't the Jews resist? Why did they simply obey the orders of the Joodse Raad? In fact, many did resist. De Jong (1990) and other scholars agree that most Jews did not accept the authority of the Joodse Raad and clearly saw it for what it was. Less well-off Jews were very aware of the privileged position of Cohen and Asscher and of those who were exempt from deportation. Their resistance was seen in their refusal to obey orders. Many Jews did not show up for their designated deportation departure dates but instead went into hiding whenever possible. Some Dutch Jews fled the Netherlands before the war, of course, but as Bob Moore points out, most saw themselves as Dutch citizens and did not imagine that they would be violated in their own country.

Class issues become pertinent here as well in that most Dutch Jews did not have the resources or the opportunity to flee or go into hiding (Moore 1997: 49). In other words, it is crucial to examine what options the Dutch Jews had when they received the dreaded letter telling them to report for deportation. Few had enough money to hire someone who could smuggle them across the border or to emigrate. Some with resources were smuggled across the border into other countries, where they survived; others were not so lucky and were turned in by such smugglers after they had collected huge sums from Jewish families. Selma Leydesdorff (1994) argues that most Jews hid if they were offered the chance; the problem is that most did not have that opportunity. In addition to the economic issue, owing to the structure of Dutch society and of the *zuilen* that kept most Jews isolated from mainstream society, few Dutch Jews had contacts with non-Jews who might have helped them to hide.

I would argue that the appropriate question to ask is not why the victims didn't do more to avoid deportation but rather, Why didn't the non-Jewish population in the Netherlands do more to resist this attack on their fellow citizens? As Presser and others point out, most Dutch non-Jews were passive at best during the process: "Dutch municipal officers collaborated in registering Jews, simply following their role models in the police and higher in the government. They placed the 'J' on the ID cards of their fellow citizens, signed Aryan declarations and dismissed

Jewish colleagues" (1988: 271). As Presser points out, not a single Dutch train ever failed to run on schedule (146) as it deported Jewish citizens to Westerbork or to points farther east. Otto Bene, the representative of the German Ministry of Foreign Affairs, reported that there were never any "incidents" affecting the trains heading east with Jewish transport. After the mass roundup of June 20, 1943, he wrote, "The Dutch population is totally opposed to the transports, but gives a general impression of a lack of interest in them" (cited in Hondius 2003: 31). Still, the 2005 apology of the Dutch rail system for its role in deporting Jews is important but unsatisfactory for those whose parents and grandparents were on board.

As the general Dutch male population sought to escape conscription by the Nazis into labor camps, approximately 300,000 people were in hiding in the Netherlands in the last years of the Occupation. Of that substantial number, only about 8 percent were Jews. Although it is impossible to know precisely, it is estimated that 20,000–25,000 Jews went into hiding in the Netherlands. Given that they went into hiding earlier than the non-Jews, this difference is striking, considering the popular notion that many Jews were hidden in Holland.

In a new study Marnix Croes (2004) found that many more Jews than has been calculated so far went into hiding at an early stage—about 28,000 instead of the 20,000–25,000 previously estimated. However, that also means that many more were detected and denounced—close to 12,000. The implications of this new assertion are that Jews were more alert to the dangers of deportation than has been argued, that more non-Jews were ready to host them, but also that more non-Jews were active in collaboration.

Although one can debate whether or not the general population of the Netherlands knew of Auschwitz during the Occupation, it is safe to assume that almost all Dutch citizens knew that Jews had been stripped of their possessions and livelihoods and were being hunted and deported. Though the Jews were in constant danger, non-Jewish Dutch citizens were much more open to hiding their fellow non-Jews. One clergyman stated that it was easier to hide ten escaped English pilots in one house than one Jew in ten houses, even if the person did not look Jewish (Mason 1984). Thus, if Dutch non-Jews were in fact willing to risk hiding someone sought by the Nazis but refused to hide those who were Jewish, then we can attribute this attitude to indifference to the Jews, at the very least, if not to anti-Semitism, whether covert or outright. Of the Jews who were able to find hiding places, approximately one-third of them were betrayed and/or caught, including Anne Frank and her family as well as two of those I interviewed and a number of the parents of interviewees. Louis de Jong notes that although the Dutch people did not accept National Socialism, "their contribution to the German war effort was not inconsiderable" (de Jong 1990: 39). We may attribute some of their activities to an adherence to bureaucratic procedures, as is clear from Mr. Lentz, but it seems clear that latent anti-Semitism can explain a fair amount as well (Hondius 2003).

RESISTANCE AND HELP

Along with the indifference and outright collusion of Dutch citizens, both spontaneous and organized forms of resistance against the Nazis were also displayed in the Netherlands, including a range of activities, from protesting to producing fliers, from finding hiding places to smuggling children into hiding. A number of books have been written about those who saved Jews, often in an attempt to understand what stimulates such altruism (Fogelman 1994; Klempner 2006). Historian Eva Fogelman points to three "types of morality" among rescuers of Jews: (1) ideological morality, based on a notion of justice that is usually political; (2) religious morality, based on a feeling of spiritual connection to Jews that was not necessarily linked to liking Jews; and (3) emotional morality, based on compassion—the rarest type. The second type was most common among those who helped to save children. Religion played an important role in hiding—some who took in Jews were strict Calvinists, and an even greater number were Catholics. Bob Moore mentions that some Christians saw saving and/or hiding Jews as a way to save souls by converting them (1997: 166).

However, this discussion of moral reasons for rescuing Jews leaves out a less common but still very real motivation—financial gain. Bob

Moore points out that the motivations among Dutch non-Jews who helped save Jews "ranged from the purely altruistic to the downright mercenary," including instances of outright profiteering and rejecting lodgers when their money ran out (167).

The general strike of February 25–26, 1941, was a rare outbreak of public resistance against the Nazis on behalf of the Jews by non-Jews. The February strike, as it is known, is a significant part of Dutch Resistance history. In early February, the paramilitary wing of the Dutch National Socialists, the Weerafdeling (WA), and German civilians were forcing cafés, restaurants, and hotels in the main Dutch cities to display signs forbidding the entry of Jewish customers (66). Their roughneck behavior led to outbreaks of violence in which young working-class Jews in small activist cells *(knokploegen)* joined with non-Jews to resist, which led to the death of one Jew from that group.[11] Shortly thereafter, an ice-cream parlor owned by two German Jewish refugees, and used as a base by one of the *knokploegen,* was vandalized. One of the owners set up a trap that would spray the WA with ammonia when they returned. However, instead of Dutch Nazis, German policemen entered and were hit with the ammonia. The owners of the parlor were arrested; indeed, one was executed two weeks later under the command of Klaus Barbie (71).

This event resulted in the Jewish quarter in Amsterdam being sealed off. Six hundred German police officers closed off the area "and began dragging people off the street and breaking down doors to find suitable victims" (Moore 1997: 71). Women and children were beaten, and about 450 young Jewish men were arrested and sent to Buchenwald and Mauthausen. However, those who were arrested were first taken to Jonas Daniël Meijerplein, a main square in the Jewish district in Amsterdam, "where they were forced to run the gauntlet through rows of policemen who beat them, and then squat down with their arms outstretched" (72). Out of that entire group of young men, only one survived the war (J. Michman 1990: 1048).

This was the first time in the Netherlands that the Germans had openly practiced their brutality. Although the raid and arrests had taken place in the Jewish quarter, Moore points out that this event took place in broad daylight "in front of hundreds, if not thousands, of non-Jews who used the shops and markets in that district. As a result, news of the raids spread like wildfire through the city" (1997: 72). The then-illegal Dutch Communist Party had been involved in several strikes against the Dutch authorities in the few months preceding this event. After word of these arrests got out, a general strike for February 25 was organized against the Germans and was joined by the general population. The strike affected the transportation system, factories, and public services, all of which came to a standstill. Jozeph Michman reports that it spread to other cities and continued into the next day (1990: 1048).

Although this strike did not prevent any Jews from being arrested or deported, and a day later the workers returned to their jobs, it features prominently as a unique European event enacted by non-Jews on behalf of their Jewish co-citizens. In her analysis of the Dutch collective memory of this event, Selma Leydesdorff refers to this strike as the "mythology of solidarity." Today in Holland there is an annual march to the monument of a dockworker that was erected on the spot where Jewish men were rounded up right before the strike, and Leydesdorff notes that this commemoration is a "symbol of the fight against intolerance" (1993: 354). However, Dutch Jews have not taken an active part in these commemorations because the same workers who went on strike returned to work the next day, transporting Jews on trams and trains that ran perfectly on schedule (355).

One of Leydesdorff's arguments is that early Jewish resistance to the Nazis by working-class youth trained in boxing, organized in *knokploegen*, has not been part of the Dutch collective memory of resistance. Instead, this collective memory reflects more of the Communist Party's version of the resistance and focuses on the later February strike. This particular version of the past renders Jews as total victims rather than recognizing their active role in the resistance. Leydesdorff demonstrates that owing to unacknowledged anti-Semitism among the Left, Jews were not accepted politically or socially and were "abandoned to their fate": "It was a bitter experience that the Social Democratic trade union, to which many Jewish proletarians belonged, was one of the first groups to let them down. Its leadership, which had been very strongly influenced by Jews, was replaced and chose to try and reach a compromise with the

Germans and promote the economic interests of the workers, even at the height of the deportations. Socialism was transformed into social cooperation" (1993: 365). In sum, while not downplaying the importance of the strike, Leydesdorff argues that the predominant role it plays in Dutch collective memory is to ignore earlier forms of Jewish resistance to the Nazis as well as anti-Semitism on the Left.

Although many individuals were involved in helping to save, smuggle, and hide Jews, resistance organizations also developed over time. The Landelijke Organisatie voor Hulp aan Onderduikers, or LO (National Organization to Help Those in Hiding) was the largest one, and it helped both Jews and non-Jews who were attempting to avoid forced labor conscription as well as those who were being hunted because of their political activities (Moore 1997: 171). Begun by an Orthodox Calvinist minister, the LO began to find hiding places in late 1942 in reaction to the deportations. By 1943 the LO was operating in and around Amsterdam as well as in the northeastern provinces, predominantly farmland, of Friesland, Groningen, and Drenthe (171–74). Many hidden children I interviewed were taken to these areas either directly or after having been in a series of hiding places, some by this organization. Still, Moore points out that hiding Jews was "perceived as posing particular problems [which] meant that their welfare often fell outside the mainstream work of the organisation" (171). The LO did not fully develop until fall 1943, "by which time it was too late to help the majority of Jews" (191). Several other resistance groups, however, had been created that focused almost completely on saving Jewish children. These groups are very relevant to the postwar history of hidden children and are discussed in the next chapter.

The Hollandse Schouwburg, a theater that was extremely popular in the 1920s, had been renamed the Joodse Schouwburg in September 1941, when only Jewish artists and Jewish audiences were allowed (Jewish Historical Museum 1993: 4). In July 1942, most likely for political reasons, it was designated as the meeting and collection point of Jews called up for deportation.[12] Most stayed in the Schouwburg for one to several days before being sent by train to Westerbork transit camp. A building opposite the Schouwburg that had been a crèche for working-class families was then used specifically for holding Jewish babies and children (Dwork 1991: 46). Walter Süsskind, a German Jewish refugee, was one of several members of the Jewish Council responsible for keeping lists of those who entered the Joodse Schouwburg. He was able to save 600 children by "losing" their registration cards, while several Resistance organizations participated in smuggling them out, into hiding (Moore 1997: 186).

The babies and young children were taken out in various ways—in potato sacks, in boxes, or in prams—and were handed over to a young member of a Resistance network. Apparently even one of the Waffen-SS guards at the Schouwburg helped expedite the escape of several children. I have interviewed some of the children who were saved in this way. Several of them had been taken to the Schouwburg after being picked up in a raid but were rescued, sometimes with their parents, by Süsskind, and then smuggled out. A recent exhibit at the Resistance Museum in Amsterdam entitled Bye, Dad, See You Tomorrow (*Dag pap, tot morgen*) featured the photos and stories of some of those saved children (Bakker 2005).

The Catholic and Protestant Churches also reacted as the Nazi occupiers tightened their grip on the Jews in the Netherlands. When the first deportations of entire families began in late June 1942, it became clear that the Germans were not simply sending them to labor camps, as they were claiming. The wholesale transportation of Jewish young children and elderly people made the Nazi effort more transparent. The Catholic and Protestant Churches sent a signed protest to Reich Commissioner Seyss-Inquart in Holland and ordered all clergy to read the text of their protest at the following Sunday's services. In an effort to quell this public protest, the Germans made a deal with the Protestant Churches, which ended up exempting baptized Protestant-Jews from deportation. However, because the Catholic Church would not renege, and the archbishop insisted that the text be read anyway, the Germans arrested all 201 Jewish converts to Roman Catholicism, some of them monks and nuns, and deported them to Auschwitz (J. Michman 1990: 1053).[13] One of the nuns deported was the German Jew Edith Stein, a Carmelite who was later beatified by the pope in the 1990s.

About 1,575 baptized Jews received exemption stamps in 1942 and 1943. In fall 1944, when almost all Dutch Jews had already been murdered, Protestant Jews were sent to Westerbork, and about 500 of them were sent to Theresienstadt. About 150 survived (Moore 1997: 129). It is thought that the Germans were more hesitant to deport these Jews because of the expected reaction from the Protestant Church and perhaps from the Dutch public (129).

Jews in mixed marriages were ignored until March 1942, when the Germans became aware that mixed marriages were increasing rather quickly. Although further mixed marriages were banned, about 8,000 Jews were in mixed marriages at that time (124), and the Jews received exemptions from the population registry. In mid-1943, a program to sterilize those Jews in mixed marriages who were childless offered a red "J" on identity cards in lieu of the yellow star. About 2,500–3,000 people were exempted from deportation through this program. It appears that most of them were given a letter by Dutch doctors certifying that they were already sterile. Apparently, the SS officer in charge accepted such letters without further questioning until he came under investigation for his leniency. In early 1944, Jews in mixed marriages were called up for labor services and put to work on various projects in the Netherlands (125–26). There was considerable ambivalence among the Germans about what to do with the Jews in mixed marriages—an ambivalence that ended up working to the advantage of these Jews. They had a better chance of surviving in Holland, especially if they were barren, had been sterilized, or were too old to have children, since it appears that most were not deported out of the Netherlands. In these cases, protests to the Germans from their non-Jewish partners kept the Jews in mixed marriages more protected. Moore explains that the exact number of Jewish survivors from mixed marriages is difficult to know, but it is approximately 8,000–9,000, most of whom were women with children and childless women. Most Jewish men in mixed marriages ultimately were not exempt (127).

After their June 1942 attempts at protest, the churches did not engage in further public, collective resistance or encourage their congregants to protest or resist. Many people I interviewed were hidden by Calvinists or Catholics who had no particular love for the Jews, and may even have disliked them, but hid them for religious reasons, a motive discussed earlier. Monsignor de Jong of Utrecht, the most senior Catholic functionary in Holland, did not give in to German pressure and protested against the deportations in part by financially supporting the hiding of Jewish children and adults through a secret fund.[14]

QUEEN WILHELMINA AND THE GOVERNMENT-IN-EXILE

Holland, a constitutional monarchy, was ruled at the time by Queen Wilhelmina, who had ascended to the throne in 1890. Although some historians claimed that Queen Wilhelmina liked the Jews and that she expressed her "empathy for her beloved people of the Old Testament," more recent scholarship is less sanguine on the matter (Moore 1997: 325). Despite the myth that the queen identified with the Jews, Gerstenfeld (2001) points out, during five years of radio speeches, she devoted a full five sentences to their fate. Others claim that her feelings for the Jews were not shared by the officials who were part of the government-in-exile. However, it seems that the queen's and the government-in-exile's practices and policies speak for themselves. Yet it is also worth noting that Louis de Jong was working for Radio Oranje in London, which broadcast to the occupied Netherlands, and shares some responsibility for the sparse attention paid to Jews in the broadcasts.

The most striking aspect of the queen's and the government-in-exile's complete indifference to the fate of their Jewish subjects is revealed by their lack of concern over the deportations. Although they were housed on the same street as the Polish government-in-exile, Dutch officials never approached the Poles to inquire about the destination of the trains that went east with Dutch Jews in them (de Jong 1990; Hondius 2003: 34). In an extension of the government-in-exile's disregard for the fate of the Dutch Jews, the Dutch Red Cross, in contrast to other national Red Crosses, was the least active in bringing help to their nationals in concentration camps (Boas 1967). Indeed, Presser argues that the Dutch inmates of Theresienstadt received the least, if anything at all, in terms of food and supplies, compared with other nationals, including the Poles (1988: 535).

In February 1943, a discussion about a possible exchange of Dutch Jews for Germans imprisoned in Dutch Surinam took place. The cabinet-in-exile rejected this possibility because, even though they agreed that Jews were most likely worse off than the rest of the Dutch population, they stated that "it is questionable whether this entitles them to privileged treatment" (Presser 1988: 333). This statement reflects the government's policy not to distinguish between Jews and non-Jews in an effort to prevent an increase in anti-Semitism. However, it ultimately translated into anti-Semitic practices in that the situation of the Jews and their treatment by the Nazis were not recognized as legitimate reasons to give them more help.

Toward the end of the war, the government made it clear that if special help was needed for the Jews, it was the responsibility of international Jewish charities or Dutch Jews who had not been deported. "It was a response which smacked at best of naivety and at worst of anti-Semitism on the part of the authorities in London" (Moore 1997: 231). At the same time, according to Dienke Hondius, the government-in-exile refused to consider creating a separate Jewish social welfare organization to deal with postwar Dutch Jews. The response of Minister of the Interior van Boeijen to this proposal was that "he did not want any special reparation measures for Jews, because that would amount to doing exactly as the Germans had done: making an exception of the Jews!" Again, this refusal of special assistance to Dutch Jews after the war was motivated by concern that special aid and attention could increase anti-Semitism in the Netherlands (Verhey in Hondius 2003: 41); however, it also ignored the fact that because the Jews had been singled out for persecution by the Nazis, they might need more assistance.

The same Resistance activists who had helped save Jewish children lobbied the government-in-exile not to make special efforts for Dutch Jews after the war. They argued that any help given to Jews should be given to them as Dutch citizens and not as Jews, and that no distinction should be made between Jewish Dutch citizens and non-Jewish Dutch citizens. In their view, such distinctions had been created by the Nazis and should not be allowed to continue once the war was over. However, as Hondius points out, these arguments show no sensitivity toward (or awareness of) Jewish interests or the existence of a Jewish community. "Christian resistance workers, together with the Dutch authorities in London, rode roughshod over Jewish interests" (2003: 35). Indeed, they felt that any aid from abroad that was designated solely for Jews should not be allowed. Hondius cites their words: "There would be unavoidable recriminations that the Jew was being helped better and faster than the person who got into trouble for helping." A 1944 document from a Resistance organization to the government-in-exile opposed any reestablishment of a Jewish community in postwar Holland: "As an objective, reestablishing the Jewish community is both incorrect and undesirable. . . . Before May 10, 1940, there was no Jewish community, there was only Jewish religious observation. This congregation must now revive inasmuch as deported Dutch Jews continue to value it. . . . We are only interested in the fate of individual Dutch citizens who have suffered deportation, the fact that they have been labeled Jews by the occupying forces takes a completely subordinate role" (Verhey, cited in Hondius 2003: 52). Although these general sentiments reflect admirable attempts to avoid the continuation of discrimination, they also reflect complete ignorance of Dutch Jewish life and identity.

In addition, in early 1944, those involved in the *Trouw* Resistance group saving Jewish children drafted a bill that would allow them a substantial role in decision making over the fate of Jewish hidden children once the war ended. This bill, which was made official after the war, will be discussed further in the following chapter. Suffice it here to say that these unusual and radical notions disenfranchised Jewish parents quite specifically, putting in place a practice of discrimination the *Trouw* group was ostensibly trying to avoid, and taking over decisions about Jewish children that traditionally had been made by the Jewish community.

Thus, the general argument against overtly differentiating between Jewish and non-Jewish Dutch citizens was directly challenged and completely contradicted by the bill on guardianship. Resistance activists tended to be young, earnest people, and clearly many felt they had a stake in the future of these Jewish children whose lives they had saved. But from a contemporary perspective, this act of social and political engineering appears as racist and repugnant as the practice in Australia of forcibly taking Aborigine children from their homes and resettling them in white homes or institutions under the guise of "helping" them to assimilate into nonindigenous society (Manne 1998).

HOW CAN IT BE EXPLAINED?

Historians have spent a great deal of effort trying to explain how a liberal and tolerant country such as the Netherlands could have allowed so many Jews to be deported, especially compared to the rate of deportation in neighboring states. The question becomes, How can we reconcile the image of Dutch Jews being rounded up and deported with that of their fellow citizens simply standing by?

In his attempt to explain the case of the Netherlands and its Jews during the 1940s, Moore argues that there is no single factor that offers a satisfactory explanation but rather a series of interrelated factors (1997: 253). However, historians may disagree about exactly what those interrelated factors are. In the English-language literature, most scholars focus on some combination of the following: (1) the structure and style of German rule, (2) the role of the Dutch civil service and the police, (3) the extent to which Dutch Jews were actually integrated in the first place, and (4) the actions of the Joodse Raad.[15]

As mentioned earlier in the chapter, Nazi involvement in the Netherlands was different from its involvement in other Western European countries, giving the Germans more control than elsewhere (Blom 1989). Other historians focus more on the compliance and obedience of the Dutch civil service and bureaucracy in accommodating the Germans' wishes, as in the example of Lentz, who created the ultrasecure identification cards. Unfortunately, Lentz was joined by other Dutch civil servants and police whose reforms aided the German effort (Moore 1997: 257; Leydesdorff 1994). The complete indifference of the Dutch government-in-exile and the queen to the fate of Dutch Jews certainly did not encourage the Dutch population to help their Jewish co-citizens resist arrest and deportation. The only way that Jozeph Michman can understand and explain the behavior of Dutch authorities and the Supreme Court under Nazi Occupation is to deduce that the "non-equality of the Jews in the

Netherlands . . . carried greater weight than their equality" (2001: 207). It is certainly very possible that equality on paper did not necessarily translate into equality and/or acceptance in practice.

Although one may point to the speed of German deportation of the Jews from the Netherlands, again it is essential to point also to the cooperation from all realms of the Dutch population that may have been involved, from arresting Jews to transporting them by trams and then trains. In comparison, the French heads of police ordered their troops *not* to arrest French Jews or to assist with transports. The Germans had to bypass the French police in their efforts to arrest and deport French Jews, which made it more difficult and slowed down the process (Moore 1997: 205–6). (Jews in France who were not French citizens, however, were more vulnerable to deportation.) In Belgium, the police slowed their efforts, and railway workers left doors of some deportation trains open so that Jews could escape (Kuper 2003: 137).

Given that Dutch Jews had certain rights, and there was a very low degree of overt anti-Semitism in the Netherlands, how can we explain the apathy of the non-Jewish population? One highly relevant analysis suggests that in seeking the explanation, we need to critically revise our notions of Holland as a safe haven for Jews historically. Jozeph Michman points out that the general impression in Dutch scholarly writings is that the "tolerant Dutch people emancipated the Jews" without friction and with the tacit approval of the majority (2001: 205). This emancipation is presented as "a gift without strings from an open-minded Dutch nation to a religious minority." This, however, Michman argues, is an "erroneous notion." Rather, the Netherlands granted the Jews in Holland "equal rights but did not guarantee them equal treatment. . . . [While] the emancipation improved the position of the Jews, . . . [it] did not raise them to the status of first-class citizens, on a par with the Protestants, or even to that of second-class citizens like the Catholics" (207). Dutch Jewish journalist Henriette Boas suggests that we rethink what she calls the "apparent integration" of Dutch Jews into pre-1940s Dutch society. Although Jews had full equality under Dutch law, Boas views this as "alleged equality" because Jews were seen as different from the mainstream, essentially as unequal (1967: 359–60).

This sense of Jews being different may have reflected or produced latent anti-Semitism, but again, it was never the overt anti-Semitism that existed in Eastern Europe. Yet the blending that occurred among Jews in Italian society never occurred in the Netherlands. Hondius describes Dutch mainstream non-Jewish attitudes toward the Jews not as active anti-Semitism but as a passive and distanced nonassociation and noninvolvement, mixed in with a fair amount of latent anti-Semitism (2003). Perhaps because of this nonconfrontational attitude historically, Dutch Jews felt at home in pre-1940s Holland, protected from the kinds of events that were occurring in Germany and Poland.

Some Dutch scholars who argue that Dutch Jews were well integrated into Dutch society also view this as an explanation for what transpired in the Netherlands. Most prominent of these is historian Hans Blom, head of the National Institute of War Documents (NIOD), who suggests that Dutch Jewish integration may have given the Jewish community "a false sense of security" so that they were "less prepared" for what was to come during the Occupation. In comparison, he points out, French Jews, long used to a more active anti-Semitism, were more alert to and perhaps more suspicious of demands made by the occupiers (1989: 282). Dutch Jews were "easy victims" because of their "deferential attitude towards public authority," something seen as a typically Dutch trait (van Galen Last and Wolfswinkel 1996: 36). Because of a tradition of accepting bureaucratic authority in Holland, Dutch Jews cooperated with the occupiers, whereas Eastern European Jews, in comparison, did not trust state authority. Essentially, Blom is suggesting that because the Jews in the Netherlands were so "Dutch," they willingly participated in the process of their own genocide. (It should also be pointed out that even if some Eastern European Jews resisted authority, it did not help them in the end.)

Van Galen Last and Wolfswinkel (1996: 68) put another spin on this notion of the very Dutch behavior of Dutch Jews and assert an interesting causal relationship. They argue that the passivity exhibited by the Jews "led to an equally passive attitude among non-Jews." In this argument, the victims are doubly blamed—for not being suspicious enough because they were too well integrated and for not being appropriate role models of resistance for their non-Jewish co-citizens.

Although Blom mentions Dutch complicity with the occupiers and views the vertical integration of Dutch society as one reason why non-Jews did not feel or demonstrate much solidarity with their Jewish co-citizens, he also finds that the "well-organized and carefully administered Jewish Council complemented the more or less cooperative and docile attitude of the Dutch Jewish community" (1989: 287). Again, this cooperation and respect for authority, Blom finds, bears a "close relationship with the earlier paradox of the greater vulnerability of the Jews in the Netherlands as related to a lack of alertness or even a false feeling of security engendered by their relatively favorable position in the pre-war Netherlands." Blom concludes his article by stating that this "interesting paradox—the relatively high vulnerability of the Jewish community in the Netherlands during the occupation . . . is in turn connected with the relatively favorable and quasi-secure position of the Jews in the Netherlands before the war" and "merits further study" (289).

At least in the English translation of Blom's article there exists a sort of self-congratulatory tone—over the fact that the Dutch were so liberal as to accept the Jews, give them equal rights, and allow them to integrate. And his underscoring of Jewish passivity can be interpreted as blaming the victim. To be fair, Blom makes a multicausal argument, of which Jewish integration is only one of three important factors and perhaps the least important. Nonetheless, the real paradox remains that non-Jews, in a society that thought of itself as highly tolerant and liberal, allowed foreign occupiers to decimate their fellow citizens.

CONCLUSIONS

To conclude, the wartime history of the relationship between the Netherlands and its Jews, most of which has been uncovered in recent times, suggests an image quite different from the one promulgated by the Anne Frank story. The majority of the Dutch non-Jewish population was not only unconcerned about what was happening to their Jewish compatriots but seemingly not too unhappy about it either. A small, brave minority of Dutch citizens did get involved and managed to save a small percentage of the Jewish population. However, the most reliable information suggests that their work was made difficult since most Dutch non-Jews did not want to house or hide Jews. This argument is, of course, meant not to demonize Dutch non-Jews but rather to deconstruct the mythos created by the Anne Frank story about a population that includes those who betrayed and arrested her family and helped send them to their deaths.

3 After the War

THE JEWS AND THE NETHERLANDS

Out of 105,000 Jews deported from the Netherlands, 4.8 percent, or 5,200, survived.[1] In sociologist Helen Fein's index ranking the proportion of Jews who survived by nation on a scale from 1 to 10 (1 being that no Jews were killed, 10 being that almost all Jews were killed), Poland rated a 10; Austria and Germany rated a 9, as did Slovakia; and the Netherlands rated an 8, along with Serbia, Croatia, Greece, and Hungary. Belgium and Norway each rated a 5. France rated a 3, Italy was one of the few countries with a 2, and only Denmark, with its tiny Jewish population that was saved by non-Jewish Danes, rated the lowest and received a 1 (Fein 1979: 52–53).

This chapter continues the themes introduced in chapter 2 by focusing on the relationship between the Jews, the Dutch population, and the state in the Netherlands after 1945, when the war ended. We begin with the vestige of an annihilated Jewish population, their return to Holland (if they had been in camps), and their reentry into Dutch society, whether they had been in camps or in hiding. Two books on this topic have been published by younger Dutch historians. Dienke Hondius's 1998 book *Terugkeer: Antisemitisme in Nederland* has been translated into English as *Return: Holocaust Survivors and Dutch Anti-Semitism* (2003), and I draw substantially from her detailed scholarship. Michal Citroen's book *U wordt door niemand verwacht: Nederlandse joden na kampen en onderduik* (1999) has not been translated yet, but the title—*Nobody Is Expecting You: Dutch Jews after Camp and Hiding*—starkly tells a large part of the story. Unfortunately, the prevalent theme of the latent anti-Semitism in Dutch society during the 1930s and the first part of the 1940s continued and, some would argue, intensified after the war's end.

After the war the state and former members of the Resistance began actively to shape the society they had envisioned during the war, one in which Jews were not differentiated from non-Jews. While this plan appeared to represent the laudable ideal of equality, it actually reflected a denial of the Nazi persecution of Jews in particular, and lacked an understanding of what genocide meant to the Jews as a collective. When these elements are factored in, such ideals end up looking a great deal like anti-Semitism in practice. This can be seen in numerous cases, from the repatriation of displaced Dutch Jews to the laws concerning hidden children. These postwar state reactions, ideologies, and policies created the context in which hidden children were rooted after the war when a parent or other kin returned to claim them.

Is the Netherlands an aberrant case compared with other European countries? While it is true that the Netherlands did much less in terms of sending aid to Dutch citizens in concentration camps than many other countries, the point here is not to measure the relative insensitivity of postwar governments in their behaviors toward their returning Jewish population. Rather, my aim is to elucidate the Dutch case, a focus that is missing in most English-language Holocaust literature, and to examine these behaviors and policies in light of the myth of Dutch tolerance.

JEWISH SURVIVORS IN DISPLACEMENT

At the war's end, the Dutch Red Cross and the government were "conspicuous by their absence" (van Galen Last and Wolfswinkel 1996: 125).

Historian Jacob Presser recounts how the Dutch government ignored appeals to help, with much-needed supplies and assistance with repatriation, Dutch survivors in Auschwitz, who were then helped by the French and American governments instead (1988: 535). This inattention, he remarks, was not new since the Dutch inmates in Theresienstadt received little or nothing from the Dutch Red Cross during the war, at variance with what inmates from other countries received.

Historians note that the Dutch state was expecting up to 1.5 million people who were either returning home to Holland or trying to get into Holland (Moore 1986: 231). Approximately 10 percent of the Dutch population (900,000 people) was displaced at the war's end; this includes those in the Netherlands and those still away. Historical evidence shows that the Dutch government was more focused on how to keep out unwanted refugees seeking a home in Holland than it was on how best to deal with returning Dutch Jewish survivors and give them the help they needed. In the end, 5,500 Jews returned.

The reception centers set up for returning Dutch Jews have been described by many as cold and unwelcoming places. Indeed, these centers mirrored the more general state-level reaction to the Jewish survivors in their cold and "frosty" attitudes (van Galen Last and Wolfswinkel 1996; Moore 1997: 249; Hondius 2003). Some returnees were given just one guilder or less, a shamefully paltry amount. One interviewee, named Bloeme, had to spend her money just to get a ride from Maastricht to Amsterdam, where she arrived penniless and with only the clothes on her back. The Dutch Jewish returnees were met by a state that was formal, distant, and indifferent in its "bureaucratic correctness" (Moore 1997: 249; Hondius 2003). For example, a bus with survivors from Dachau was stopped at the border near Vaals for passport control but was not allowed to cross since those aboard did not have valid papers. "That they came from Dachau was 'irrelevant' to the border official" (Hondius 2003: 93).

Some returning Jews were quarantined, a situation that echoed the Nazi portrayal of Jews as vermin. Gerhard Durlacher, a German Jew who was deported from the Netherlands to Auschwitz, described his return through France and how coldly and suspiciously he was treated at the Dutch reception center. He felt that the returnees were "treated like lepers" and sent straightaway to doctors for medical clearance; the cold, mistrustful treatment made him feel like "Oliver Twist" (1991: 90–91). Hondius tells of a group of Jews put in quarantine, who then fled after ten days. Some were tracked down by the police and told either to return to the police station or to pay a fine for fleeing illegally (2003: 94).

Hondius recounts another incident in which a Jewish military officer, Captain Gassan, found his wife and children in a reception center in Maastricht and took them to a clinic in Amsterdam for medical care, with the permission of the head of the reception center. He was reprimanded by the Maastricht Security Detachment head, who sent a report through the bureaucracy about this "inappropriate intervention" (Hondius 2003: 95). That no one stopped to think of the human aspect of this intervention provides us with some insight into why and how the Dutch system worked for the Nazis.

Pieter Lagrou found that the Dutch "welcoming committees" and centers clearly were notches below those in other Western European countries (1997: 209). One Dutch Jew said that her reception in Holland was a great disappointment compared with her reception in Belgium, where "doctors and nurses did everything they could to assist and help us in every way" (Hondius 2003: 94).

German Jews who had emigrated to Holland after Hitler's rise to power and who returned to the Netherlands after the war were badly treated by the Dutch government. Because Nazi Germany had revoked the citizenship of the German Jews, they were stateless and did not have any kind of residency permit from the Netherlands. Austrian and German Jews were considered German by the Dutch bureaucracy and by lower-level civil servants, and therefore were seen as enemies. The fact that they were Jews made no difference to the civil servants concerned, one effect of the policy of not differentiating between Jews and non-Jews (Hondius 2003). Hondius and others recount numerous and horrendous incidents caused by this policy. Some German Jews were arrested and given prisoner numbers; others were incarcerated in prisoner-of-war camps with Dutch and German Nazis, who taunted them (Moore 1997: 232; Hess 1991). Some of them had their belongings taken away and never given back. They were treated as slave labor and even punished. Historians feel that there were clearly some anti-Semites among those

Dutch men running the postwar camps. Hondius recounts one case in a camp in which 140 German Jews reattached their yellow Stars of David in protest against being housed and confined with Dutch and German Nazis (2003: 89). Their actions drew attention, and within a day or two, almost all these stateless Jews were released.

In addition to those returning from concentration camps, Jewish survivors in Holland who had been hidden were also reentering society. Presser underscores how painful the return from camps or from hiding was for many Dutch Jews, who experienced hostility from some of their former neighbors and friends. Otherwise "respectable" Dutch citizens were quoted as saying that there had been too many Jews anyway, and that Holland was better off without them (1988: 543). Although some were surprised and pleased to see their neighbors or friends return, historians have been more struck by the negative responses among the Dutch. Dienke Hondius examined seventy-five cases of Dutch Jews returning to Holland after the war, from interviews, memoirs, and documents, in order to analyze the kinds of welcomes they received. She found that although some had positive experiences, the majority did not. Hondius distinguished between anti-Semitic prejudices and overt anti-Semitism, arguing that overt anti-Semitism increased in the Netherlands after the end of the war.

Presser speculates that considerable guilt lay behind the anti-Semitism expressed by Dutch non-Jews, since most of them had not been in the Resistance, and returning Jews served as a constant reminder of their failings. The cultural anti-Semitism of the 1930s had reappeared, Moore argues, but in a more virulent form. When these upstanding citizens heard the experiences of former Jewish neighbors and friends recounted, they responded with disbelief, incomprehension, and denial. Jewish returnees often encountered non-Jews who claimed that they had suffered more, not unlike the way many Germans claimed to be victims after the war (Moeller 2001). One Jewish woman who went to her neighbor to reclaim her fur coat was told, "Well, quite a lot of your kind came back. Just be happy that you were not here! What we have suffered from hunger!"[2] Another woman went to see her doctor and told him about her experience in hiding: "I became very emotional, and this doctor interrupted me and

said: 'Do you know what happened to me? The Germans took my bicycle'" (Hondius 2003: 57). Durlacher and others, former Amsterdam
mayor Ed van Thijn (2001) among them, describe how a "conspiracy of
silence" descended when they returned to their former communities.
Among their parents' friends and neighbors, "some decent and some not,
each had their own story of the hardships of the occupation which made
me choke back the unspeakable" (Durlacher 1991: 100). Van Thijn recounts, "If, on occasion, in an unguarded or intimate moment, I told
something of my personal history, a deep silence would descend as if I
had spoken in an incomprehensible dialect—in some cases it abruptly
ended what was expected to become a passionate romance. Oddly
enough, I had similar experiences with my Jewish friends. We never
spoke about what we had been through" (2001: 267).

While some non-Jews returned property that they were keeping for
Jewish neighbors and friends or that they had taken from their resi-
dences after they had been deported, others refused to return such property and/or denied possession of it (Moore 1997: 240, 250). Some sold the
items, assuming they were theirs to do with what they liked. Hondius
found that many returning Dutch Jews experienced their former friends'
and neighbors' selfishness and "unashamed materialism." Others told
returnees that their or their parents' possessions had been stolen, even
when the items were right there before the returnees' eyes. During the
war, the term *bewariër* was used in a neutral sense to mean a non-Jew
who took care of the goods of Jews (it is a combination of the word *be-
waren*—"to keep"—and the word *Aryan*) (de Haan 2001: 410). After the
war, those who did not return Jewish properties, especially apartments,
were termed *bewariërs,* but the word took on a different and pejorative
meaning.

Two of Hondius's accounts are excellent examples of how some Dutch
Jews struggled to reclaim what was once theirs. One woman visited a
former neighbor in her flat, only to discover many of her parents' former
possessions. She describes the strange experience of being served coffee
in "mother's porcelain Meissner cups, dark blue with a gilded edge,
beautiful," with her mother's lacy tablecloth on the table, all the while realizing that the neighbor was not about to give these things back and that
she had to keep silent about them (Hondius 2003: 107). In another ac-

count, a Jewish doctor came back from hiding and returned to the doctor who had taken over his practice. The returning doctor described the scene: "[He acted] like we were stealing when we came to pick up things from our home." The doctor's father, a clergyman, also had some of their belongings and returned them with a message that he didn't want anything more to do with the family, acting as though they had no right to their own possessions (108).

One of my respondents, Louis D., recounted how in 1963 a family friend took him to his parents' former home, where he had been born. Louis found a neighbor who knew him and his parents and who described how his parents had escaped out the back door during *razzias* (raids). Then the family friend said to the neighbor,

"Do you know, because the couple [Louis and his wife] *just married, where all the nice things are?"* [The former neighbor] *said, "I didn't take anything, but maybe over there and over there are still the same people, and maybe they took something. I didn't see anything. We didn't take anything." So we had a nice talk for hours and hours. We were sitting there, and then the husband came in. The husband's height was like my father—he was tall. . . . And strong. . . . And I remember him coming in, and his wife told him about me. The first ten minutes he started crying. He was so emotional. And then he didn't say anything. He took my hand and went upstairs, and he said, "Listen, this bed,"—it was a very big bed, of wood—"this bed is the bed of your parents." And then I was shocked, because the lady told me she didn't steal anything from my parents. I was so shocked because I saw a lovely lady telling me the truth, but she was not telling me the truth.*

After this experience, Louis suspended his visits to old family friends. He did not take the bed.

In addition to losing their belongings, returning Dutch Jews confronted financial hardships because they were held responsible for paying rent and insurance premiums to cover the time they had been in hiding or in camps. Hondius reports that in these cases compassion was the exception (2003: 59). The general policy of the state not to treat Jews any differently from non-Jews had been adopted by insurance companies and landlords. Thus, if life insurance policies had not been paid up, the policies lapsed. Tax officials also attempted to collect back taxes from those who had been in hiding or in camps (95). One of my interviewees, who had emigrated to the United States with her mother, reported to me that her mother had successfully evaded paying her "back taxes" before she left Holland.

The government tried to collect taxes or the like from Louis D. on the shops owned by his family. Government officials were going to sue him for these monies but would desist if he sold them the shops. His foster father sold them all (on paper) and felt quite proud that he had saved Louis from distress. Louis has never attempted to collect on these properties, even though the state essentially stole them from his family through this shady interaction.

Anti-Semitism also became more public during this postwar period. Hondius cites quite a number of publications, some by those who were in the Resistance and who therefore had excellent "credentials," that were directly and clearly anti-Semitic. I found my surprise deepening as I read Hondius's book because of just how many examples she found. I must include several here, if only to give the reader a taste of the kind of anti-Semitism that was apparent at that time.

In the writings of some former Resistance members, Jews were portrayed as the "Other" in some very frank discussions of their "objectionable" qualities. According to Hondius, no negative reactions to these publications were reported. In 1946 one former Resistance member, Anne de Vries, wrote in a memorial publication *Den vijand wederstaan* (Resisting the Enemy):

> Let us honestly admit it and frankly write it down because only honesty can set us free: *we didn't like the Jews*. Despite the fact that we associated with them daily and did business with them, all of us were what we, using an imprecise term, usually call "anti-Semitic." Even as children, we were struck by the foreign, separate, completely distinct atmosphere of Jewish families. . . . And later, was it their adeptness, their cunning, their merciless business instinct that we feared? Or was it their often thoroughly materialistic attitude to life that aroused our aversion? (Hondius 2003: 97, my emphasis)

In 1946 the lawyer H. Sannes wrote a book in reaction to what he perceived as increased anti-Semitism in Holland. Although it seems as though he was concerned about this trend, he too wrote about the Jews as undesirable Others. At one point, he describes Jews, as perceived by himself and others, as being exuberant; gesturing while speaking; using a different sentence structure and intonation; being immodest, arrogant, pushy, and brazen; hogging the conversation; bragging, boasting, and swaggering; being parvenus and show-offy; being loud; indulging in "Jewish flattery" (i.e., building up others and complimenting them on qualities they do not actually possess). He describes the Jews' laziness, deviousness, treacherousness, criminality, lechery, and parasitism and their lack of a culture of their own. He also inevitably cites the imminence of Jewish global dominance.

The most widespread criticism Sanne notes (and seems to agree with) is "their lack of manners, the fuss and bother, the hoo-ha, the boasting, the bragging, the arrogance" (cited in Hondius 2003: 98). Although often there are threads of truth in every stereotype, Sanne leaves no stone unturned and falls back on traditional anti-Semitic images.

Hondius found another reaction to returning Jews among Dutch non-Jews. Many found it necessary to issue "warnings" to their fellow citizens to watch themselves and their demands and to show modesty and gratitude. Some warnings were expressed in benevolent terms; others were more sinister in tone. She includes an excerpt from a resistance magazine *De Patriot*, published in early July 1945, that is well worth including here, as an example of what Dutch Jews faced on their return. Published anonymously, this piece was on the "Jewish question":

> All the Jews who have come out of hiding owe their lives to Dutch people who sheltered them for humanitarian reasons, and who ran the risk of losing their homes, possessions and their lives.... The returning Jews may thank God for this assistance, and feel humbled. Maybe some superior people were lost because of all this. And this is something those who have returned need to keep in mind too: there is a lot to make up for.... Now the Jews must abstain from excesses, and they should be constantly aware that they need to be thankful. They should demonstrate their gratitude by assuming responsibility for making amends to those who became victims themselves for helping Jews.... Truly, they are not the only ones who had a hard time and suffered. (Hondius 2003: 59)

Others wrote the Jews brought anti-Semitism on themselves, adding that they needed to change their behavior. In 1945 another author in a Resistance newspaper, *Het Parool* (The Watchword), argued that only the Jews can prevent another genocide: "The only thing that can be done to prevent this is to give as little offence as possible. As I stated before, the Jews are different from other Dutch people. Let them attempt to adopt a little of our greater modesty" (Hondius 2003: 59). Hondius found another form of postwar anti-Semitism, which she termed "institutional anti-Semitism"—in which individuals sought market protection against a possible invasion of Jewish workers and professionals. They called for quotas in certain professions so that Jews would not exceed a proportion beyond what they represented in the population (107–8).

All in all, the receptions Dutch Jews got when they returned and/or reintegrated into society were mostly unexpected and quite negative. The lack of empathy was conjoined with a lack of support, both moral and material. At the community, society, and state levels, there was little help to be had. Rather, there was a "temporary revival and increase of antisemitism . . . a mostly latent, relatively mild form . . . [i]n which tolerance and indifference are hard to separate" (Hondius 2003: 63–64). This was most evident in the fact that the state and the majority of the Dutch people kept their distance from Jewish survivors rather than becoming involved or showing any solidarity toward this minority population. Although Hondius views this increase in anti-Semitism as temporary, lasting no more than six months, Evelien Gans felt that it continued for years (cited in Hondius 2003: 157). Hondius suggests that traditional Dutch tolerance evolved into a kind of indifference and a laissez-faire attitude then reflected in state bureaucratic dealings with surviving Jews.

Although scholars refer to a "mild form" of anti-Semitism that existed in prewar Holland, especially when compared with that in other countries, it was part of the fabric of Dutch society. However, after the Occupation and the war, during which Jews had lost everything, including their families, Dutch Jewish citizens no longer viewed this mild anti-Semitism and its increase after the war as benign. As Dutch citizens, many felt betrayed by their country and by their compatriots. The prewar attitude of tolerance and of keeping to one's group was now experienced as "gross indifference, a lack of understanding, and denial of what had happened" (Hondius 2003: 155).

THE STATE AND DUTCH JEWS AFTER THE WAR

As discussed, after the war official Dutch state policy was consistent with previous dealings with the Jewish community. No special status was accorded to these survivors. Instead, it was immediately accorded to those who had been in the Resistance. A postwar "spirit of the Resistance" allowed the Dutch populace to hide behind the nationalized myth that "we were all in the Resistance" (de Haan 2001). "A small, ideological diverse resistance movement was proclaimed the vanguard of national resurrection" (Romijn 1995: 311). This kept the question and practice of collaboration and anti-Semitism out of the public debate and, more important, out of collective memory (1995).[3] The spirit of the resistance was synonymous with anti-German sentiment, which still runs strong in the Netherlands. This popular image of resistance, common in France as well, created a binary between the enemy (the Nazis) and the victims (the general population), thereby "de-Judaizing" the real victims (Lagrou 1977: 184).

In what Hondius calls this "new order" in which Resistance fighters were granted the highest rung, all other returnees, including Jews, fell much lower in the hierarchy. Jews, Lagrou argues, were placed at the bottom of the "hierarchy of martyrs" because Resistance victims could be integrated into a "national epic and an ideological discourse" in a way that Jewish victims could not (1997: 222). Furthermore, a focus on the Resistance allowed for national pride, whereas a focus on the huge number of Dutch-Jewish victims inevitably brought up shame, guilt, and questions about collaboration (220, 222).

"There was a strong consensus that former members of the resistance deserved something extra" (Hondius 2003: 79). A pension plan drafted by former Resistance members and those related to them was approved in 1947. Citizens entitled to receive a pension included those who were in hiding for political principles—*principiële onderduiker*—making it clear that those who were forced into hiding because of racism and genocide were not deserving of extra attention or help. Special centers were opened for former Resistance fighters and for them alone. In the 1930s the queen had had "serious reservations" about a proposal to establish a temporary camp for Jewish refugees that was to be located near her palace, yet in 1945 she made a whole wing of her palace available to former Resistance fighters, with whom she sometimes socialized (80).

The state's quest for equality meant that Jews had to be treated no better than any other Dutch citizen who had not been a Resistance fighter. Perhaps with that standard in mind, the minister of justice declared that former Jewish property owners and the current owners had the same rights. If the Jewish owner could prove that the current owner had acquired the property in bad faith, only then could he or she make a claim on it. Thus, those whose homes had been robbed from the Jews were innocent until proven guilty, and it was the Jews who bore the burden of proof. Rather than making Jews equal to non-Jews, these kinds of orders and laws privileged non-Jewish Dutch citizens who were not in hiding or camps during the war.

Another law stated that if the Jewish owner of a property had died during the war, the heirs needed a death certificate before they could reclaim it (de Haan 2001: 408). Procuring a certificate was, of course, extremely difficult in cases when the deceased had been killed in a concentration camp. Only in 1949, four years later, did the state finally agree to exempt Jews from that law, acknowledging that there might be special circumstances. The state also deemed transactions from Lippman Rosenthal Bank, the bank to which the Jews were forced to turn over all their wealth during the Occupation, legal and fully acceptable after the war (205). As Presser aptly noted, in light of Nazi genocide, this kind of strict legalistic egalitarianism after the war amounted to discrimination against Dutch Jews (cited in de Haan 1998: 203).

In his accounting of judicial and administrative process, van Schie (1984) describes in detail, and to a great extent defends, the workings of Dutch bureaucracy when Jews tried to reclaim their property after the war. In example after example, it is clear that the burden of proof was on the returned Jewish victim who, according to van Schie (1984: 407) "thought goods should be returned without fuss." Van Schie's statement mirrors the state-held attitude that Jews once again (or still) were acting entitled and demanding too much. Although van Schie agrees that the "state could and should have settled accounts more quickly," which would have been "less of an affront" (419), he explains that the state's priority was to fight the nationalist movement in Indonesia, which was very expensive. Only direct damage, such as that from war bombs, was considered for compensation. And it was only Dutch *non-Jews* who received such recompense.

"For all other damages—the so-called intangible or immaterial damage—neither the Jews were compensated nor other war victims such as those persecuted for their political or religious convictions, hostages or people repatriated from Indonesia" (420). Thus, Jewish suffering was equated with the sufferings of all others, including returned Dutch colonials, and even ranked lower than that of those whose houses had been bombed. Van Schie feels that government restitution has been fair: "Due to clashing interests, it was impossible to give everyone that which *he thought himself entitled to*" (420, my emphasis). Here we see a barely concealed notion that Jews wanted more than they deserved. Van Schie represents a mainstream view and helps us to understand the unsympathetic context that Jacob Presser described: each returning Jew "was forced to build up his entire life anew, in an environment that too often refused to receive him, in which he felt unwelcome, which took it amiss when he asserted his claims to former possessions, indeed, which simply resented his very existence and often treated him with suspicion, dislike and scorn" (537).

Compare van Schie's defense of the state with Jozeph Michman's account:

> The reintegration of Jews into Dutch society after the war was a protracted and painful process. The Netherlands had suffered more from the German occupation than any other country outside Eastern Europe. There was also an anti-Semitic streak in government circles and an inclination not to permit the Jews to regain the position they had had before the war. A determined struggle had to be waged by the Jews to gain recognition of their claims to the property that had been stolen from them. A government proposal to reimburse the holders of LIRO accounts with only 70 percent of the balance was vehemently denounced by the country's leading jurists and in the end, the government retracted. (J. Michman 1990: 1056)

How does the Dutch Jews' experience fare comparatively? In his research on postwar France, Belgium, and the Netherlands, Lagrou found
that in general the ideology of resistance dominated most Western European nations after the war and that there was considerable hostility toward Jewish survivors. Lagrou notes that in contrast to France and Belgium, the majority in the Netherlands were "unimpressed and unmoved
by the return of concentration camp prisoners," who went unnoticed
and unacknowledged (1997: 209). In France and Belgium, Jewish survivors and political prisoners constituted "the most active and respected
milieux de mémoires," whereas in the Netherlands, the majority of Jewish
war victims were deprived of initial postwar help and reparations (209).
It took close to thirty years for Holland to grant the kind of recognition to
Jewish victims that France and Belgium gave to Jewish returnees directly
after the war (201).

We might also note another difference, for example, in the way that
Jewish properties were handled. In Denmark, Jews forced to leave their
homes turned over their keys to state officials, who kept them until the
occupants returned. The funds of Jewish families were administered by a
Danish lawyer. While one may argue that the occupational regime in the
Netherlands differed from that in Denmark and made such safekeeping
of Jewish properties impossible, it is also true that there was absolutely
no effort on the part of Dutch state bureaucrats to thwart Nazi thievery
of Jewish property. Indeed, the Dutch state ended up with some of this
Jewish booty, and not a few Dutch non-Jewish families ended up with
the possessions of their Jewish neighbors. Between 1950 and 1964, most
Dutch citizens convicted for persecuting Jews were pardoned and released, including the group of volunteers who specialized in "Jew hunt-
ing" and were directly responsible for the deportation of thousands (de
Haan 2001).

JEWS, VICTIMHOOD, AND NATIONAL IDEOLOGIES

A shift in national ideology occurred in the early 1960s when a television
documentary called *The Occupation,* narrated by Louis de Jong, deeply
affected the public. Only in 1968 could those persecuted during the war

make disability or pension claims (de Haan 1998). This new public awareness led to a belated recognition by the Dutch parliament and state in 1972 of its responsibility to Jewish survivors. In 1973 the WUV was created (Act for Benefits for Victims of Persecution), and in 1977 the ICODO (Coordination of Services to Victims of War) was founded (206). More than thirty years after the war had ended, the psychological needs of war victims were finally recognized.

Although about six of those I interviewed reported that they were able to get funds from the WUV for their emotional disabilities, illness, or other needs, others found the organization to be frustratingly bureaucratic and completely insensitive to the fact that it was treating Holocaust survivors. I heard comments that were somewhat similar to the descriptions of the so-called welcoming centers set up by the Dutch state to greet returning Dutch Jews. One was, "They're nasty and smug, but they act like they're wonderful." That woman told me she felt that the attitude of the WUV demonstrated that the Dutch "have not recognized their collaboration." Another reaction was, "Those bastards—it took them years to file my claim and send me money. My father always said, 'The Dutch are *krentekakkers'*" ("currant shitters," in this context meaning overly concerned with little things). One respondent feared applying to the WUV for help because she did not want to be seen or recognized as Jewish.

Sociologist Abram de Swaan argues that another important aspect of this ideological shift was the invasion of psychology into politics. He notes that in the late 1960s, the vocabulary of psychology and psychiatry individualized the issues of war and persecution. This shift transformed a social and collective political phenomenon and reduced it to an individual problem. Political strife was reduced to a mental health problem. De Swaan argues that Holland's past is so shameful to Dutch society that the "political history of murder was transformed into a succession of complaints in the consulting room" (1990: 198). This is not to discount the traumatic effects of war on individuals and their families; however, reducing such trauma to psychological effects, such as PTSD, depoliticizes the causes of that trauma. Focusing on the individual mental health effects of the war medicalizes the Shoah and transforms public issues into private ailments (196). Thus, although de Swaan would never deny the trauma individuals experienced because of the war, he is critical of the way in which the trauma framework has been used to deny broader political culpability.

De Swaan asserts that while the psychic stress that occurred because of the Shoah is easily understood and accepted, for each survivor, "there is a story that cannot be told," a horrendous past that cannot be articulated in a public venue. This "unspoken" history then returns disguised as "symptoms, uncomprehended behavior, or physical disorders" (197). Doctors, lawyers, and social workers end up fulfilling the same functions as therapists—acting as a "buffer zone between the private troubles of individual survivors and the society of their contemporaries, between the private and public domains" (198). Yet, de Swaan argues, these private problems that survivors experience as a result of murder in the death camps cannot be resolved by individuals. "History cannot be dealt with only in the consulting room; as a historical and political problem, it must be coped with in public discussion" (198).

Historian Ido de Haan focuses on how psychological terms leaked into national discourse and on how "persecution became a national trauma anyone could suffer from" (de Haan 1998: 207).[4] The discourses of trauma and victimhood applied to everyone alike—Jews, the children of Dutch Nazis, those who suffered from crime, and victims of incest. Thus, once again, the playing field was leveled, and everyone became a "survivor." De Haan pushes his analysis further by claiming that it is an "outright insult" to call the Occupation a national trauma because it implies that everyone—perpetrators and victims alike—suffered equally. He argues that we should directly name the Occupation for what it was: "The persecution of the Jews in the Netherlands was a *crime of organized violence committed by German occupying forces in collaboration with Dutch officials and facilitated by Dutch institutions, rules, and morals*" (213, my emphasis). Keeping the discourse focused on politics rather than on psychology might have allowed the Netherlands to deal publicly with its collective memory and practices, as the Germans have done. "Because indeed, the very same Dutch society that is said to have suffered so much from the persecution of the Jews was also the context for its effective execution" (212).

Memory and identity are both social constructions and cannot be understood as individual and private, states de Haan. "The way in which people conceive the past and their own position in that past, as well as its meaning for their current identity, is subject to processes of public deliberation, political struggle and conflicts of interest" (2001: 434). De Swaan asserts that the Dutch view their history in the past sixty years as one of powerlessness—they could not manage to hold on to their empire, they could not prevent the Nazi Occupation or the deportation of their citizens to extermination camps. "Quite understandably, as a nation they prefer to remain silent about it, and quite understandably they indignantly deny either this silence or else the very facts" (1990: 201–3).

One positive effect of this shift toward a psychological understanding of the Shoah was that it put the Jews in the limelight, and in the 1980s, both in the Netherlands and in the United States, they were finally able to talk about the persecution in their own words. Survivors became a more popular topic in the media. However, de Haan points out, this shift also used the language and images of victimhood. Although survivors and their offspring were victims of the Shoah, portraying the Jews solely in these terms did not mesh with contemporary Jewish life in the Netherlands. Some scholars view the pendulum as having swung too far, almost to a state of "philo-Semitism." De Haan feels that this respect for the Jewish "point of view" that was so prominent in the 1980s, though it decreased in the 1990s, still remains strong (2001: 431).

At the same time, current political events in Israel and Palestine have led to more anti-Israel sentiment among a sector of the Dutch population, and some believe that anti-Semitism has increased as a result. However, the number of anti-Semitic occurrences remains relatively low, and it is crucial that we not conflate anti-Israel protest with anti-Semitism. Since the intifada, viewing Jews solely as victims has shifted somewhat in Holland and elsewhere (Moore 1997).

WHO OWNS HIDDEN CHILDREN?

As mentioned earlier, before the war ended, various Resistance group representatives met to plan for the care and guardianship of Jewish children they had helped to hide. Scholars suggest that these young, childless idealistic activists felt an attachment to the children they protected and wanted to have a say in the children's future. Indeed, it seems as though they felt they had a right to be involved with the children's futures because they had saved their lives. Resistance members prepared a bill allowing them to have a say in the children's future and circulated it to the government-in-exile, where it found support (Fishman 1973: 31). This bill took away a parent's natural right of guardianship over their child, if he or she had given that child to someone else and not returned after the end of the war within one month, and gave it to the state. A memo that was part of the proposal stated: "Parents who do not report within one month will presumably be those who have been transported somewhere else from the Netherlands. They will probably not be capable of taking on their parental duties the way that they should. They shall not be permitted to resume their parental authority until they have demonstrated that they are fit to do so" (Brasz 1995: 65).

In fall 1944, when some thought that the end of the war was imminent, the Samenwerkende Ondergrondse Groepen voor het Kinderwerk (Association of Resistance Groups for Youth Work) distributed a pamphlet to Dutch families hiding Jewish children that stated: "While waiting for this [the bill to become legislation], we urgently request you to keep the children as long as possible and to give them up to no one, not even the parents, without receiving permission from the bureau" (63).

In August 1945 this bill became official, and Royal Decree No. 137 was issued. By agreeing to the Resistance's proposed bill, historian Joel Fishman argues, the state "officially recognized the claim of the Resistance groups to be consulted in determining the children's future" (1973: 31). When the bill became law, the government officially formed the Commissie voor Oorlogspleegkinderen, or OPK (Commission for War Foster Children).

Fishman asserts that a crucial semantic point exists in the state's definition of these children. They were legally defined as foster children (*pleegkinderen*), since in most cases it was not clear whether or not their parents had survived—it would have been presumptuous and insulting to have called them orphans without knowing if their parents were alive or not. In the case of foster children more generally, the state severed parental rights, citing abandonment or neglect and took over the children's guardianship (cited in Moore 1997: 233). Jewish parents, however, had *not* abandoned or neglected their children, whose lives they were attempting to save by sending them into hiding. What this particular legal definition suggested was that parents consciously or unconsciously abandoned their responsibilities *as parents* and in doing so, willfully *abandoned their children*. Furthermore, after the war, transportation was chaotic within Holland and across Europe. Given the lack of quick assistance from the state, Dutch citizens who were liberated from camps may not have been able to return home within a month's time, even if they were physically able to do so.

Dr. Gesina van der Molen, a lecturer in international law at the Free University of Amsterdam who had been active in the Resistance as a member of the *Trouw* group, was named chair of the state commission. She belonged to the Calvinist Church (Gereformeered), which believed that Jews did not have theological legitimacy and should be converted. Chaya Brasz acknowledges that though van der Molen may have been sincerely motivated by a desire to help children, she was strongly influenced by her church's beliefs and edicts, which may explain her somewhat allergic reaction to the notion of the Jewish community's continuation (1995: 75). Former members of the Resistance were given a privileged position in the OPK (Fishman 1978a; Moore 1997). Initially, there were twenty-five members of the committee, eleven of whom were Jewish. Four of those eleven were "avowedly assimilationist" (Moore 1997: 233), and one was baptized (Fishman 1973: 24).

The committee's charge was to determine "the best interests of the child" in making decisions about the child's future guardian—an extremely difficult and contentious concept to define under the best of circumstances, since multiple perspectives often exist. In this case, not surprisingly, there was a strong division between the views of the Christian majority and those of the Jewish minority. Fishman points out that the tradition in Dutch family law had always been that "an orphan should be brought up in the faith of his deceased parents" (1973: 32). As discussed in the last chapter, within vertical distinctions in Dutch society (*zuilen*) each group, such as the Catholics, the Protestants, and the Jews, traditionally had had the right to autonomy over its own affairs, such as the care of foster children and orphans (1973: 34).

The Jewish community, only a remnant of what it once was, felt that state intervention into this issue was a clear violation of Dutch civil tradition. They wanted a Jewish organization to make the rulings or to advise on these cases. The Jewish organization L'Ezrat ha-Yeled was founded in August 1945, which many Jews hoped would replace and supersede the OPK.[5] However, there was no Dutch law that turned over the fate of orphans to their parents' community, simply a tradition. Thus, while the OPK and its decisions were fully legal (Moore 1997: 234), this kind of crossover process was highly unusual. As some scholars have suggested, it is inconceivable that the reverse—a Jewish majority committee having a major say in the future of Dutch Protestant foster children or orphans—would have or could have occurred.

The Dutch Jewish community was numerically small and politically weak after the war. They had few tools with which to fight off this affront. Furthermore, the creation and composition of the OPK reflected a general strengthening of the Protestant idea that being Jewish is a punishment and a liability that Jewish child survivors should not be made to suffer. Thus, the weakness of the Jewish community and the religious zealotry of the Protestants combined to run roughshod over the Dutch tradition of respecting each *zuil*'s determinations.

Van der Molen argued that if the children in foster families were loved and doing well, there was no need to alter "God's will." It was a very Christian God that was seen to be actively involved in Jewish children's lives, and the fact that the children were living with Christian families was interpreted as a progressive change and as their destiny. Those on the OPK who were Orthodox Calvinists, including Chairwoman van der Molen, were accused by the Jewish community of not taking into account the pressures Jewish parents confronted when giving up their children to the Resistance. Opponents who supported the OPK argued that they assumed that Jewish children "who had the good fortune to end up with a Christian family" should not necessarily be returned to Jewish kin (Michman, Beem, and Michman, cited in Moore 1997: 233).

The majority on the OPK argued that these children were Dutch first and Jewish second as a way of justifying whatever setup the government had agreed to. Indeed, the whole idea of Jews affirming their identity as Jews or having an interest in the perpetuation of their community seems to have created discomfort, if not hostility, among many OPK members and among Dutch citizens more broadly. These former Resistance members who now sat on the OPK, Fishman argues, had "utopian visions of ideal postwar society" and saw the OPK as a way to turn their dreams of a society without divisions or racism into a reality (1978a: 425).

Jews had been invited to join the commission as individuals and were selected according to criteria designated by former Resistance members. They wanted to avoid having Jews on the committee who represented what they felt was an "extremist minority"—that is, Orthodox or Zionist—and preferred those whom they believed were "true representatives" of the Jewish community. They selected Jews who were not too identified or outspoken as Jews and certainly not religious (Fishman 1978a: 424). "The State and the Resistance did not envisage a meaningful role of the Dutch Jewish Community on the Commission since they chose the Jewish members and they ruled on the Jewishness of the deceased parents" (429). Scholars also point out that van der Molen did not believe that a Jewish community existed; rather, she felt that the majority of Dutch Jews were "Dutch-inclined" and that there existed only an "extremist" minority of Orthodox Jews and/or Zionists. That the OPK and its edicts were created by non-Jews (from the Resistance), provoking state intervention into matters normally left to the Jewish community, is now seen by many as ranging from highly insensitive to blatantly anti-Semitic. Fishman asserts that the actions of the OPK and the personal opinions of van der Molen demonstrate an "us-them" attitude, one in which the majority identified Jews in a negative manner, as Dutch citizens with dual loyalty (429).[6] This viewpoint may very well have reflected general Dutch sentiment.

Right after the war's end, most foster families were willing to turn over their Jewish foster child if and when parents returned. Widowed fathers tended not to claim children unless they were living with other female relatives or had remarried because of a strong family ideology that linked a child's welfare to having a mother. However, some foster families wanted to keep the child they had hidden and possibly even adopt him or her. As mentioned, in some cases parents were simply not told the whereabouts of their child. Elma Verhey's first book opens with the story of a Dutch woman named Monica Nieuwkerk who, along with her sister, thought she had been orphaned. Only when she married in the late 1950s and needed her parents' consent did she find out that her mother was still alive. After meeting her mother, Liselotte, Monica discovered that after the war, parental authority had been taken from her. Guardianship authorities had judged her incapable of bringing up her own children. She had no house, no relatives, no money, and no husband, and the authorities refused to tell her where her children were living. Liselotte had gone to search for them; when she found them, the foster parents refused to let her in the house (Verhey 1991: 1–2).[7]

Liselotte's two adult daughters could never quite believe their mother's story and were upset that their mother had not rescued them from their painful youth. However, when Monica saw Elma Verhey on a TV talk show in 1991, she "could not believe her ears." It was only then that she found out about the law that prevented hidden Jewish children from being returned to their parents after the war. She and her sister finally believed their mother (Verhey 1991).

It is estimated that 3,500 Jewish children survived the war, 1,417 of whom were reunited with one or both surviving parents.[8] Jozeph Michman reports that 1,540 were returned to at least one parent. Two thousand and forty-one were completely orphaned, about 1,300 of whom were under the age of 15. The OPK dealt with those 1,300 children. If the parents did not return, often close kin wanted guardianship over the child. Sometimes this was contested by the foster family if it wanted to keep the child. Other options were having the child's guardianship transferred to L'Ezrat ha-Yeled, which then put the child either in an orphanage or in a foster or adoptive Jewish family.

When a decision had to be made, the OPK considered the "best interests of the child" in psychological terms and within his or her "current setting." What this means is that specialists evaluated the child's psychological, nutritional, and physical conditions. The majority of OPK members felt that such evaluations were a sufficient basis for making decisions and recommendations. However, the Jewish minority on the OPK felt that the good of the collective—the then-decimated Jewish community— had to be considered, in addition to the biological parents' identities and affiliations. The OPK rejected any notion that Jewish suffering had created a common interest or common rights (de Haan 1998: 205).

When considering each child, the committee, particularly the majority members, made a judgment about the parents' Jewishness, and that was calculated into their final recommendation. Majority members did not consider parents as "really Jewish" unless they had belonged to a synagogue, attended synagogue, kept a kosher household, and/or were Zionists. If parents had strayed from these demonstrations of Jewishness, the OPK majority deemed them "not really Jewish" and, therefore, highly assimilated. That was interpreted by the majority to mean that the child did not need to be in a Jewish environment.

It is clear that OPK majority members had a very narrow understanding of Jewishness and Jewish identity that was based solely on strong religious observance. However, most Dutch Jews before the war were cultural and secular Jews. For example, if parents had been married under a *chuppah* and had circumcised their son but had not been observant otherwise, OPK majority members would interpret the couple/family as being not really Jewish and on the way to full assimilation. They argued that those acts demonstrating Jewish affiliation, such as a Jewish wedding or a *bris*, reflected pressure from the grandparents and the community (Brasz 1995: 79). But for the majority of Dutch Jews, their wedding, their son's circumcision, and their funeral were the main markers of their Jewishness (Bregstein and Bloemgarten 2004), even if they did not observe any other Jewish religious rituals.

For obvious reasons, there was disagreement and strife on the committee over these kinds of interpretations and decisions. Gesina van der Molen and other majority OPK members created their own inaccurate definition of Jewishness and stuck to it. That they refused to be swayed by the explanations and views of the Jews on the committee reflects their strong sense of superiority and smugness (Hondius 2003). Indeed, through a contemporary lens, these attitudes smack of a kind of paternalistic anti-Semitism. In a 1991 interview, Mrs. W. G. Doorn-Pleiter, former head of the legal section of the OPK, stated: "The Christian majority of this Commission were unable to empathize with Jewish interests. They saw their own Christian identity as something so self evident and so positive that they naturally wanted to extend it to the Jewish children" (36). In her analysis of the attitudes held by OPK members, Dienke Hondius does not mince words: "The history of the aid to Jewish children in hiding by mostly Christian resistance workers reveals how closely linked the chain of compassion, help, self-sacrifice, interference, condescension and arrogation could be. The denial of Jewish interests, Jewish identity and the Jewish community was the last link in this chain" (36).

Fishman (1978b) points out that because of the OPK, the Jewish community in the Netherlands found itself in the uncomfortable position of arguing with its benefactors. These Jews were seen as being "ungrateful" by those who rescued them. Although many individuals who helped and hid Jews did so for a variety of reasons—religious, humanitarian, political (anti-German and/or socialist)—the perpetuation of a Jewish community was usually not one of them. In June 1946 the chief rabbi of Palestine, Isaac Herzog, visited the Netherlands and pleaded before the queen, the prime minister, and the minister of justice to return Jewish children to the Jewish community, to no avail (Brasz 1995: 80).

OPK chairwoman van der Molen wrote an article in an Orthodox Protestant newspaper about how to define the best interests of the child, which, Fishman asserts, explained that "the rescue of Jewish lives in the Netherlands did not necessarily imply the intent to preserve them as Jews": "According to some people they [the children] must be given back to the Jewish community. In most cases, the children were entrusted by the parents to resistance workers. . . . Does the Jewish community now simply have the right to demand these children? Did these children really belong to the Jewish community alone? Even when the parents did not have a single tie further with Judaism? Even when they felt themselves to be more Dutch than Jewish?" (Fishman 1978b: 83).

For less than a year, the commission made evaluations case by case, making recommendations both about orphaned Jewish children and about those whose parents were claiming them but who were unable to get them back from foster parents. As Jacob Presser wrote, "there were quite a few cases in which judges saw fit to set aside the natural right of parents, as though their suffering during the war had not been more than most people could bear" (1988: 543). Internal strife on the commission over decisions such as these led to the Jewish members withdrawing from the OPK in July 1946, under the leadership of Professor Kisch. They sent a letter of explanation to the minister of justice and met with the minister the following month. The minister created the Meijers Commission to investigate, and it was decided in January 1947 that if the OPK was not unanimous on a case, the minority could submit its own recommendations to the court.

In February the Jewish minority members returned to the OPK, which had continued to make decisions during the seven months of their absence. Two years later, the Jewish minority members were still dissatisfied and took their concerns to the Jewish press. In June 1949 this led to a demonstration against the OPK that was attended by 1,500 Jews—6 percent of the country's remaining Jewish population. This extraordinary turnout challenged Chairwoman van der Molen's contention that only a small fraction of "extremist Jews" wanted the children returned to the Jewish community. One month later the minister of justice dissolved the OPK, but by then most cases had been decided.

The numbers on hidden children vary somewhat but hover within a similar range. Jozeph Michman states that in the end 360 children remained with non-Jewish families (1990: 1056); Joel Fishman states that about 500 remained in non-Jewish surroundings, although some returned to Judaism on their own (1973: 35). He explains that by 1967, 264 Jewish orphans from the Netherlands had immigrated to Israel with the help of L'Ezrat ha-Yeled. (Two such orphans appear in this book.) When the OPK was dissolved in 1949, of the 1,300 Jewish children whose fate the committee had discussed, 601 went to Jewish households—either to relatives or to a foster Jewish family—and 403 to non-Jewish households, which I assume means that they stayed with their hiding family, and 359 cases were still unresolved. Those cases went to the Minors Protection Board of Amsterdam (Moore 1997: 236). Of the 2,041 orphans (minors and nonminors), 1,500 were in Jewish foster homes or in Israel, and about 500 were left with non-Jewish families (239).

Elma Verhey's first book (1991) brought the workings of the OPK and the long-term ramifications of their decisions to light for the Dutch public as well as for the affected families of former hidden children. Her 2005 book presents a devastating look at how Jewish children were dealt with after the war, including conditions in the Jewish orphanages. One aspect is particularly relevant here—the reports she found from social workers sent by the OPK to evaluate the situation of former hidden children, their foster families, and/or their biological parents, in order to give the OPK information that would help members decide whether the children should be returned to their biological parents.

She gleaned comments from the reports such as the following descriptions of Jewish parents who survived the war: "Weak character, superficial, they spoil their children. They look unpleasant, they speak like a traveling salesman. When they visit the foster parents, they can't help but do business with the Canadian soldiers living there" (2005: 54). The Jewish adopted father of a boy is reported to be "typically Jewish. . . . He is clearly primitive" (*Zijn primitiviteit is evident*) (2005: 54). Indeed, the description *typisch joods*, "typically Jewish," seems to pervade these reports, and it was clearly not meant as a positive evaluation.

These are the comments about a child named Chava: "She is modest and hasn't got the character that most Jews have." About 5-year-old Sally (nickname for Solomon): "A typical tendency to earn money. When he went to play on the street, he started to sing. Later on, he did it only for money. This was reported to me by children in the village" (54). About a girl named Caroline K.: "She is typically Jewish—sneaky."

In one report, a social worker wrote that "Hitler was right" (*Hitler had gelijk*), although she also stated that valuable Jews do exist (55). And a director of a hospital reported on a girl who survived Auschwitz, stating that the girl thinks she should be spoiled. "She can't imagine how difficult it was in our society." The director noted that nothing she did for the girl "was good enough for her." She added that "the Jewish patients almost created a revolution like political delinquents—they circumvented in a very devious way the rule that visitors were forbidden" (55). Given that she was writing about camp survivors, many of them children, the lack of empathy coupled with blatant anti-Semitism is jolting. Verhey also points out that this kind of anti-Semitic atmosphere was disastrous for the children, who were very much in limbo, trying to reconcile their conflicting identities.

KIDNAPPING AND THE CATHOLIC CHURCH

Dutch citizens do not seem to have been concerned with the workings of the OPK or the protests of the Jewish community. However, one case in particular caught the public's attention, that of Anneke Beekman (Fishman 1978a; Moore 1997; Brasz 1995). Anneke Beekman was born in November 1940 to an Orthodox Jewish family in Amsterdam. When she was 2 $^1/_2$, her parents got help from the Resistance in finding her a hiding place in a Catholic setting, which they believed to be a temporary but life-saving plan. Anneke's parents were deported and murdered in Sobibor a few months later, in June 1943 (Fishman 1978a: 3). Anneke had been placed with five Catholic sisters in the van Moorst family. After the war, her surviving kin asked of L'Ezrat ha-Yeled that she be transferred to and raised by a Jewish family. The OPK recommended this as well because of her Orthodox background and because they did not view the five sisters as constituting a "normal family" (4). The committee recommended to the court that her guardianship be transferred to L'Ezrat ha-Yeled, which had found a potential Jewish foster family.

The district court of Amsterdam, however, awarded custody to Anneke's Catholic foster mother in 1948 (Brasz 1995: 93). A court battle followed, and the district court's decision was overturned on appeal. The sisters appealed to the Netherlands Supreme Court, but the appeal was rejected. Anneke's custody was awarded to L'Ezrat ha-Yeled by the district court in 1950; she was then about 10 years old. However, Anneke was nowhere to be found; in 1949 she had been baptized and then kidnapped by the Catholic sisters and taken into hiding in a Belgian convent.

Another Dutch Jewish girl, Rebecca Meljado, had been kidnapped by the sisters and taken to the same convent. Dutch detectives raided the convent in March 1954 and found Rebecca, but Anneke had already been taken by her foster mother and had disappeared again (Brasz 1995: 93). The Church's response was to state that Anneke was following Catholicism of her own free will and that the Jews should cease persecuting her (Fishman 1978a: 8). The Jewish community's response was to reject the notion of a child in such a situation being capable of exercising her free will.

The Catholic sisters refused to compromise and would accept only the legalization of their guardianship over Anneke. One of the sisters was brought to trial in 1954 for helping Rebecca hide and was sentenced to twelve months in prison. She received eight more months for hiding Anneke. The case was appealed, and her sentence was reduced, but still no Anneke. De Haan states that when it became clear that Catholic clergymen had been involved in Anneke's abduction to a convent in Belgium, "protests at least appeared in the press," but at the same time, the state dismissed the public prosecutor who had ordered the arrest of her abductors (2001: 409). According to Fishman, the Anneke Beekman affair led to anti-Jewish writings in the newspaper, and public opinion was against the Jewish position (1978a: 11). Indeed, at the 1954 trial of the van Moorst sister, her attorney intimated that "in the event of a conviction, *Jews in a future Holocaust might not be certain of aid from the Catholic community*" (Fishman 1978a: 19; my emphasis).

In 1961 one of the van Moorst sisters appeared in Maastricht with a 20-year-old Anneke, who had just returned from France and was no longer a minor. Anneke stated that there had been no kidnapping and that she had willingly become a Catholic. She responded in the negative to questions from journalists such as did she know anything about Judaism or did she know how many Jews were killed during World War II.

Sociologists tend not to focus on outliers that constitute only a few cases out of hundreds, but historians have extensively mined this particular story. It is useful not because of any pattern that it exemplifies, but because it demonstrates what could, and did, happen in extreme cases. Here, the state can be credited for prosecuting the civilians who refused to obey the courts and return the children. In France, where there are many more convents than in Holland and where many Jewish children were hidden, there were many more cases of the Church's involvement in keeping Jewish children.[9]

To my great surprise, in early January 2005, a 1946 Vatican document surfaced in Church archives near Paris that had advised French Church authorities that "Jewish children baptized as Roman Catholics, for safety or other reasons, should remain within the Church—even if that meant not returning them to their families." If a child's family had survived the Holocaust, the Church advised that he or she be returned "as long as they had not been baptized." The letter had been approved by Pope Pius XII, and its tone was cold and impersonal; "it makes no mention of the horrors of the Holocaust" (Sciolino and Horowitz 2005). Given the pope's silence on the Nazi death camps, the publication of this document reopened old wounds for many Jews. Reminiscent of the workings of the postwar Dutch bureaucracy, the directive demonstrates the "very bureaucratic and very icy attitude of the Catholic Church in these types of things," claimed Italian religious historian Alberto Melloni. Also similar to the Dutch context, it reflects a Church with no understanding of the Holocaust as a major catastrophe for the Jewish people (cited in Doland 2005; Sciolino and Horowitz 2005).

CONCLUSIONS

In 1995 Queen Beatrix addressed the Israeli Knesset and acknowledged that only a small minority of Dutch people had taken part in the Resistance and that they, rather than the majority of the population, were the "exceptional ones." However, she then went on to state that "the people of the Netherlands could not prevent the destruction of their Jewish fellow-citizens" (quoted in van Galen Last and Wolfswinkel 1996: 122). This statement portrays the Dutch population as rather passive but at the same time almost suggests that they were victims too in their inability to act. Furthermore, it bifurcates the perpetrators as Germans and the victims as the Dutch and the Dutch Jews. In this speech the queen completely ignored the role of Dutch citizens in aiding and abetting, if not approving of, the destruction of their "Jewish fellow-citizens."

Two years later, some students' discovery of Ministry of Finance archives in an Amsterdam attic sent a serious shock wave throughout Dutch society. These archives, from the 1940s, directly concerned unclaimed Jewish properties, many of which had remained in the possession of the Dutch state. Finally, in 2000, the Dutch government admitted error and failure with regard to its Jewish citizens in the postwar era. The Ministry of Finance published a "Final Report of the World War II Assets Committee" and concluded that although the restoration of rights to Jewish victims reflected consideration of their specific situation, "the implementation was unsatisfactory":

> In retrospect, special arrangements should have been made for Jewish victims of persecution. The restoration of rights itself [was] extremely time consuming and engulfed in legal and administrative red tape. The concerned individuals were often left in uncertainty for many years. They found the system painful and lacking in understanding and compassion for their sufferings. . . . In retrospect certain aspects of the restoration of rights, the return of stolen property and government actions were certainly unfair or inequitable. Insofar as these situations were attributable to the actions of the government or government bodies, the government should in our view acknowledge its responsibility. (cited in Hondius 2003: xv)

Most of the historians I have cited, and the Dutch Jewish citizens who lived through this ordeal, would strongly disagree with the government's contention that the laws set up to deal with returning Jews' rights were satisfactory but that the problem lay in their implementation. Indeed, especially by today's standards, the way in which the postwar legal rights of returning Jews were delineated appears unequal. In this legalistic language, the original Dutch may be satisfactory to those who suffered, but in translation, the wording that "they found the system painful" is a passive way of avoiding laying any direct blame on the government. Perhaps solace can be found in knowing that the state acknowledged its errors, joining other European countries, although the fact that it took fifty-five years makes it difficult to wholly accept that it is "better late than never." What does not provide solace is that it took a serendipitous event—the accidental discovery of papers by students—

to trigger this admission of wrongdoing, an event that just as easily might not have occurred.

In the late 1990s, the government decided to make restitution to all war refugees—Dutch Jewish survivors, German Jewish refugees to Holland, Roma (Gypsies), and those who were refugees from the Dutch East Indies, now Indonesia. Each group had its own representatives. The committee that represented these Jews was named Maror, an apt description of this restitution. The word *maror* refers to bitter herbs, one of the ritual foods on the Passover seder plate. One eats a small amount of *maror*, symbolized by fresh horseradish, which bites and causes tearing, to remember the bitterness of slavery in Egypt. By bearing this name, the committee reflected the bitter nature of this restitution. As mentioned in the introduction, in September 2005, the Dutch railway system officially apologized for transporting Jews during the Occupation and war. It is clear that the Netherlands is attempting to come to grips with its past, accepting that its citizens were not only victims but also passive bystanders and active participants. A new publication in comic book form for children copublished by the Anne Frank House and the Resistance Museum in Friesland attempts to teach the collaborative aspects of Dutch behavior in the 1940s (Heuvel 2005). In it a boy discovers some family "secrets" in his grandmother's attic, and she tells him a story. His grandmother's father was a gruff policeman who seemed to follow orders under Nazi rule. His family thought he had turned in his daughter's young Jewish friend, but in the end, grandmother and grandson find out that he had saved her and secretly helped her go into hiding. Thus, a well-meaning effort to educate children about World War II in the Netherlands basically ends with the discovery of a relative's decency and heroism in saving rather than betraying a Jew. Although some Dutch citizens did save Jews, unfortunately, they were fewer and much farther between than this surprising (and happy) ending might suggest.

4 "My Mother Screamed and Screamed"

MEMORIES OF OCCUPATION, WAR, AND HIDING

We begin with the changing lives of Jewish children and their families during the Occupation, when they faced the possibility of separation, deportation, and death. This chapter will deal with the perceptions of these children as danger enveloped their lives and as they began the "descent" into hiding. (The term for hiding in Dutch—*onderduiken*—literally means "to dive under.")[1] We will also examine the vast range of their experiences while in hiding, setting the stage for the next several chapters on postwar family reconstruction.

Documentation of children's lives during the Occupation and war is fragmentary at best. Diaries such as Anne Frank's were relatively rare, and no one I interviewed had written one. It was very risky to keep a journal or diary, particularly if such materials were found during a raid (Dwork 1991: xxiii). And most of those in hiding whom I interviewed were too young to have engaged in diary writing. It is also the case that many hiding families were very religious and/or poor and would not have encouraged such an activity, because it would have been seen either as frivolous or as too costly. If anything, children in hiding were encouraged to forget their identities and to erase any signs of the past.

Not surprisingly, children's memories of the Occupation vary greatly depending on their age. Most respondents who were young children at the time do not recall this period, even if it was full of radical life changes. Some childhood memories are strong and clear; others are vague and shadowy but still created enough of an impression that respondents were able to describe their feelings about an event. I am reminded here of Wilkomirski's now-discredited memoir *Fragments* in which he vividly describes the space of childhood memories as "a rubble field of isolated images and events . . . mostly a chaotic jumble, with very little chronological fit" (1996: 4). Although fabricated, these descriptions seem apt.

THE EXPERIENCE OF OCCUPATION

Many respondents who were between the ages of 3 and 5 during the Occupation recall that there was a great deal of whispering and nervousness among the adults, reminiscent of scenes from Bergman's film *Fanny and Alexander*. Young children had no inkling of what it meant to be Jewish, but they were able to sense the fear and danger growing around them. Some recalled seeing their parents cry, an unsettling event that most likely had not occurred in the past. Others spoke about feeling fearful or being aware of danger simply by the way a parent held their hand or by the silence in the house. Lea, who was 4 or 5 years old at that time, remembers thinking that her family members and others were criminals because they were all being arrested. Although Peter was only 3 when he first saw German soldiers, he knew they represented danger and was fearful of them.

Mary was 4 when there was a raid, and she remembered "a lot of noise. . . . And my mother screamed and screamed." Sophia was 5 when her father was taken away but has no recollection of it. She does recall, however, wanting to wear a yellow star like her older sister (children younger than 6 did not have to wear one). In 1943 Peter V. was 5, when, after being tipped off, police raided his apartment and dragged his grandmother away. He wept as he recounted what must have been a horrendous scene, remembering the shouting, the crying, his mother's helplessness. Riwka was about 6 when her father was taken away. She recalls that before departing, he told her that her mother's birthday was the next day and that he had hidden her present but would be back in time to give it to her. They never heard from him again, apart from receiving a card in the mail stating that he had died. As mentioned in the introduction, Max L. was about 6 when his mother left the house at a time when it was too dangerous to do so and never returned; he has no recollection of her disappearance. Since he is able to recall other events from that time, it seems he has completely repressed this memory.

Those who were of school age during the Occupation recall having to leave public school and attend an all-Jewish school. These children were ever aware of all the restrictions increasingly heaped on Jews because they directly affected their lives. Louis G. recalls the tension during summer holiday when, owing to suffocating restrictions, he and his friends could no longer ride a bicycle, roller-skate, play soccer, swim, take a tram or train, listen to the radio, go to the movies, or even enter a park. They were all branded by the yellow star they were forced to wear outside the house. Louis recalls playing in a park despite these restrictions and being chased out by a former classmate who had joined a Nazi youth group.

Catarina found it traumatic to go to school because everyone stared at the star on her coat. Like other Jewish children, she stopped going to public school, but after a few months, she was one of the few Jewish children who was allowed to return to a "mixed" public school. When she returned to her school, the teachers told the other children, "You're not going to stare at her. She is one of us, and nobody is going to mention the star." She stayed at that school until she went into hiding. Her teachers there clearly were unusual and courageous.

David G. was in the same class as Anne Frank in the Jewish school. He and many other respondents recalled how, one by one, classmates disappeared from one day to the next without a word. Their classmates were left to wonder whether they had emigrated, been picked up in *razzias*, or gone into hiding. If these children had gone into hiding, it was done in the utmost secrecy, and they could not say good-bye to their friends or often even their relatives. Mirjam's parents did not even tell her paternal grandmother, who was living with them, that they were going into hiding, because "they did not trust that she wouldn't talk with people about it. . . . They left a note for her to go to her daughter's because they were in hiding and they left."[2]

During this period, serious reconstellations of family life took place as the Nazis laid their groundwork. Most fathers lost their jobs or had to close their stores, with the exception of those who were grocers, since they were allowed to sell to Jews during certain hours. As economic resources dwindled because of unemployment, some families had to move or have relatives move in with them. Often there was covert if not overt tension in the air, particularly in crowded quarters. Many families had their bags packed so that they would be ready in case of a raid.

When raids were imminent, some families moved around, staying with different relatives or friends, or they sent their children to sleep elsewhere. Several respondents told me how their parents concocted contagious diseases for them as a way to avoid being raided or being taken during a raid. These children were put in bed, where they faked smallpox or scarlet fever, and a sign on their apartment door warned outsiders about the danger of entering due to contagious disease. The police tended not to enter such dwellings. This ruse was also used later during raids when children were in hiding.

A number of those I interviewed barely escaped being picked up by the Germans. Jaap A. was 14 on June 21, 1943, when he, his parents, and some other family members were captured. At his parents' urging, Jaap was able to escape. His mother told him to go to a family friend in Amsterdam to whom they had given money and who was hiding his younger brother. When Jaap arrived, the woman said to him, "I don't want your brother; you can take him with you. I have nothing from your family; sorry, I can't do it." Jaap recalled, "It was so terrible for me. I was young and had a brother of 3 years old by my side. . . . I didn't know what to do. I longed to go to my parents. I wanted to give up." He and his brother walked and walked. They ran into a relative who then helped arrange hiding places for both boys. His parents and the other captured family members died in Sobibor two and a half weeks later.

Ed was 15 in October 1942 when his family received the summons to report to a labor camp in Germany. The Jewish Council had advised the summoned Jews to pack a backpack with warm clothes and blankets. "So my mother put nice warm blankets and socks and so on, we had backpacks with our names on them, my father painted names on them. We were all set to go . . . to work-relief in Germany. And then my grandfather Isaac came from Amsterdam, where they had begun dragging Jews out of their apartments." He told them that "there are rumors that the Germans are lying to us. . . . Don't go on those trains. . . . You must go into hiding." Ed attributes his parents' willingness to obey the law to a general attitude among the Dutch Jews that "we'll be alright." His was one of the few families that survived in its entirety, with its members hiding separately, however.

Louis D. was less than a year old when he and his parents were betrayed in hiding and "sold to the Germans." Once in the Schouwburg, his father was asked if he'd like his child to go underground. He believes that his father said yes because, as Louis explained, "normally no mother could say good-bye to her child." His parents were killed, and Louis alone survived in hiding.[3]

German Jewish Children as Refugees in Holland

Several people in my sample were born in Germany and were there when Hitler came to power. Their experience differs considerably from that of Jews who were born and raised in the Netherlands, and their memories of terror begin much earlier. Ruth J. was only a year old when Hitler came to power but recalls Kristallnacht occurring five years later, after which her family fled to the Netherlands. Hans lived in Berlin and recalled the day Hitler was elected, even though he was only 5. When he began school a year later, he was taught the Nazi salute. His family left Berlin in 1937 for England and then in 1938 went to the Netherlands, where he attended the Joods Lyceum, the same school as Anne Frank. His brother worked for the Joodse Raad, the Jewish Council, and accompanied the SS on nightly raids, to calm those being taken away. His brother's German must have come in handy in such situations since there were so many German Jewish refugees living in the Netherlands. Carla was Dutch, born to a German Jewish mother and a Dutch Jewish father. Until 1938 her parents had sent her to Germany to stay with her maternal grandparents during summer vacations. After Kristallnacht, her grandparents moved to Holland.

Ilse left Vienna after Kristallnacht, at age 13, and was sent to a cousin in Amsterdam. The cousin could not take in Ilse and arranged for her to stay with another couple, who after two months decided that they did not want her because she was "too old." They had recently lost a child and wanted someone younger to foster. Ilse exclaimed, "Can you imagine leaving my own parents, to be all alone in this strange country and coming to a family who doesn't even want you?" Luckily, another Jewish foster family was found through a Jewish agency. Ilse's parents tried to emigrate to Holland, and her father had a job secured at the Dutch mint, but they never made it and were killed. In May 1942 Ilse received a letter, the same one received by the Frank family and all other German Jews registered in the Netherlands, telling her to report to the train station the next night at midnight, in order to go to a German labor camp. Instead she went into hiding.

Flora lived on Birneplatz, across the street from a synagogue in Frankfurt. She was 8 years old when she was woken up on Kristallnacht, when what Flora called "hooligans" rang their bell and then threw them out of their apartment. Her father was picked up and sent to Buchenwald and was let out some months later. Flora and two of her siblings were on a special transport of German Jewish children sent to live with Jewish families and/or in a children's home in Holland after Kristallnacht. The Germans did not want to let the train cross the border into Holland and held up the train for about twelve hours. Yet what was likely a harrowing experience for many felt like an adventure to Flora.

I heard more about such experiences at a reunion of those who were on the Kindertransport, in Burlingame, California, in October 2004. Some of the *Kinder* described their terror as German police trolled the train and sometimes made the train stop and wait for hours. They described their relief and exultation after crossing the border into Holland, when they opened the windows and sang. Most striking was their gratitude to the "Dutch Ladies," non-Jewish Dutch women who met the trains and provided hot cocoa and snacks—cookies, crackers, or bread— to the children. At the conference, Nobel laureate Dr. Walter Kohn recalled how it was the first time he had seen and tasted white bread, causing his audience to laugh and nod their heads as he described how it felt wet and rubbery compared with the hearty brown breads on which he had been raised. One woman explained how the welcome from the Dutch Ladies felt especially warm and wonderful after feeling hated by German and Austrian citizens for years.

Louis G. lived in Arnhem, close to the German border, and was very aware of Kristallnacht, after which hundreds of German Jews fled and crossed the border into Holland. Some refugees stayed with his family for a few days, and they also housed some of the children who were on the Kindertransport. He recalled a 5-year-old girl who cried continuously; his father went out and bought her a doll to comfort her.

GOING INTO HIDING

At some point, the Dutch Jewish parents among those I interviewed decided to send their child(ren) into hiding. The German or Austrian Jewish parents who sent their children on transports to the Netherlands, though they had sent their children away to safety, had not made the decision to send them into hiding once in the Netherlands. My guess is that if they were willing to separate their family to keep their children safe early on, they would likely have made the decision to send their children into hiding as well. For most parents, the decision was made when raids came closer to home, sometimes after a close relative or perhaps even a spouse had been picked up. I cannot even fathom the anguish parents must have experienced as they considered this option; however, it was clearly a desperate decision made during desperate times. Nor is it possible, as a parent myself, to imagine how they felt when they put their child into the hands of someone else, often a stranger, and said what were sometimes their final good-byes.

Hiding occurred informally with family networks or friends, or through a Resistance organization. As mentioned in chapter 2, it is believed that many more Jews would have hidden had they had contacts with non-Jews willing to help them. It is also believed that those with more resources were at some advantage in finding hiding places because they could offer money to those who hid them. In Holland, several organizations focused on saving and hiding Jews, and some, such as the Amsterdamse Studentengroup, the Utrechtse Kindercomité, or the Naamloze Vennootschap (NV), focused solely on saving Jewish children. The first two of these organizations consisted of university students (Moore 1997), and it was in part their youth that allowed them to translate their indignation into courageous and risky activities.

Children in particular were easier to hide than adults because they did not need papers, and if they were caught en route to or once with their hiding family, it was easier to fabricate a lie to justify their presence (Dwork 1991: 34). The Resistance felt that it was preferable to separate families for two reasons. First, it was easier to find hiding places—Dutch families were more likely (and perhaps more able) to accept an individual rather than a group of people. Hiding several people required more space and access to more food, which was rationed at the time. Second, breaking up the family lowered the risk of everyone being caught. That rationale may have made it easier for some parents to give up their child(ren) to a stranger. Therefore, with the exception of a few cases, almost everyone I interviewed went into hiding without his or her parents. Again, the case of Anne Frank's family hiding with another intact family was very unusual.

Those in the Resistance found that families willing to hide a Jewish child tended to have preferences for gender and age—Dwork cites a former Resistance participant who stated that most requested "a girl of four years old. For a girl of four or five years old, you could get as many places as you wanted." Dwork attributes some of the preference for girls to the mark of circumcision on Jewish boys, which would have distinguished them from non-Jewish Dutch males. However, two Resistance members felt that the preference for girls had more to do with foster parents' images about girls being easier to deal with than boys. In his interviews with former Resistance workers, Bob Moore found that children who did not "'look' Jewish were easy enough to place, but if they were, for example, circumcised young boys who did 'look' Jewish, then it was far more difficult" (179). And in general, those he interviewed stated that it was far easier to place a Jewish baby in hiding than a Jewish adult.

From her interviews with two former Resistance activists about the numbers of male and female children they saved, Dwork concludes that in the end, despite their stated preferences, foster parents took whatever child they received, and that age and gender ultimately were not relevant (1991: 53–54). Yet the gender and age breakdown of my sample does reflect a preference for younger girls, followed next by younger boys. Because we do not have a full accounting of those children who went into hiding (since we assume that many of them were betrayed and killed), it is impossible to substantiate either conclusion.

Sixty percent of my sample was female, and the average age at hiding was about 7.3 for both males and females. The median age at hiding for both boys and girls was 4 years old. Two-thirds of the girls and about half the boys in my sample were hidden at age 5 or younger. However, older children, in their mid-teens, were hidden as well.

Taking Leave of Parents

German and Austrian Jewish parents whose children were sent on the Kindertransport to England were able to prepare for their children's departure and talk with them openly about the transition. Parents carefully chose and packed their child's clothing and other belongings in preparation for their first voyage alone, and an international one at that. They were also able to openly accompany their children to the train station, although times were already quite dangerous. In films such as *Into the Arms of Strangers* and *The Power of Good,* former *Kinder* describe their departure as they entered the train, some of them quite excited, and waved good-bye to parents, who were usually in tears. The small children were often crying and had no idea what was transpiring. While the children may have expected their separation to be short-term, lasting only until their parents joined them, parents knew it might be the last time they would see their child. One *Kind* describes looking back as the train pulled out of the station to see her strong and brave mother suddenly collapse into her father's arms.

In contrast, children going into hiding seem to have had little time to prepare for their separation. They needed to keep their whereabouts secret, and in some cases, arrangements were made quickly and without much warning.

Those who were very young children have little or no recollection of leaving their parents, but about half my sample spoke of the separation. As they relate it, they were suddenly told to go with a stranger but were not prepared for what was to happen. The separation and transition into hiding took place in a matter-of-fact manner, sometimes without discussion or explanation. Some children were advised to "be good" girls or boys, to watch their manners, and to eat everything they were given, since they were going to live with strangers. Chava was 5 when she last saw her parents. She describes how her mother prepared her:

My mother told me that I had to leave and that I will be brought to a very distant place, where I will have to be till they came back. She explained it clearly to me that I will have to behave myself because I was a little bit spoiled. I had to eat everything and not be rude, as I sometimes was rebellious, and to behave nice. I think she told me that the people I am going to be with are not Jewish so their customs will be different from our customs and their food will be different and their language would be totally different from what I was used to.

Several recalled their last hug with their parents; others recalled seeing a parent cry. Although Naomi was only 3 when she was separated from her parents, she stated, "That's such a trauma, you always remember that." She cried herself to sleep at night and was told by her hiding family to cry more softly. Naomi was moved to four different hiding places; she said, "All I did was cry." At the fourth place, she sat under the table and cried until an adult put her on his lap and spoke with her. Naomi thinks that he must have been able to reason with her because she finally was able to stop weeping. Her mother had left a note in Naomi's suitcase addressed to the strangers who would be her foster parents that stated, "Please treat her well," but it was burned for security reasons.

Naomi, now a mother and grandmother, cried as she recalled this part of her narrative. Her mother did not survive the war, and it is clear that her note would have been a precious keepsake.

Catarina was 7 when she returned from school to find a stranger in their living room. Her mother introduced him as "Oom Stemberger" (Uncle Stemberger) and told Catarina and her younger sister, Rita, that they were to go with him. Catarina cried, "I didn't want to go with that strange man. . . . And they told me, 'You don't have any choice. That's the way it is and we hope we'll see you as soon as possible.' I don't exactly remember what they told me, except for, 'We have to go.'" Rita was blonde, blue-eyed, and fair, quite different from her dark-haired, more Jewish-looking older sister. On the train with Oom Stemberger, 3-year-old Rita loudly exclaimed, "Catri, you're not wearing your star!"

Deborah Dwork found that Dutch Resistance activists who were helping to rescue and transport children realized, especially as they aged, that "they were able to do this work precisely because they themselves did not have children. At that time they simply did not understand or comprehend the intensity of the parent-child relationship." One former Resistance member told her, "Now as parents and grandparents you start thinking. What would your reaction be if a youngster, twenty years old, comes and knocks on your door? Would you so willingly trust them enough to give your child away?" (1991: 51). Another former Resistance fighter explained,

> Of course it makes an impression on you if you see it—if you go to the parents and they give their child away, and they don't know if they'll ever see the child again. But as a boy of twenty-one you don't realize what it means. You think it's very unpleasant; you can cry about it, but you don't realize. And I think that's good; that's why we could do it. . . . For a Jewish mother to give away her son or her daughter to a strange goy, that's something. It took a lot of courage in my opinion, and foresight. (51–52)

Along with the heart-wrenching descriptions of separating from parents, I also heard stories of a distinctly different reaction from a handful of those I interviewed—that of excitement and adventure. Ies found it "frightening and exciting." Josef could recall all the details of the separation, which occurred when he was 6: "I remember the car, even. As a child, there are certain details you remember. . . . The car was black with yellow . . . and the model I later realized was an Audi; at the time it was called DKW. And the colors I remember distinctly. And I also remember it was a two-door car, and we had to go through the front seat to the back." Although his sister cried, he didn't because he saw it as an "adventure" although he "didn't fully realize what was happening."

Ellen said that when their father was taken away, she and her siblings did not have much of a reaction since he was often away anyway, on business trips. To this 13-year-old, her departure also "felt a little like an adventure." Five-year-old Henny said that although her brother cried when they left their parents, she felt "excited to go on an adventure." And 15-year-old Hans was not particularly unhappy about the separation, or at least he was able to make light of it: "When I talk to kids in the classroom I say, you know, to be in hiding with my mother for a year and a half [laughs]. I don't know if I would have survived that [laughs]! I don't think she would have been a joy to be around for a year and a half."

Adjusting to a New Home

After getting over their initial shock at separating from their parents, children sent into hiding then had to adjust to their new settings. Besides adopting a new identity (discussed in more detail below), they had to adjust to a different family life, since many hid with those who were less well-off than their own families; rarely did a child move up in status when he or she went into hiding. The rules were different, expectations were different, and the diet was different. The few who came from kosher households were forced to acquire very different dietary habits. Moving from a Jewish family where eating was frequently encouraged to a more Calvinist one where sparseness was the norm could be jarring. Most children did their best to adapt, to blend in, and not to cause trouble, a pattern Evers-Emden and Flim found in their research as well (1995). Indeed, many did their best to please their hiding parents, to show their gratitude.

Many children reacted regressively to separating from their parents and adapting to a new home—they wet their beds or refused to eat—often with dire consequences. Rob's older brother, who was 10 when he went into hiding, was very unhappy and wet his bed. As a result, their foster father sent him back home to his parents, and he was deported and killed with them. Betty, age 3, cried nightly for her parents and was shaken and threatened with a spanking for doing so by her foster parents.

Peter was sent into hiding at age 3 as an experiment, but he wouldn't stop crying and was taken back home. He did not recall that episode, but a few months later, he was taken to another family, which he remembered clearly:

I remember the first night. When they took me to bed, and I started to cry, "I want to go home!" But I couldn't go home. I cried the whole night. And then I got out of bed and was lying on a rug. And then I remember that I was still feeling very strange, . . . I realized that you can go on crying, but it doesn't help. So you better stop and go to sleep. So I went to bed again, and I slept. I awoke very early in the morning and took a biscuit out of a tin. And when they came down, they were very angry at me for having done that.

The Resistance worked feverishly to find hiding places but clearly did not have the resources, time, or ability to evaluate who would make "good parents," even if temporarily. Indeed, they did not have the luxury of rejecting any volunteers since there were more Jews to hide than people willing to hide them. The result was that not everyone who hid a Jewish child was a good temporary guardian since "it was neither a love match nor a true adoption." Those who hid adults could view them as hidden boarders for whom they needed to procure food. Children, however, needed much more than simply room and board. Mismatches occurred, and when the Underground was aware of them and could move the children, they did so. Dwork states that many children were made to feel inadequate by their foster family, "not only unaccepted, but unacceptable. It was not a situation in which self-worth flourished" (1991: 79). While I concur that many hidden children did not receive affection or empathy from their hiding parents, some did flourish during this period, and therefore, based on my data, I would not be able make the same generalization.

THE INS AND OUTS OF HIDING

Jewish children were often brought to hiding places by strangers, members of the Resistance. Two-thirds of those I interviewed were hidden in more than one location. The average was three hiding places, with a range of one to fifteen and a median of two. The seventy people I interviewed had been in a total of two hundred hiding places. Three respondents were too young to know in how many places they had been hidden; all three were orphaned after the war, which may contribute to their lack of knowledge. Their hiding places would add anywhere from three to twenty to the two hundred already calculated.

There were two types of hiding: clandestine, such as Anne Frank's, in which the outside world was not supposed to know that the child was with a particular family or in their house, and what I would call "integrated hiding," in which the child was integrated into the family and community, albeit with a false identity. The majority of my respondents fell into the latter category, and about one-third of them were in clandestine hiding at least once. Sometimes, those who were kept in the house with one family were allowed out with another, so some children experienced both types of hiding. Some who had to stay inside the house had to hide even within the house so that other family members would not know they were there, or so that neighbors could not hear them. One of my respondents lived in a hayloft, and another in the attic; both had very limited interaction with family members, but that kind of hiding did not occur often and would have been impossible with young children. A few were allowed outside in the garden, but only after dark.[4] Two sisters who hid together in the same house were given different rules—the fair one was allowed to integrate and could go outside freely, but the darker one with the "Jewish nose" was kept inside.

Clandestine Hiding

Those kept inside were usually free to be in all parts of the house except near the windows and in the front room, where outsiders could look in. Some were able to move about the house and to talk during the day but not at night. During a period when there were many raids, which often took place at night, 12-year-old Mirjam and the other girls hidden with her could not sleep in their bedrooms. They were put in a safer hiding place, in a crawl space under the kitchen floor, from 7 P.M. on, with one small flashlight and no toilet facilities. They were not allowed to talk or leave the space to use the toilet. These restrictions made Mirjam very nervous, since she anticipated needing to go to the bathroom. And of course, her nervousness usually caused her to need to go more often than normally. Sometimes she would hold it in, but sometimes she could not manage and would quietly open the trap door and the linoleum that covered it to use the toilet. "And when I got caught, they were very mad at me for doing that."

How did those who were hidden clandestinely spend their days and nights? Mieke spent the first three years of her life in hiding and remembers how fearful she was of the bombing. She recalls being under the table a lot and keeping quiet. Most likely, small children could entertain themselves with a few toys or household items. Maarten spent a great deal of time in cupboards, under sinks, and in cellars and attics. By war's end he could crawl but not walk or talk, because these cramped conditions did not allow his motor or verbal skills to develop. Those who were older and had been attending school described the boredom of having to pass the time with nothing to do. A few were lucky enough to have some books, which they reread multiple times; others reported being in houses where there was only a Bible. They were forced to entertain themselves with few props other than their imaginations. Some were able to draw, but again, that depended on the family's resources. Between the ages of 5 and 7 Chava was in clandestine hiding. She read, played, and was taught how to embroider, knit, sew, and do other crafts. She also helped around the house. "I loved it, because it made me feel important, to do something."

It is hard to imagine the almost unbearable difficulty of the lives of those who were hidden in small spaces for long periods of time, unable to use the toilet or to talk. As Moore points out, it was difficult for both adults and children to deal with days and weeks of "enforced idleness . . . although it was undoubtedly true that some people were better psychologically predisposed to deal with the pressures than others" (1997: 158). He notes cases of some adults succumbing to depression and even suicide, and several of those I interviewed told of mothers who had to be tranquilized while in hiding, because they could not cope with the separation from their children. Moore underscores how strong the feeling of helplessness was, and I would add that of dependency.

Right after receiving their summons to appear with their luggage, Thea and her family hid in a friend's warehouse, where they stayed for five months. "Suddenly I had no more family life—the extended family, we didn't know if they were still home or rounded up. There were no friends. There were no toys. There was no daylight. . . . This was a storage place. There was never any activity at night [in the warehouse], so you could not flush the toilet, could not talk loud, could not do anything."

Although some hidden children, like Chava, were happy to be given chores, since they helped distract them, sometimes these chores went too far. One boy was forced to do piecework for the family to sell and was only given his meal if he had completed a certain number of these jobs. A few older girls were forced to spend all their time cleaning, cooking, and looking after the children, as unpaid maids. However, the majority who stayed inside were left to their own devices. In one case, a hidden child was allowed to practice piano, but that was rare, for obvious reasons. One young man who was alone in an apartment during the day spent a considerable amount of time masturbating. "I was so goddamned horny. I was a teenager, had never been kissed, and here I was locked up in a little room. . . . And thought about girls a lot, but it was impossible. So it's funny that I remember that. . . . What else was there to do?" I suspect that others may have also dealt with their sexuality in this way while in hiding; however, it is also likely that the fear and worry experienced by many may have decreased their libido.

Integrated Hiding

How did families explain the sudden arrival of a new child who was subsequently seen on the streets and perhaps in school and at church? The arrival of those who were openly integrated was usually attributed to the bombings in Rotterdam. Some children were portrayed as a sibling's or cousin's child, perhaps orphaned by the bombings. State documents were also destroyed during these bombings, so escaping from Rotterdam became the excuse of choice, since no one could follow up and check on the children's identities. The Resistance often used the addresses of bombed-out houses in Rotterdam when fabricating identities for hidden Jews. A few were supposedly some relative's child from the Dutch East Indies—colonial Indonesia—where the relative remained. One man I interviewed, Josef, looks as though he could be part Asian because of the shape of his eyes. (See figures 3 and 4.) The man who took in him and his sister temporarily (in the black-and-yellow car) thought that 6-year-old Josef could pass as half-Asian and made up a story that he was Indonesian, from a Chinese mother and Dutch father. Josef told me, "I was Indonesian until the end of the war, and I even believed it myself. . . . I started to slowly believe that I was really born in Indonesia. . . . It was very exciting; I was somebody that was not ordinary like everybody else. I came from far away, from a place people told stories about."

In order to integrate, children had to lose any trace of their pasts and their Jewish identities. Especially among younger children, any knowledge or memory could be dangerous to them and their hiding family. First, names were changed. Often children were given the hiding family's last name, but if not, they were given a "typically Dutch" name. Their first names were changed as well—Rozette became Rita, Josef became Johannes, Rutie became Clarry, Lea became Wiesje, Riwka became Ria, David became Dirk, and Naomi became Toosje. (In Dutch, the "tje" or "je" ending indicates a diminutive.) They were usually told a story that they had to memorize about where they were from and where their parents were, and eventually, like Josef, some of them came to believe that story. Most important, they could not say anything that would indicate that they were Jewish. Most were told never to answer adults who asked questions; a few were told to cry or to run home if that occurred.

That children adopted these new identities as their own is not surprising. In her research on the psychology of memory, countering that of the repressed memory movement, Elizabeth Loftus found that it is very possible to create and implant in children false memories of events that never occurred. "[O]nce implanted, these memories can come to be experienced by the rememberer as real" (quoted in Prager 1998: 87). So it is understandable that Rita forgot she was Rozette or that Josef thought he was from Indonesia—and that most children had no idea they were Jewish.

Three-year-old Jeannette recounted a story about discarding bits of her past: "[I had] a little suitcase with clothes . . . that my parents had given me. And when they pulled out clothes I said, 'Oh, that's my Shabbes [Sabbath] dress.' Well that dress had to go, of course." Josef describes bicycling with his foster mother: "I used a word which she identified as a Yiddish word. I don't remember the incident but she said *never* to use that word again; it was a dirty word. I don't know what it was. After the war, she apologized and said, 'I'm so sorry I had to say that to you.' She remembered, but I didn't." There were some close calls with small children who did not understand the dangers. For example, one young girl bragged to her friend, the daughter of a Dutch Nazi (NSB), "*My* mother had a yellow star on her coat"; she was quickly spirited away on a bicycle that night, in a burlap sack, to another hiding place.

One poignant story that reflects the innocence of children caught in a situation they don't understand came from Joop, who was told by a boy at school that he was Jewish and that it's very beautiful to be Jewish. Joop recalls yelling to his foster mother down the street, "Did you know I'm Jewish?" Although nothing came of this incident, it demonstrates how thin the line could be between safety and death for Jewish children and the families that took the risk to hide them. Three-year-old Naomi told the maid that she was Jewish and was later told, 'Listen, if you *ever* say again you are Jewish, you are going to a concentration camp.'. . . So I didn't talk about it anymore." Luckily the maid kept that information to herself.

Quite a number of hidden children were exposed to Christianity during the war and became active participants. As mentioned earlier, those who were fully integrated into family and community life went to church with their family on Sunday, sometimes up to three times if the family was Orthodox Calvinist. However, not all families went to church; those who were socialist tended not to. Among the more religious families, children joined in the family's prayers before each meal and before bed. In some very religious families, they prayed three times a day.

Jill was put in a Catholic orphanage as an infant and recalls how much she loved going to church and the nuns who took care of her. She felt that she was well taken care of and in the interview referred to "my nuns." Ruth was hiding in Southern Holland, which was mostly Catholic, and she went to a Catholic elementary school.

Like Jill, many hidden children mentioned how much they enjoyed going to church. Lore lived with a very religious Roman Catholic family. "I loved the rosary, it's just exciting for me, going into this beautiful church, the whole family together. The celebrations that we had [at their home] were very sparse. I mean, they lived a very spartan existence." Many hidden children adapted to their hiding family's religion, knew the prayers and hymns; many looked forward to Sundays. It is not surprising that many former hidden children still feel more comfortable in a church than in a synagogue today.

PARENT-CHILD CONTACT

Twenty-seven of those I interviewed had some contact with their parents while they were hiding, through either a letter or a visit, or both. Several were able to hide with their parents for short periods, but only one hid the whole time with her mother and brother. Six were able to write to or receive letters from their parents, although sometimes the letters were written by and read aloud by foster parents if the child was too young. These letters were infrequent because of the risk and difficulties involved in delivering them, but they constituted a lifeline for parents and children. However, the letters also brought up other emotions in some children. When his foster parents told him his mother might still be alive, Max A. (age 3 or 4 at the time) apparently pleaded with his foster parents, "Please don't give me away!" Another respondent reported that although she was able to write letters to her mother and even had a visit from her, she was confused because she felt she loved her foster mother more. Lore wrote many postcards to her parents, but they were never sent; it seems her foster mother encouraged her to do this to help her remember her parents, but for safety's sake, never sent them. This was unusual because foster parents tended to encourage their charges to forget the past. (I did not count Lore as one of the six letter writers since hers were never sent.)

Eleven children either were visited by a parent or parents or were able to visit them; two of those children also wrote and received letters. In some cases, the children were too young to remember their parent or the visit; in one case, the daughter was not at home both times her father was able to visit. In other cases, reunions brought up considerable emotions for the child involved.

Ruth W. was 9 when she first went into hiding; she ended up hiding with about fourteen different families. Her biological mother had died when Ruth was young, and her stepmother was very much her "real mother." (See figures 5 and 6.) Nonetheless, Ruth had a very difficult time separating from her parents and five half-siblings, and she acted out her anger. She explained that she stole small things from the families with whom she lived and that she lied: "Everyone was nice in my hiding places—it was me who wasn't always nice." Her stepmother was able to visit her once while she was in hiding, even though to do so was very dangerous. Ruth recalls this visit and how terrible the departure was: "I sat on my mommy's lap and said, 'I'm not letting you go! I want to go with you!'" Little Ruthie held on tight, and it took other adults to physically restrain her so that her stepmother could leave. The next time her stepmother left her hiding place to come visit Ruth, she was caught, deported, and killed in a concentration camp. Of course, Ruth did not know this for quite a while.

At one house, Ruth stole what she thought was a diamond ring for her stepmother. She hid it inside her doll's stuffing, determined to surprise her stepmother when she came back:

I knew that I had to be good. And I was always doing everything to give people presents. So I was making presents, stealing flowers from somewhere else, and I had an incredible fantasy life, of course. I was learning how to lie, and I loved it. I was making up the most unbelievable stories. . . . They took me for a visit to somebody, and I was left alone in the house to play. I came to a bedroom where there was a beautiful box with jewelry. I opened the box and . . . I stole a ring. I was going to keep this ring with me to give my mother when she came back. She would tell my father, "Moishe, look what she got for me! This beautiful ring!" and it would be glittering on her hand.

Ruth lost the ring during a street celebration at Liberation. "I was furious with myself and angry; I scratched my face. I just hated myself—how could I do such a thing?" She feared that her stepmother would feel forgotten if she returned and Ruthie did not have this gift for her. After finding the ring on the street, Ruth said, "It was as if I had given myself a duty or a task to guard this, and if this ring wouldn't be there, my mother wouldn't come back." Some time later, she lost it again in the sand dunes in The Hague. "When I came home that evening, the ring was gone. And from then on, I knew my mother would not come back. And she didn't."

Rozette's father visited his infant daughter several times, but her foster father finally had to ask him not to come because of the danger involved. Then her father was killed in a concentration camp. After the war, her foster father cried when recounting this to Rozette, since the image of her father standing on the street looking in still haunted him. Catarina wrote to her parents but can't recall her mother's visits, even though she was 8 or 9. "She came once or twice, but it didn't make a big impression." She thinks this is perhaps in part because she felt her hiding mother was more a mother to her than her biological mother ever had been.

While some children pined to see their parents, 11-year-old Ruth J. found her visit with her mother and father in their hiding quarters too difficult:

They were in this tiny little room. They couldn't really talk loudly, normally. . . . We couldn't really walk and then we played cards forever . . . without speaking. . . . They had to be careful walking because the kids were underneath. . . . So the mother, whenever she was desperate for somebody to tell off the kids, she said, "I tell the bogeyman," and with the broomstick she would go against the ceiling, and my father and my mother would stamp their feet. And so when I came there, there was this bed; I remember a tiny coffee table and a window. And in order to eat, we had to sit on the bed, and then when we went to sleep it meant that we had to sleep all three in that bed. And all day long we played cards. I didn't know at any moment [whether] *it was day, night; I was so miserable, and besides, I had lice. . . . I had the worst diarrhea. I was homesick, I guess. I missed them, and then I saw them . . . it felt like seeing strangers. . . . So I decided to leave them* [and go back to my hiding family]. *I was glad to leave them.*

Because they were in the same village, Ruth was able to walk to the corner where her parents lived, once a week at a certain time, and her father would signal to her that they were OK by standing on the toilet in the bathroom and showing his balding head at the window. Ruth found this system anxiety-producing, worrying that someone might see her, and frustrating, because she could not speak with her father and never saw her mother. One day her father was not there at the appointed time, and she became very upset. She was able to find out from a Resistance activist who was having an affair with her foster mother that her parents had been moved for their safety. At the end of the war, her parents requested that their family hide together, so Ruth was with them for a few months. However, she found it extremely difficult to see her parents in such a vulnerable position: "I had the same feeling of being claustrophobic when I was with them because they were always in small rooms, they always were running, hiding, and even though I was doing that [too], it is different to see your parents do that."

Louis G. was about 14 when he had to leave his fourth hiding place, and he joined his parents and sister in hiding for a short period while others continued to seek another hiding place for him. Contrary to Ruth's experience, Louis has very positive memories of this period:

We spent a lot of time together as a family. My father taught us how to play bridge. So we spent almost every afternoon playing bridge with very long discussions of the hands that were played. . . . We spent wonderful time together, really, as limited as it was, because it was really a time that I think back on when the family was very close. We had only one table. Nobody could go sit at the other table. We all had to sit together, share the small space, which was the living room and a bedroom. . . . While my parents had made the preparations to go into hiding, and we were the children, by now we were like partners in the same ad-

venture, so we were treated differently. Much more information was shared with us.

The striking differences between Ruth's and Louis's experiences with their parents in hiding might be related to several factors. Louis was older than Ruth, and from his description, I sense that he was already fairly mature at age 14. Ruth was still quite young and in need of more protection and clearly needed to see her parents in a position of more strength. Ruth's parents' hiding space was much smaller and more limited than that of Louis's parents, who could talk and walk around. It also appears that Louis's parents had one main room as well as a small sleeping room, which, even if it was small, was considerably larger than Ruth's parents' tiny attic space. Louis's age allowed his parents to talk with him in a more egalitarian way, which would have helped him feel more in control, while Ruth was still very much a child and could not be part of any such discussion. Finally, personalities also played a role. According to Ruth, her mother was "very neurotic" and deeply affected by the hiding experience. It sounds as though Louis's parents were able to adjust to their limited environment, although perhaps we should not underestimate the difference it would make to be able to walk around and talk freely.

Sixteen-year-old Ed had a fearless mother who visited him and his two brothers, all in their separate hiding places. He described the difficulty of one hiding place and how she was able to boost his morale:

Hiding was a time of darkness [last word said in a heavy, whispering voice]. *I see it as gray dark clouds* [same emphasis] *hanging over everything. . . . There were no lights, and the days were gray and dangerous, and anybody arriving on the horizon through that flat Dutch land might be a German coming to get me. So I couldn't stand the strain, and I decided I'd give myself up. Then my mother talked me out of it, gave me a little mantra* [chuckles] *which was* "This also shall pass." "Remember, say this to yourself."

In the meantime, his mother got in touch with someone who found him another hiding place. She was finally arrested while trying to take care of one of his brothers, who was ill, and was sent to Bergen-Belsen. Ed found out about her capture and left his hiding place to find his father and brothers. During the war his mother had rented a summer cottage in the country, supposedly to spend some time with her family for a week. Ed's brothers and father all stayed together for some months until Liberation. They survived by stealing food from farms and by begging. Ed felt bonded to his father for the first time and to his brothers because they all functioned "as a team."

A RANGE OF HIDING EXPERIENCES

As my respondents described them, hiding experiences ranged from "wonderful" to "terrible," with the majority somewhere in between. Although everyone's story is important and different, below I give brief summaries to suggest the various types of hiding experiences children confronted. It is also vital to understand that since the majority of those I interviewed hid in more than one place, most individuals had more than one experience, and these experiences usually differed. Although no one person experienced the full range from excellent to terrible, most did live through a range of hiding experiences that were somewhat more moderate.

The majority of hiding experiences, which were acceptable or at least livable, fall within a large gray zone. Respondents did not tend to elaborate on those experiences that were basically "OK" and unremarkable. A few stated that their foster parents were not nice but did not expand on any major problems. Quite a number of children were hidden in families in which they were not shown any affection or love; however, the majority of these also stated that because the parents did not show affection to their biological children either, they did not feel singled out. But for those used to more warmth at home, it was clearly missed during a crucial period of development.

Finally, during the last winter before the war's end in 1944—the Hunger Winter—many of those who hid went hungry, along with their hiding families. It caused some to come out of hiding in order to search for food. Although some mentioned how difficult that period was, it was a condition general to the entire population, not something that specifically affected Jews in hiding. Thus, though one respondent wept as he described eating tulip bulbs and sugar beets during that winter, as awful as that situation was, I do not attribute these hardships to his hiding family's negligence.

"It Was a Marvelous War": Good Experiences

While several people reported having had a good experience in one hiding place, five of them were extremely positive about one hiding family, which, for most, was the only family with which they hid. When attempting to analyze what factors might have made these particular situations different from the others, it was difficult to find one prevalent theme. Two of those hidden were boys, and three were girls. Two were infants when they were taken in. Two of the foster families had lost babies or young children who bore some similarity to the Jewish children in need of help. One family was childless; another had already raised their children and had an empty nest. In one case, the family had been friends with the child's parents. Thus, there was not necessarily one factor explaining these cases, but rather an unpredictable factor or a combination of factors. I will briefly explore each of these situations, starting with the youngest child in hiding.

Sjef was less than a year old when he was picked up by a young woman in the Resistance to be taken to a family that turned out to be unable or unwilling to take him. For fear that postponing his departure from home would endanger him, the young woman brought Sjef home to her mother, who did not want a sixth child or to take on the risks involved in hiding a Jewish child. So the young woman's mother took Sjef back to Amsterdam to his parents and only then found out what his name was—Sjef, short for Josef. She had lost a baby with the same name on that same date in 1934. "She felt it was an obligation for her to get a baby who was alive and had the same name of her dead child." So she brought him home, and because he was orphaned by the war's end, he lived with them until he married. "I was one of the few who were very lucky in what happened to him. . . . I was one of the few who was raised in a good family." (See figures 7–11.)

Eva was 3 when she went into hiding, in the south of Holland, brought to safety by the NV. A very attractive and artsy woman at age 61 when I interviewed her, she no doubt had been a beautiful child. She told me about her hiding family: "[They] wanted to keep me not only because of that [her attractive looks] but because they had a little daughter who died, and her birthday was the same day as my birthday." She stayed with them for three years. When I asked her if they treated her like their own child, she responded, "Oh, yes, more than that. . . . I was so happy to be in their family. I mean, afterward, realizing the risks, it was a marvelous family to stay with . . . for me it was a marvelous war." In Eva's view, that was the best period of her childhood, which ended and changed radically with the war's end. (See figures 12 and 13.)

In her second hiding place 5-year-old Lore was taken in by an older couple who had a dairy farm. They were more like grandparents to her, since their five children had already grown up and were out of the house. "I completely loved the scene. I was on a farm. I was riding cows, making butter, making milk; everybody adored me. They were wonderful. They were probably my replacement grandparents; I never knew anyone but my grandfather." It seems significant in Lore's case that she was the only young child in the household at the time.

Mirjam was 10 when she first hid with her parents' friends, who were not Jewish. She told me, "I loved being there." This couple had a girl who was a bit older than Mirjam and a boy who was a bit younger. The father was the head of the Van Gogh Museum in Utrecht, and the mother was an artist, making them unusual foster parents—this was the most educated hiding family in my sample. After her foster father was detained by the Germans, they felt it would be safer for her to leave, and so after six months, she was sent to a family of strangers, with whom she was much less happy. Every year on her birthday while she was hiding, her first foster mother visited and brought food and gifts, making Mirjam feel special. German-born Hans A. was about 14 when he hid with a poor socialist family with two younger boys. They gave him one of the boys' beds, and he feels that if anything, they gave him more food than they gave to the others. "We became lifelong friends—I derived a lot of my values from them."

These kinds of experiences were summed up in Aviva Slesin's documentary *Secret Lives: Hidden Children and Their Rescuers in Nazi Europe,* in which a middle-aged Jewish man wearing a *kippah* and sitting next to his hiding mother shyly states, "It's shameful to say it—I had a lovely time during the war. . . . She made it as lovely as possible."

"It Was Hell": Terrible Hiding Experiences

Six interviewees described particularly negative hiding situations, but again, no one factor distinguishes their hiding families from the others. Two of these hidden children were in openly anti-Semitic households, two were in institutions, and two were on farms where conditions were especially difficult. I categorized two of these experiences as being among the worst, even though those I interviewed may not have identified them as such. The other four did describe their hiding experiences as extremely negative.

Harry, age 11, and Betty, age 3, were both placed in anti-Semitic households. Harry was with a farm family for a year and a half and described the family as "horrible, punitive, Calvinistic, and anti-Semitic." They seem to have had rather antiquated views about Jews, since Harry was forbidden to look at the pregnant wife. He was not allowed to bathe in the tub they used once a week but instead was given a small can filled with warm water and told to wash in the barn near the cows. While they bicycled to church three times on Sundays, Harry was forced to make the eight-kilometer round-trip on foot. "I was punished for what [they said] my people did two thousand years ago!" He never felt any kindness coming from them, although he said that they fed him well. By the war's end, he and the other Jewish boy they were hiding no longer wished to be Jews but wanted to please Jesus. His mother arrived before he was able to convert.

Betty was 3 when she was taken into a family that kept her until she was 21. She recalled that when she cried nightly for her mother, her foster mother and aunt shook her and threatened her with a spanking. Most of her memories, however, are from after the war since she stayed on with that family until she was an adult. Betty recounted that she never received any kindness and always felt like a stranger in their home. Without question, they kept her for no other reason than the 75 guilders they received monthly; indeed, they seemed to be anti-Semitic. (See figures 14 and 15.)

David H.'s non-Jewish Austrian mother was pregnant with him when she married his Dutch-Jewish widower father, who brought eight children to the marriage. All were arrested on the day of the wedding, but the German officer told his mother to run away, which she did and lived to regret. Her new husband and stepchildren were all rounded up. Shortly after David was born, his mother brought him to the Salvation Army because she feared that her half-Jewish son would be caught. David felt very much at home with this group of streetwise children, but he also describes a brutal environment in the Salvation Army home. Although he did not describe his Salvation Army upbringing in negative terms, since that was all he knew, his descriptions of it led me to categorize it here as poor.

Henny was 5 when she went into hiding. Smuggled out of the crèche of the Joodse Schouwburg with her family, she eventually ended up hiding with one foster family throughout the war. The father worked with the Underground and was rarely around. Henny became the wife's "little servant": "I took care of the kids; I was 5 and they were 3 and 1. I cleaned the house; I was a kind of a Cinderella. She didn't treat me very nicely. I didn't like her, and I don't think she liked me." If they had better food to eat, Henny was sent outside and didn't get any. If the wife wanted to bathe her children in hot water, Henny was sent to get coal but did not get the benefit of a hot bath. She was put in the cellar when she disobeyed. When the husband returned when his wife was out, he touched Henny sexually. "It was not something that offended me or that hurt me or disturbed me. He was kind; he wasn't aggressive." Although Henny claims not to be disturbed by his sexual advances, she was by the mistreatment of the wife, whom she now thinks was reacting to her rocky marriage and to her husband's affairs.

Louis G. was 13 when he was moved from one hiding place to another with a communist working-class family. Although Louis's parents were paying them for his room and board, they were still in need of money. As a result, and without his parents' knowledge, they had Louis make envelopes, since he was at home all day with nothing to do. (Making envelopes is the kind of piecework prisoners in Holland's jails were given at that time.) He was given a small unheated room in the winter and had to make about two hundred envelopes before they gave him dinner, which consisted of their leftovers. He had no soap, no showers, no clean linen, and no clean clothes; he never got a haircut. When his cousin came to visit, she said, "You stink!" and began to call him "Sabu," meaning a child who grew up in the jungle.

After an incident in which the family accused Louis's cousin of stealing some bread and Louis defended her, the foster mother informed Louis's father of his son's bad behavior. So that they would think her kind, she brought Louis's parents butter and sugar when she went to collect his room and board. Louis's father decided to visit in order to set Louis straight, having no idea that this woman was taking his money, barely feeding his son, and exploiting Louis as though he was a prisoner (which, in fact, he was). The family got Louis cleaned up and cut his hair. He was able to go to his parents' hiding place for a while. Although Louis was very skinny by that time, his father did not believe Louis's story initially. However, his parents began to believe him and found another hiding place for him. He had been in that family for a good six months.

At one point, Ed, whose story was told earlier in this chapter, was so depressed, scared, and hopeless that he was about to give himself up. He was living on a farm as a laborer, helping out the farmer who was paid by Ed's mother for room and board.

It was absolute hell. I was a city kid. . . . [I had] never worked hard with my hands, and here I had to learn to milk cows at five o'clock in the morning out in the ice-cold rain. . . . I learned to dig ditches with blistered hands, walked in wooden shoes with bleeding feet. . . . And [I] never complained because it was all too dangerous. The food was abominable, it was medieval. . . . What was bad was the strain of constantly being alert. . . . In a normal conversation, let's say, with the farmer, I had to watch every word, that I wouldn't say one wrong thing; I mean, he might just get an idea in his mind. I had to stay with the lie, and it was grinding. Even at night, you had to sleep lightly because the Germans might come to the farm. . . . So I couldn't stand the strain, and I decided I'd give myself up.

As mentioned, Ed's mother came out of hiding at considerable risk and paid him a visit on the farm.[5] She also got in touch with someone who found him another hiding place; his story continues in the next section.

Two other respondents were exploited by the family, forced to do housework and childcare, but neither seemed to find this situation too horrible. At least three mentioned that the family hid them for the money they received either from the child's parents or from the Resistance or for the money they hoped to receive at war's end.

OTHER ASPECTS OF THE HIDING EXPERIENCE

Gaining Foster Siblings

When hidden children joined foster families where there were already children present, gaining a new sibling was not necessarily a neutral experience. Some foster children welcomed their new sister or brother. In the film *Secret Lives,* one Dutch woman recounts that she and her new foster sister were both 4 years old and that she was delighted to have a new playmate. "I loved her. . . . We pretended we were twins," she chuckled, since the Jewish girl in hiding had dark hair and olive skin and the speaker was blond and fair. However, the filmmaker interviewed another foster sister who was older by two years and who found the new 4-year-old to be "a pain in the ass." This older sister described her long-term resentment and anger toward her parents: "The Jewish kids always came first. I was always sharing my parents with others, and felt I was shoved aside." She describes how keeping Jewish children meant that she and her other siblings were the ones who "really did the work": "We were schlepping the food, keeping secrets, taking care of the kids. We were supposed to lie to the outside world, but if we lied at home, we got punished. I've been angry most of my life. They risked our lives as well as their own, but that's their business if they want to risk their lives." Thus, although I did not interview foster siblings, I knew from my respondents that the degree of closeness between foster siblings and hidden children seemed to vary quite a bit. Like their hiding experiences, relationships with siblings were fine for the most part, with a few that were awful (Betty) and a few that were excellent.

Sexual Exploitation

Unfortunately, sexuality sometimes played a negative role in my respondents' hiding experiences. Several young women were approached sexually by either the father or a brother in their hiding family. One man touched a young woman when his wife left the house. "I wasn't unhappy, but it wasn't comfortable either," she told me. At least two of those whom I interviewed were fairly sure that their mothers had had an affair with the head of the household who was hiding the mother (and who was sometimes hiding her husband as well), although it is unclear whether these "affairs" were consensual. In her beautiful memoir filled with her art about that period, Ruth Jacobsen, whom I also interviewed for my study, described hiding with a childless couple, who had wanted a girl, when she was 11 or 12 (2001: 43). Like the rest of the family, she took a weekly bath in an aluminum tub in the kitchen:

Tante [Aunt] *Hanny insisted on washing me. Her presence in the kitchen made me uncomfortable, but at the same time, I knew that it was my responsibility to be grateful. These people were putting their lives in danger for me. I told Tante Hanny I was too old, that I had been washing myself for a long time. She would not listen. One day the washing turned into a massage. I could not stop her. The expression in her eyes frightened me. In that moment, all my fury at her took over, and I splashed her with water. She never touched me again.*

Bloeme Evers-Emden and Bert-Jan Flim (1995) also report that quite a few hidden children had to deal with unwanted sexual advances. My assumption is that generally it was females receiving unwanted attention from males. In some cases it was tolerated, while in others, it caused problems for the young woman, since she needed the family's help and loyalty. If she complained, she risked the ire of her foster mother, who might blame her for her husband's or son's errant ways. Thus, a minority of hidden children in my study were exploited either sexually or for their household labor—or both. In Evers-Emden and Flim's survey of 310 hidden children, 112 of them (36 percent) felt resentment toward their foster parents. Among the reasons listed (including hard work, being undervalued, and anti-Semitism) was sexual abuse (1995: 51).

Dangerous Encounters

Several hidden children old enough to understand the situation felt the strain of constant fear, but not many referred to it except when they were in an actual raid. When I attended a reunion of those on the Kindertransport (in Burlingame, California, October 2004), I was surprised during my various conversations with *Kinder* at how much they share as a group with hidden children. Yet all those I spoke with disagreed with my contention, saying, "We did not live with constant fear of being found out, as did the hidden children." The younger hidden children I interviewed, however, never gave me the impression that they lived in all-consuming fear. Many lived through dangerous situations, but many had fairly normal lives as well. Under certain circumstances, some people may normalize their experiences, while others may exaggerate them. These reactions are a reflection of age, personality, and culture, among other factors.

Ten of the former hidden children I interviewed experienced raids while in hiding, and at least another six experienced them before going into hiding. Two of them had been betrayed. Many more were in danger while with their hiding family and were sent away for a few days or weeks, or secretly hidden within the house. Indeed, most hiding families had a plan for where the child should go in the event of a raid. Of course, there was not always a warning or enough time for the child to find his or her new hiding place. The plan B for Lore was to hide inside the hayloft in the family's barn:

It was a little house that was covered with hay that you couldn't see, and the only access to it was underneath the floor of a closet that you walked down and then back up into this little room, where you sat quiet as a mouse. You didn't dare move because if you did, everybody would hear you. . . . So it was very scary, because I remember that . . . there were no lights, no electricity, so it was pitch-black and they [the others in there with her] *weren't people I knew. . . . Sometimes it felt like I was there all day. . . . That's why I have claustrophobia. I don't do well . . . I get really claustrophobic in tunnels or in elevators.*

A few people I interviewed had been betrayed and survived, but many more recounted that one of their siblings had been betrayed and killed. Twelve-year-old Louis G. was hiding clandestinely but believes that because the walls were "paper-thin," the neighbors, who were NSBers, heard and betrayed him. The local police came and said to the adults hiding there, "[We know] you have a Jewish boy hiding here.

And if the kid has a place to go, we'll help him to get there, because you know we have to arrest him." Louis requested to go to Amsterdam, so they explained that the next morning they would arrest him "in full view of the neighbors so that they will know we did our job. One of us will travel with you to Amsterdam," and they did as they said. Louis thanked the policeman at the Amsterdam train station and was able to walk to his parents' hiding place. Max L. was integrated into village life in Friesland. A friend of his, Dolphy, was named after Adolf Hitler by his NSB parents. Dolphy's father told Max that he knew he was Jewish but never betrayed him. A number of those I interviewed believed that some neighbors suspected that they were Jewish but did not report them. Bloeme, already a young woman, was betrayed, captured, and deported.

Ed left the farm where he was so miserable and was brought to a group of seven men who worked with the Resistance in a small wooded area. His job was to go to the edge of the woods next to a convent to pick up containers of food provided by one of the sisters and to clean up the hut where they lived. Two pilots, one from England and one from Canada, who had been shot down were brought to the hut where, because of Ed's proficiency in English, he was asked to interview them. Thus, as a 17-year-old Jewish boy in hiding, he was in a rather dangerous and exciting position. (See figures 16–18.) Ed was on guard duty from four to eight in the morning with another man, watching for German soldiers after the Resistance intercepted a message to the Germans concerning suspicions about their area.

Five German trucks quietly arrived at 5 A.M. He and his partner returned to the hut and started to yell, "It's a raid! Wake up! Save yourselves—it's the SS!"

And then we started to pull the blankets off the bunk beds where the men were sleeping. It was pitch-dark in there, and they couldn't light any light because it was too dangerous. There was just pandemonium, men trying to find shoes and trying to find clothes to get the hell out. When my buddy and I saw that they were all out of their beds . . . we ran. . . . It was the worst day of my life, the most frightening day.

Ed found his father in a nearby town and told him about the raid, and then he returned to the woods, where the men were to regroup that evening. Ed's father told Ed's mother, who decided to rescue him. Waiting in the silent, dark woods, the men heard a noise, saw a tiny flashlight, and realized it was a bicycle. Then somebody got off the bike.

For the second time that day, my heart stopped. I thought this is it, it's a trap. But nothing further happened, and we waited quite a while, and then we approached the bike rider with drawn guns. It was not a German, and it was not one of our men. . . . It was my mother!

She said, "You don't know it, but you have walked back in a trap. We're surrounded here by a circle of Germans, all around. There are hundreds of them, and they are still looking for you." All the men had escaped, but the Germans had found the hut and the weapons. My mother said, "You've got to bury those weapons. If they catch us with the weapons, they might execute us right on the spot. Bury the guns, and maybe we stand a chance."

One of the men buried the guns. Ed's mother suggested to Ed that they pretend to be lovers:

"When we get to the German guards, we will put our arms around each other and our heads together, and you must talk loud and laugh." By this time, I was close to a nervous breakdown, but I had to do this, and this is what we did. When we saw a German standing there with a shouldered rifle, we began to laugh and to talk and to giggle and to put our heads together and arms around each other like lovers. We waved to him. . . . He couldn't figure these were the dangerous Resistance men he was told to watch out for, of course, so he waved us on.

Although Catarina was often sent to relatives and friends for a night or two when a raid seemed imminent, and her hiding family had other hiding places for her in the house should a raid occur, one day they were caught off guard. Catarina was quickly put into bed with a scarf around her head as though she had a contagious disease. This did not stop the Germans from entering her bedroom, but they were satisfied by the explanation. Peter H.'s foster mother was a nurse to mothers who had recently given birth. She had given him to some nurses in a clinic for a few days when there was a raid. He too was put into bed, feigning scarlet fever. Bert's hiding family put a sign on their barn when the Germans were in their area, warning about a contagious disease in their household.

Sometimes the Germans did random checks of households looking for hidden Jews or for Dutch men avoiding labor conscription; at other times someone had betrayed the hidden person, and the soldiers or police were looking for someone in particular. In one random check, Peter had to flee out his foster family's back door and cross through the reeds to a neighbor's house. Others report being safely in their hiding places during a raid—below a trapdoor in a closet, a hidden space behind a wall, a crawl space in the cellar floor. Maarten experienced multiple raids as an infant and toddler. In one family that clearly did not have a contingency plan, he was thrown into the pig house during one raid and almost died from the cold. When the tension level rose as the neighborhood anticipated a raid, 13-year-old Ellen, who was being hidden by a prominent Dutch judge, would "go outside and climb into a tree and wait it out in the tree." In the event of a raid, she was supposed to get inside a box in the attic, behind other suitcases and boxes. Ellen's story is hair-raising:

They came to the house during the daytime, and the only one that was home was Len [her 18-year-old foster sister]. And the first inkling I had is that I heard loud voices, and I heard Len say, "I don't have a key." I had locked the attic door. She said, "My mother has the key," and so they broke the door down. And I went into my box, and a man came upstairs and he looked around. . . . Len . . . just wanted to show how unconcerned she was, so she went and played the piano, and I could hear how badly she played, compared to what she usually does. And so they searched it, and they came back and they searched again, and I heard them go through all the other rooms, and I could see the shadow falling over [the box] and I could hear them farting and muttering to themselves. And luckily he was not one of the ones with bayonets, you know they just stuck the bayonets into everything. It was just great, great luck. And he moved boxes but did not come to my box. . . . At a certain point during this thing, I decided I would try and get downstairs and hide somewhere else because they seemed to be so interested in this attic, they kept on coming back up. So I was just working my way

down the attic stairs, and Len came running around the corner, and she said,
"Come, come," and they had left except they had left one soldier on guard in the
front yard. I was barefoot, and I managed to go all the way down and escape into
the backyard and went into a meadow and was there all day long. Even with all
this going on I could still feel how wonderful it was just to be outdoors . . . at
dusk I ran across the heather to a neighbor's house, and they had sort of been ex-
pecting me, and so they made a sandwich because I hadn't eaten all day. And I
was still standing at the table, I hadn't even sat down yet, and all of a sudden
there was knocking on the door, and they were doing door-to-door razzia. . . . I
hadn't even seen a hiding place, I didn't know their house. So the man takes me
and he pushes me up the stairs, but I couldn't get up the stairs. It was dark and
the stairs were crooked and I kept hitting the wall. . . . He pushes me into a room
and closes the door. But the soldiers were right behind him. . . . I think they were
Dutch.

The soldier found Ellen trying to hide behind the bed in a bedroom, and she tried to act demented, but it appears that he did not tell the others about her. When he left, she climbed into the bed and acted like a scared child. The other men checked the room but left her alone. As was the norm with raids, they returned later to the same house, but they did not search again. The next morning, the family got her out of the house to yet another family for safekeeping, but that family was afraid to keep her and told her she could hide in the bombed-out house next door. After Ellen had been there for a day or two, Len came on her bicycle, picked her up, and took her to the next family, who lived in a fancy house. As they rode up to the house, Ellen did not see the soldiers coming up the path. She was put into a hiding space under a false floor in the attic, where two young non-Jewish Dutch men were hiding. The house was searched, but the police seemed interested only in the wine they had found. The next day Ellen was moved to yet another hiding family.

When Elly was caught in a raid her family pushed her into another apartment. She was unable to get away during another raid in which they were looking for her foster brother, who was active in the Resistance; when asked, she told them that she was from Indonesia. Ies was about 7 years old when there was a raid on the farm where he was hiding. He explained to me that because Friesland is so flat, the family could see the car coming from far away, giving them time to hide the two Jewish boys, the two Dutch young men who were wanted for conscription, and two of the family's sons who were also avoiding conscription. Ies and the other Jewish boy were put in bed, supposedly with diphtheria. The raids inspired a great deal of creativity. Because the family had had some warning, they were able to bury the other young men in cow dung, up to their necks, in the barn. The family also spread pepper to distract any dogs brought by the police who were trying to pick up the scent of those in hiding.

CONCLUSIONS

The Nazi Occupation and Jewish genocide brought with them a radical disjuncture in the lives of Jewish children in the Netherlands, as they did elsewhere in Europe. These children learned firsthand the meanings of danger, destruction, ostracism, death, and exile. The transition from family life to hiding life also forced children to cope with separation from their parents, strangeness and strangers, and uncertainty at a young age. However, most children learned to adapt, to be grateful for what they were given, and not to make trouble. Indeed, it is difficult to fathom how such young children learned to deal with such dangerous situations. Some hidden children lost not only years of schooling but also the normalcy of childhood. Others who were fully integrated remained in school, and some had what we might consider a quasi-normal family life in their hiding household.

In this chapter I have explored the range of hiding experiences as recounted by those in my sample. A small minority of hidden children feel that they were exceptionally well treated and parented and look back at this period as one of the best in their childhoods. Some hidden children (and hidden adults) were exploited for their labor and/or their sexuality and lived in unacceptable, sometimes unbearable, situations. Nonetheless, it appears that most hid in places that were acceptable and unremarkable. Hidden children may not have been well parented in this period; however, the standards of family life, like most everything else, change radically during war.

1. Max L. and his biological mother. He does not remember her.

2. Max L. and his hiding family in Friesland.

3. Josef with his family before the Occupation. His mother is holding him (right); his aunt is holding his sister, Robbie, and his father is seated on the left, ca. 1937. Josef's parents, sister, and aunt were killed.

4. Josef and Robbie (second from left), with friends, ca. 1942, before Josef went into hiding. Because of the shape of his eyes, Josef was able to pass as Indonesian during the war.

5. Ruth W. with her beloved stepmother, ca. 1938. Her stepmother was caught and deported on her way to secretly visit Ruth in hiding.

6. Ruth W. (back, right) behind her half-sister, Annie, who is holding her two children, who were conceived with her second husband (left) after the war. He is holding Chaja, Annie's daughter by her first husband, who was killed in the war. Ruth, then age 14, desperately wanted Annie to be her mother.

CLOCKWISE FROM ABOVE:

7. Baby Sjef with his mother in occupied Holland, ca. 1942, before he went into hiding and she and her older two children were deported.

8. Sjef with his hiding mother, who had lost a baby with the same name.

9. Sjef with his hiding sister.

10. Sjef (second from left) was brought up as a Roman Catholic. This photograph was taken at a special occasion at school, ca. 1948.

11. Sjef at his foster sister's wedding, after the war.

12. Eva with her older foster sister and two younger foster brothers. "For me, it was a marvelous war."

13. Eva at Liberation walking by the American soldiers.

14. Betty on a picnic with her family; this is the only surviving photo in which she is shown with her father.

15. Betty as a young girl. Her anti-Semitic hiding family kept her after the war.

16. Ed (left) as a young man, in a hut in the forest, working with the Resistance.

17. At night, one person read while the others listened and drank tea. Ed (second from left) calls this photo "The Last Supper."

18. Ed (right) with his father and brothers after the war, before his mother returned.

19. Baby Rozette with her mother and grandfather, neither of whom survived.

20. Rozette with her hiding mother and new baby brother.

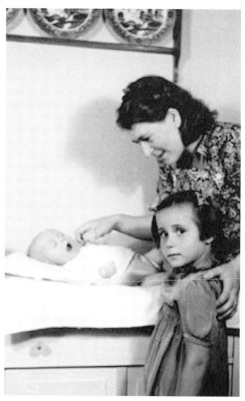

21. Louis G. (left) and other boys from the Joods Jongenstehuis (Jewish Boys' Home) in Amsterdam, playing soccer behind the Reichsmuseum, fall 1947.

22. Louis G. (front, right) with other young Dutch men training in Palestine for the Haganah, April 1948, a month before Israeli statehood was declared. Another boy from the Amsterdam orphanage is to the left of Louis.

23. Statue by Ruth W. done in Bhopal, India, with community participation, after the Bhopal poisoning disaster. The statue depicts a mother blinded by the gas, running with her baby in her arms, with her daughter pulling on her from behind. The mother and baby died; the young girl survived and inspired the memorial.

24. After my talk at the conference of the Jewish Child Survivors of the Holocaust in Amsterdam in 2005, with some of those in the book, from left to right. Top row: Jeannette, Josef, Diane, Sophia, and Sanne. Bottom row: Eva, Louis D., Leidie.

5 "I Came Home, but I Was Homesick"

WHEN BOTH PARENTS RETURNED

In this chapter I will examine and analyze the beginnings of the postwar family experience for hidden children who had both parents return. We will look at the postwar reunion of parents and children, paying attention to the age of the children and their relationships with their foster family. We will then explore the dynamics and relationships of postwar family life. Among my respondents, twenty-three hidden children (32 percent) found their natal family intact after the Shoah. These children were and still are considered lucky by many of their peers, although their postwar family lives do not reflect such good fortune.

The data strongly suggest that in general, regardless of a child's age at the time of hiding, postwar relationships between children and their parents, particularly their mothers, were not close. Indeed, it is striking, although perhaps understandable, that so many in this group, still envied today by their peers for not having lost either parent, describe their relationships with their parents after the Shoah as distant, cold, and detached. Interestingly, this is true regardless of the relationship between the hidden child and his or her foster family. Gender plays a role in this dynamic, since the males in this group do not seem to experience the high degree of dissatisfaction in their relationships with their parents that the females do, especially with their mothers. That females are brought up to be more relationship-oriented and emotionally aware may explain this difference in experience.

In this chapter we will hear a great deal from the former hidden children's point of view. While reading about the distanced behavior of parents, particularly mothers, we need to keep in mind that, in general, hidden children as a group tend to have developed strong feelings of distrust during their wartime experience. Many felt abandoned by their parents and can still call up those feelings, even though as adults they understand the reasoning behind their parents' decisions. While in hiding, many of them learned to repress their feelings and to maintain silence about them. As psychologist Eva Fogelman points out, since they had to be "good children," many adapted by not being seen or heard. While "continual distrust of the outside world, of new acquaintances, and of new situations actually protected the child in extreme danger," such feelings may have played a detrimental role in children's ability to reestablish close and trusting relationships with their parents after the war (Fogelman 1993: 295).

Almost half of those whose parents returned went into hiding under the age of 3, while two-thirds were under the age of 5. This group consists of fourteen females and nine males. The number of places in which they hid also fits the general pattern. One-quarter of them were in one home for the duration of the hiding experience, about four years on average. Another quarter were in two hiding places, while most of the remainder ended up in four to six hiding places. In one case, a newborn baby who was taken into hiding when only a few hours old was told that he had been in at least fifteen hiding places. Another former hidden child who also went into hiding as a young infant simply did not know his hiding history.

After Liberation, how did parents find their children? And how did these children, having spent several years in hiding, react to their parents' return? These are some of the questions I will examine in the sections below.

LIBERATION

Several interviewees recalled Liberation and the excitement that ensued. For many hidden children, it was a celebration of the end of fear and of near-starvation much more than it was a celebration of a renewed life with their parents. The obvious reason is that most hidden children I interviewed had forgotten their parents. In effect, because of the length of the war, young children's memories of their parents had been temporarily repressed, if not completely erased. For most hidden children, family memory reflected the present constellation of their foster family, not of their past family.

Rita, who was 7 at the time, describes her experience of Liberation:

It was very exciting. It was late at night and the fourth of May, and there was always somebody who had a secret radio with them, and apparently it went from mouth to mouth and we heard the Germans were fleeing. And she [my foster mother] *kept a big box of biscuits. . . . And she always said, "We will not open it until we really get hungry." So that evening she said* [laughing], *"We are opening the box of biscuits. Now the war is over." I remember her saying that. . . . The following morning, we all ran out to the street. We were suddenly free, and the flags were out, and it was very exciting. It was the fifth of May.*

Rita's 10-year-old sister, Catarina, had been in hiding with her. Fair-haired Rita had been allowed outside during the war, whereas darker-haired and more Jewish-looking Catarina spent those years indoors. She has a different recollection of Liberation, owing in great part to her wartime experience:

We were already in bed, and they came to tell us. We were sleeping, the two of us in one bed. . . . We left our bed and we went to the street, and for me, it was the first time that there was, ahhhh! Outside! But then things got a little bit dangerous because some of the Germans were still not captured.

Lea, now living in Israel, recalls being liberated when she was 7-year-old "Wiesje":

It was fantastic the Germans lost the war. And I saw them running through the streets of Holland with their hands held high over their heads in surrender, and I was just as happy as everyone else.

What was striking about interviewees' memories of Liberation is that no one mentioned the thought of seeing their parents again. Liberation was celebrated as an end to the overwhelming fear of the Germans and to German occupation.

Young children witnessed the surrender of German soldiers and sometimes the anger of Dutch crowds attacking citizens who were suspected of collaboration with the Germans. Ruth J.'s family fled Nazi Germany for the Netherlands, where they hid after the Nazi invasion. Having hidden with her parents for the last few months of the war, 13-year-old Ruth, with her father, went outside for the first time after Liberation:

There was a whole group of Dutch men having literally captured women that had slept with German soldiers, and they were proceeding to shave their heads. And my father went through the crowd, and with his German accent, which was deadly, he told them that they should be ashamed of themselves. They stopped.

This was an important moment for Ruth, one she did not forget, if only because it had been difficult for her to see her parents' vulnerability for the several years of Nazi Occupation. Here her father returned to his old self, guided not by fear and weakness but by morality and strength.

Alfred was 15 and has a strong memory of the German retreat:

The Germans mined the streets before they left. The streets were cobblestone, and so they took a number of cobblestones, removed them, put the mines underneath, and put the cobblestones back on. But fortunately one of their own trucks hit it and it exploded, and I recall seeing body parts all over, in trees, everywhere. But it was their own.

THE MOTHER AND CHILD REUNION

The word *chaotic* best describes life in Europe immediately after Liberation. In September 2001 we got a glimpse of the kind of confusion and disorientation that can reign when we saw relatives of those killed in the World Trade Center wandering from hospital to hospital, shell-shocked, posting photos of their loved ones in the days following the attack. In postwar Europe, many adult survivors of the war did not have photographs of the children they were looking for, and even if they did, the babies and toddlers of 1941 or 1942 looked much different three to four years later.

In this section I will use interviewees' narratives to illustrate the nature of the reunion between parents and children after the war. The younger the child was when she went into hiding, the less likely she was to recognize her parents on their return. For most of these reunited families, the lack of reconnection experienced when they first met after the war became a leitmotif in their family dynamics thereafter.

The fact that most hidden Jewish children had been given another name, identity, and family background added to the difficulty of tracking them down. Children had been taught to memorize a new name, a new city of origin, an untrue story about their parents (usually, that they were killed in the bombing of Rotterdam), and a new religious identity. In most cases, foster parents did not talk about the child's biological parents with them because such knowledge could be deadly. Young children cannot fully be trusted to keep the truth hidden and, therefore, it was safest to encourage them to forget their parents. Some parents knew where their children were hidden, but others did not. Those who did not know had to rely on word-of-mouth, putting advertisements in the newspaper and searching village to village, door to door. Some accounts make it clear that a small number of foster parents did not want to give up their hidden child and therefore did not register him or her at the local town hall or respond to any advertisements. In at least one case, it was a neighbor who helped connect parents to their child, since the foster family deliberately had not responded to an advertisement in the newspaper. The fact that public transportation was impeded and rubber was not available for making bicycle wheels did not stop parents from searching for their children. What they found, however, diverged radically from their expectations.

I present the narratives of parent-child reunions beginning with the youngest person interviewed in this category, proceeding to the older ones. This continuum demonstrates the range of children's reactions to seeing their parents, from having no memory of parents, to having a faint recollection, to having full recognition. However, owing to their ages at hiding of the majority interviewed, most children fall into the first two groups.

"I Kicked Him in the Shins":
Children with No Memory of Their Parents

Born toward the end of the war in winter 1944, in a hole in the ground in a forest, Aaron was taken into hiding when he was only a few hours old. He was 1 $^1/_2$ years old when the war ended and obviously had no memory of his biological parents. Although his parents found him shortly after the war, very soon after that, they asked his foster mother to take him back because their housing situation was poor. He remained with his foster parents until 1947, when his biological sister was born. Returned to his biological parents at age 3 $^1/_2$, he has little recollection of the separation from his foster parents or the return home. Yet he does recall feeling attached to his foster mother and grandmother.

Sent into hiding as a 6-month-old baby, 2 $^1/_2$-year-old Maarten did not recognize his parents when they came to pick him up, even though his mother had taken the risk of visiting him toward the end of the war. He explains that there are two versions of his postwar reunion with his parents: his mother's story and his father's. Although his mother was not present at this reunion, she used to tell him, "You recognized your father, and it was as if you knew who your biological father was. And you immediately went home with him." Maarten, however, believes the story his father recounted, and he tells it here in his own words: "He wanted to kiss me, and I kicked him in his shins. And he came in and stayed for a few hours and then came back the next day for a few hours, and so on. And after a week, he stayed for a night, and it took four or five weeks to bring me home again." Indeed, in several cases, parents and foster parents together worked out a transition period for children so that they could slowly grow accustomed to their biological parents again. Others who went into hiding at a young age report similar kinds of bewilderment when parents returned. The transition proved more complicated in Peter H.'s case. Peter was born in 1939 and was 3 when he went into hiding and ended up staying with an unmarried woman, a nurse who helped out mothers right after the birth of their babies. His "Tante [Aunt] Cor," as he called her, usually took him with her on her rounds, but sometimes she left him with some other nurses in a clinic or with a poor family in Amsterdam that ended up being abusive. Toward the end of the war, when he was 6, he was temporarily parked with yet another family during an air raid, and he was hit by a grenade and taken to a hospital. Because he had already lost so much blood, they could not risk operating to remove pieces of the grenade. He was paralyzed on his left side and put in a wheelchair:

I was still in a wheelchair during the Liberation. And then my parents came back on the day of Liberation, but they were in very bad shape. They were hidden in Utrecht, and so was I, but they didn't know where I was and hadn't seen me during the whole war. And then they walked from the southern part of Utrecht to the northern part, where I lived. A very long walk; they were in very bad shape. I was very nervous when they told me that my parents had come. My parents didn't know that I was wounded so they had a terrible shock to see me in a wheelchair. And I didn't recognize them. So I felt very miserable.

My mother was just crying and saying nothing. My father was just standing there; he had not had a haircut for a long time, so he had very long curly black hair. Very strange man. I didn't recognize him, I didn't feel anything for him, of course. But they were my parents. So they stayed until the night, and then they went back to the place where they had been hidden. And they came back the next day, and my father stood there with a sailing boat in his hands. He had, while he was hidden, made a sailing boat and it was very important for them to try this sailing boat out with me. So they were pushing me in the wheelchair and they couldn't walk. They really couldn't walk, they were so weak. All my father had eaten in the past few days was machine oil with ground peas. And that's very heavy and dangerous. And he was bent over from stomachaches. But they wanted to try this boat with me. So they pushed me out of town until we found a small place with water where we could put the boat in. My father crawled down to the water with the sailing boat, put it in the water, and it immediately capsized.

His parents visited him every day for about two weeks and then took him with them to their former hiding place; however, Tante Cor came along.

It was very embarrassing, because I didn't know who to go with. I was expected to tend to my parents, but I didn't, because I didn't know them anymore. And Tante Cor was very possessive; she didn't want to let me go to my parents. She wanted to have me as her child. She was not invited, but she just went with me and also lived there.

When his parents finally found a house of their own, Tante Cor simply came along, uninvited, and lived with them. This family story is unusual, since foster parents usually didn't end up sharing a house with biological parents, but it illustrates in the extreme the postwar tug-of-war between two sets of parents experienced by many hidden children.

Also born in 1939, Ria was reunited with her parents at age 6. Her parents had placed an ad in the newspaper to find their three children. They found their two other daughters but did not know where Ria lived. It is still unclear whether her foster parents did not answer the advertisement because they were trying to keep her or because they did not see it. Since there was only one local paper, the latter explanation is fairly unlikely. Ria explained how her parents found her:

They were walking around, and they saw a little dress on the laundry line. So they went to that house, and I was in the garden. My foster parents were very hospitable, so they put my parents in the beautiful room. My foster mother went to get me, and she said, "Come, come, your parents are here." I always used to say "mijn eigen papa en mama" [my real parents]. And [lowers voice] I didn't recognize them. That was terrible, terrible. They stayed the whole day, and I didn't eat the whole day. It's a sad story. I held on to my foster mother the whole day. And I said to her, "I won't go with them—he [her foster brother] can go with them, I won't!" I was afraid to go with them. They went back to their room, and I was glad they were gone. After a short time, it was Easter. They came again, and I was baptized with my mother in their church.

Her parents converted to Catholicism out of gratitude to those who had hidden them. Ria was baptized Maria, or Mary, the name she now uses.

Having a mother in Indonesia was part of Elly's alibi for living with her hiding family, and that is what she believed. Six years old at the war's end, Elly locked herself in a room when her mother came. She referred to her mother as *"mijn tante-moeder"* (my aunt-mother) and was completely confused: "I said 'Tante' to my mother and 'Moeder' to my aunt [foster mother], and 'my real mother lives in Indonesia'!" When discussing that time in her life, Elly stated succinctly and directly about her mother: *I didn't like her at all.* And that statement contrasts starkly with her feelings about her foster mother, who held her on her lap, rocked her, and sang to her.

Chana, now living in Jerusalem, recalls how her foster parents always reminded her that she had real parents and did not allow her to call them "Mama" and "Papa." Her parents came to visit after Liberation when she was 6 years old, her name changed to Hanneke:

I heard that they're my parents and that I had to go with them. I hid behind the skirt of my aunt [foster mother]. *I screamed. My parents were also in shock because they left me as a 3-year-old. When they saw me, I had hair that was not their style, so curly and wild. It was very traumatic. And then afterward they said they will take me later and will sleep at my foster parents' house for a while, until one day they told me, "Well, we soiled the bed and can't sleep here anymore." So I went with them, but I always said to my parents, "I will go back to Tante Fiet."*

Seven-year-old Wiesje (née Lea) saw her parents approach:

I was standing in front of the window and looking outside and seeing Germans with their hands held over their heads. And then I saw a couple, a man and a woman, on bicycles . . . with wooden wheels like the Dutch had after the war, because there were no normal tires. And I looked at them because there was nothing else to look at, and no one was supposed to be outside, and how could they be cycling? That was very dangerous, and it was also forbidden. And I looked at them, and looked at them, and looked at them, and they looked at me. And the woman fell off her bicycle. And then I knew that horrible things were going to happen, dramatic things. And I hated drama. And I hated tears and screams and cries. And I ran away to the only place where I could lock a door, and it was the lavatory. And very soon, people knocked on the door telling me I had to come out, and I didn't want to, and I said that I didn't want to [laughs]. And in the end, I gave in and came out in the corridor. And the woman screamed and she fell on her knees next to me as one does with little children, and she put her hands on my head and said something which I remember. She said, "Yivarech Elohim ke Rivka, Lea ve Sarah," *and I didn't say anything.*[1] *And I looked at the man, who was crying [pause]. I didn't like men crying [laughs] . . . and I looked at him again and said,* "Daddy" *[long silence]. And he lifted me up as he always used to do. That was my daddy [soft, shaken voice] and my mother.*

Seven-year-old Rita did not recognize her parents but followed her sister, Catarina, who was 8 when she went into hiding and 11 when their parents returned. Both went straight to their father, a warm man. They had never felt connected to their mother but felt very close to Tante Paula, the woman who had hidden and nurtured them.

Lore was 5 when she went into two years of hiding and grew very attached to her foster family. When her foster mother told her the "wonderful news" that her parents were coming for her, Lore had a strong reaction:

[I said,] "I don't want to go!" *I had no interest in leaving them. I had made friends, I had a family, I had a school, I had everything I wanted, what did I want those people for? They left me! I didn't want to go back with them. And when I think, if I try to reverse the situation [teary], I mean just the horror of it, can you imagine, it's probably all they lived for. They came back and found out that I didn't want to go with them*

When asked if she recognized them, she replied:

I don't know.

And when I asked if she hugged or kissed them, she said:

Hug them? Kiss them? I wouldn't even leave Cornelia's skirt!
They stayed for about a week till we got acclimated to each other again, but I really didn't trust them. I thought they would leave me again. I just didn't trust them because they never told me where they were going, whether I was going to

see them again, they never explained anything to me. . . . I think that the reunion really determined my relationship for a long, long time after. You just don't know how to act with somebody who doesn't come running into your arms after two years. Then it gets worse and worse, and then you stop doing it [showing affection] because it's so strange. You know, if I had gone running into their arms, it would have been such a different kind of meeting.

Lore's narrative reflects two very different points of view—that of the 7-year-old child who is repelled by strangers and that of an adult who is also a mother and can empathize with her parents' pain. It also demonstrates how the danger of the Occupation and war and traditional views of childhood colluded, leading most parents to say nothing or very little to their child before separating and going into hiding. This pattern was repeated in many Jewish families.

Henny was taken in by a family when she was 5 $\frac{1}{2}$. She explained how she adapted to her new family: "Slowly your memory gets lost, somewhere on the road. You don't remember your parents afterward, you don't remember your brother, the life which was. And you start something new." One day, after the war had ended, her foster mother went out shopping and left her at home. She was 8 years old at the time:

Somebody rang the doorbell. So I went over; in those days, you still opened doors. There was a woman standing there, and she asked me, "Is your mother at home?" I said, "No, my mother has gone out shopping." "Will she be home soon?" she asked. I said, "Yes, probably." She said, "Can I come in?" and I said, "Yes, of course, come in." That was my mother, my real mother! She just stood there, and she heard me saying that my mother had gone shopping. She didn't say anything, she just walked in. She walked in and sat down, and then my foster mother came back. I went off to play again.

But one of the questions she asked me at a certain stage was, "Do you remember that a while ago you used to live in a different place and there was a shop and there was chocolate in the shop and you loved to eat peanuts?" I said, "Yes, I remember." She said, "Do you remember you had a little coat in Turkish blue . . . ?" I said, "Yes, I remember." "And you used to go to kindergarten?" I said, "Yes, I remember." "Do you remember you had a little brother?" I said, "Uh-uh" [no]. "And your father, you remember?" "No." I didn't remember.

Henny's parents, survivors of Bergen-Belsen who had escaped from a train headed for Auschwitz, had nowhere to live and therefore could not take Henny even once they had found her. Henny was taken to Amsterdam some time later and stayed in a DP (Displaced Persons) center for a few days. Then she and her brother were sent to Denmark for six months to recover. Other children were sent to Switzerland or Sweden for recovery.

I loved adventure. I had nowhere to be in Amsterdam; I stayed in this DP camp, which was nothing. I didn't have any connection with my real parents; I had no past, I didn't know about the future. For me, to get on the train or bus and go somewhere was fun! I loved it!

Right after a two-and-a-half-year separation from her parents and a brief reunion, 8-year-old Henny and her 5-year-old brother were separated from each other again and from their parents and were sent to live with different Jewish families in Denmark. After being treated like a servant and living like "Cinderella" for two and a half years with a hiding family, she was placed with a warm and loving family in Denmark:

I was a little princess. I got the most beautiful clothes. I had a big room for myself. I had two foster sisters—one was 13, and the other one was 17. We got along very, very well together. I went to school. And I didn't want to leave. I was just in heaven. I had a very big family, which was closely knit—a lot of nephews and nieces and weddings and parties. . . . And when I came back after half a year, I had a big suitcase full of beautiful clothes, which I loved; I never had things like that before.

Henny's brother, however, was younger and much less adventurous and did not want to leave. He had much more trouble separating from their biological parents both when they went into hiding and after the war, when they were sent to Denmark. "My brother cried; he always cried. He didn't want to be taken from my mother. And I loved it."

"Seeing Strangers": Recognizing Parents

Although older children recognized their parents, often that did not make the reunion any easier. As the ages of hidden children in my sample increase, so does their recognition of their parents after the war. Harry was sent into hiding when he was 11 years old, an age at which one's memory can withstand absence. His last hiding place was the worst, and he had been there for one and a half years, exposed to strong anti-Semitism. His mother came to his school to find him. The teacher told him, "Ari [his hiding name], your mother is here": "I thought it was my foster mother. And I turned to look, and she was there. I wore my wooden shoes, and I had an open wound near my ankle. But I ran anyway to my mother."

Ruth J. and her parents left Dusseldorf, Germany, in 1939 and traveled to Holland by train. They were among the last Jews to leave Germany. The family was housed by a wealthy friend of the family, who took care of them. In 1941, when the Germans required Jews to register, and Ruth was 10 years old, the children were hidden with a farm family. After that, Ruth was hidden in at least five places, with several more short-term hiding places in between. Early on, she was able to visit her parents where they were hiding for a weekend. As mentioned, she found their living conditions difficult. In the attic in which her parents hid, "the tiniest room you can imagine," all three of them had to sit on their small bed during the day, the same bed they all slept in at night. They played cards all day without speaking so that no one would be able to hear them. "I didn't know any moment if it was day or night. I was miserable." In addition to feeling stifled, Ruth missed her foster family. "I was homesick, I guess. I missed them. And then with my parents, it felt like seeing strangers."

After a short visit, she was glad to leave and return to her foster family. Ruth saw her parents again later in the war, at a distance while in hiding, since they lived near each other. Toward the end of the war, her parents asked the Resistance to bring them together, and the family was hidden in another town for a few months. Ruth was about 13 at the time. The whole family dined with the family that housed them. One evening, someone forgot to lock the door, and a man walked in, most likely a neighbor. Ruth's father slipped under the table and began to act strange. The hiding family explained to the man that he had emotional problems, which they hoped would distract the visitor from thinking that he was Jewish. It was difficult for Ruth once again to see her parents act so helpless.

Ruth, like other children who were older when they went into hiding, was disturbed to see her parents' vulnerability and defenselessness. While she recognized her parents, Ruth felt an emotional distance from them, as though they were strangers. Seeing them weakened and unable to protect her alienated her even more.

The next case illustrates the effects of age on family reunions. In 1938 Alfred's parents sent him and his two sisters from their German home to the safety of the Netherlands. He was 8 years old at the time. A Jewish agency placed them in separate Jewish homes. After the Nazi invasion in 1941, Alfred narrowly escaped deportation and death twice, hiding with five different families as "Willie Becker." His parents were deported from their home in Germany in 1941 and sent to concentration camps, along with Alfred's grandparents. Though his grandparents were killed, his parents survived. After they were liberated they were sent to Sweden to recover for about nine months, and Alfred was placed with a Jewish family. Through various organizations such as the Red Cross and the Hebrew Immigrant Aid Society (HIAS), his parents and surviving family members were all able to contact each other. One of his sisters had been deported and killed at age 16, but Alfred and his younger sister remained in Holland.

Alfred and his sister were sent to Sweden to be reunited with their parents. They had not seen them for six years, twice the amount of time most Dutch Jewish children were separated from their parents. Fourteen-year-old Alfred was excited to see his parents and had no trouble communicating with them. His younger sister was 4 when she last saw her parents; at the time of their reunion, she was 10 and no longer recognized them. She had been living with a foster family who considered and treated her as their own child. Not only was she traumatized by having to separate from her foster family, but she could no longer communicate with her parents, since they spoke German and she spoke Dutch. This case is similar to the cases of the children in the Kindertransport who were separated from their parents for many years, during which time they spoke no German.

The final story in this section is of Ed, the oldest child in this group, who because he was 16 when he went into hiding in 1941 was fairly secure in his identity. During the war, his mother risked traveling to visit her three sons, all hiding in different locations. She was caught en route, just after locating a doctor for one of her sons who was ill, and deported to Bergen-Belsen. For the last ten months of the war, Ed and his two brothers lived in a small cottage with their father. In 1945 his mother was listed by the Red Cross as located in a United Nations rehabilitation camp called "Jeanne d'Arc" in Algiers. Ed, his father, and his two brothers settled in an apartment in Delft, and the three brothers returned to school (figure 18). In fall 1945, Ed returned home one evening to see an English army truck in front of their house:

As I walked by the truck, out from under the camouflage canvas comes this voice saying, "Oh sir, would you know where the Lessings live?" It was the voice of my mother. I could barely answer [weeping]. I said, "It's me, Mom, it's Eddie, it's me." And there she was, back. We had seen [photos of] the skeletons, the piles of bodies, we expected the worst, and out comes this all-tanned woman in an army jumpsuit. We had saved one cigarette and one bar of chocolate for my mother for when she would come back, if she ever did.

His mother's return provoked a spiritual reaction in Ed. Having promised God that he would be a good Jew if God saved his family, Ed recalled, "I realized then that God had kept his end of the deal, despite my bacon eating and the other sins" (Marks 1993: 246).

The anti-Semitism some hidden children picked up in their environments also affected many reunions. In the film *Secret Lives,* an elderly Polish-born Jewish mother, with her middle-aged daughter by her side, describes how she felt when she gave away her baby girl in the hopes of saving her. Then her daughter describes how she experienced her parents' return from camp. Her father had been in the hospital for a while after having been in a concentration camp, but she says at least "he looked human," implying that her mother did not. Her mother, whom she did not recognize, had no hair and looked "terrible." The daughter was covered with lice: "She was picking the lice off me, touching me. I said, 'Don't touch me!' I didn't believe she was my mother." The mother continues, "She was in a very Christian family and said, 'Don't touch me with your Jewish hands!'" The mother reiterates how she didn't blame her daughter for such feelings and was clearly very grateful that a family had saved her. As she recounted this story, it was clear that it stirred up painful memories for her daughter, but in the film we can't really tell what she is feeling or thinking. "But now she loves me," laughed the mother. The daughter also smiled, tears in her eyes, and it was clear that she had strong feelings; however, it is not clear exactly what those feelings were.

To summarize, if children were 5 years or younger at the time of hiding, they did not remember their parents enough to recognize them when reunited. But this is not to say that they had no memory of their early years—many do have fragments of memories, even if these children were very young. The older the children were—those 5 and older—the more often they recognized their parents. This section has also made clear that whether or not children recognized their parents, they experienced problems with reconnecting, especially the girls.

POSTWAR FAMILY LIFE

After parent-child reunions and transitions that often lasted up to a few months, almost all hidden children in this category returned to their parents and to a new home in 1945 or shortly thereafter. What ensued was a complex multifrontal attempt to regain and remake a home, a livelihood, and a family.

Creating a Home

The first issue at hand was to find a place to live and to create a new home. Most families returned to their hometowns to find that others were living in their apartments or houses and that their furnishings and possessions were gone. Some families had asked friends and neighbors to safeguard some of their possessions, which otherwise would have been confiscated by the Nazis. After the war, these families did not always get back the goods they had entrusted to their Gentile friends. Several examples suffice to demonstrate the range of situations that families confronted after the war, most of them difficult.

Thea's father had entrusted his son's teacher with some of their possessions. He had given her the key to their apartment, and after they left to go into hiding, she took things that she liked. After the war, she refused to return them, claiming that if the Germans had taken these goods, the family would not be getting them back either: "We visited there once and saw the coatrack, the vases, the clock, whatever, it was all ours. . . . And without any shame. I never saw her again. I don't know if she is still alive or not." Yet the family then had some very unusual luck—when Thea's father's boss heard that he had returned, he hired him back, promoted him, and found the family an apartment in Amsterdam.

Mary's parents had a similar experience with reclaiming possessions. They had given some friends several important household possessions, including their silver, for safeguarding. After the war, not all of their "friends" would return their possessions, and they had to fight to get them back.

In contrast, Maarten's parents were able to regain their belongings, which had been hidden with friends and also buried in a barrel in the ground. Peter's father had hidden their antiques in burlap sacks that he hung inside the chimney of their old-fashioned stove. His father returned to their old house, which by then was occupied by other people. Using a big hammer, he smashed the chimney and removed the sacks. He told the speechless woman who was watching, "Look, these are sacks completely full of diamonds and gold! and I'm taking them home!" "Well," said Peter, "it was a very pleasant moment for him" [laughs].

Lore's father was able to rent his butcher shop again after the war, and her family moved into an apartment that had been used by the Nazis. All their belongings had been stripped from their house and stolen, except for their Rosenthal china, which a friend had kept for them. Later they were given a "beautiful, high-class," fully furnished apartment. Chana's parents were not as lucky at first—both their apartment and shop were gone—but soon thereafter, they opened another shoe store in an upscale shopping area and quickly found a house. Harry's father found their four-story building, which had housed his bakery, in complete ruins, since people had taken whatever wood there was during the Hunger Winter of 1945 when food and fuel were scarce. The government paid him only a small amount for the ruined property, despite the fact that his insurance policy covered him for more.

Elly describes, "Germans lived in our house and took *everything* away. So we got our house back, and I have the memory that there was nothing in the house left, not even the sinks!" Since most families returned to nothing or next to nothing, parents were completely occupied with the basics of living, from finding a decent place to live and furnishing it to securing an income. Furthermore, as chapter 3 delineated, the state made making any claims very difficult for surviving Jews.

Creating Family

Along with reconstituting their homes and livelihoods, reunited families were faced with the challenge of reconnecting after a long absence. The majority of respondents with an intact nuclear family after the war described poor and distant relationships between themselves and their parents, regardless of their age at hiding and the strength of their connection to their foster families. And their narratives point to highly gendered differences. In all cases but one, the fourteen women in this category reported that they did not reconnect with their mothers after the war, although several of them felt close to their fathers. The nine men in this category follow a different pattern in that their relationships with their parents were less problematic for them and perhaps more mixed. Four men seem to have reconnected with their parents, although two of them had some difficulties in the beginning. What clearly distinguishes the men from the women in this category, however, is that parent-child relations are more prominent in women's narratives than they are in the men's. In several men's narratives, I was unable to get a sense of their postwar relationships with their parents because they did not or could not elaborate on emotional issues in general.

To fully understand how the separation during the war affected parent-child relationships, we would need to compare the state of these relationships before and after the war. Perhaps some parents were not warm toward their children before the war and this dynamic simply continued; in other cases, perhaps the wartime experience catalyzed a change in the adults' ability to parent their children. Most of the children in this sample (and in general) were too young to recall their prewar family relationships, making it impossible to conduct a comparative analysis. However, a few older hidden children were able to conjure up memories that are useful to consider.

Two women recalled their closeness to their mothers and families before the war; both these women had very different postwar family experiences. Another woman reported a warm, large, connected family before the war and seems to have had a good relationship with her parents afterward. And one interviewee recalled her prewar family life by stating that their maid was warm and nice, but that her mother was cold. She and her sister, both of whom are in this study, continued to experience this coldness from their mother after the war. There are not a sufficient number of comparative cases to allow a more general statement, but these few responses indicate that both continuity and change were evident.

Finally, it is essential to remember that these narratives represent children's views as filtered through adult lenses. Their parents would likely tell a very different story about themselves and their children. Many children were very difficult after they returned to their parents. They were angry at their parents for abandoning them, and they did not trust them; some mourned the loss of their foster family and were upset with their parents for taking them away. Many acted out after years of adjusting to strange environments and trying to please others. Dutch psychologist Bloeme Evers-Emden points out that many hidden children left their sweet characters behind in their foster families and became difficult and rebellious once they returned to their parents (Evers-Emden and Flim 1995: 128). These reactions were manifested in a number of different ways—aggression, psychosomatic reactions, depression, and so on.

In reconstituting their family lives, parents were also anxious to find out which family members had survived the war. It was the rare family that was not heavily affected by losses. Lea described this process:

And it was so terrible, because my parents were waiting for my grandparents and uncles and aunts, and they went to all those different homes that I slightly remembered—this is where my Aunt Eva used to live, this is where my grand-mother used to live, this is where Uncle Alexander lived, who I especially remembered—and all those homes were empty and they stayed empty and the people weren't there anymore. It was like being in a horrible dream all the time. . . . Everyone was always crying and screaming, just like before the war. So in my eyes, nothing had changed.

A majority of children in this group lost close relatives, often grand-parents. In Thea's large extended Sephardic family, only one cousin survived: her grandparents, aunts, uncles, and cousins were all killed in Auschwitz and Sobibor. Thus, parents were often coping with the additional burden of intense, irreconcilable loss. Here the status of hidden children as both survivors and children of survivors came into play. These children lost their grandparents, aunts, uncles, and cousins, and in the next chapter, we will meet children who lost a parent as well. Additionally, they felt their parents' pain at losing their parents, siblings, nieces, and nephews, which often resulted in unresolved grief. Immersed in their own distress, parents were unable to deal with their children's. Thus, hidden children carried a double burden, that of mourning their own losses as well as that of living with grieving parents who transmitted their own pain.

Evers-Emden and Flim point out that the adults had

suffered loss but were never able to express their anger about the impossible situation which was forced upon them. They could not easily express their sorrow toward their friends and family and they did not have the opportunity to grieve over dear ones. Those returned from camps had to go through unimaginable stress and did not receive a warm welcome in Holland after the war. . . . Parents were traumatized and very angry at what had been done to them. They were also jealous of foster parents who had their child for years and had strong connections with them. (16, 110; my translation)

Within that context, it is likely that parents engaged in a fair amount of emotional repression in order to carry on from day to day. Depending on the kinds of losses they had suffered and the level of emotional repression, it is very likely that this constraint spilled over into family relationships and created a rift between parents and children. In addition, many parents returned from the war suffering from malnutrition, poor health, or physical wounds inflicted in concentration camps. Two of the women's mothers were sedated during hiding because they were so agitated and distraught about the safety of their children. They were given either tranquilizers or sleeping pills, to which they became addicted. One of the daughters realized that as a result, her mother had begun to distance herself emotionally in order to survive.

Five hidden children were very attached to their foster families and did not reconnect with their parents after the war. Conversely, four who reported being able to reconnect with at least one parent after the war were not attached to their foster families. This might begin to suggest some kind of inverse relationship between the child's connection to his or her biological parents and to the foster family; however, the data also demonstrate that the most common category among this group of hidden children were the six people who connected neither with their biological parents after the war nor with their foster family during the war. As alluded to above, there are also five males whose attachments to either family are difficult to categorize.

YOUNGER CHILDREN AFTER THE WAR

In the earlier discussion of parent-child reunions, it was most relevant to organize and analyze the narratives according to the age of the hidden child. Although gender rather than age is a determining factor in the nature of postwar family relations, for the sake of continuity here I will present the narratives grouped by both gender and age. The younger group consists of those who were younger than 5 when they went into hiding; those in this group did not recognize their parents on their return. The older group starts with those who were at least age 6 when they went into hiding and includes two who were in puberty while in hiding. The first group consists of thirteen people, four of whom are male, while the older group consists of ten people, four of whom are male. I will begin with those in the younger group, starting with the females.

Younger Girls

Of the nine females in this group of girls who did not recognize their parents, none felt that they were able to connect with their mothers after the war. Lore was 7 when she returned to her parents. Lore, who earlier was quoted as saying that her resistance to her parents during their postwar reunion set the tone for their later relationship, felt that her relationship with her parents was "somber, very somber": "I was afraid to ask them any questions probably because they didn't ask me any questions, so I thought it was a taboo subject." She describes feeling that her family was constantly "treading on eggshells":

I think they didn't want to ask me anything about anything, and I probably didn't volunteer anything because I didn't know if they wanted to know anything. So they busied themselves with the work at hand. My father went to work, my mother went to work, I went to school. When we came home, we had dinner and we went to sleep and we got up.

There was no physical affection between Lore and her parents:

They loved me very, very much, but I think they had difficulty showing it because they just didn't know how to do that. . . . I think that that reunion was really the thing that determined my relationship for a long, long time after. . . . I didn't trust them and didn't feel that anything I would ask them I would really get an honest answer for. About ten years ago, I started trusting my mother—it took that long! I tried to work on my father, and I had a strong relationship with him, you know, inside, but he was even more closed than my mother. I'd ask them to help me with my homework, and he would say I should ask my teacher, that sort of thing.

When 6-year-old Chana returned home she immediately missed her foster family. Her parents took in and later adopted their nephew, whose parents had perished in the Shoah. Although they attempted to treat both children equally so as to not make the boy feel different, Chana felt that they took his side, and she felt inferior to him. When this kind of emotion is evident in the narratives, the child's voice is clearly speaking, usually referring to some kind of inequality. Chana noted that her father was affectionate but was also the disciplinarian; her mother, however, was neither. Her father sold shoes and noticed women's fashion. Chana felt her parents constantly criticized her for being chubby:

I felt miserable actually and lonely. . . . I was slow and insecure. [My father] liked a nicely dressed doll, and I was a little plump. They were very critical, and on the other hand, I had these foster parents who accepted me without restrictions. They never said, "You have to do this and you have to behave like that."

Chana was also aware of feeling guilty because when she was with her biological parents, she longed for her foster parents. And she also felt guilty because her family's socioeconomic status was higher than that of her foster family, something she was aware of at even an early age. She remembers saying to her foster parents, "It's not important, money, it's the atmosphere at home what is more important," a rather astute statement for a child. Although she concedes that her parents were very nice people, her memory of her childhood after the war is an unhappy one.

Also 6 when she was reunited with her parents, Mary was very close to her foster parents, especially her foster mother, who had made matching dresses for the two of them during the war; it was Mary's dress on the clothesline that had helped her parents find her. After a transition period, during which her foster sister stayed with her as she readjusted to her biological parents, the atmosphere at home was not easy for Mary:

It was so strange . . . I couldn't believe it. I could not understand it. I was 6, and it was such a change for me. I could not believe that it was my mother because she never gave me a hug—never! And my foster mother, she was always kissing and hugging me.

She is also very aware that the postwar era was difficult for her parents—"the family was dead"—and that her parents were fighting in great part because of all the difficulties:

They were very sweet. And they tried to have a good family after the war. You have to write this in your book—everything was for the children. They had to build a new life—there was no money, nothing!

When Mary was 9, her parents had another baby, who received the kind of physical and emotional affection Mary was craving. After the baby was born, Mary received even less attention than she had before.

Confused by having two very different mothers, Mary spent every vacation with her foster parents in Houthem, during which time her foster mother always had clothes made for her. She recalls always talking about "Mama in Houthem" or "Papa in Houthem" until finally her older sister said: "You have your parents here! These are your parents!" During a difficult adolescence, Mary recalls being very upset and screaming at her parents, asking them why they had given her away during the war. "I was always homesick," Mary explains. "It was terrible!" Mary always considered her foster parents her "real parents." Their opinion of her choice of fiancé and all her other life decisions was more important to her than her biological parents'.

Six-year-old Elly experienced even more complications than did most hidden children. Her parents did not live together again after the war and divorced right away. Thus, her family had survived the war, but not intact. Her father remarried in 1946 and immediately had another child with a woman whose husband and children had been gassed. Elly and her mother moved around a lot until they moved back into their former apartment. Her mother was manic-depressive and had been hospitalized right after the war and given a "sleeping cure":

It was chaos, chaos, chaos all over. Some years ago, my brother showed me some letters he wrote to his foster family, and he wrote that I was crying so much all the time, and he understood that very well.

When I asked what she was crying about, she replied:

The loss of my foster parents. There was nobody who could understand what all this crying was about. It was seen as overacting with no reason whatsoever.

Because of Elly's crying, her mother took her to a psychologist:

According to my mother, [he] said that it would be better if I didn't see my foster parents for a half a year or a year, to be able to bond to my mother, which didn't work, of course. I felt no support from my mother.

Eventually Elly resumed contact with her foster mother, who came to visit during the holidays to spend time with her:

It was a positive point in my life because I knew I was welcome with these people. My mother didn't know how to take care of a child; I was more taking care of her than she of me. I remember doing her nails, putting nail polish on them, sewing a button on her dress, or packing her suitcase. And my foster mother, she would sew my clothes.

Elly adored her stepmother, who adored her in turn, perhaps, Elly thinks, in part because she filled in for her stepmother's murdered children. Thus, Elly felt bonded both to her foster mother and to her stepmother, but not to her biological mother. When Elly was 10, her mother remarried as well. At night, Elly's stepfather would bring her to bed and then tongue-kiss her.

Since I wasn't used to much affection, I thought, "Oh, this must be some adult way of kissing, but I don't like it." . . . but I preferred getting some attention to getting nothing. And I would also look for it in that I would go to his bed on Sunday mornings, stay in his bed and lie with him to be stroked. I liked the stroking; you get touched on your body, it feels better. But even when my mother was present in the room, she was not aware of that.

This sexual abuse was soon joined with violent beatings. "He could beat my mother up, he could beat me up, I was afraid he would kill her." When I asked Elly if her mother ever tried to stop him from beating her, she replied:

I don't know. I don't remember that she stopped him.

Unfortunately for Elly, her father, stepmother, and half-sister moved to the United States when she was 12 or 13, so she had no refuge from her stepfather until his death, when she was 16. And this move also cut Elly off from her beloved stepmother, who gave her the affection she craved. It is interesting to note that Elly never felt connected to her father, not even when she visited him and his family in the States when she was 16, in great part because of the way her mother had talked about him. While she readily acknowledges that her abusive stepfather did some positive things for her as well, she also stated, "I really lived around sick people—my mother and my stepfather. They were both sick." Because of the separations, disruptions, violence, and incest, family life in Elly's postwar household was not the norm of this sample; yet unfortunately, we will see cases like hers in the next chapter, when other stepparents enter the picture.

In Lea's family, she and her younger sister returned home, but her younger sister was traumatized by being separated from her foster mother and father. "She was completely devastated, and she would cry day and night and night and day. I held her hand. I wanted to sleep with her so that she wouldn't run away." When I asked if her parents were able to reconnect with her, she responded, "I tell you, this was not possible." Using the analogy of mother animals being separated from their offspring and rejecting them later, she continued,

There is an instinct, "This is my baby," and then they take her away, and it is for such a long time. She was only a baby, now she is 6 years old. She is so strange. She is completely different. She looks different, she acts differently, it's hardly possible to recognize her. Of course it is your child, and you'll love it, but it will never be the same. And I saw this when my mother later had other children. She had two more children. . . . And there is a great difference, we understand that now. We are all of us grandmothers, the four sisters, and we often talk, we try to understand.

Lea's mother was sedated while she was in hiding to stop her from crying and screaming about being separated from her daughters. Lea feels that her mother learned to distance herself in order to survive: "And when you do that, there is no way back. And when my parents came back after everything, their whole world had collapsed. They had to rebuild what could not be rebuilt. . . . There was nothing normal ever again in our family." Like other parents, they did not ask her anything about her hiding experience, Lea feels, because they did not want to know.

Rita at first found it exciting to return home with her parents

because it was new, and the freedom was fantastic. That summer, we went to the swimming pool, and we were given these secondhand bikes and were taught how to ride on a bike, which all the children in Holland knew long before us, we were lagging behind. But at the same time, we missed Tante Paula. My mother told me that we often said to her, "Tante Paula did it different," or, "We don't do it like that, we want to do it the way Tante Paula did it." And she was very upset about it and said, "From now on, I'm your mother and I don't want to hear this anymore."

Rita's mother was not a warm or affectionate person by nature, so Rita and her older sister had never connected with her, even before the war. But their father was a warmer person with whom they had a more affectionate relationship. He was humorous and even joked about the war. But neither parent ever asked their daughters what happened to them while they were in hiding: "What happened to us was not important. We were only children, you see, and they thought we had forgotten." Rita depended on her older sister, Catarina, for connection and guidance. (Catarina's narrative follows in the next section.)

Unlike Mary and Rita, Henny did not feel attached to her foster family; rather, she felt exploited since they used her as their maid. Still, her lack of attachment to her foster family did not help her reconnect to her parents. After spending six months recuperating after the war with a well-off Jewish family in Denmark, where she felt adored and attended to, she returned to a very different lifestyle. Her parents had found a small grocery store to run, and her "tiny room" was behind the store. "I didn't like it. I didn't like anything after all I had in Denmark."

Henny felt that her father was scarred by the war, while her mother maintained her determination despite frequent nightmares from which she awoke screaming. The war experience intensified her father's introversion, and he never talked about the war or anything much at all; Henny thinks that he only survived because of her mother's strength.

My father was a very closed person. He couldn't show his love. I know that he loved me very much, but he couldn't show it. Now, my mother was much more outgoing, but I had nothing in common with her. [DW: Did she hug you?] She never did. And she used to say, in years afterward, "I don't want you to feel what I felt when I had to leave my mother, the longing for my mother. I don't want you to have it."

Henny also feels that she did not connect much with her parents because they were extremely busy rebuilding their lives. "They didn't have any strength to do so [to be with their children]. My brother was still quite small. I don't know how they managed with us." Henny feels that she and her brother were more or less left on their own to make their own way.

This premature push for their children's independence was not uncommon among parent-survivors who wanted to make sure (consciously or unconsciously) that their children would be tough enough to survive another war on their own. We will see more of this dynamic in chapter 9, where hidden children discuss having their own children. Sadly, part of this strategy often included emotional distancing, which prevented closeness between parents and children.

Although none of the women who went into hiding before age 5 felt they could reconnect with their mothers, about three did feel close to their fathers. These mother-daughter disconnections persisted regardless of whether or not the daughter had a close relationship with her foster family. In the following examples of the four males, we will see a gendered pattern of much less focus on the parent-child relationship in general.

Younger Boys

Aaron remained with his foster family for two years after the war while his parents reestablished themselves; when his younger sister was born, he returned home, at age $3 \frac{1}{2}$. His parents did take back his brother, who was two years older than Aaron, because he had been hidden with some nuns in a hospital. Because Aaron was in a better situation, they let him stay there longer. He does not describe a close relationship with his foster parents, although he knows that his foster grandmother was very attached to him.

It was difficult to get a sense of Aaron's relationship with his parents or of his family life after the war; my interview with him was fairly unemotional and nondescript:

There were tensions sometimes, but . . . it wasn't really [regularly] *tense. Was it warm? Yes. But also,* ja . . . *one of the things looking back is that my mother had difficulties. She was expecting her brothers, but only her sister came back from Auschwitz. She couldn't cope with the fact that her brothers weren't coming back. And this has marked part of our existence, knowing she has this sorrow and not being able to help her.*

When I asked him how she expressed this sorrow, he said:

By a lot of weeping and telling about it and even saying that she hoped that someday from Russia, one of her brothers would reappear. . . . I have been made aware of that all the time. . . . I felt powerless to help her and felt pity and did all the things to do my best at school in order at least to give a good impression. That was the only thing I could do. But I couldn't bring her brothers back. . . . I think nonetheless, she could give enough affection to all of her children. But sometimes, I also had the feeling that perhaps, in fact, we were a kind of compensation.

Sometimes, Aaron stated, he and his siblings felt they were taking care of her.

Maarten was hidden as a baby and toddler in approximately fifteen different places. He was not quite 3 when the war ended, having spent his first few years being hidden in cabinets, under sinks, and in cellars and attics. "I could crawl very well, but it was very bad in the beginning. Everything was delayed—walking and speaking and everything." Although he stated that the hiding experience "creates a strange relationship with your parents," Maarten's parents were warm and affectionate toward him and his three siblings born after the war. "We always kissed each other, and they were very good parents, without a doubt." His parents, he recalls, always wanted to take care of their children, even into their adulthood. "It's still the same with my mother, who will be ninety in October. When we come to visit her, although she almost can't walk anymore, she gets all kinds of sweets and things and wants to spoil us." Maarten recalls starting his own vegetable garden at about age 4 or 5, "in case war start[ed] again."

Although he has some memories of his time in hiding, his parents never asked him about it, assuming that a small child could not remember such things. At the end of the interview when I asked him if we had missed anything relevant about how hiding had affected him, he began to reflect more critically on his relationship with his parents:

What we haven't discussed, in fact, is the only thing that is of importance to me with regard to the hiding period, and that is that you will never reach a normal attitude toward your parents, a normal relationship with your parents. I wouldn't say that they are strangers to me, of course not. But when I observe the relationship between my parents and my younger brothers and sister, it is different. When I see the relationship between my children and me, it is different than the relationship that I have with my parents. It is more emotionally bound.

Similar to Lea, who drew an analogy to animals, Maarten began to describe the problems with young gorillas who are taken from their mothers when they are young and then later do not know how to nurture their own offspring in zoos:

Then I looked in the literature for humans and found out that it is incredibly important for young people, babies, that they stay with their parents from six months to at least about three years, almost three years. And then I suddenly realized what was probably wrong with me.

The literature on attachment, however, makes it clear that children separated from their biological parents can attach to people other than their parents; what's important is that the child attach to *someone*. What Maarten is expressing here is his feeling that his parents lost an important connection to him.

As described earlier, when Peter returned to his parents and their new home, his wartime protector, "Tante Cor," followed right along, without being invited. Although his parents told him all about their trials and tribulations during the war, including his mother's jump from a two-story building to escape the Germans, they never asked him about his experiences. Indeed, his mother did not even want to read the book he later wrote about his experiences, although about ten years ago he was able to convince her to do so:

I was never recognized. I would say I don't blame my parents, but in fact I do blame my parents. . . . I would want to know what happened to my children! You should give the problems of your children a place, and they never did. The reaction was always, "What happened to us was much worse—what are you talking about?"

Indeed, Peter's parents always threw this line at him to downplay any of his concerns. They also remained passive when it became clear that Tante Cor was becoming abusive toward Peter:

They didn't dare resist her because they felt they should be grateful. And they didn't know how to handle this problem. I remember very well, my parents said, "You don't have to pray anymore" [referring to the Catholic prayers Cor forced him to say]. *And I was very happy that I didn't have to pray anymore. She returned from visiting her father, and when she came back, I was very triumphant and said to her, "I don't have to pray anymore!" So she became very angry and hit me. And my parents didn't dare to say anything! And she was hitting me! And there were my parents. . . . She saved my life, but on the other hand, I'm not very grateful. It's a double feeling. I should be very grateful, but it was a rotten time.*

His family remained in contact with the head schoolteacher in whose house Peter had hidden early on. The teacher's wife encouraged Peter's mother to resist Cor, but his parents had felt so intimidated during the war that they found it difficult to assert themselves afterward. Peter felt torn between his parents and Cor, although as time progressed, he was less conflicted. Finally, a good six months after Liberation, his parents told Cor to leave. Once again she tried to get Peter to pray and again tried to hit him for not obeying. This time, although they did not stop her, Peter's parents encouraged him to resist her, which he did. She finally left his home but

she remained very cruel; she found a room not far from our home, and she came very often and she didn't let go until she died. And she died in about 1975. And when I wrote my thesis, even, in '72, after defending my thesis, everyone was congratulating me. And she was standing next to my parents . . . she's standing there as if she's my mother! Even when I was 33 years old! It's unbelievable. And we wanted to show our gratitude, but we didn't like her. It was a very strange situation.

Peter said that after he had been home for a few months, he grew accustomed to his parents again. He was 6 at the time. "I felt connected to them. That took some time, but not very long. I'm always surprised about that. Something of the old feeling came back." It is clear that the three were united in disliking Cor and wanting her to leave, yet, all the same, it is difficult to imagine that Peter was not angry with his parents at some level for not protecting him from Cor's malevolence. As stated earlier, although this case is unusual because of Cor's presence in the household, it magnifies the way in which children often felt torn between two different sets of parents. It also exemplifies to the extreme how Jewish parents felt both vulnerable after the war and grateful to those who had saved their children's lives.

The final male in this group of younger children, Bert, granted me the shortest and leanest interview in this project. He recalled crying when he was separated from his foster mother to leave with his parents at age 6. An only child, he recalled his parents hugging and kissing him, and during the first weeks of their reunion, giving him everything he wanted—toys, his own room, even a Dutch military uniform. He remained an only child, since his parents had no more children after the war. Bert's parents never discussed the war with him, perhaps in part because they were grieving for their siblings, who had perished. It was difficult to elicit much information about his relationship with his parents (or with anyone else) beyond his stating that his parents were "very warm and very nice."

OLDER CHILDREN AFTER THE WAR

Those in this group of older children were at least 6 when they went into hiding. There are five women and four men in this group. Here the gendered trend of women not connecting with their mothers continues.

Older Girls

Phia's nuclear family survived intact, but it grew with the addition of other kin. Her parents adopted two of her cousins after the war. She already had two older brothers and then two male cousins when, in 1947, her mother gave birth to a girl. There were then six children in her household. "My parents had never asked what happened to me during the war. They never knew where I had been! My father has never known, and my mother didn't want to know. When I tried to say something, the subject was changed." She felt that there was "nothing positive" in her family life, even as she grew older.

When I asked what family relationships were like, she responded, "Well, there has never been any love, really. I mean, my mother has never in her life said she loves me. It was just going on with what you do, what they expect you to do. I was a very bad student, but I was so nice, so there were no complaints." She felt that her cousins got more attention and less punishment because as orphans they were treated as special. Again, the subject of unequal treatment in families tends to tap into some very early feelings. However, most of those in my sample who were, like her cousins, orphaned and taken in by other relatives felt much more like stepchildren than privileged. Of course, it's possible that the cousins' views of their intrafamilial relationships are the inverse.

Catarina, the older sister of Rita, featured in the younger group, elaborated on what her younger sister had told me. Both were very attached to their hiding mother, Tante Paula, and both found it difficult to leave her. Back at home, they talked about her and wrote to her constantly. Catarina discovered later that although her parents wanted to have more children after the war, her mother felt it would be better for the family if they did not. Even though Catarina admires her mother's decision, she also feels that her mother failed in her attempts to heal her family, and the girls' attachment to Paula did not subside.

Catarina had a breakdown in high school, a few years after the war ended, and left school without a degree. When I asked her what was happening for her emotionally at that time, she elaborated:

Very quickly after the war, I got all kinds of new friends. . . . Later on they said, "You know, we never asked you, we knew you were Jewish and never asked you 'Where have you been?' We never let you talk about it. You were just one of us, and you wanted to be one of us. But why shouldn't we have asked you all kinds of questions that would help you to get over all those problematic years?"

In the interview, Catarina had stated that her mother was not warm before the war, so there was no shift. "She wasn't very warm. She didn't have a clue, I think, about child rearing." One example she provided is from that same year, when Catarina was not well: her mother planned a vacation away with her father during September, missing Catarina's birthday. Catarina and Rita, today both living in Israel, frequently visit their aging mother in the Netherlands, but it is clearly not something they do with pleasure. Catarina feels that having had Paula in her life helped her a lot, "because every child, everybody needs someone to relate to and she was always there." Tante Paula provided an alternative to what Catarina and Rita experienced at home: "In those fifteen months, Tante Paula had been more of a mother for me than my own mother all those years."

In a sense, both Rita and Catarina were lucky to have had a warm parental figure in their lives, since their own mother did not play this role very well. It is an irony of the war that despite the devastating ramifications, some hidden children benefited from having parental figures who were emotionally available, even if they weren't kin. As stated earlier, what's important for a child is having one or more primary attachments; whether it is with a surrogate parent or a biological parent is much less important.

Thea was the only one in my sample who hid with both her parents throughout the war. Thus, there was no trauma of separation and reunification, but they did have harrowing experiences in multiple hiding places. Her relationship with her parents seems to have been strong and steady throughout those years and also in the postwar years. As mentioned above, Thea's father received his job back with a promotion, and his boss found them an apartment. At the same time, the person to whom they had entrusted their possessions refused to return them. Once a large, extended Sephardic family, everyone except one cousin had been killed, creating a somber tone in her postwar family life. Thea was also the only female in my sample who did not mention feeling alienated from her mother.

The war exacerbated problems in the family that had existed beforehand. Ruth J. reports having been close to her mother before the war but says that her father "simply wasn't there, physically as well as emotionally." He was a traveling salesman, very outgoing, and Ruth is sure that he was a womanizer. Her mother, though she had a good sense of humor, was not outgoing. She believes that her mother had a nervous break-down before the war when Ruth was a little girl.

After the war, Ruth's mother paid attention to her and talked with her, something no one else had done during the war years. But although Ruth was becoming more open to her parents, her mother became in-creasingly depressed, and her father was rarely there:

I took her to psychiatrists, to hypnotists, and her depression got worse. She would sleep a lot and was complaining forever. Everything just got worse and worse. I would sit with her, but I was afraid to touch her, because I thought I would get this disease of depression. . . . Nobody was able to help her.

Unlike many other parents in this chapter, Ruth's mother still had her two siblings; however, she did not get along with them "and there was a lot of venom. They did not give her any support." She tried shock treat-ment when Ruth was about 17 but had to stop when it began to affect her heart. "She came home, and her mind was really quite scrambled, and she took an overdose of sleeping pills." She was found still alive and sent to a sanatorium.

Because the shock treatment damaged the mother's ability to func-tion, Ruth's family had a number of maids to do the cooking and clean-ing while her mother slept, an effect of the sleeping pills she was still tak-ing. Her father hired one maid with whom he had an affair, something Ruth and her mother knew about. At this point her mother was receiving lower dosages of shock treatment as an outpatient, and Ruth had to es-cort her to the hospital and take care of her. This included dressing her after treatments, when she was in a state of complete bewilderment. Ruth's father turned over more and more power to the maid. When he declared that Rosha, the maid, would be the guard and dispenser of her mother's sleeping pills, Ruth was offended and told her father that either "Rosha goes, or I go." He chose the maid, and Ruth left home at age 19.

Ruth feels that her mother had suffered from an underlying depres-sion before the war. She came from a family Ruth called "neurotic and very hypochondriacal," and she feels that the war was simply too diffi-cult for her to integrate. Ruth's parents were planning to divorce during this postwar period, and Ruth and her mother were planning to emigrate to America. However, neither plan was realized. When Ruth was 20, her mother drowned herself. Ruth's father married the maid, and Ruth emigrated to the United States. She never saw her father again but heard that he was deeply in debt and drinking heavily. He too committed suicide. Although his will stated that he had bequeathed her parents' wedding rings to Ruth, Rosha never sent them.

The final female in this group is Mirjam, who was 14 when the war ended. She describes her prewar family life in very positive terms—she recalled her parents' affection and had memories of hearing a lot of classical music at home. "My mother was happy. They never screamed at us. They never punished us, they never hit us or anything like that. We were their main focus, and we all went to a Montessori school because they were very concerned about our well-being." While her parents were hiding, her father gave her mother sleeping pills because she was so agitated and could not stay quiet all day. As a result, she became addicted to the pills, a problem that lasted for ten years after the war. "It's like having a drunk in your house, really. And then we had nowhere to go. We had no more furniture. We had nothing." Mirjam's father was a pharmacist who had worked for the Dutch army in Indonesia, where she was born, and then for the city of Rotterdam. He got his job back, and they received a house that had been inhabited by Nazis.

Her mother's family sustained huge losses from the war—her sister's four sons did not return, and neither did her other sister, brother-in-law, and two nieces; her oldest and youngest brothers died in a camp, as did her mother. "So every time they heard the news, they were upset, they were crying, they were always whispering. And they didn't want to make us too upset, yet we knew about it."

Mirjam and her sisters joined Zionist organizations as a way to escape home. At age 16, Mirjam met her future husband at the 1947 celebration of the founding of Israel. Mirjam joined Hachshara, a Zionist group that prepared young people for emigration to Israel. She quit high school before graduating and stayed with Hachshara, going home on weekends.

At home things were tense. Her parents tried to care for their daughters, but Mirjam did not get along with her mother. "I was impatient with her, I was embarrassed by her because she was many times not fully there. And I felt sorry for my father. I wasn't very happy to be home." Her mother was still addicted to the sleeping pills. Even though Mirjam's father had forbidden all pharmacies in Rotterdam to sell her mother pills, she was somehow always able to obtain them. At age 18, Mirjam emigrated to Israel.

Older Boys

Finally, there were four men in the group of children who were 6 or older after the war. In two cases, it was difficult to get any sense of family relationships; in one case they were problematic; and in the most emotional interview, family relations were reported as being good. It is not necessary to elaborate on the two interviews in which it was difficult to get a sense of parent-child relations. One was a highly disjointed interview that was difficult to follow. That respondent stated that family life was good after the war but also said that postwar, his parents were strangers to their children. The other interview, in which I got sparse responses and no elaboration, was mentioned earlier. Although both these interviewees were positive about parent-child relations, it was impossible to get them to elaborate, which makes me wonder about what was left out.

The more problematic story of parent-child relations was told by Hans V., who explained that he never had a good relationship with his parents, not before the war and not after. In 1938, when Hans was 5 years old, his parents sent him to a children's home. This was a very unusual move since children's homes were for orphans, sick children, or those whose parents could not care for them. He said that he and his mother did not get along: "There were problems with me, I don't know. I was always the black sheep of the family." When the Nazis invaded in 1941, his parents picked him up and put him and their other children into hiding. After the war, he returned to school and was sent to a therapist. Although Hans describes himself as a "problem child" before the war and after, his description also suggests that he suffered from what we now would call ADHD, attention deficit hyperactivity disorder. He simply could not sit still at school and left after sixth grade. His parents' relationship deteriorated after the war, which he blames on the trauma of the war.

In the most positive case of parent-child relations, Ed described a warm and lively family life before he, his two brothers, and his parents all went into hiding. Earlier, I described his mother's return from Algiers, on an army truck. His descriptions of family life after the war also evince a sense of warmth and of happiness to be together. Shortly after the war, his parents got a visa to go to the United States, so Ed, then 20, went with his father. However, that ended his life with his family, since his parents now lived in different places because of work demands. Shortly thereafter, he married his Dutch-Jewish girlfriend, also part of this study, and they emigrated to Israel.

CONCLUSIONS

This chapter has delved into the immediate postwar family lives of those hidden children considered to be the "lucky" ones. What becomes clear from these narratives is that family life was either good or neutral for the males and tended to range from difficult to disastrous for the females. Although I expected to find more problems in parent-child relations among hidden children who had been strongly connected to their foster parents, that hypothesis did not hold. That is not to say, however, that a child's relationship with his or her foster family was totally irrelevant. In fact, it is very likely that this bond may have intensified the distance between parents and their children, upsetting parents and pulling children further away from them. On the positive side, it gave some children, usually girls, a wider choice of parents; this was especially constructive given that so many of these children had aunts and uncles who had been killed. It also allowed many of them to experience unconditional love, something they did not always receive from their biological parents.

The gendered nature of both the hidden child–foster parent relation as well as postwar parent-child relations was not an outcome I expected. However, in light of differences in socialization among males and females, it is not surprising that females would put more emphasis on interpersonal dynamics and on family relations, compared with males, who are often encouraged to be independent. Additionally, although most men in my sample elaborated very little on parent-child relations after the war, it is possible that such relationships were very complicated, but either they were simply not a major focus in their lives or it was difficult for them to admit to such problems. Conventional gender dynamics, in which women feel more at ease revealing problems, may well be at play here, in addition to a traditional focus on family. Regardless of causes, what becomes clear is that the women in this category were more likely to experience both the closeness of ties with foster parents and rejection and distance from their biological parents.

Despite parents' assumptions that children were not capable of remembering the war—or their hope that their children would forget—this chapter has illustrated the tremendous range of feelings and reactions children had to the war and its aftermath. Many clearly wanted and needed to discuss and process their wartime experience but found that their parents did not want to or could not bear to hear about it. This absence of discussion likely widened the emotional gap that many experienced between them and their parents after the war.

Parents were often motivated to deny their children's war histories by other, more complicated, factors. While some dismissed their children's memories as implausible, it's also likely that parents felt tremendous guilt about abandoning their children to strangers. Eva Fogelman (1993) points out that some parents were quite jealous of the relationships that developed between their child and his or her foster parents, which might have led them to avoid asking about this period. Further, the kind of competitive victimization Peter and others experienced reflects parents' wounded and vulnerable states. Many of these parents were already dealing with the deaths of parents and siblings, and their children's stories were the only wartime experiences they could avoid.

In her extensive research, Evers-Emden (1996) has found that hidden children's relationships with their parents suffered irreparable damage, a finding that has been partially corroborated here, albeit with a gendered twist. Although these children were fortunate compared with their peers whose parents had been murdered, most of them did not feel all that fortunate—rather, they felt unhappy, if not downright miserable. As

Mieke put it, "Everyone told me I'm exceptionally lucky. But I never felt happy." Family life did not provide the kind of haven they needed and wanted. At the same time, it seems likely that their parents may have felt similarly in light of the tremendous burdens they bore. These narratives challenge the stereotype of overbearing, overprotective Jewish mothers, instead presenting mothers who are more distant and detached. These narratives also challenge notions of the warmth, comfort, and closeness of Jewish families by presenting some of the chaos, dysfunction, and human fallibility that inevitably occur after war and genocide.

Jack, the husband of one of my respondents, framed the issue poignantly: "I had four parents. The parents I had before the war were not the ones who returned." This sad observation is unfortunately true for many, if not most, of those discussed in this chapter.

6 "They Were Out of Their Minds"

The focus of this chapter will be on hidden children who lost one parent during the war and who were reunited with their remaining parent afterward. Although the families of children with one surviving parent fall into the same category as the families described in the previous chapter—that is, they are defined as a nuclear family—there are sufficient differences between the two groups to merit separate chapters. The hidden children featured in this chapter had to confront not only the death of a parent, but also, for many, the addition of a new stepparent and sometimes a blended family, with stepsiblings and/or half-siblings. All this added yet another layer of complexity to an already problematic family context. These specific differences constitute my focus in this chapter.

Gender also plays an important role in the analysis of this group, but for different reasons than it did in the previous chapter's examination of those with two parents. Gender ideologies regarding parenting determined whether or not a hidden Jewish child could and would go home with his or her parent. Widowed fathers on their own were not considered "proper parents" and would not usually take their child unless and until they remarried. Even if they wanted to take their child, others let them know that doing so would be inappropriate. If they did not remarry, their children usually did not live with them, and the family unit basically dissolved. In other words, younger children with a surviving father were seen and treated as orphans. In contrast, there was never any question about the ability of mothers to care for their children on their own. And, as the narratives unfold, it will become obvious that assumptions about parenting abilities based solely on gender can be very wrong.

In my sample, seventeen of the seventy former hidden children interviewed had one living parent after the war. In this group ten mothers and five fathers survived the war, in addition to one non-Jewish mother and one non-Jewish father, both of whom had been married to Jewish spouses. It is no coincidence that more mothers survived than fathers. Nazi policies at first aimed at deporting able-bodied Jewish men, although eventually every Jew, regardless of gender or age, was sought. Four of the five Jewish fathers who survived were in hiding. The fifth father was a German Jew and was picked up in Germany right after Kristallnacht in 1939 and sent to Buchenwald. He was released and fled to England. One hidden child's father had committed suicide in 1936, before the war. Of the seventeen surviving parents in this group, four women and three men remarried. Thus, seven children, about 40 percent in this category, had to cope with and adjust to living with a stepparent.

So it seems natural to ask, Did the loss of one parent create a stronger bond between the remaining parent and his or her child compared with the parent-child bonds discussed in the previous chapter? Generally, the pattern discerned in the last chapter in which postwar relationships with mothers in particular were poor, tends to be replicated in this group. Most of those with surviving mothers did not have good relationships with them after the war. Although some hidden children featured in the last chapter had better relationships with their fathers, none of those with surviving fathers in this group established good relationships with them after the war. And this being the case, did the addition of a new stepparent then provide a viable adult with whom the former hidden children might more successfully bond? Unfortunately, relationships between stepparents and stepchildren did not tend to fare very well.

Hidden children's reunions with a single parent did not differ considerably from those discussed in the previous chapter, in that the younger the children, the less they recognized their parent after the war. What differed was that on top of reuniting with a parent they may or may not have recognized, these children also had to contend with the death of their other parent. In some cases, the news of that parent's death came early, and in others, the remaining family waited hopefully as Jewish war survivors made their way back from concentration camps until they heard something definitive, either from the Red Cross or from someone else who knew when and how the parent was killed. The death of a loved one in a concentration camp (or in any other type of anonymous mass killing) deprives the survivors of the opportunity to say a final good-bye and of the rituals attached to this. Thus, to get any kind of closure without a body, a coffin, a funeral, a burial, and sitting shivah, the traditional form of Jewish mourning, was often very difficult. The abstractness of the death also fed a continued hope that the missing person was still alive and would eventually return.

Children's reactions to the loss of a parent very much depended on their age and whether they remembered their parent and therefore noticed his or her absence. In keeping with the general tendency in society at that time to involve children as little as possible in certain emotional issues, most surviving parents did not discuss their spouse's death much with their children. So although the absence of the parent was very marked, it was not spoken of between parent and children. Indeed, most parents who returned were sufficiently occupied .with, if not overwhelmed by, simply surviving and providing the basics for their children.

In this chapter I will analyze and compare postwar families in two subgroups of this category—those children whose parents did not remarry, and those whose parents did. As they were in the previous chapter, cases will be presented chronologically by age, starting with the youngest hidden children.

The majority of parents of former hidden children in my sample whose spouses did not return from the war—six women and four men—did not remarry. How was family life reconfigured after the war among these adults and their children? Were these parents able to reestablish a functional family life? Out of these ten cases, three worked out relatively well, four worked out badly, and another three were somewhere in the middle. What is most striking here, particularly given the findings of the last chapter, is that three family contexts *did* work out well.

To illustrate some of the unfortunate results stemming from gendered stereotypes, we will first look at two cases—one in which only a father survived and another in which only a mother did. In both cases, the children involved were 10 or younger when the war ended. Erica's mother was Austrian Jewish, and her father was a Dutch non-Jew. Her parents had divorced in the mid-1930s, and her mother had returned with her to Austria until the Anschluss, at which point they returned to the Netherlands. In the early 1940s, Erica's father married his ex-wife's sister in an attempt to save her from the Nazis, but they never lived together. She survived and divorced him right after the war. Erica's mother was deported in 1942 and did not survive. After the war, only Erica's father returned for her. While in hiding, Erica ended up at a Christian children's home, the Maartas Stichting. Other Jewish children were there as well. The home was "dark, cold, wet, and stinking," Erica recalled. She lived in a group of forty girls supervised by one woman, who beat them. After the war, her father lived with his father, her beloved Opa, and the children's home would not release Erica to live with two single men. Her mother's entire family had been killed except for one of Erica's aunts. Erica does not know whether her aunt requested that Erica live with her or not, or if the OPK simply decided in favor of Erica's staying in a Christian institution. Regardless, Erica stayed in this children's home until she was 19. Her father visited her and was kind to her, "but there was no bond." She was, however, connected to her grandfather. Thus, despite having a father and grandfather who were able and willing to care for her, Erica was forced to stay in an institution. These social and legal restrictions prevented her from having any semblance of a normal family life after the Shoah.

Another tragic story counters the opposite assumption—that mothers are capable of caring for their children simply because they are women. Peter's parents were socialists and very active in the Resistance. His father was not Jewish, a fact that initially protected Peter's mother. When Peter was 4, he watched as Nazis dragged his maternal grandmother from their apartment, while her daughter tried to prevent it. In 1942 he hid with his parents for six months, and then he was sent to live with a family. His father was caught and arrested and eventually killed. His aunt found Peter after the war and brought him to Amsterdam, to his mother. He was 7:

My aunt brought me into the room and there was sitting someone who was apparently my mother, and I had no real memory but it was clear to me that this was my mother, and she had a little baby on her lap. And then my aunt said, "That's your brother." . . . I stiffened. . . . I said, "Dag, Mevrouw" [Hello, madame], *and my mother, as I recall, was very upset and distant.*

When I asked him if his mother tried to hug or touch him, the answer was simply, "No."

Peter's mother was able to use the skills she had learned in the Underground to help the postwar government. Every day she went to the central train station and checked the identification papers of those attempting to enter Holland. Since she could tell whether these papers were real or had been falsified, she was able to help identify Dutch and German Nazis who had fled Holland and were attempting to return. Apparently Peter's mother assumed her husband was dead, but when she found out definitively, "She went crazy, crying, screaming; she really flipped out." Although she continued to function, she did not take good care of her two young children. One cold winter day, her sister found the two boys at home alone with no food and no heating; at that time, Peter's younger brother was 2$\frac{1}{2}$. She took the two boys, and Peter stayed with friends of the family for two weeks. He was by then 8. When the father of the family with whom he was staying approached him one day, Peter saw that "he was very sad":

I could tell something very terrible had happened, and I told him my mother had died, and he said "Yes." . . . I recall that I stiffened, and this was my thought, that from now on, I am all alone. And because he was so sad, I decided, OK, I will be a brave boy about it.

Peter's mother had returned to the house the night her sons were taken and had swallowed the cyanide that Resistance activists carried in case of torture. Peter is still angry that he was not told earlier of his mother's death or allowed to attend her funeral. His aunt and the family with which he was staying ended up living together in Peter's house in order to provide the two boys with a more extended family. Now a psychologist, Peter reflects back on that time:

People were completely crazy. For me, the crazy world started after the war, not during the war. They were out of their minds, everybody; that's how I remember them. They tried to do the best they could, but they were not in this world anymore, none of them.

Although his aunt tried to be a mother to him, Peter kept her at a distance and has a poor relationship with her to this day. Peter's case also exemplifies a novel attempt at family reconstruction with friends, although after some years, a fight led to the family moving out.

The majority of the remaining stories, though perhaps less extreme, did not have happy endings. One of the youngest in this group, Ineke (née Sarah), was born in 1942 and was rescued that same year from the Joodse Schouwburg crèche. Her parents were deported to Auschwitz, and her father survived. She has no memories of her hiding family, with whom she stayed for two and a half years. According to Ineke, after her father returned a broken man, he paid a somewhat older, childless Jewish couple to take care of her. Although she lived with them in Utrecht, her father appears to have lived elsewhere. He visited her a few times every year, but they did not develop a strong bond. Ineke believes that her father was an alcoholic. In any case, she recounted that he refused to discuss the war but would often begin crying. He once stated, and Ineke

agreed, at least to me, that it would have been better had her mother returned rather than him. Ineke felt that her life with the couple in Utrecht
was not harsh, but neither was it warm or pleasant. She did not particularly like either of the two adults with whom she lived. Her father eventually remarried, and though he was available as a grandfather to Ineke's
children, she feels that he was never a father to her.

One year after the war ended, Bob's mother finally found his sister
and him, when he was 15, and they were able to secure the house of a former Dutch Nazi in Amsterdam. The three of them resumed their lives, although they were much poorer than they had been before. Bob resumed
his schooling, but his family could not afford the kind of school he would
have liked to attend. He admired his mother's courage, but when asked
if he felt connected to her he stated,

*I respect her, and she was very brave in the war, but she was not a mother who
put an arm around you and, I was not a boy who put his arms around his
mother. I didn't have a lot of emotional love for her, no, I didn't. I love my mother,
of course, but not like my sister does. I had more trouble [with the fact] that my
father didn't come back. This was a very heavy blow that he didn't show up after
the war. It was very emotional for me.*

When his mother found out that her husband had been killed by the Germans, Bob recounts, it was difficult for all of them. "That my father
didn't come back was more important for me than having my sister and
my mother."

Two years later, in 1948, he lived with his aunt for a year because she
liked having him around his younger cousins. His interview reflected
the emotional distance he felt from his mother and the tremendous effects the loss of his father had on him. Ironically, had his father come
back instead of his mother, it is likely that Bob would not have ended up
living with him, because of the stigma attached to single fathers.

David G., who like Bob was 15 when the war ended, was reunited
with his mother after the war.

*It was hard to adjust to normal life because I was kind of more on my own then.
I went back to school, and like I said, my mother didn't understand kids and we
never got along very well.*

In part because of this relationship with his mother and in part because he didn't know what to do in the Netherlands, when he was 16, he joined Hachshara, and left home. David worked in a kibbutz-like setting in Holland until 1947, when he traveled, via Marseilles, to Palestine, where he stayed until 1948. Once in Israel, he entered the army right away, met and married another Dutch former hidden child, also interviewed for this book, and had two children on a kibbutz before emigrating to the United States. After David left home, his mother also emigrated to the United States and eventually remarried.

When Ellen was very young, in the early 1930s, her family left Berlin for the Netherlands, where her father was eventually picked up by the Nazis as a "criminal" because he had left Germany clandestinely, without paying the exit taxes demanded of Jews by the Nazis. Her brother had been sent to school in England in great part to keep calm in the family because he and his father did not get along. Ellen describes her upbringing in her bourgeois German Jewish family as typical, one in which a nanny took care of the children and the mother took care of other family and social affairs. The mother traveled with the father, "or knitted or had *kaffeeklatsches*, and the kids were paraded out and they did their little . . . bow, and then they were paraded back again, and there was very little interaction, really, between the parents and children." Ellen also described how their nanny hit her and her sister but adored their older brother. She described her father as a very nervous person with a mean streak. Her mother, she recalls, was a very good person, and a very soft and gentle woman, but also very determined.

Ellen told me about her brother's visit from England, where he had spent many years, including the war years:

He was like a complete stranger. Since he was 12 years old, he just lived a completely different life. It was very weird for him, and he had a lot of resentment against my mother, because during vacations, they didn't always let him come home to Holland, and it wasn't about the money. . . . He was often alone in the school with the very few kids who for some reason couldn't go home. My mother once said that the relationship between my father and my brother was so bad, she figured it was better to keep them apart. He has a lifelong resentment about that. Later on, he cut himself off from my mother just about completely.

Most likely Ellen's brother was sent abroad both because of Hitler and because of his poor relationship with his father. Regardless, we can see that he understood the strategy that saved his life as abandonment, something for which he never forgave his mother.

Ellen returned to school and, with her sister, joined a Zionist group. Eventually, her sister became Orthodox and emigrated to Israel. Her brother returned to England. Ellen's mother adjusted and took care of her children on her own. In 1947 Ellen and her mother left for the United States; however, they left illegally: "The Dutch government wanted back taxes for the years that we were in hiding, and my mother was really ticked off at that and said, 'No way!'" They settled in Washington Heights in New York, an area full of German Jewish refugees and immigrants.

Born in 1930 in Frankfurt am Main, Flora was put on a train to Holland, to "safety," after Kristallnacht in 1938. Between the ages of 8 and 12, she lived with an Orthodox Sephardic Jewish family in Amsterdam. Her mother was shot, but her father was released from Buchenwald and made his way to England. Eventually, Flora and the Jewish family with whom she had stayed for a few years all went into hiding, but separately.

Her foster father, a well-known rabbi, found her after the war and sent her to England to be reunited with her father. Flora had seen her father once, when he left Germany for England and came to visit her in prewar Holland. Flora spent a year with him in England as they waited for visas to emigrate either to Palestine, where she had several brothers, or to the United States, where she had one brother. Her father, an Orthodox Jew, preferred going to Palestine, but since the papers for the States came through first, they went there, to her brother's in New Jersey. Their papers for Palestine had come through while they were in transit, and her father left New Jersey, shortly after they arrived, for Palestine. Flora was 17 by then. She lived with her brother's family and developed a close relationship with her niece and nephew. Eventually she went to nursing school, married, and had children. She saw her father one more time, when he used his reparations money from Germany to travel to the United States. Her father really did not offer her much in the way of family or security, and her mother's death was never discussed.

Finally, Leo, whose story is similar to Flora's, was already 20 when the war ended and was too old to continue his education. Directly after the war he began working in various businesses but did not set up a household with his surviving father. The above cases demonstrate that several families were never reconstituted, in part owing to family dynamics, the age of the hidden child, emigration, or some combination of these factors.

Three people in my sample with one surviving parent after the war enjoyed relatively good family dynamics after the war. Carla was 7 when her father killed himself in 1936, at which point she was sent to stay temporarily with her grandparents in Germany. In 1942, back in Holland, she was 13 when she went into hiding with her mother and brother, and they stayed together throughout the war, which was very unusual. Carla did not have to suffer any separation from her mother. They were liberated when she was 15—undernourished, undeveloped, but alive. They moved to The Hague, where she resumed school and joined a Zionist organization. Her brother decided to emigrate to Palestine illegally rather than be drafted into the army to serve in Indonesia.

After the war, "there was no reconstitution of family life." Carla's brother was gone, many relatives and friends were dead, her mother had a difficult time making a living, and Carla spent all her spare time involved with other young Jewish people. In 1949, when Carla was 19, she and her mother emigrated to the Unites States, sponsored by Carla's uncle, and six weeks later, Carla married Ed, a former hidden child whom she had met at the Zionist organization in Holland. She strongly feels that her family as she knew it was no more after the war, since it was split apart by geographical distances, fractured by loss, and affected by the emotional difficulties they experienced with their sponsoring uncle. Nonetheless, Carla's relationship with her mother is one of the few that seems to have survived intact, perhaps because there was no physical hiatus. However, as noted in Ruth J.'s case, being together as a family during the war was no guarantee of a good connection among family members afterward. It is also significant that Carla's mother already had adjusted to being a single parent for five years *before* the Nazi invasion of Holland. Thus, neither Carla nor her mother had to confront the death of

Carla's father after the war and had one less shock to deal with than other families highlighted in this chapter.

Sophia was 7 when she and her sister went into hiding, first in a Jewish children's home for six months, where they were together. When it became too dangerous to be hidden together, they split up and were hidden separately. After Liberation, her mother was able to move Sophia to the village where her sister lived, and they stayed there another six months while the mother set up housing. Her father did not return.

I never missed him. I don't think I asked about him so much. I think, as a child, you feel there is something wrong. If your mother is fetching you and you live all together and your father isn't there, I think you understand he's gone, he's dead.

Sophia's maternal grandparents, her aunt and uncle and their families, and her paternal grandfather were all killed, but she does not recall her mother being upset, at least when she and her sister were around. She feels her mother was a good parent who was available to her daughters:

We were very close. I was always sitting on her lap, I think until I was 16! I could tell her everything, and I could ask her everything. And she told me everything. I was always asking, curious; I always wanted to know everything.

A quick-witted attractive woman who is direct about her feelings, Sophia saw her aging mother every week until she died in 2004 and was not shy about telling her (or anyone else) what she thought. Sophia is strong-willed, optimistic, and humorous and speaks her mind, a trait she attributes to her family background, since her grandmother sold goods in the Jewish market. This mother-daughter relationship was one of the least complicated in my sample, and Sophia was one of the happiest people I interviewed. It was a relatively short interview, and while humorous in parts, it was not very emotional, although Sophia did tear up at one point. Well treated during hiding, she had some harrowing experiences all the same. The separation did not appear to create long-term damage in her relationship with her mother. Sophia did not seem to engage in much introspection or self-reflection; this is one of the several cases in which personality structure seemed to soften the deleterious effects of hiding and separation.

The final case of a relatively good family life is that of Max A., who went into hiding at age 2½ and stayed with one family for three years. He was well treated by the family and formed a close bond with his foster sister, who was ten years his senior. His mother had been caught and detained three times but managed to escape. When she came to take him home three years later, he did not recognize her. His foster parents invited them both back to visit and stay, which encouraged a healthy, inclusive relationship for the two families. Max's mother waited for the trains coming from the East, to see if any relatives would come back. One day, she saw a woman she did not recognize, but she did recognize the material of the woman's dress, since she had made a dress for her mother out of that same fabric. Her mother had become so thin that her own daughter did not know her. Max's foster family took them all in and helped nurse his grandmother back to health. Eventually, Max, his mother, and his grandmother lived in a small house together. Max did not remember his father and seems not to have asked about him, but his mother talked about his antifascist activism.

Max bonded with his grandmother in particular; he described her as lively, humorous, warm, and nice and openly admired her strength in the face of all the deaths in her family. It sounds as though there was more distance between him and his mother:

With my mother, this was a little bit more difficult. My mother was more emotional and would have her moments. Then she had headaches, and you couldn't approach her. She's a difficult woman, anyway. But when she became a grandmother, she was a wonderful *grandmother. And they* [his sons] *really like her very much.*

Max's father had fought the Dutch fascists and in 1942 was jailed for six months. He was then sent to Auschwitz, where he was killed early on. When the war ended, Max was only 5½. He thinks that at that time the loss of his father did not affect him one way or the other. Nonetheless, Max, like many other hidden children, was forced to deal with his father's death later in life. When he was 45, his foster parents died, and he became so depressed that he entered therapy. Only then did he seek out the facts and find out definitively that his father had died in Auschwitz. He then traveled to Auschwitz with ninety other Dutch Jews who belonged to the

Auschwitz Committee. Max depicts how difficult it was to accept the finality of a death that is not tangible, a feeling shared by many who lost parents in camps. His trip to Auschwitz was also an important journey:

It helped to make it real, absolutely. There was always confusion where he died. They thought he had died in Mauthausen. Somebody had said that he had seen him dead. There must have been confusion, but everything was very vague. People were deported, they didn't come back, but the rest was a black box. That was not only [the case] for a small child, but it was also for my grandmother, you must remember. . . . She had an older daughter, and her whole family was killed in Auschwitz.

Max did well at school, where he studied political science, and today is a well-known journalist in the Netherlands. Although he appears "successful" and well adjusted in many ways, he has struggled quite a bit with his past. His father's death took a long time for him to accept, digest, and integrate. Max explains, "It took more than forty years before I really understood that he was murdered in Auschwitz and what happened to him."

My sense is that Max's family story had a happier ending because both Max and his mother had his grandmother as a source of support. The grandmother sounds rather unusual in her ability to offer succor, since a number of surviving grandmothers seem to have been very understandably engulfed by their own grief. Max's mother was not left completely alone and was spared the grief of losing her mother in addition to her husband. As mentioned above, Max's relationship with his mother was not easy or close, and he was more connected to his grandmother. Generally those males whose only primary family relationship was with their mothers tended not to have a good relationship with them, and that negativity may have been intensified by the fact that most of them had no other positive female relatives with whom they connected closely, as Max did.

WHEN PARENTS REMARRIED:
BLENDED POST-SHOAH FAMILIES

My sample included seven cases of hidden children whose parents remarried. In the five cases in which a parent remarried while his or her child was relatively young—that is, 10 years old or younger—the relationship between the stepparent and the hidden child did not tend to go well for the child. In three of those cases, the results were brutal. In the two other cases, the hidden children were 16 and 17 years old at the war's end, and their parents' remarriages had fewer serious long-term effects on their lives and psyches. To the three brutal cases involving a young child and a stepparent, we can add another one from the previous chapter, in which Elly's parents both returned from the war but divorced directly afterward. Although her father remarried a warm woman who treated Elly well, her mother remarried when Elly was 10, and her stepfather sexually abused and beat her. Thus, out of the seven cases involving stepparents (counting Elly's), four of them involved abuse. We will begin with the youngest child in this category of children whose sole returning parent remarried.

Sanne was sent into hiding at 3 months old, and was 3 years old when the war ended. Both her parents were in camps, and her mother was killed. Her father returned from the camps and spent some time working for American intelligence interrogating those claiming to be Jews or war survivors but who were suspected of being Nazis. Six months or so after Liberation, just as her foster family was beginning to start the adoption process, her father showed up and claimed her. He was still working for the American army, so he visited her with the intention of taking her back as soon as he could.

Once 4-year-old Sanne realized that she would be leaving her foster family, she began to show signs of emotional disturbance—she wet her bed and became angry and upset in ways that affected the entire family, including her foster siblings. Because of these difficulties, her foster family felt they could no longer handle her, and she was placed in a Jewish orphanage, where she lived for six months, another difficult transition for a very young child. Indeed, the strong message she received during this transition, the first one she can remember, is that attachments are not permanent and cannot be trusted. At the time, she had a chronic but undiagnosed mastoid infection, which the doctors believed was simply her way of trying to get attention. When it was finally diagnosed, at age 4, she was already permanently deaf in one ear, and major surgery ended up causing permanent paralysis on one side of her face.

Her father remarried quickly, and she joined him and her stepmother in Amsterdam. Her stepmother was older than her father and childless. Sanne feels that neither of them had any sense of a child's needs; for example, she was still sleeping in a crib at 5 years of age. As to living with them, she recalls, "I hated it. Totally and completely hated it. I had no desire to be there. They made me this lovely room, it was in the attic, and although I liked being away from everybody, it was scary."

Sanne still wet her bed and wanted to return to her foster family. Her parents made it clear that she should not discuss her foster parents, and they severed all contact with them. They also told her that her foster parents had not treated her properly, which she knew was untrue. The result was that she never trusted either her stepmother or her father. She had called her foster parents the equivalent of "mommy" and "daddy," as any child would, and was then being pushed to call her father and stepmother by those same names. "I couldn't, there was no way. *These people stole me from my parents!* [my emphasis]." Although Sanne looks back at these dynamics with sympathy for her father, she observes astutely that one of the problems was, "How do you connect to a child whom you don't really know and [who is] already formed?" While she readily admits that her father was affectionate with her and that they had some good times, she insightfully points out that they all had to quickly assume unfamiliar roles: "What is a mother? What is a father? What is a child in this situation? And that wasn't easy."

Sanne had been embraced first by her foster family's extended network of kin, and then by her stepmother's large family; she realizes that she benefited from having experienced these family environments. When she was 8 her half-sister was born, and once again her family moved, and once again Sanne felt isolated and had to adapt. It also removed her from her stepmother's mother, her grandmother (Oma). Although the content of her interview suggested that her family was much more progressive and open than others I've heard about, this fact did not help Sanne feel connected to or trusting of her father or her stepmother.

In 1951, when Sanne was 9, the family emigrated to the United States. Her stepmother had been a psychiatric social worker in Holland and had worked for a Jewish agency, seeking Jewish children who had been hidden by and were still with Christian families. Once in the United

States, the stepmother found that her degrees were not valid, and the only alternative—cleaning other people's houses—was unacceptable to her. Unfortunately, she remained unemployed and isolated at home. The job her father had been promised fell through when they arrived, and so the family made multiple moves. When they finally settled down, Sanne's half-brother was born.

As Sanne describes it, family life was tense, and her father was always either busy or gone. Sanne now believes that her stepmother was manic-depressive; at the very least, she seems to have been depressed. About a year and a half before her death, Sanne's stepmother had had surgery—what kind, Sanne still does not know. Since she remembers watching her stepmother grow thinner, Sanne now thinks that she had cancer. In 1961, when Sanne was 19 and away in nursing school, and her stepsiblings were 11 and 9, her stepmother tried to kill herself. Her father refused to take Sanne to the hospital to see her stepmother, who was in a coma; instead, he took his lady friend and had Sanne baby-sit the younger children.

Her father remarried within a few months, and Sanne was furious because she felt she already had lost two mothers, the implication being that she did not want to lose yet a third. In reality, she had already lost three mothers (her biological, foster, and first stepmother). Other incidents reinforced her strong feeling that her father did not tell the truth and could not be trusted. One of his most heinous omissions was revealed when Sanne was in her 20s, when her father acknowledged that he and her biological mother had had another child during the war and that Sanne's baby sister had been killed in the camp, along with her mother. Finding out decades later that she had had a baby sister she had never met and that this baby had been murdered in Auschwitz added yet another loss to her already substantial list of sorrows. Thus, themes of loss and separation and the disappearance of her adult caretakers were threaded throughout Sanne's young life and deeply affected her ability to trust others later.

David H., like Sanne, was born in 1942. His father was a Dutch Jew, a widower with eight children who married an Austrian non-Jewish woman when she was pregnant with David. As mentioned earlier, on the day they married, David's father and eight half-siblings were taken dur-

ing a raid, later deported to Westerbork, and then murdered in Auschwitz. During the raid, the German soldier saw that David's mother was
pregnant and told her to run away to save her life. This decision haunted
her for the rest of her life. "She felt herself to be a traitor to her husband
and her children. And my mother went crazy. During her life, she was
really crazy."

Because David was half-Jewish, she took him to the Salvation Army's
children's home, where many other Jewish children were living and hiding. He grew up with adults who beat them regularly.

*Every Sunday, for example, we had to line up, and we were beaten up because
they always thought that we had done something that we shouldn't have, and we
never confessed. We were beaten by the sisters, and they were like the military—
captains, majors, and soldiers. And it was crazy! But the first few times it took
getting used to, and then it was alright. In my case, I always was put away,
locked away in a cellar, because I always started to scream.*

He explained how the children had created a hierarchy in which age
determined one's position: "The smallest had to be obedient to all the
elders. If not, they were punished, but not cruelly; you would just show
them your place. And when you grew up, you did the same [to the
younger children]."

David stated that his mother did not visit him until 1948 because she
worked as a maid in a family that demanded her time and because she
had been emotionally ill. I assume this explanation is a combination of
what he was told and what he presumed.

*There was this woman who was a stranger, and she told me that she was my
mother, and I didn't even know what that meant. I don't think I understood what
that was. But she took me out, and she took me away, and I got some things to
eat. But she always said, "Don't tell anyone, don't ever, ever tell someone that
you're Jewish or that you have a Jewish father."*

Until that time, David did not know he was Jewish, and it's unlikely that
he even understood what that meant.

David recalls that after the first contact, she rarely came to visit. Additionally, she had a male friend whom she eventually married and who,

according to David, did not like him because of his poor socialization in the children's home. "He didn't like me at all because I was very strange. I came out of this home, and I didn't know how to act or react to the outside world. He didn't like me at all." David lived in the children's home until he was 13, at which point his mother, pregnant with her next son, finally brought him home. David's mother left him in the children's home for *an additional nine years* after the war's end—until 1954.

Bringing David home created a very problematic situation. "I had a bad temper. When this man told me what to do, I just attacked him, kicked him and stuff. And then he would beat me up, and then my mother jumped in between." David feels that his mother never recovered from the deportation and death of her first husband and stepchildren: "[She] was kaput; my mother was crazy after the war. She hated me because I was the reason that she left my father." Indeed, it appears that she blamed David "incessantly":

She always shouted and screamed that it was my fault that she was still alive and kaput. She would always, *always call me names like "damn Jew" and that sort of thing. She would say, "Your father was bad, and you are even worse." She was hysterical. It was a crazy time.*

Although his stepfather only lived for three more years, until 1957, David describes those three years of family life as "terrible": "My stepfather drank a lot, and when he drank, he was very nasty, especially to my little brother. He tried to hit him, and my mother jumped in between, screaming all over the place." Apparently, he also beat David's mother. When I asked David how she treated her infant son, once again I heard an animal analogy when he compared her to a gorilla mother who did not know how to treat her baby. Because of his experience with smaller children in the children's home, David was more at ease taking care of his brother than his mother was. He also felt that his mother loved his little brother but not him. He explained why he thought this:

I was a nasty boy; I would never shut up. I was a difficult child. No one could handle me. I was very, *very bad, very naughty. I always screamed, and I loved to do it. I don't know why, I was like a kettle filled with pressure. I had to scream all the time, so very hard.*

Another sign of David's troubles appeared when he started a new school after moving home. In class, he invented a father and often spoke in great detail of all the things they did together. When the teacher called in his mother to discuss David's difficulties at school, he mentioned David's father, which shocked and angered his mother. "She blew up, but she didn't understand me." Luckily, this male teacher was very kind to David, especially after realizing that David's wonderful father was a complete fabrication.

A gentle, soft-spoken man who now lives in a communal setting and is a macrobiotic sushi chef, David has struggled his entire life with this tumultuous background and spent fifteen years taking drugs, traveling around the world, living on the margins. His harsh and cold upbringing took a serious toll on his ability to interact with others, and he is unable to express his feelings. As a troubled child, David did not make things easy for the adults in his life. At the same time, his mother appears to have been deeply disturbed and perhaps anti-Semitic. His story and others are not meant to demonize the parents, who themselves were victims. These hidden children came home with problems, needs, and damaged psyches and were dependent on parents who had their own set of traumas and problems. In a later chapter, we will see how David's lack of connection with any adult figure foreshadowed his problematic family life.

The next three cases involve hidden children who lived with stepparents after the war and were between the ages of 5 and 7 when they went into hiding, somewhat older than David. Two of the three cases included serious physical abuse, similar to David's case, but they also included sexual abuse, similar to Elly's in the previous chapter.

Margot, today an accountant in The Hague, went into hiding at the age of 7. Her mother returned from multiple concentration camps to find her 10-year-old daughter fully involved in Catholicism and an anti-Semite. "So here comes my mother—a Jew! What am I going to do with her? I was embarrassed to death!" Although Margot recognized her mother, she did not approach her, and it seems that her mother did not hug her, either. Margot found out that her father was not coming back but kept thinking, "What am I going to do with the Jews? Who wants to be involved with Jews?" Eventually, Margot moved back to Amsterdam and lived with her mother and younger sister. "It was awful. I never built up any bond with her."

Her mother agreed to take in two young men in their early twenties who were recovering from TB they had contracted in the camps. Eventually, her mother, then 37, had an affair with one of the young men, who was about 23 years old. This relationship developed into a marriage that has lasted to this day. Unfortunately, this union also led to a dysfunctional family life.

Margot and her sister, Edith, slept upstairs in a dingy room with a pipe in the middle:

The pipe was like from the sewer—it smelled awful. We didn't have a toilet upstairs. On Sundays we were not allowed to come down before nine o'clock, so if we had to go to the bathroom, too bad; we just had to hold it. There were so many restrictions. And then, we were just very much unwanted. We were intruders. And they didn't try to camouflage it or anything. So if we came downstairs at nine o'clock, we always had to go out again. We were never allowed to sit in the apartment, so we were always out on the street.

Margot still prayed twice daily with her rosary, and she came home one day to find that her stepfather had thrown out "everything":

The two medals [of saints] *that saved my life during the war, my church book, my rosary, everything was abandoned. "This is a* Jewish *home!" he said. And they didn't do anything like go to* shul, *nothing! So here my whole life is shattered again. It was such a terrible thing that these things that saved my life were thrown away, just demolished.*

Margot's stepfather also hit her often and was sadistic at times. Once he asked her to check whether the water was boiling in the kitchen while Margot was busily knitting. When she didn't respond immediately, he called her into the kitchen. She cried as she told this story:

"Margot, come here for a minute," and I walked into the kitchen. He put my hand and arm in the boiling water, *to teach me a lesson because I was lazy. He did other things like this, threw me out of the house if I did something wrong.*

I had to peel potatoes to make French fries on Sunday, and if I wasn't fast enough, he came after me and threw all the potatoes and the knife and everything at me. And then I ran away.

When she was 13 and her mother was in the hospital after having given birth to a daughter, Margot's stepfather raped her. "Of course I knew it was wrong, but I was scared of him. But I could never understand how you can combine making love with hitting?" Margot left home at age 16 and found out only recently that he also sexually abused her younger sister after Margot left. Margot explains how she has protected herself from this abusive past: "See, if I tell you, it's like it didn't happen to me; it's like another person. I think if I realized that it happened to me, I just couldn't handle it. So it's some protection, I just pull down this shade."

When she was 16, Margot ran away to the house of a relative, who persuaded Margot to tell her story of the sexual abuse to a social worker. The case was brought to court, and the judge gave her the option to drop the case, which Margot gladly did. However, she recalls her mother telling her something in the courthouse that she repeated many times to Margot: "I will never throw away my husband for my children." It was clear to Margot that the only way to protect herself was to leave home. So at age 16 she married someone she did not love as a way to escape her family life. This marriage did not last, and the children born to it did not have an easy time or a good relationship with their mother, a story that will be explored in more detail in a later chapter. For our purposes here, what is clear from Margot's narrative is that the re-creation of two-parent Jewish families did not necessarily guarantee a positive outcome.

Finally, we have two cases of children who were born in 1936 and went into hiding, one at age 5, and the other at 6. Before he was taken away, Riwka's father told her that he had hidden her mother's birthday present "but that he'd be back so we could give it to her the next day." He was transported to Westerbork and killed in Mauthausen. Riwka went into hiding when she was 5 years old; her hiding places included a hayloft on a farm and, later, a home for the illegitimate children of un-wed mothers. She was liberated late in 1944 and ended up living with a baptized Jewish family, as an evacuee. During the half-year that she lived with them, they taught her how to talk normally because until then she had spoken only in whispers.

In 1945 her mother arrived and introduced herself and Riwka's sister. Riwka's younger sister was now a Catholic, and Riwka and her mother were Protestants after the war. Riwka mentioned frequently during this part of the interview that her mother was a difficult, unpleasant woman who frequently lost her temper and hit her children with rattan carpet beaters. In 1947 Riwka's mother married a widower; Riwka described him as a kind and friendly man who worked in a matzo factory. He brought his 18-year-old son into the marriage, creating a blended family.

Riwka's experience with her stepfather was much more pleasant than were other hidden children's. Her major complaint about him was that she felt that he always sided with her mother and never with her. However, he was the rare stepparent, at least in my sample, in that he did not hit his stepdaughter. A few years after the families blended, her stepbrother, then about age 20, attempted to get into 14-year-old Riwka's bed. When she finally told her mother about these incidents, the stepbrother denied it, and her mother did not believe her.

Riwka stopped school early, at age 14, because she was not doing well, and took on different sorts of low-skilled jobs. She left home at age 19, although there was an argument over her departure—she wanted to leave home, and her mother and stepfather, who needed the income from her job as a movie usher, wanted her to stay. When Riwka left she continued working at various jobs, eventually becoming a servant in a Jewish household, where she only lasted for a few months because her employer kept attempting to seduce her. She married at age 20. Throughout Riwka's interview, it became clear that she had a poor relationship with her mother and, it seems, later in life, with others as well.

Max L., whose story opens this book, was 9 years old at the war's end. Because his foster parents wanted to keep him, and because his father was on his own, he was able to stay with his foster parents for another three years, until he was 12. As described in the introduction, Max L.'s postwar family life was problematic—he wanted to return to the warmth and love of his foster family but lived with the coldness, distance, and punishment of his blended family. Only at age 13 did Max find out that he was Jewish and that his "real" (biological) mother had been killed. And when he was 14, his stepmother forced him to begin a sexual relationship that lasted several years and continued to be coupled with harsh physical punishments.

Max's father was only home on the weekends because of work, but over time he stayed away longer, owing to his involvement with another woman. By leaving Max alone with his angry and frustrated wife, Max's father was essentially abandoning him and abdicating his role as a parent. In a sense, he had long ago abandoned Max emotionally; he never tried to protect or understand him. Max is one of several former hidden children who were beaten and one of four who were sexually violated by a stepparent.

The final example of a hidden child who gained a stepparent after the war falls into a somewhat different category because he was substantially older than those previously discussed. Hans A. was born in Berlin in 1928 and was about 15 when he first hid. At the war's end, he was 17. Hans's mother was remarried to a British man: "It was not a love marriage. She had never earned a penny in her life, and she didn't want to be a burden on us kids, so she decided the best she could do was find somebody to take care of her." She moved to England about half a year after the war. Hans did not join her. He often described his mother as "lethal" during the interview, a depiction that at least in part explains his decision. Hans's mother did not appear to take much care of her sons:

She had trouble taking care of herself at that point. So basically, we were on our own. And that was pretty scary, actually. That was more scary than being in hiding because all of a sudden I had to face the real world. And during hiding, the expectations of after the war were so great that in a way it was a comedown when I had to face the real world, and my father didn't come back. I had nothing to hold on to.

Although some young Jewish people his age returned to an intensive program at school to try to catch up, after trying it for a few days, Hans felt he was "beyond that": "They treated us like kids. Had they taken into consideration what all of us had gone through?" Instead he got a job in a matzo factory through a former school friend. Hans and his older brother, both former German citizens living in Holland without Dutch citizenship, were stateless, and in 1948, when Hans was 20, they emigrated to the United States. Once in the States Hans went to school and graduated from high school a short time later.

It is clear that when Hans's family broke up after the war his mother was unable to take care of her sons as a single parent. However, Hans's interview also made clear that he found his mother to be a cold person whose attention he did not seek. Thus, the war and its effects, particularly the death of Hans's father, ended up destroying Hans's family prematurely.

CONCLUSIONS

In some cases, the family lives of hidden children who had one parent return replicate those of children who had both parents return, in that there was an attempt to return to normal family life, even with a missing parent or spouse. However, a fulfilling family life was rarely the result in this group. In the majority of cases, there were two possible outcomes. The first was that the family fell apart and family life was never resumed. This could have been due to a widowed father who could not be granted guardianship of his child, or to a mother who could not take care of her children and family on top of trying to manage her grief. Traditional gender ideologies persisted at that time that deprived many children whose only surviving parent was their father of a return to some kind of family life. This was particularly cruel in light of the fact that some mothers were not necessarily adept at parenting.

The second outcome was a reconstituted blended family in which the hidden child gained a stepparent—often a third mother or father, counting foster parents. In very few cases did a stepparent make a close connection with his or her stepchild. In fact, remarriage tended to have disastrous consequences for the former hidden children. These children were in great need of attention and understanding but instead received inappropriate, insufficient, or even violent attention. To be fair, many children acted out tremendously after the war when they could finally vent their frustrations and anger, and parents and stepparents were often victims themselves, dealing with their own grief and anger. However, this does not excuse the physical and sexual abuse that was perpetrated. Children who were abused in these ways were scarred even further, often permanently. One of the women I interviewed who was sexually abused seemed to blame herself, at least partially, when she explained that she was craving the attention she never got from her mother. She liked being noticed by her young stepfather and was perhaps flirtatious; this understandable behavior, however, does not justify what occurred. Although many hidden children acted out after the war, their parents had the responsibility of protecting their children and of knowing appropriate limits.

Of the four cases in which a stepparent beat a stepchild, three of the stepparents also became sexually abusive. While the combination of sexual and physical abuse may be common, I certainly did not expect to find it in postwar Jewish or partially Jewish families because of the myth that such patterns do not exist in Jewish families. That I found several cases of this kind of abuse suggests that many others existed. This pattern reflects how destructive the war was for many Jewish children, long after it was over. It also suggests that the stepparents who perpetrated this kind of violence were damaged and brutalized by the war or perhaps by other events as well.

A final point is that abuse occurs in all types of families, cutting across racial, ethnic, religious, and class lines. That is, Jewish families are not exempt from patterns found in other families.[1] I had attributed these cases of sexual and physical abuse to the effects of the war on individuals and families, implying that if not for the war these abuses would not have taken place. Perhaps both possibilities are true—the war may have resulted in more instances of sexual and physical abuse, but these abuses might still have occurred without the war.

This chapter also included a few instances of reasonable postwar family life; all three of these involved a mother who survived. But these cases seem to be the exception rather than the rule; in both this chapter and the previous one most of the stories demonstrate that distance, conflict, and dysfunction appear to have been the norm in postwar Jewish family life.

7 "Who Am I?"

ORPHANS LIVING WITH FAMILIES

This chapter and the next will focus on the distinct experiences of Jewish orphans in the Netherlands after the war. In my sample, twenty-six people—more than one-third—were orphaned after surviving the war in hiding. For these orphaned children, there were four options: (1) staying with their (non-Jewish) foster family, (2) moving in with kin, (3) being adopted by a Jewish family that was not related, or (4) living in an orphanage in the Netherlands. A fifth option was available to those in orphanages only after 1949—going to Israel. Children younger than 18 who went to Israel usually lived with other orphans, but males aged 18 or older were immediately drafted into the army. This chapter covers options one to three; option four will be covered in the next chapter.

The postwar trajectories of orphans were not necessarily limited to only one of these options. Some children experienced multiple moves and situations. Sometimes orphans simply moved from one family of their kin to another, but more often than not, they moved between families and institutions, as when they were adopted from an orphanage by kin or by an unrelated Jewish family, or were sent to an orphanage after a stint with a family that didn't work out.

Some postwar contexts created and reproduced a sense of displacement and caused more trauma, while others were more successful. Although some orphanages were notoriously cold and cruel, most orphans who lived in them developed a camaraderie with the other children that they maintain today. In the better orphanages, some had a very positive experience. Those who were enthusiastic about their postwar living situations were living either in an orphanage or with their original foster family. Rarely was any enthusiasm expressed by those who had lived with Jewish kin or another Jewish family who were nonkin.

Of the hidden children who were orphaned after the war, seven stayed with their non-Jewish hiding families, nine went to relatives, and two went to nonkin Jewish families. Thirteen were sent to Jewish orphanages, at least at some point in their childhoods. Of those who were in orphanages, the majority of them (seven) lived with a family, either kin or an adoptive Jewish family, at some point. Again, not all paths were linear; some who left the orphanage to live with a family did not stay with that family and ended up back in an orphanage, usually by choice. Therefore, one cannot simply add up the numbers above, since some orphans were in more than one setting. Those orphans who experienced multiple living situations after the war will be categorized by the situation in which they spent the most time, although their experiences in other living arrangements will be mentioned. I interviewed a few hidden children who were adults by the war's end and were too old for any of the options listed above; ready or not, in 1945 they were on their own.[1] I will begin with a discussion of the first option—staying with hiding parents—the only one that did not include a major move.

STAYING ON WITH FOSTER PARENTS

With the war's end, many foster families were able to verify that what they feared had occurred—that the parents of the child they were hiding had been killed. As previous chapters have demonstrated, some foster families were not prepared to keep the child any longer than they had to, while others very much wanted to do so.

What precipitated the decision for foster families to keep their hidden Jewish child? Who made this decision, and how was it made? The data presented here are clearly partial, since I did not seek out (nor would I have been given permission to view) primary documents kept in the Jewish social service agency that would have depicted struggles, if there had been any, between the foster family and surviving kin or Jewish agencies over the child's guardianship. Some respondents knew of these struggles and/or had seen their files directly; others may not have known of them and still do not want to look at their files. But what did become clear is that in several of these cases, state intervention determined a child's postwar family context.

What unfolds from the narratives is that most Jewish children kept by their foster families were in an environment that ranged from adequate and agreeable to loving and nurturing. One living situation was highly unsatisfactory. Although a single case has no statistical significance, it does alert us to the unfortunate fact that occasionally there was abuse. Yet highly problematic environments were not exclusive to Dutch non-Jewish foster families but occurred in Jewish families as well. Although we are dealing with small numbers, those who had a good experience in this category suggest that most situations with foster parents were acceptable, at the very least, and in some cases were better than other possible options. I will begin with the youngest children.

Rob was 3 months old in spring 1942, when he was put into hiding with a childless couple. Rob's parents were betrayed while in hiding and deported; neither survived. After the war, 3-year-old Rob's foster parents initially lied about him to state officials, stating that he was their child. They also said that he was not circumcised, as partial proof that he was theirs. However, unable to live with their bad consciences, they finally came forward and told the authorities, in Rob's words, "He is not our child, but we are so afraid to lose him."

Rob's surviving aunt was then able to locate him. Rob described her reaction:

She was very much impressed by my father and also by my mother, who was kind and took her hand; she was moved. She decided I would be better off there. My older brothers had to go to the orphanage. My brother Shmuel was angry when he realized that he had to grow up in the orphanage. Only a couple of months ago, my cousin explained to us that it was forbidden, that my aunt didn't get permission [to keep the brothers]. *I never knew.*

Rob's foster parents strongly desired to keep the toddler they had raised almost from infancy, a child who knew no other parents but them. Furthermore, it appears that his widowed aunt had requested guardianship of his brothers, but was denied it by the OPK, probably because of her status as a single woman. Although widowed mothers were privileged by the OPK over widowed fathers for guardianship, they did not automatically regain custody over their child(ren). Among the orphans in my study, none was allowed to be transferred to a widowed aunt if she had not remarried.

Sjef, Rozette, and Fia V., also born in 1942, were sent into hiding at 8, 9, and 13 months of age, respectively. Sjef's mother and his two brothers were deported the day after he went into hiding. Along with his father, they were all killed. I was struck by the photographs Sjef showed me of his two toddler-aged brothers and his sister, all of whom had dark eyes and dark curly hair. That photo was mirrored by others, placed in a large frame, of Sjef's children at a young age, with similarly dark eyes and curly hair. When I saw the photo of Sjef's young mother, in her thin winter coat adorned by a yellow Jewish star, holding him for the last time in Amsterdam on the day he went into hiding, I could not speak (figure 7). As the mother of a young child, I could not help but wonder what she was thinking as she prepared to hand over her baby to strangers. Another framed photo on the wall showed a young Sjef on the lap of his foster sister, his dark features in contrast to her fair skin and long, straight blond braids (figure 9). At that moment, these photos transmitted both the tragedy of the deaths of so many innocents and the good fortune of those who were saved.

In Sjef's case, there were no adult survivors in his entire family and, therefore, no contestations about his staying with his foster family. The last he heard from his mother was a postcard she sent from Westerbork to neighbors, requesting a bottle of water. From our interview, I got the impression that his foster parents treated him like their own son and never considered sending him to an orphanage. Sjef was ten years younger than his foster parents' youngest child and feels that he was treated better than his foster siblings.

His sister, however, was less fortunate. She was hidden during the war, and her parents had asked their neighbors (who were not hiding her) to take her if they didn't return after the war. Apparently, the neighbors agreed, but grudgingly. Furthermore, they had many of the parents' belongings but never offered any of them to Sjef or his sister when they became adults.

Sjef recalls visits from social workers from the Jewish community who were checking on his situation, asking him how he was doing in school. Later in life, he asked the Jewish Social Work Agency (JMW) to investigate whether his parents and grandparents had owned property before the war, but he found them uncooperative. However, the JMW was able to establish how much money his father and grandfather had had in their pockets when they arrived at Westerbork—a total of sixty-one guilders—which Sjef received back at five times that amount. With the help of his son, a notary, Sjef claimed those monies (about three hundred dollars at the time). This moment was important to him perhaps in a similar way that Max A.'s trip to Auschwitz, discussed in the last chapter, was for him. The return of stolen family money both verified Sjef's father's and grandfather's deaths and linked Sjef to them. Like Rob's, Sjef's is one of the few cases in which a child felt accepted and loved by his foster family and was able to bond with at least one foster parent.

Rozette's father visited her several times when she had already been hidden with her foster family, before he and her mother were deported. During one visit, her foster father asked a neighbor to witness Rozette's father's answer to his question, "What should we do if you don't return?" Rozette's father responded, "Take care of her as if she were your own," which Rozette's foster parents were happy to do. The social workers and the courts felt that 3-year-old Rozette (then called Rita, her de-Judaized hiding and postwar name) was safe and happy with her foster family. The neighbor's witnessing of her father's request was enough to persuade the courts to deny an uncle's later claim to his niece. The government did not deem it important to place Rozette in a Jewish home. As she explained, "Jewishness was not a motive for the government to make these decisions. After the war, they wanted to see everyone as equal." Rozette frequently visited her uncle, yet he refused to discuss the past with her. (See figures 19 and 20.)

Fia's uncle fought to get her after the war but lost his claim, and she stayed with her foster parents. She believes that had her surviving aunts claimed her, she would have been sent to them, although it was never clear in our interviews why they didn't claim her. It is very possible that they tried to, but the court was not likely to send Jewish orphans to their widowed relatives if a married couple wanted them.

Like the three hidden children just described, Louis D. was born in 1942. He went into hiding with his parents, and they were all betrayed. He was probably just over 1 year old when this occurred. Louis was one of the children smuggled out of the Joodse Schouwburg; he was then hidden with a farm family in Friesland. The father, a widower, did not want to take care of a baby, but his eldest daughter agreed to do so; baby Louis called her "Mama." When she married and left home with her husband, she took Louis, nicknamed Loekie, with her.

His mother's kin in The Hague wanted to adopt him, but the OPK decided that Louis should stay where he was. His foster parents did not allow his relatives to visit him. Today, having emigrated to Israel, he is still angry that the OPK made this decision, though the commission was fully aware that he did not know he was Jewish and did not plan to tell him. "Forget about being Jewish! Forget that my parents were killed and that my family died! They weren't murdered because they were Dutch, but because they were Jews!"

Betty was almost 4 when she went into hiding. None of her family survived; all that remained of her large family were their hundred or more names in a memory book listing all Dutch Jews who were killed. She stayed with her foster family until she was 21, in fact, until the day of her twenty-first birthday. This situation is explained in more detail later in this chapter.

Philip was 10 at the war's end, living with a foster family in a situation I would describe as adequate. He was unhappy during the war and often stayed in his room, in his bed, for long periods. That he did not want to go to the toilet between the ages of 6 and 10 and instead eliminated in his room suggests that he was deeply unhappy and traumatized. Although his foster parents were not abusive to him, there was no warmth or affection, and he had little interaction with his foster mother.

The two older hidden children in this category, Jaap A. and Feena, were 16 and 19 respectively, at the end of the war. All of Jaap's relatives had been killed, and he stayed on with his foster family. Even though he felt loved by his foster family, they told him after the war that he had to work to pay them for his upkeep. Jaap began working at a young age and left his foster family by the age of 19 to seek his independence. Feena would have preferred to live with her relatives, but her foster mother wanted to keep her and her younger sister. Out of gratitude, Feena's relatives felt that her foster mother's wishes should be granted because she had saved their lives. Feena agreed to stay with her foster mother in large part because she knew that she'd be leaving for nursing school one year later. Her sister stayed longer. In both Jaap's and Feena's interviews, it was very difficult to get a strong sense of the texture of family dynamics. Their situations seemed acceptable and perhaps even good at times, but neither seemed deeply connected to their foster parents, and both were quite ready to leave and become independent as soon as they could.

Learning the Truth

Since this is the only group in the study that did not experience a radical disruption and/or move, I asked those in this category when and how they found out that they were orphaned—and that they were Jewish as well. Because these foster children were not going anywhere, there was more flexibility in the timing of the decision to tell them about the fate of their biological parents, especially in the case of younger children who thought that their hiding parents *were* their parents. Rob explained that there were many relatives in his life, from his first foster mother to his second (his first foster mother died). He told me about discovering one more. He and his foster family visited a family in Amsterdam, and Rob took notice—the woman was small, and "the culture was different." His foster mother said, "This is your own aunt," and based on that one comment, Rob feels that he knew and understood his situation at some level.

Sjef was told at age 7 that he was Jewish, although his foster family continued to raise him as a Roman Catholic. Fia explained that she always knew her foster parents weren't her real parents and that there was something about her that set her apart.[2] However, when Fia asked what it was, her foster mother would not discuss it. Rozette's foster mother was advised by a well-meaning German Jewish social worker, who worked under the famous psychiatrist Hans Keilson in L'Ezrat ha-Yeled, to tell her the truth the evening before her sixth birthday so that her sadness would be countered by the joy of her birthday the following day:

I remember sitting on the lap of my father, my papa. And he's telling me a very, very sad story about a girl and a papa and a mama. And the papa and the mama were killed. And they were dead, but the madmen could not find the little girl because she was hidden somewhere in safety. I don't remember anything else. I just remember the feeling of uncertainty because everything changed. I felt sadness, and everything was strange. I have been in therapy for years and years, and now I call this the time "when he took away my foundation." From that moment, I was not the one I had thought I was. He was not my father, and my mother was not who I thought she was. He said, "Of course, you don't have to go away, you can always stay with us. We love you." But nevertheless, he was not who I thought he was.

Rozette and her foster parents never discussed her situation again, but she thought of it daily; "I became a stranger to myself," she explained, and as her life unfolded, she experienced substantial psychological difficulties. In this case, Rozette became estranged and emotionally unhinged, even though her narrative suggests that her foster parents were thoughtful and very caring people.

Louis D., then Loekie, did not find out until he was 14 that his name was Louis D., not Louis Rienstra. This occurred one day when a teacher punished him for not knowing his own name by pulling his hair and taking him to the headmaster. The headmaster was kind and understanding, however. He didn't tell Louis anything but sent him home early. Completely confused about what was happening, Louis asked his mother to explain who Louis D. was:

And then my mother started crying. She wouldn't tell me. She said, "OK, you should wait. Father comes home at twelve o'clock, and maybe he will talk to you." So we waited, and at lunchtime, they told me that I was not their child, I was a Jewish child. So I had one terrible week, but in school you had examinations . . . the pressure, everything continues. . . . So after a week, two weeks, you forget all about it. I continued to be Louis Rienstra in the school, because everything was fixed again, my name was back, and it was OK.

Although he claims that life went back to normal, Louis also recounted that this news was shocking because he hated Jews and hated being Jewish.

Philip's foster parents told him that his parents were dead when he was about 12 years old. However, they failed to tell him that he had surviving siblings—a brother and a sister. He recalls that the starkness of his parents' deaths made him sad but also very angry. Philip recalls that he was even "more terrible" than before, fighting more with his foster mother.

Older children were told about their parents' deaths, or they guessed it, as they waited for parents to return and no one came. Later in life, many of these orphans were given memorabilia and photos of their parents by relatives, and many have framed and hung these photos in prominent places in their homes. Among other items, Sjef "inherited" an invitation to his parents' wedding and the haunting postcard already mentioned sent by his mother from the transit camp. At age 18, Rozette received her parents' wedding rings, which had been smuggled out of Westerbork and given to her foster father. Understandably, all these orphans felt a need to connect with their parents and their past in some way, even if they had had a relatively happy life with their foster parents.

Orphans, Identities, and Family Life

Of the twelve children in my sample who stayed on at their hiding parents' homes after the war, three described situations that were good, with two of the men reporting that as boys, they were very bonded to their foster mothers. Two others said little about the quality of their relationships with their foster parents (or with most others in their lives), and it was difficult to get a grasp of family dynamics.[3] Three seemed to have had difficult childhoods in their foster homes. Two stayed with their foster families until they were adults, while one who fought a lot with his foster mother was finally thrown out of the house and sent to an orphanage at age 15.

Rob was one of the two males who did well with his foster family. His foster mother died in 1949, which was a shock for him, but it appears that during the two years before his foster father remarried, he and Rob grew very close. "To my father, I was his real son. He was fond of me, he spoiled me. We had been together, the two of us, for a couple of years alone." Rob was 6 when his foster mother died and 8 when he gained a new stepmother, but it appears that both women had good relationships with him. "I've got two fathers and three mothers!" he remarked jovially. In his case, it seems especially relevant that he was taken in by a childless couple and that he remained their only child. It is also instructive that a widower was, in fact, very able to care for a child on his own and that this period was an important time for them as a family. Interestingly, Rob was not removed from this family when his foster father was widowed, perhaps because he was Protestant.

Rob's foster father played a role in the Reform Protestant Church, and Rob was brought up in that church. He fondly recalls how his father used to bring him peppermints on Sundays during church. In the army as a young man, Rob was seen by his peers as a Jew and was given some Jewish education, but he felt he was living in two worlds. It resulted in a "problem of loyalty": "I wanted to be loyal to my father, who was a good Christian and who wanted me to become one too. I could never discuss this with him." Unfortunately, Rob's foster father died young (when Rob was 15), and they never had this conversation. Rob married a non-Jewish woman in a church; later in their marriage his wife decided to convert to Judaism. Rob accompanied her and also gained a Jewish education. Now he has a strong Jewish identity, they have a distinctly Jewish family life, and Rob is a leader in the Jewish community.

Sjef remarked, "I'm one of the few who is lucky in what happened to him after the war since I was raised in a good family," echoing Rob's experience. Sjef's foster family remained his family throughout his adult years, and his foster siblings have been aunts and uncles to his children. As a young adult, his nascent Jewish identity, however, put a wedge between Sjef and his foster parents and siblings. At university, Sjef became involved with a Jewish student organization, and two years later, at age 20, he went to Israel on a student trip. When he became involved with a Jewish woman, his foster mother did not want to meet her, in part, he believes, because she was jealous, and in part, because she was not happy that his girlfriend was Jewish. His foster parents had a mixed reaction to his Jewish wedding, although he thinks they were glad that at least it was a religious rather than a secular wedding. One foster sibling felt Sjef was "stupid" to take on his Jewish identity because it was riskier for his descendants. Yet Sjef felt an obligation to perpetuate the Jewish community.

Whatever Jewish education Sjef had, he obtained in adulthood. He is not only a member but also the vice-chairman of an Orthodox synagogue. Although his beliefs are closer to those of Reform Judaism, he did not join the liberal synagogue—the other choice in the Netherlands—because he had become accustomed to the Orthodox approach he had experienced in the Jewish student organization. It also makes him feel connected to his parents and his past, even though his parents were not Orthodox. The irony is that when Sjef's rabbi urged him to learn more Hebrew, Sjef responded to him: "When I look at the translation [in the prayerbook], I don't like it at all because for me it is nonsense. No normal man says things like this! And I didn't quit the Roman Catholic Church to do something like that in another religion!" Thus, for Sjef, rather than reflecting his own belief system, his dedication to the Orthodox synagogue fulfills an obligation he feels toward the Jewish community in Holland and maintains his connection with his parents.

Rozette was well treated by her foster family. She seems to have had a better relationship with her foster father than with her foster mother, whom she described as overbearing. She felt protected by her foster father, and from her descriptions of his dealings with her biological father, it was clear that she admired him. Indeed, I had the sense that Rozette's foster parents were considerate and sensitive people, and I did not understand the roots of her unhappiness. After our interview, I emailed Rozette, asking her just that. This is her reply:

The problem has been the fact that my foster parents tried to bring me up as if I were their own child, acting like they were my parents, without giving any credit to my real parents, who were so loving and brave (and desperate) that they gave me to them in order to save me. The systematic neglect of my biological parents caused the real damage.

Yet Rozette also explained that when she asked her foster father why they did not adopt her, he responded, "How could we have taken your name away from you too?" This response reveals a fair amount of sensitivity, more than Rozette may have felt or been able to acknowledge. After many years of therapy, Rozette is finally able to appreciate her foster parents' efforts: "I am able to see now that they did their utmost, they did what they were able to, they gave everything they had to offer."

Rozette's Jewish identity evolved as she grew into an adult. Her Jewish boyfriend, who became her first husband, initially introduced her to his friends at the university by her real name, Rozette, a Jewish-sounding name that had been changed to Rita when she went into hiding as an infant. She very much liked returning to her real name. Her wedding was paid for by a Jewish organization with the proviso that it be Jewish. So, two days after their civil marriage, Rozette and her husband were wedded under a *chuppah* in the synagogue. Although her foster father and brother attended both weddings, her foster mother only attended the former. She would not attend the synagogue wedding, telling Rozette: "You were not brought up Jewish. Why should you have a Jewish wedding? You are not a religious person." Two people from L'Ezrat ha-Yeled stood in for Rozette's parents during the ceremony.

Rozette has learned more about Jewish holidays through her involvement with an association for child survivors of the Shoah. She sees herself as an Amsterdam Jew, someone who is culturally rather than religiously Jewish, but is not particularly Zionist. While her Jewish identity has helped her to forge meaningful connections with other hidden children, she remarks wistfully, "I feel lost as a Jew and can't make up for the loss of having a family that teaches you." Her Jewish identity is clearly an important link to her parents and her family that perished. At the same time, it was not welcomed by her foster mother, an apparently common reaction among foster parents who wanted their foster children to reflect them. These reactions echo what scholars have argued about the discomfort non-Jewish Dutch citizens had with their co-citizens' Jewish identity and Jewishness.

Fia felt that she was treated differently from her foster siblings, enough so that it was clear that her parents were not her parents and her family was not her family. Her foster parents never discussed the past with her. Fia's life has been full of psychological adversity. She has been hospitalized multiple times, once for six years, diagnosed with depression and post-traumatic stress syndrome. Her past as a hidden child has emerged more intensely in recent years, and she is trying to confront it as best she can. When I met her, she was planning to go to Auschwitz with a group organized by the Auschwitz Committee in Holland, because she feels she has not yet said farewell to her parents.

She described her feelings of survivor guilt, that she failed her parents somehow. Neither her foster family nor her kin (except for her three children) have stayed connected to her, perhaps because of her psychological difficulties. Given that she has three children, it was strikingly sad to hear how alone she feels. Fia seems never to have had a primary bond with an adult and has been unable to establish meaningful connections to others. It seems that her two dogs remain her closest companions.

In her modest flat, Fia proudly displays elements of Judaica (e.g., Shabbat candlesticks and a menorah) and many Jewish books on her shelves, as well as a photo of her parents. She clearly identifies as Jewish, although she has not had any Jewish education. Her main Jewish activity is to read the Dutch Jewish liberal newspaper; indeed, she answered my ad looking for volunteers to interview. Fia was kind and hospitable but seemed very fragile. She cried a lot during the interview and detailed her history of depression and hospitalizations. My Dutch teacher, who translated, and I both felt that we had to tread very lightly, and we asked her several times during the interview whether she'd like to stop. We also asked if she had someone she could call after the interview, and she assured us that she did. Nevertheless, we deliberately kept the interview short, and we kept any probing to a minimum, seeking only to clarify her statements. At the end, she told us that she was proud of herself for doing the interview because only now, in her late fifties, is she able to cry about her past.

Louis D. hid in Friesland, in a very poor household, and stayed there after the war. He loved his foster mother, and she loved him, but his foster father was strict and punishing. Louis recalled that if didn't eat all the food on his plate, his father would punish and even force-feed him. All the same, Louis claims that he respected his father. When Louis entered the army, his father wrote down his real last name and told him to register with that name. He then checked the box for religion, choosing Protestant. Apparently, a rabbi who served Jewish men in the army "had often seen names like Shmuel Levi with the Roman Catholic box checked" and knew what had happened. One day Louis was sent to Arnhem by the head commander and had no idea why. He thought that perhaps it had something to do with military intelligence. He was given an address, and when he couldn't find it asked someone on the street, telling him that it had something to do with the army:

He said, "No, it has nothing to do with the army. There is a shul, and normally at ten o'clock in the morning the rabbi is in after shul." I didn't know what a shul was, I didn't know what a rabbi was. So I knocked on the door. And then the rabbi came. For me at 20, he was an old guy—maybe he was 40 or 60. He went to a dark room where they have this office. I was nervous again. So then he started shouting, "What happened to you, Louis D——! Protestant? You are a Jew! What happened to you?" So I start crying. I said, "I don't know what happened to me."

Louis D. went to Talmud Torah once a week while in the army and got Fridays and Saturdays off, even though he was not observant. Before marrying his non-Jewish fiancé, he agreed to visit Israel and considered staying there. He married, had children, and threw himself into work, at which he was very successful; he was driven by the poverty he had experienced as a child and vowed never to be poor again. But all that came at a price. Louis was a workaholic who slept little and saw his children even less. When his children were still young, he sold his stores and moved his family to Israel. In response to my asking why, he answered philosophically.

Am I the product of my education, which was Christian, or am I the product of everything that preceded? My question was not, "Who is a Jew?" and not, "Am I a Jew?" but *"Who am I?"* [with emphasis on each word]. *Am I the sum of my total memories, not just from my birth, but also the collective of national Jewish memory? Is that inside of me? Where do I belong?*

And, he explained, his only wish was to have Jewish grandchildren, something that was unlikely to occur if they stayed in the Netherlands.

His case is a mixed one. He loved his foster mother and still does—his foster parents were grandparents to Louis's children, and now Louis's children bring their children to Friesland to meet them. However, he feels that the poverty in which he grew up was extremely harsh and that he had had a hard life. When he expressed a desire to go to business school, his foster father informed him that Louis would have to pay for it. His foster parents were unhappy with his Jewishness because they wanted him to be Christian, like them, and they still feel that because he does not believe in Christ, he is damned.

Earlier in life, by his own admission, Louis channeled his energies into work and was a very rigid, strict, and aggressive person who was businesslike but not warm or available to his children. Now, he is well-off economically; he flew his foster parents to Israel and had them stay in one of his homes. He has found his Jewish roots and is thrilled to have three Jewish grandchildren. During our interview, he was very direct and wanted to get to the point without any of the usual small talk that preceded other interviews. At the same time, he was unusually kind and insisted on driving me back to the city where I was staying, something others did not do. When I saw him again five years later in Amsterdam at the Conference for Jewish Child Survivors of the Holocaust, Louis was extremely warm and very sweet.

After the war's end, 6-year-old Betty was sent by L'Ezrat ha-Yeled from her foster family in Holland to Switzerland for three months, to live with an Orthodox Jewish family. Betty recalls that she did not understand why she was there and did not eat or sleep for days. At the end of the three months, the Jewish family told L'Ezrat ha-Yeled that Betty should go to a Jewish family, and they agreed. A Jewish family was waiting for her at the train station in Utrecht when she returned; however, somehow her foster mother had come to be there and was also waiting for her. The new Jewish foster mother had a photo of Betty, while the wartime foster mother had her letters. The police were called in to resolve the conflict, and they decided to send Betty home with her wartime foster mother. After that, the legal process went to the OPK, which recommended that she stay with her foster family.

Betty's family life after the war was shockingly rife with resentment and anger. She recalls that her foster mother would not let the visiting social workers speak with Betty directly and bitterly regrets that the social workers never asked her whether she was happy. She recalls being "miserable": "Living with that family for so many years after the war . . . I never felt love from them, never." Her foster parents often referred to her Jewish sexuality, something they saw as very different and much more menacing than the sexuality of non-Jews. They told her that she was a bad girl, meaning a loose one; they even called her a degenerate, suggesting that Jewish girls develop earlier and are more sexual than non-Jewish girls. She felt her foster sister's unkindness ("I hated her!") and felt completely ignored by her older foster brother ("I was air for him—he didn't look at me"), although she did get along well with her younger foster brother.

Her foster father was very authoritarian, and when they disagreed, he would say to Betty, *"Your blood and mine don't talk,"* a reminder that not only did they not get along, but also that they were not related. In his anger, he would say, *"When you are 21, you're leaving! You are going out!"* Understandably, Betty told me, "I always say that *for me, the war lasted till my twenty-first year."* She rented an apartment in Amsterdam the week before she turned 21, packed her bags, and on her birthday, the fifth of September, announced that she was leaving. Her father said, "Now? You can wait." "No," Betty responded, "you said 21, and I'm now 21, I'm going!" She said, "He didn't tell me to leave, but I left by myself. I was very happy to go; I thanked God I was 21!" Before leaving, she purchased and gave her foster father a television table and her foster mother a watch in her parents' names, so they would not think her ungrateful.

Although Betty had many friends, she also recognized that her experiences had forced her to be very protective of herself:

I had built a wall around me so that nobody could hurt me. But I was jealous of my friends who had parents, girlfriends who met with their mothers and went shopping. When I had problems, I had no one to go to.

Betty married another former hidden child when she was 29 and went on to build a strong family life, with two children.

In the early 1990s, when she was 50, Betty decided to read her file documenting her years as an orphan and a minor. Betty had to visit the JMW about ten times to read her thick dossier, in which she found shocking information about her past. First, it became clear that her foster family had only wanted her for financial reasons. They received 75 guilders monthly for her care, and her foster father documented and claimed every minute item she consumed, including the cost of the stamp that was on the letter he sent to make the claims! Second, she discovered that several Jewish families had wanted to adopt her after the war. Because she had had such an awful time in her foster family, this news, which she received only in middle age, sent her reeling. When the psychologist at JMW checked on her when she was done reading this part of her dossier, Betty recounts telling her, "It's a pity my foster parents are dead." "Why?" the social worker responded. "Because if they were alive, I would tell them to drop dead!" Betty also found out that when her case went to court, her foster father claimed that he had promised Betty's father that he would keep her until she was 21 if her parents did not return. The intermediary, the courier who brought Betty to her hiding family, attested to Betty much later in life that her father and foster father had never had such a conversation.

Betty's case occupies one end of the spectrum of experiences in foster families in postwar Holland. She is a warm and generous person, as is her husband; clearly, she had received warmth and love from her biological parents during her first three years of life. And although she's disappointed about the lost possibilities of being adopted by a loving family, she is not a bitter person. She's angry when she speaks about it, but she has not let it cloud her life. Despite her intense hatred of her foster family, she faithfully visited them until her foster parents died. She felt that she did that because of her parents' name and reputation. Betty did not want to enable her foster family to add to their list of anti-Semitic views the notion that Jews are ungrateful.

Philip was 10 years old at the war's end and stayed on with his foster family, not realizing that his sister and brother were alive elsewhere in Holland. It was not clear to him why his foster parents had not told him about their survival. Philip felt connected to his foster father but not to his foster mother. His foster father wanted to keep him after the war, but he believes that his foster mother wanted to send him to a children's home. After the war, he went to school, but he was an unhappy child who fought a lot at home. He also realizes that he became a difficult child, especially after he learned of his parents' deaths. During the seven years he stayed with his foster parents, the fights intensified. One night at dinner, during a fight, his foster mother threw a glass at Philip, and it cut him on the neck. According to the doctor, it was a dangerous cut. His foster mother could no longer cope with him, and he was sent to a children's home at age 15.

We have a mixed set of outcomes for those who stayed with their hiding families after the war. Although the transition into postwar family life went smoothly, it was not an easy situation for all these orphans. However, apart from the one case of outright greed and anti-Semitism, most of the other environments presented appear to have been fairly loving, and several hidden children who stayed with their foster families were very content. These narratives also demonstrate that their postwar experience did not always dictate how these former hidden children would react to it later. Betty is an excellent example of someone who was able to deal with a difficult environment successfully, while Rozette was in what seems to have been a good environment but has experienced considerable pain in coping with her past.

In August 2005 I had the privilege of presenting some of my findings to hidden children at the annual Conference of Jewish Child Survivors of the Holocaust in Amsterdam. About forty people attended, six of whom were in my study. The discussion after my talk went for forty-five minutes and could have gone longer, but we had to stop for the next session. I taped the discussion and include here some of the comments. One attractive woman with a Polish accent was an unusual example of an orphan:

> I would like to say that listening to you made me aware that the word *sociology* has value for me. I did like your explanation and your astute observation, and in comparison to the psychological studies I've read until now, I prefer yours. . . . Yours is much more objective. . . . You made me aware [for the] first time in my life that I'm an orphan. . . . It's valuable information, thank you very much. I was raised by a wonderful family. I never realized I was an orphan, though. But my parents *did* vanish and I *was* an orphan. And this was a wonderful way of categorizing, really. You should feel proud of your work. Thank you.

Many in the audience had strong verbal reactions to her statement, most of them shocked. One former hidden child said, "I'd like to know how come she didn't know she was an orphan." The Polish-born woman reiterated, "I just said I was raised by another family but a wonderful family, and I never thought about myself as an orphan, logically and psychologically." We do not know what her Polish foster family told her or how and when they told her, but clearly she felt grateful to and fulfilled by her foster family.

LEAVING FOSTER FAMILIES FOR OTHER FAMILIES

For the fifteen orphans who did not stay on with their foster families, the end of the war signified the beginning of life elsewhere, either with another family or in a children's home. In this section, I will focus on those who went to a family to which they were related. These eight females and one male ranged in age from 4 to 12. The four children who were under the age of 6 at the war's end still have no memory of their biological parents. Of the three girls who were 7 at the war's end, only one seems clearly to recall her parents.

What is striking about this group is the evidence that not all moves to the households of Jewish kin or of adoptive Jewish families improved or even maintained the child's well-being. Although the initial scandal that drew me to this study concerned the workings of the OPK and its decisions concerning the placement of Jewish war orphans, some of which may have been decidedly anti-Semitic, the narratives of such war orphans draw our attention to a less well-known phenomenon—problems *within* the Jewish families in which some war orphans were placed.

Another less-known fact that emerged from these narratives concerns not so much the fight over a Jewish child's guardianship between Jewish kin and non-Jewish foster families through the OPK but, rather, fights *among* Jewish kin over the orphan. These fights were usually between the two different sides of the orphan's family. While these orphans were fortunate to have some surviving relatives on both sides of their family, these kinds of fights had long-term detrimental effects. They sometimes meant that eventually ties were cut by the side that had "won" the child, restricting the orphan's access to other surviving relatives and a broader network of kin. The fact that so few Dutch Jews survived and that once-large families were reduced to a few surviving individuals highlights the tragedy of such estrangements. Any estrangement in the family was to the detriment of the child.

One last pattern clearly emerged concerning postwar family life and attachments. Of these nine orphans, three had had what they considered a wonderful connection with their foster family during the war, and the other six had lived in acceptable situations. However, when discussing their postwar lives as part of a relative's family, six still had acceptable situations, but three ended up in terrible, abusive ones. On the whole, then, the transfer of orphans to the homes of Jewish relatives ended up being problematic and made them unhappier than they had been when living with foster parents and in hiding during the war. For some orphans, the shocking rupture in their happy lives at the war's end created a lifelong pattern of detachment or other problems. And the three who experienced a bitter and unhappy postwar family life with relatives were exposed to continuous conflict, if not trauma. In making such an argument, I am in no way being an apologist for the OPK. Even if leaving some Jewish children in their foster homes would have been easier on them, if not better for them emotionally, this does not justify the heinous ways in which the OPK marginalized and ignored the Jewish community in its processes and decisions concerning Jewish orphans. And this argument is also not meant to blame some Jewish families for their dysfunction, which, in the cases of those who survived the war, is understandable. However, while dysfunction may be understandable, abuse is not and cannot be legitimized by the war.

The following sections will depict the shift made by this group of orphans, from Liberation to departure from their foster families to joining their new families. In this next section, I will depict individuals starting with the youngest; following that, I will analyze those whose postwar family lives were acceptable and then those who endured highly problematic family lives.

In the early 1940s, Yvonne's pediatrician had connected her biological family with a non-Jewish family who had lost a full-term baby and who took her into hiding. About her war years she says, "[They were] my happiest years, my lucky years." Her foster mother treated Yvonne like her own child: "I got all the love and everything that I needed. I was just their kid. . . . It was fun. I had everything, even a little brother." Yvonne's aunt was in hiding with the same family but appears not to have interacted with Yvonne during this period.

After the war, Yvonne's foster parents wanted to adopt her. They felt it was in her best interests, since they had raised her from infancy. However, Yvonne's aunt (her mother's sister), despite neither liking nor wanting children, claimed Yvonne because, as Yvonne explained, she detested the foster mother and did not want her to have Yvonne. Thus, Yvonne understands her aunt's desire to have her as driven more by competition with and spite for Yvonne's foster mother than by affection for Yvonne or loyalty to kin. Yvonne's paternal grandmother also wanted her since she had lost her son and Yvonne was her only grandchild. The grandmother had lived with Yvonne and her parents after Yvonne was born and felt "she had a right" to her. As Yvonne put it, "and so the fight started." This conflict was somewhat unusual in that it was a three-way fight. According to Yvonne, her OPK file displays that it was a "total mess . . . with constant fights" taking a good six months to resolve. Yvonne first went to her grandmother's house, and then was brought to her aunt and uncle's home.

The one male in this group, Jaap T., was less than a year old when he went into hiding with one family, with whom he stayed for almost four years. Jaap T.'s hiding time was fine as far as he can remember, although he admits that he may have repressed some memories. His foster parents were childless and had functioned as intermediaries for Jewish children in hiding. Their house served as a kind of transit station for children whose hiding destination was to be elsewhere. However, they ended up keeping Jaap T. "out of love" because it became too dangerous to pass him to another home. While he admires his foster mother for her strength—she told neighbors that if they betrayed Jaap T., she would kill them—he also readily acknowledges their limits. They were "poor, un-educated, good people" but "not fond of Jews"; they found Jews to be strange, a people very different from their own.

All of Jaap's grandparents and an aunt and uncle survived the war; his mother died in Auschwitz-Birkenau, and his father died in Ebensee after surviving Auschwitz and a death march. Jaap's biological family wanted him back, since his parents and aunt had agreed that they would care for each other's children should anything happen to any of them. However, his foster parents also wanted to keep him, ar-guing that they had no children, that they loved him, and that he was happy with them. A fight for custody developed into a lawsuit, with the OPK involved in the decision making. His aunt and uncle argued that *they* were his family and that the foster parents were "simple peo-ple." Furthermore, the foster parents were not technically married, which was held against them; they subsequently married to help their case. His aunt and uncle won the case, and Jaap T. joined their family, along with their daughter, who was a year younger than him, and a brother, who was three years younger. Later, another sister was born in 1949.

Jeannette and Eva were both about 3 years old when they were sent into hiding in 1942. Jeannette was hidden in eight different places, end-ing up with a young childless couple for two years, while Eva spent three years with a family who had recently lost a young daughter whose birth date was the same as Eva's. Jeannette's foster parents (the last couple with whom she stayed) were young and active in the Resistance. She felt fine about her foster father but did not like her foster mother, whom she described as "unkind, judgmental, not warm, and not nice. . . . I never felt any warmth from her." Jeannette describes her hiding period as neither easy nor particularly nice, but bearable.

Eva was one of the hidden children who felt that the best years of her childhood were spent with her hiding family. She was the one who told me several times that she had a "marvelous war." Eva believes that her foster family wanted to keep her after the war once it was clear that her parents would not return, and their wartime behavior suggests that she is correct. However, a woman who was not a blood relative but was related to Eva's half-brothers found her and took her back to Amsterdam.[4] Although Eva did not discuss that rupture specifically, her postwar years with this woman were dramatically different from her hiding years.

Jeannette, in contrast, also 6 years old at the war's end, had an uncle and a grandmother who survived, along with her younger brother. Jeannette's family tried to discover her whereabouts through an advertisement in the newspaper, to which a previous foster family responded; the current foster family ignored it, in the hopes of keeping her. Jeannette's uncle came to get her in July because he knew that in August the Oorlogspleegkinderen law, the War Orphan Law, was about to go into effect. Jeannette believes that her uncle appeared suddenly and took her immediately because he wanted to avoid a conflict with her foster family over her guardianship.

Jeannette did not recognize her uncle but vividly remembers the trip back to Amsterdam as a child. She particularly recalled getting on the train and fearing the big gap between the platform and the train car. Interestingly, she cannot recall if it was difficult to leave her foster family, but she does remember her uncle chatting with her on the train, telling her about a cousin and other relatives she would soon see. Jeannette explained that one adaptive strategy she developed as a 6-year-old who had lived with nine different families, including her own parents, was simply to "leave when [she had] to" without looking back or making a fuss.

Naomi was 3 when she went into hiding, and even though she somehow knew that her foster parents were not her "real" parents, it was traumatic for her to separate from them at the war's end. She believes that her foster parents treated her like their own child, but stating that they were "Northern people" from Friesland was a coded way of saying that they were not demonstrative, warm, or affectionate. When her guardian came to claim her, Naomi's foster parents refused to give her up. Naomi expressed several times how the trauma of separation never leaves. "One never forgets," she said.

Her parents had been very observant Jews, her father a *chazzan* (cantor) and Jewish teacher. They had asked older, childless friends who lived on their street to take Naomi and her two brothers after the war, should they not survive. When this new father arrived with one of her biological brothers, Naomi recognized her brother, but her foster parents would not give her up to anyone but her parents. Her foster parents fought to keep her, but finally their minister advised them to let her live with her two brothers, since her parents were no longer alive.

They agreed, and I was taken away. It was a drama, terrible. . . . I saw that all my stuff, all my toys, everything was lying there in front of this bus [with which they fetched me], *and I had to go away. So there we were standing, all of us were crying.*

Marian, who was 8 at the war's end, was very connected to her foster family. She had been with them for two and a half years, from age 5 $^1/_2$ until 8. Marian's parents had fled Germany in the early 1930s and met and married in Holland. They were killed, and Marian had no siblings or surviving grandparents. Two uncles, however, were alive, one of whom lived in the United States. Her foster family had started the adoption proceedings when her uncle arrived in his U.S. Army uniform to claim her.

Some time later, Marian was brought to Amsterdam and remembers being unhappy there. She was put on a plane to New York, and someone was asked to watch over her. Her aunt and uncle, whom she had never met, picked her up at the airport. As they drove her to her future home, their house, they argued in German, a language she no longer understood. This argument was only the first of many to come in Marian's life with them. At that time, she could not understand how her foster parents could let her depart:

Mostly, I was angry that they would have let me go. How could they love me yet let me go? This was explained to me. . . . I think they probably loved me more than the family I came to here [relatives in the United States].

Ruth W. was the oldest in this group—she was 9 when she went into hiding and hid with about fourteen different families. Ruth did not seem to have trouble leaving her last hiding family after the war. She had one surviving half-sister, Annie, and one surviving half-brother; they were both older than she. Ruth was happy to be living with Annie, who lived with her own daughter and her new partner, also widowed by the war (figure 6). During the war, Annie's daughter and husband had been in hiding, while Annie had been in a concentration camp, and only Annie and her daughter survived.

When I presented the findings from my research to participants in the 2005 Conference of Jewish Child Survivors, after my talk, at least two people brought up the issue of whether my research considers the feelings of the foster parents. One woman recounted that she had been hidden by a widow and her two sons but only found out much later in life that this foster mother had been attached to her. She told her, "You were the daughter I never had"; however, that sentiment had never been picked up on by the hidden child. Another woman corroborated that her foster mother also had been very attached to her but that she had never known it. Only some years ago did her foster mother tell her that she had mourned when this hidden child had left; however, the child had assumed that her foster mother didn't want her and had given her up "quite readily." Both these women encouraged me to find out more about the feelings foster parents had for the children in their charge, concerned that foster parents have been ignored in my research.

I agree with their basic argument; the reactions of foster parents and also of foster siblings are all important. However, my goal was to focus on the hidden child's perspective, even though there are clearly other views besides his or hers. Also, at this point most foster parents are dead. About fifteen years ago, Bloeme Evers-Emden did research on foster parents, which resulted in her book *Geleende Kinderen* (Borrowed Children, 1994). Many foster parents were deeply attached to their foster child, but

not all foster children felt their foster parents' deep attachment to them—
although clearly some did. Indeed, it is yet another very unfortunate aspect of this history that hidden children felt abandoned by foster parents,
some of whom were forced to give them up and would gladly have kept
them.

Life with Relatives

Three orphans, all girls, who went to live with kin ended up in tumultuous households where there was constant conflict and where they
were abused by their aunts. First I will describe these postwar family
lives, and then turn to other, less tempestuous, ones. It is vital to understand that while those in the latter group were not emotionally or physically abused by their postwar parents, almost none of them seemed to
bond with their families or to feel content in those homes.

After the war ended, an aunt found 7-year-old Lilly and brought her
home. Lilly's new blended family consisted of her aunt, the aunt's
daughter (who was age 15), and the daughter of her husband's brother
(who was 19). "Then my war started because I was old enough to understand. That for me was when the Second World War started, honest to
God." Lilly described how she was sent to the kitchen to be with the
maid when company came, was hit many times, and was given very different treatment than the other two girls. When Lilly began living with
her aunt, she continued to kneel down and pray before bedtime, as she
had been taught to do. "Instead of explaining it to me, she hit it out of
me." Lilly recalls an annual fair *(Kermis)* that occurred in a nearby village
that all the children attended: "The other two girls in the family were allowed to go, but I had to be at home, knitting from sheep wool for her
long underwear. I was honestly an *assepoester,* a Cinderella."

Late in life, Lilly found out that her aunt had received a monthly
stipend for her, just as the foster father had in Betty's case:

But that doesn't matter. She-yiheye la-briut.[5] *I don't care. But the fact is that
she forced me to take gymnastics, and that cost ten cents. Every Saturday I had
to ask for this stupid ten cents, and then she said, "You only cost me money, and*

you are a piece of shit," and she said much more to me, and worse. . . . She hit me
here on the back, you can still see it, with a spoon out of a boiling pot. . . . I tell
you, the war for me started after the war. [my emphasis]

Because Lilly was unable to concentrate in school, by age 9, the OPK
arranged for her to see a psychologist in Amsterdam. "I remember that
every question she asked me, I said 'I don't know, because I am crazy. I
know that I am crazy.' That was, of course, not true." A year later, in 1948,
when Lilly was 10 years old, a relative reported to the OPK that Lilly's
home life was not working. Lilly and her aunt were asked to come to
Amsterdam, where again a psychologist talked with Lilly. Subsequently,
the OPK removed her from her aunt's home. She was then placed in a
Jewish orphanage, which worked out well for Lilly, but the sad irony is
that her original foster family had been prepared to keep her all along.

Yvonne, described above as happy and beloved by her foster family,
went into hiding at about 10 months of age and was wanted by three different parties after the war. The OPK had to intervene in her case to resolve this conflict. Her paternal grandmother wanted her, since Yvonne
was her only grandchild, and they had lived together before the war. Her
aunt, her mother's sister, with whom Yvonne had been in hiding, also
wanted Yvonne, although she was not a child-friendly person. And finally, her foster parents loved her and fought to keep her ensconced in
their stable family life.

According to Yvonne's description, her aunt was a very difficult person who was impatient and highly critical. She had not gotten along well
with Yvonne's foster mother, who had also hidden her. Therefore,
Yvonne interprets her aunt's sudden interest in having her as being motivated more by the aunt's spite for Yvonne's foster mother than by her
interest in Yvonne's welfare. Yvonne's OPK dossier includes her foster
mother's negative opinion of the aunt as a possible foster mother for
Yvonne, a viewpoint that was apparently verified by others who were
less involved. The ongoing fight took its toll on Yvonne's foster parents,
and finally they gave up their quest to keep her. They decided, apparently on their own, to take Yvonne to her grandmother, who lived with
her unmarried daughter, Yvonne's paternal aunt, in Bussum. It seems as

though they realized they could not win custody of Yvonne, but they also wanted to subvert her maternal aunt's request for custody. Yvonne told me about her time in Bussum:

When I came to Bussum, I think that's where all my problems began. Whatever went on when I was in the war, I had safety. You know, I had a family, I had a brother, I had loving parents. I don't remember leaving them. What I remember, the next view I had, is that I walked into a room with people, I had my little toy elephant. . . . After a day or so, I said, "I want to go home, I want to go home to Papa and Mama, to Frank" [her foster brother]. *And I remember she* [her grandmother] *said, "Those people are not your parents, they don't ever want to see you again. . . . Don't even mention them." And that was that. . . . So this was a total abrupt ending of a life when I had just turned 4.*

Although most foster parents wanted to maintain contact with their foster child once he or she had moved, Yvonne's foster mother must have decided that it would be too painful to do so, and she cut all ties. Yvonne acknowledges, "Everyone did the best they could from pain, from their own sadness, from handing over a kid that they raised to people that weren't the parents." At the same time, today we are fully aware that such a dramatic change can feel like a rejection to a child. Indeed, Yvonne only found out decades later from her foster brother that when he returned home that day and asked for her, he was told, "Don't ever ask about her again": "And that was that. He never asked again until he was 35, and then he still wasn't told."

After crying a lot and not eating, she eventually adjusted to life with her Oma and her aunt. Her grandmother would point to a photo of her son and say, "That's your father": "I didn't know who the fuck it was . . . my own parents were an abstract thing." All in all, by the time she adjusted and began to feel better, her aunt and uncle found out that Yvonne had been moved illegally (without OPK permission) from the foster family to her grandmother's house in Bussum. Again they fought for her through the OPK, arguing that it was not healthy for a young girl to sleep in the same bed and spend the whole day with an older woman, while the aunt went to work and was not available. They, on the other hand, could offer her a room of her own and an aunt who would be home all day.

The OPK agreed to let her go to her aunt, who was put on probation for one year until it could be verified that she could handle having a child. Yvonne's first memory of entering her third family was arriving in Amsterdam and "being pulled out of the tram": "She pulled me impatiently because I didn't walk fast enough. She dragged me along, I had my little Dumbo elephant under one arm, [and I remember] her saying 'hurry hurry, hurry up!'" Yvonne was instructed to call her aunt and uncle "Mama and Papa."

By then, I had already hardened myself. You don't ask, you don't talk about anything. You keep your mouth shut, go with the flow. And close off. That's why I was a happy, well-adjusted little girl on the outside and on the inside, just dead.

That first year was not a good one for Yvonne, since her aunt criticized and berated everyone Yvonne held dear—her foster parents, her biological father, her living grandmother and aunt, even Yvonne's deceased mother, the aunt's own sister. Yvonne recounted that her aunt also felt free to criticize Yvonne, telling her that she was spoiled, that she ate too slowly, that she was stupid.

Everything, everybody I loved was pushed into the ground. There I was, 4 years old. I had no resources for even discussing this or defending myself or saying "that's not true." You just stand there, you swallow it. My aunt was a horror. That year she kind of behaved because she stayed home, but she was absolutely horrible. She had no patience.

Yvonne's aunt also abused her physically: "She used to beat the hell out of me to get rid of all those things that irritated her in me." After the year of probation ended and Yvonne was in nursery school, her aunt took a job and Yvonne became a "latchkey kid."

Yvonne's uncle was kind to her and took care of her when he wasn't working. However, he was not able fully to override the negative effects his wife had on Yvonne. It was also helpful to Yvonne that she could visit her paternal grandmother and her maternal grandfather, who had remarried. However, a fight between the aunt and the aunt's father (Yvonne's maternal grandfather) led to a long-term break in communication, and Yvonne saw her grandfather less. Although her aunt and uncle had made the argument that Yvonne should be in a Jewish home, they did not engage in any Jewish practices or observe any holidays. Indeed, Yvonne recalls sitting on her uncle's lap and being told the story of Maria, Joseph, and baby Jesus, and enjoying their Christmas tree! Yvonne now understands how she began to cut herself off from her feelings to tolerate the abuse and to survive, and she understands how that pattern led to a lifetime of disassociation, emotional turmoil, and very low self-esteem.

The last person in this group, Marian, was surrounded by constant bickering and quarreling: "I never saw a sign of affection between them [her aunt and uncle]." Marian found out much later that her uncle, a doctor, had been having a long-term affair with one of his patients. She also concedes, "I must have been a difficult and remote child too by this time. . . . I just remember always feeling uncomfortable because my aunt was very needy. This made my life difficult."

Marian recalls an unhappy childhood and adolescence in the United States and a depression that only lifted much later when her aunt died. She also recalls being a "goody-goody." Marian never asked her new parents about the war or her biological parents—by not asking, she convinced herself that her aunt and uncle were her real family. Even though she finds Holland claustrophobic when she returns to visit, she is adamant that her life would have been better had she stayed with her Dutch foster family—"they were liberal, nice, good people" to whom she was deeply attached. Her aunt became verbally abusive to Marian and resentful that Marian didn't love her. They were estranged later when Marian became an adult.

The other six orphans in this category were not in dire straits when they lived with their relatives, but they did not fare particularly well either. I separated these two groups because of the highly problematic familial contexts in which the three orphans discussed above found themselves. Although the children I describe below also had some difficulties, these conflicts were more passive than direct.

The first case concerns an orphan who had been hidden, discovered, and then interned in two concentration camps and sent to a Jewish orphanage briefly at the war's end. Greet was born in 1942, and in 1943, she was hidden but betrayed.[6] She was sent to Westerbork under conditions about which she knows very little. Her parents and a baby brother born in hiding were also sent to Westerbork and killed in a concentration camp. At age 2, Greet was part of a transport of fifty-one *unbekannte Kinder* (unknown children) sent from Westerbork to Bergen-Belsen. She ended up in Theresienstadt. According to Greet, at a reunion of the children on the transport, a Dutch woman who had accompanied the children on the train told the following poignant story:

[I] *had been unable to forget a small child named Greetje who was crying, crying, crying twenty-four hours a day. She couldn't stop crying, and I didn't know where she was getting all those tears from. Poor child, she had very itchy arms, she had eczema. I made bandages so that it didn't hurt her so much. And I was thinking all my life about this little girl, if she survived, and if she was OK.*

And that child was Greet, who had no memory of this period.

Greet survived two camps and dysentery and at the end of the war, she was sent to a Jewish children's home for a few months. Both sides of her family wanted her and fought over her guardianship. Her uncle, her father's brother, was supposed to be her guardian after the war. He had three children. However, another uncle, a widower whose wife had been Greet's father's eldest sister, also claimed her. He and his wife had been sent to Auschwitz, and she never returned. He married a widow after the war, adopted a child eleven years older than Greet, and also wanted Greet to join their new family. This fight was taken to the OPK, and Greet's guardianship was granted to the deceased aunt's husband, perhaps because he did not have any children of his own.

Greet loved her "stepfather," as she called him, but her stepmother was "just stupid. She didn't know how to handle things." Family life seems to have been fine, and both adults were warm and affectionate with Greet, a person who has learned to shield her feelings. Her stepfather died young, when Greet was 21, and her stepmother clearly expected Greet to devote her life to her. Her stepmother had never allowed the relatives who did not get guardianship to see Greet. She had claimed they were terrible people—crooks and cheats. When Greet was 22, her other uncle called and wanted to meet. The stepmother told Greet, " 'If you do so, then you will never inherit my money.' So I said, 'OK, then I won't inherit your money; I go to my uncle.' That was the [laughs] choice I had to make, and she kept her promise."

When Greet met her husband, Rob (different from the Rob in this study), her stepmother again demanded that Greet make a choice— between Rob and the stepmother. Luckily Greet was strong enough to choose Rob; her stepmother did not even come to their wedding. As her stepmother aged, Greet helped her out with transportation, and she seemed to soften a bit. However, she clearly reiterated to Greet, "It's all very nice and well that we see each other again. But when I die, you will never have any money. Everything goes to your sister." Greet didn't respond but always felt that it was "her [the stepmother's] problem."

Although Greet was very capable of making her own decisions, unhampered by her stepmother's hostility, she admitted that it was upsetting to be treated so badly and especially to see her children treated poorly by their grandmother. Greet's stepsister (the other girl who was adopted after the war) did not tell her that her stepmother had died until the funeral was over, because the stepmother had not wanted Greet to be present. Thus, not only did her stepmother hold a very long-term and seemingly unreasonable grudge against Greet, taking it out on Greet's children, but Greet's stepsister clearly collaborated with the stepmother against her. Given that there was an inheritance involved, it is possible that Greet's stepsister did not want Greet present at the funeral so that she could demonstrate who was the better daughter.

My interview with Greet was interesting yet contradictory. Greet was attractive, pleasant, and easygoing, but it was difficult to elicit much emotion from her about the effects of her past. She never cried during the interview, which seemed unusual, given her history. However, one might argue that in light of her history—being separated from her parents before the age of 2 and sent to concentration camps—this emotional distance is completely understandable. While this was not a case in which abuse occurred during childhood, one might argue that the stepmother was emotionally abusive toward Greet after her husband's death. After all, most would agree that not letting a child meet a relative who knew her dead parents in addition to asking her to give up the chance for a husband and family in order to serve her stepmother are both unreasonable, to say the least. Perhaps the stepmother felt that Greet owed her a great deal because she and her husband had "saved" her; however, she also seemed to feel that Greet should pay with her life. Cases such as this one and some that follow suggest that family was hardly a haven for these young Jewish people; indeed, some might have been happier in orphanages.

Six-year-old Eva, the orphan who had described her foster father as "fantastic," was taken by 50-year-old Borah (short for Deborah) to live with her in Amsterdam. As mentioned earlier, Borah was related to Eva's father's deceased first wife. Eva was plucked from a caring environment in which she was very happy, perhaps the happiest she had ever been, and taken to live with a woman who meant well but was not warm. Eva found it strange and regretted that Borah did not also take in Eva's half-brother (Borah's nephew), since he had lived with Borah after his mother's death before the war. "He lived with a foster family from 1945 to 1947, and they wanted to get rid of him." A Jewish organization found some relatives of theirs in New York and sent him there. "It was a decision which makes me very angry until today, that they separated us siblings. I think that's the worst thing they could have done to us. We were just the two of us from this family, and they separated us, which is a terrible thing to do." Apparently the relatives in New York were wealthy but heartless, and he left them when he was 17 years old, severing contact for over forty years.

Eva believes that Borah did not take her brother because he was seen as too difficult and traumatized, since he had a tic and still wet his bed. "I think she expected more complications with bringing him up than with bringing me up, and that was a mistake because I was worse [laughs]. I turned out to be worse. I was a rebel, and he is so nice, so easy and so sweet." Eva's paternal grandparents survived the war in the south of France, and so she was able to visit them when they returned to Holland after the war. They were too old to take in their surviving grandchildren, but it was yet another loss for the grandparents that "they lost him alive," meaning that they lost their surviving grandson when he emigrated to the United States.

Eva was clearly not fond of Borah, who she acknowledges "was doing her best": "She couldn't help it that I didn't love her." As I tried to get more of a sense of the dynamic between Eva and Borah, Eva explained, "She was not a talking person like I am. She talked as little as possible. She was a working woman; she was cleaning the house and selling her things and trying to forget about the war and those experiences, trying to forget all those nasty things."

Although her time with Borah was not remarkable in any way, Eva also reflected on how she learned to contain a great deal of her anger about her past. Well into her adult life, when she was under emotional stress, Eva turned this anger against herself by tearing out her hair and scratching her scalp until it bled. Although I found her to be a lovely and engaging person, and I enjoyed talking with her, she described to me how she unconsciously has cut off many of her feelings as a result of this rupture in trust when she was moved out of her foster family's house. Much to her consternation, this detachment continues today, at times with her own family.

Jeannette, who, like Eva, was also about 6 years old at the war's end, was brought back to her surviving relatives in Amsterdam by her uncle. Shortly thereafter, she was reintroduced to her 3-year-old brother, with whom she had little connection at the time. She was sent to live with her mother's cousin and her husband in Amsterdam, whose son was about her age and also had been in hiding. Their family was adjusting to being back together after losing those crucial years, and it was very difficult. Jeannette and her cousin fought a lot, which was also unpleasant. Jeannette described her aunt: "[She] was not very nice to me in many ways. She tried to be very nice, but it was a difficult situation. I was not really part of the family. She wasn't very warm." She recalls a number of rules that she and her cousin had to follow; for example, she was not allowed to hum. Jeannette explained that as a 6-year-old, she hummed "constantly as a defense mechanism, to shut out the world."

There was a conflict between her father's and mother's sides of the family over Jeannette and her brother. Her father was one of five siblings, four of whom survived. Three of those who survived were unmarried women, one of whom wanted to take care of Jeannette and her brother.

She told me that her uncle, her mother's brother, would not hear of this: "He didn't want us to grow up in a household with spinsters; he wanted a real family for us." Shortly after his marriage, this uncle took Jeannette's 3-year-old brother. His wife was pregnant and gave birth to a premature baby, and shortly after that, Jeannette joined their household. So, as she jokingly states, her aunt had three children in one year. This means that Jeannette stayed with relatives from the paternal side of her family for about one year before moving to be with her maternal uncle and aunt. She was joining her eleventh family at the age of 7. When asked what it was like to begin yet again, she explained, matter-of-factly, "I just did it"; she learned to draw on her highly evolved adaptive abilities. "I just kind of adapted; you didn't have much choice. No one really talked about anything."

Jeanette does not recall having been told that her parents died, but when she asked her aunt where her grandparents were, she was told, "They are on vacation." "And I *remember* that answer. I *know* she said it, and I *knew* it was a lie, right then and there. So when people lie like that, then you know you can't really talk to them."

After seven to eight years, her uncle and aunt decided to emigrate to the United States. By then they had two children of their own, in addition to Jeannette and her brother. Fourteen-year-old Jeannette once again had to separate from family unwillingly. She had to leave her aunts, a cousin to whom she was close, and her grandmother, with whom she had lunch every week. Like most 14-year-olds, she did not want to move and was happily ensconced in her school, social life, and family life in Amsterdam:

That was a little difficult, because I really loved, I just loved, being in Amsterdam, and I really didn't want to leave at all. Leaving my grandmother, I suppose, it's again one of those things. It was hard, and yet that was just one of those things that I did because I had no choice.

She never saw her grandmother again.

Jeannette's interview offered a glimpse of a textured family life. She felt closer to her uncle than to her aunt but basically never felt as though she belonged to their family. Although she believes that they felt like parents toward her and her brother, she says that she and her brother always felt like stepchildren: "You really felt that she had made this giant sacrifice in her life to have us, but I was never their child." She always felt she had to be grateful for what her aunt and uncle had done for them, and she tried to be "good." Her brother, however, acted out, and as a result, he was hit frequently. Another relative told her much later in life that from his observations, she and her brother were clearly not treated the same as her aunt and uncle's biological children:

It's hard to know exactly how. It's just that with children, . . . you let them get away with things because you have this unconditional love. Well [voice fades somewhat], *no one ever had that* [for me] [tears well up in her eyes]. *No one.*

Although no expense was spared for Jeannette's education, she realized as an adult, when she was in college, that her uncle was paying for her education (and later her wedding) with money left by her parents. "It was weird when I realized that. . . . The accounting was so exact, it made you feel that maybe you weren't really part of the family after all, even though my uncle had done it with great love and care." This distinct sense of having received different treatment than her aunt and uncle's own children continued as Jeannette had her own family after her uncle's death:

Although she [the aunt] *was definitely their grandmother, there was definitely a "but." She never wanted to have them overnight, she was always afraid to have them by herself. So there was a real relationship, but I never felt it was as much as . . . it would have been nice, but, you know.*

Jeannette saw a real difference in the way her aunt treated her biological grandchildren compared with how she was with her adopted grandchildren.

Jaap T. lived with his aunt and uncle after they won the fight over who would raise him and after they took him from his foster parents. He did not have a particularly bad experience, but neither did he have a positive one. He went to live with them, by then his third family, at about age 5 and was told later that he was a difficult child. While they did not punish him, there was definitely not enough understanding. "There was love, sincere and real, both from aunt and uncle, whom I called mom and dad, and from the whole family. I had a happy youth in spite of everything. But definitely, they were unwise people." Jaap was an anxious boy, and rather than help him with his anxieties, his uncle made fun of him.

Jaap recalls his aunt as someone who was unable to show affection to anyone; he was clearly not connected to her. His relationship with his uncle was better. He remembers his grandmother as loving, but he didn't want her affection. His uncle and aunt had a difficult time telling him about his family's past and about the fate of his real parents. Social workers from L'Ezrat ha-Yeled urged them to tell him, as he later read in his dossier. Although Jaap had some clues about his parents, he did not really know the truth:

My grandmother made me crazy because I had to visit her every day. She lived around the corner and had a big photograph of my real parents on the wall. And of course I could only call them "uncle," my real parents, because I didn't know. So every day she said, "Look at them. Oom Sam and Tante Esther. They were good people." She made me crazy, so to speak.

Jaap is an accomplished professional and admits that he is doing well; however, he told me, "The most difficult part of my experience was losing my parents, and for several years during my childhood living in uncertainty about my own identity."

Chava was 8 years old at the end of the war. Her parents had been killed in Sobibor. She was sent to a Jewish orphanage, even though Bep, the unmarried woman who sheltered her, wanted to keep her. However, her aunt, her mother's sister, survived, and Chava had expected to be adopted by her. Apparently, though, none of the surviving aunts or uncles was willing to take her, and the OPK would not let Bep, an unmarried woman, adopt her. Although Bep had good intentions, she also had made it clear that she wanted to baptize Chava. Chava's sister was allowed to stay with her Protestant hiding family after the war, but Chava was sent to the children's home in Hilversum, and Bep moved to a nearby village. Chava explained that her biological mother had made her intentions known during the war, saying, "*Mijn kind niet naar een in-*

stituut": My child should not be sent to an institution. However, Chava was sent to a children's home for four years, and she looks back at that time with great fondness.

In 1949, when Chava was 12, Israel became a state, and she was sent there to live with her uncle:

He had three of his own children, younger than me. I think it was a difficult time, to put an adolescent in the family, very difficult. I think it was not a very good decision. . . . I had to be with my uncle in Eretz Yisrael [the land of Israel], *which was the Zionist solution for me because my parents* [had] *ultimately wanted to emigrate.*

Sometimes Chava felt like a daughter to her aunt and uncle, sometimes not. After being with them for a few months, she visited the group of Dutch Jewish orphans with whom she had traveled and returned home visibly different—she was happy. Because of the noticeable change in her mood, her aunt asked her if she'd prefer to be in a children's home, but Chava said she would not.

Family life had its tense moments. Chava was rebellious, and there were quarrels; she felt that her aunt and uncle were not tolerant of her. She realizes that she was angry with her uncle because she had arrived with unrealistically high expectations and ended up being disappointed. On top of that, their economic situation was not good. Chava described to me what in retrospect she feels would have been the "wisest decision":

I would have gone to a children's home [in Israel] *with all the other children and been able to come often to my family—weekends, holidays, and vacation—and I think that would have been the best solution. It was not only the adjustment to my family, it was difficult to adjust to class, Israeli children. I had to adjust in too many areas.*

In Chava's case, a better solution in her eyes would have entailed remaining in a home for orphans rather than living with extended family.

Ruth W. was the oldest in this group of orphans—age 12 at the war's end. As mentioned above, she was thrilled to find and be with her half-sister, Annie, an older woman (age 31) who had cared for Ruth when she was very young and her biological mother had died (figure 6). However, Annie, a young survivor of Auschwitz, had her 5-year-old daughter, Chaja (Chaya), to care for as well; and their separation during the war had its effects on Chaja and on their relationship. Chaja had been in hiding with her mother and father during the war, but they were betrayed. When the police came to take them away, the hiding mother claimed that Chaja was her own child. Chaja's father did not survive Auschwitz. When Annie came to claim Chaja, she was greeted by a child who, like many I have already described, no longer recognized her mother. Thus, there was already considerable emotional turmoil in this family.

In the midst of all this, it was clear that little "Ruthie" was a difficult child, and a very needy one at that:

I was happy, but I was a very wounded child, an impossible child, really impossible—with puberty and all the scars from the war. When I talk with Annie about it today, she says, "What the hell *did we know about this?"*

After about two years, Annie ended up living with and marrying another survivor, a man who had been in the Resistance and had been friends with her and her deceased husband before the war. Chaja had a difficult time accepting her new stepfather, and at some point, it was too much for Annie to cope with Ruth's needs on top of everything else. Ruth was sent to live at her half-brother's home, where she felt very alone and unhappy:

It was a disaster; I just hated his wife. She was a very cold character with no warm feelings for me. It was just a terrible house. If ever I was not treated well, it was by my sister-in-law. The most terrible memories I have is that I couldn't live with my sister and her children, and I couldn't live with my brother. . . . For the first time, I became aware that they were not my real *brothers and sister, that they were my half-brothers and sister. So what did I have? I had nobody, you know? And I went to a Jewish girls' home.*

The girls' home ended up being a good option for Ruth, and she very much liked the director, a Jewish woman and a psychologist. However, the home was closed when it was revealed that the director was having an affair with the orphanage's doctor. Again Ruthie was afloat, and this time she was sent by L'Ezrat ha-Yeled to a Christian family that wanted her to convert. She left that house and went to a half-Jewish home in which the people had been in the Resistance. She flourished in this home, but when she was 17, right after finishing school, her brother (and guardian) decided that she needed to go to Israel and meet a Jewish man. He sent her to Israel supposedly for a three-month vacation to a childless aunt and uncle, who took her passport and wouldn't let her leave. Because Ruth knew that they all wanted her to marry a Jew, her rebellious streak guided her, leading her to decide, "I'm going to look for a black Arab! [laughs] I didn't quite succeed, but I found a black Moroccan Jew [laughter] as a boyfriend, and my family threw me out! They said, 'She's impossible!' and I said, 'But he's a *Jew,* for God's sake!' [laughs]."

LIVING IN A NEW HOME WITH A NEW FAMILY

In some cases, Jewish families in the Netherlands wanted, or at least offered, to adopt an orphan after the war. Two young men who appear in the next chapter were offered this option, and both refused. They did not want to become ensconced in a situation that might not work out, and even if it did, they did not want to feel obligated to people they might not love. These refusals were influenced by their experiences with families during the war, in hiding. However, some orphans, such as Chava and Greet, were not asked their opinions about such choices—the decisions were made about them and for them by the OPK, and as their narratives suggest, they may have been happier remaining with other children in orphanages.

This section presents the narratives of two people in my sample who lived with a Jewish family that wasn't kin. Naomi's was one of the least troubled cases in this subcategory. There was a fight over Naomi as well. Her mother had had seven siblings. Naomi's grandmother hid with her youngest daughter and son-in-law, and they were the only ones to survive—all the seven other siblings, with their spouses and children, were murdered. No one returned from her father's side of the family. Her grandmother and aunt did not want Naomi's two older brothers, but they did want custody of Naomi. Naomi stated, "I am so glad that my foster parents said, 'No, she is living with her brothers, and that is so important because they are the nearest relatives, so she should stay with us.'" After the war she and her brothers grew up with a highly religious Orthodox Jewish family who had been friends of their parents. She no longer knew Jewish life, and relearning it felt strange and awkward to her:

They said I had to eat kosher. When I came there, I didn't know what kosher was. The first Shabbat, I wanted to do something, I wanted to play, and you are not allowed to do many things on Shabbat. So I thought I wanted to draw. No, I wasn't allowed to [sighs]. I know a little bit how to knit. No, I wasn't allowed to. The only thing what you could do was read. So I read much [laughs], I must say. We went to the Beit ha-knesset—to the synagogue. I didn't understand it too much. It was different from what I saw in the church, and I couldn't read [the prayerbook]. My father always said, "Now when you are living with us, we live in the Jewish way. Afterward when you want to live different, you live different."

I did not get a strong sense of family dynamics from Naomi, although she talked about having been a difficult teenager. She only commented that she tried to please and to be nice and that she "hardly dared to breathe": "I always thought that when I am a good girl, they will treat me well." She was aware that the OPK was checking on them, to make sure that everything was working out. She believes that had it not worked well, she would have been put into an orphanage and not necessarily sent to her grandmother.

Naomi was already working as a kindergarten teacher when at age 24 she went to Israel for a month of vacation, at her family's urging. She liked it so much that she returned two years later to make aliyah. Of all the hidden children interviewed, Naomi stayed at home the longest. My sense is that this decision was due to an acceptable, if not good, atmosphere at home, in addition to her previous two traumas of having separated from her parents and then from her foster parents, something she referred to several times during our interview.

Lidy, age 7, was initially in an orphanage for a few years and remembers being happy there, especially in comparison to the household of her punitive hiding family. When she was 10, Lidy agreed to be adopted by a couple from Gouda. The man was Jewish, and the wife was not; they had one child, who was two years older than Lidy:

And they promised me everything—I don't have to eat what I don't like to eat and so many things, and I thought, "Wow, that's great." So after a couple of visits, I went there. Till today, I regret it because I had a terrible time over there. I was then 10 years old. When I was 11, he raped me. Several times. He tried it many times, but he didn't always succeed. And then I called the OPK when I was 12. First I tried to tell my stepmother, and she was shouting at me and saying, "You are lying." So the OPK came here to take a look at how everything was going, and I was afraid to tell. So I phoned Amsterdam and asked them to come because I want to talk to them. Nobody believed me. . . . And that was going on for four years, and then I ran away.

At age 16, Lidy returned to the orphanage in Amsterdam for asylum but was sent back to her foster parents; still no one believed her:

He came [to me] in the bathroom, or he asked me to come into his bed in the morning when my mother left the bed . . . to make breakfast. It was such a terrible time; it is very difficult for me to talk about it because it was a stamp on all my life. And I can't tell you, I can't express my anger still to that man because not only did he touch me all the time, but he made me feel dirty . . . and nobody believed me. Till now, I don't understand why. It's very difficult for me to talk about it. It's the most terrible thing that can happen to a little girl when she's alone. . . . And I was there another two years, and it didn't happen so many times, almost never, because I was fighting. And then I really ran away and never came back. I went to the same kinderhuis *[orphanage].*

They did not send 17-year-old Lidy back this second time. Understandably, she could not concentrate in school and quit early:

But till today, it influences my life. I can't see a movie where there is a rape. I have eight grandchildren, that means five girls, and the big one is 16. When I see her, I am so afraid. That was the bad story of my whole life—that time in Gouda. You have no idea. You have no idea.

Years later the couple's younger son told Lidy that he believed her story because his father also had sexually abused him. This acknowledgment from one family member was extremely meaningful to Lidy, in light of everyone's else's denial:

I had Jewish lessons from somebody in Rotterdam. I tried to tell him, he was a Rav [rabbi], and he phoned Amsterdam. Nobody believed him. I can't express my feelings to the OPK. How is that possible that children are crying for help, but they don't believe them? It's a stamp on your whole life because you are always afraid. . . . When I heard that he [the father] was ill—he had cancer—I was only praying that it would take a very long time. That's very bad to say; it was my wish, and I was disappointed that it went so quickly. I didn't go to the funeral. I was so glad.

Lidy suffered from depression for twenty years and was in therapy and on medication. As it does for others who have suffered from sexual abuse, the rape took center stage in her life. It overshadowed any possibility of dealing with her parents' deaths. As an adult, Lidy saw her dossier at JMW and was shocked to find that nothing about the rape or her running away to the orphanage had been written up, another sign that no one had believed her. "The most proof I have came from the second son when he said, 'I believe you. I knew it. I knew it.'"

After having a stroke nine months before I met her, she was diagnosed with thyroid cancer and had surgery. "Suddenly I thought since I could handle that beast over there, I can handle this also." When I interviewed her in 2000, Lidy (then age 63) emphasized that her main focus and joy is her grandchildren. She explained that the love she gets from all eight of them soothes her: "It makes so many things good. . . . That's the biggest gift God gave me—grandchildren." There seems to be a healing quality to her relationship with her grandchildren, perhaps especially since she tries to ensure that her granddaughters are protected and safe from the kind of abuse she experienced.

CONCLUSIONS

This chapter detailed the family lives of those orphans who spent most of their postwar childhood and adolescent years with a family—either remaining with their hiding family, moving to the home of other relatives, or, in two cases, moving to the home of a nonrelated Jewish family. For the most part, these narratives are not happy ones. In general, the most satisfying and connected postwar family experience occurred among the three who stayed on with their hiding families; perhaps I would also include that of Naomi, who lived with her parents' friends and her siblings. With one exception, hiding parents who kept their Jewish foster child did so because of their attachment to and love for the child. In other words, keeping a Jewish child until he or she became an adult was much more of a conscious choice for these families than hiding them in the first place might have been. Some hiding families were so attached to their Jewish foster children that they would have been very willing to keep them on, had their parent(s) not survived. Indeed, we have seen situations in which foster parents did not want their child to be found. Further, several foster parents were willing (and happy) to keep their foster child but were convinced by Jewish social workers to let the child go to allow him or her to live with a Jewish family. In a number of cases in which the Jewish child was happily ensconced in a foster family, he or she was removed but never adopted by another family.

Jewish children who were taken in by Jewish kin did not fare well as a group. Most of them felt like stepchildren and never felt fully accepted and loved. Indeed, we have seen several cases in which young girls were treated abusively by their aunts, as though being orphaned were not painful enough. As in the previous chapters on children whose parents returned, we can imagine that a number of these young people would have fared better had they stayed with their foster families who adored them rather than going to live with blood relatives who were coping with the fallout from the war. Although the children found themselves in a more Jewish environment when they lived with their kin, the poor quality of family relations may have mitigated some of the positive effects of being raised in their own culture and religion. We also saw that in some Jewish families, very little Judaism or Jewish culture was actually present.

Indeed, many of the narratives in this chapter and in previous ones suggest that blood is not necessarily thicker than water and that a notion of the family based on biology was sometimes too limiting, if not harmful. This study underscores the possibility and importance of attachments formed among nonkin, relationships that are sometimes superior to those in a "real" (biological) family. In such cases, it would have been in the best interests of the children to have kept them with their hiding families, if the families wanted them and if the children were doing well. To mitigate the effects of being raised in a non-Jewish household, the Jewish community could have arranged for some kind of Jewish education on a regular basis, including summer camps during school holidays.

8 "There Was Never a Kind Word"

LIFE IN JEWISH ORPHANAGES

If an orphan did not end up living with a family, the only other option for him or her was to stay in an orphanage. Several Jewish orphanages existed in the Netherlands after the war, and they seem to have been of greatly varying quality. These orphanages provoked strong feelings in those who lived there, everything from love to hatred, and sometimes both. While this chapter illuminates the various twists and turns of postwar life for certain Jewish orphans, it also points to the uneven and in some cases heinous conditions of some Jewish orphanages. However, even in the better-run orphanages, the one gift that the Jewish community could and should have bequeathed to its postwar children but did not is ironically one of the most highly valued Jewish traditions—that of education. With few exceptions, those who ended up in orphanages received little education beyond high school and were not trained in vocational skills. Thus, they entered adulthood and the labor force greatly unprepared. They had only their own common sense and strengths on which to rely, and most remain bitter about the shortsightedness of the Jewish community in an area that had long-term implications for their well-being.

The previous chapter on orphans who lived in a family for most of their postwar years included several cases in which children initially spent some time after the war in an orphanage but ultimately left for a family, either kin, near-kin, or a new adoptive family. The time spent in an orphanage ranged from a few months to five years. Already discussed were two cases of orphans who were removed from their postwar family settings and sent to an orphanage. In both cases, this change worked out well for the children. We will begin with those who had short-term stays in an orphanage, and then turn to the other orphans, all males, who spent most of their postwar years as minors in an orphanage. The oldest one spent only a few years in an orphanage, but the younger ones spent up to eleven years in one. In most cases either they were not wanted by surviving relatives, or the surviving relatives were not mentally fit to care for them. Their experiences in different Jewish boys' homes are mixed—two males were able to attain a higher education and became professionals, owing to luck and circumstances, but others were not as fortunate. This chapter focuses somewhat more on the former two— Louis G. and Josef—in great part because of the detail provided in their narratives.

TEMPORARY STAYS

Five orphans, mostly female, spent some time in an orphanage, but not all their postwar years, as minors. For them, the orphanage was either the first stop on the way to somewhere else or the last stop after having lived with a family where things did not work out. In all these cases, former hidden children remember their time in the orphanage with great fondness and nostalgia. Some of this attitude reflects the different approaches of the various orphanages, since some were more rigid and cold than others. However, it is likely that some of this nostalgia also reflects how much better the orphanage was for those children who had been in difficult family situations. There may be a little overromanticization at play in some of these fond memories, but if so, it only serves to emphasize how much worse these children's family settings must have been.

After the war, 8-year-old Chava was not allowed to continue living with her foster mother, a single woman, so she was sent to an orphanage in Hilversum, where she lived for four years. She loved the children's home:

I know other children did not love it, but I loved it . . . there was no tension. It was Orthodox, but not depressing, and we had a lot of freedom to do or not to do [whatever we wanted]. *We could amuse ourselves. We were allowed to meet children from school, non-Jewish children, and we went to a non-Jewish school. We could visit friends at their houses but not eat there.*

Chava was happy to return to the children's home after spending weekends with her relatives, and she did well in school. When she was 12, in the year of Israeli independence, she was sent to live with an uncle in Israel, a situation that was not optimal. As mentioned in the last chapter, her favorite times in Israel were when she got together with the other Dutch Jewish orphans, and she now feels that she would have been happier living with them.

Lidy was one of the orphans who started off in an orphanage, a period that she remembers fondly. Lidy's hiding family had punished her for wetting her bed and for not eating her dinner. She believes that they hid her for what they had hoped would be financial rewards after the war. Her parents did not survive the war, and when she was 8, her brother arrived at her foster home with a representative from the OPK. Lidy was taken to a coed Jewish orphanage in Amsterdam, while her brother remained with his foster family. "I was very glad to leave, even though nobody told me where I was going." She never returned to visit her foster family because, she claims, of their intention to baptize her.

She stayed in the *kinderhuis* (children's home) for two years. "I had a very, very nice time over there. I did. Very, very nice [with emphasis]. [The couple who cared for the children was] very kind and very warm, and it was great. It was like I was a newborn." When she continued with her Catholic prayers, they gently explained to her that she needed to stop because she was Jewish. Clearly, there was kindness in this setting, and no one tried to change her behavior by beating her with a belt, as her hiding family had. Her uncle in Antwerp wanted to adopt her, but because he had taken his niece as a lover and was living with her, it was not allowed. Her stay at the orphanage remained a pleasant time for the two years. "I was very happy there, and was laughing and having fun. I went to school, and people were nice. That was a great time."

The rest of Lidy's narrative appeared in the previous chapter, since she was adopted from the children's home by a Jewish man and his Gentile wife. As discussed, he raped her over the course of many years, and although Lidy voiced complaints about it and ran away to the children's home, no one believed her. When she ran away to the orphanage a second time at age 17, she was finally allowed to stay. In her case, compared to her experiences with her hiding family and her postwar adoptive family, especially her Jewish adoptive father, living at the children's home evoked her fondest memories.

Since she first moved in with Jewish kin, Lilly was introduced in the previous chapter. A 7-year-old at the war's end, she was taken home by an aunt who had found her but who then treated her like a maid, or, as Lilly stated, like Cinderella *(assepoester)*. However, after the OPK noticed that Lilly's home life was not working, she was moved to the Beerstichting (Beer Foundation), a coed Jewish orphanage, where Lilly had "a wonderful time": "It was fantastic [delight in her voice]. I had girlfriends, I was laughing, we were together, we did stupid things together . . . it was unbelievable fun." In comparison to where she had been her previous few years, the orphanage was a relief and a welcome change. Lilly's aunt never visited her in the orphanage, where she lived for eight years. However, Lilly had to visit her aunt once a year, and she described how a week before she had to go, she began to dread it and feel ill.

Ruth W. went to a girls' home after things did not work out well when she lived first with her half-sister and her family, and then with her half-brother and his family. The girls' home ended up being a good option for Ruth, and she very much liked the director. The director appears to have been very interested in the girls' development, but then the home was closed, and Ruth was sent to another family and then eventually to Israel, to live with a family there.

Philip was 10 at the war's end and ended up staying with his hiding family for ten years. However, as mentioned in the previous chapter, he became more and more difficult after he learned of his parents' deaths, and he and his foster mother fought a great deal. When he was 15, after an especially bad fight, they sent him to a children's home. This was far from a bad ending; Philip was happy to leave and went to an Orthodox Jewish boys' home in Amsterdam. Coming as he had from a life of daily Bible reading and weekly church attendance, he welcomed this change. Philip quickly befriended other young men in the orphanage. (Indeed, I met him through another orphan who had lived at the same orphanage and with whom he has remained in close touch.) He stayed there for three years until he decided to quit school and seek a job. When Philip's attempt to find a job did not work out, it was decided, with the help of psychiatrist Dr. Keilson, that he was not a good influence on the other boys. They wanted to send him to a home in Amersfoort for Jewish boys and girls who were mentally ill, disabled, and retarded. Philip refused and left the orphanage to be on his own, even though he was still a minor. Because they were responsible for him until age 21, the JMW found a room that he could rent in the home of a Jewish woman in Amsterdam, and later another orphan in this study joined him.

LONG-TERM STAYS

I interviewed Marcel at his house on a *moshav*, a privatized farm, in Israel, sitting outside with the scent of ripened mangoes in the air. Marcel went into hiding in 1943 at age 4 and stayed, with his brother, in one foster home the entire time—for three years. He called his foster mother "Moe" (pronounced "moo," an abbreviation of *Moeder*, mother) and remembers her as a warm person. His parents were picked up in a raid the day after he and his brother went into hiding. From Westerbork, they were sent to Sobibor, where they were killed on arrival, after spending three days in cattle cars. As Marcel recounted this part of his family history, I turned off the tape recorder until his weeping had subsided and he felt able to continue.

Out of his entire family, only one relative, a nephew of his father's, survived. This man became his and his brother's guardian. In 1946 both boys ended up in an Orthodox Jewish boys' home in Hilversum:

The children who were there were not Orthodox, and we tried to run away from everything that was according to Jewish orthodoxy. We didn't like it at all. We didn't want it. I can remember that, until I left there, all of the kids didn't like it at all. But the strange thing about it, when I saw my OPK file, it was written there that my parents asked before they put us into hiding, "Don't give the children a Jewish education because only bad things can happen being Jewish." So it's not just that they gave us a Jewish education but that they knew my parents didn't want it.

Although Marcel's hiding family might have kept him after the war, they had let him and his brother go because they were told, most likely by a Jewish social worker, that the boys would be adopted by a Jewish family. They felt the boys might be better off in a Jewish environment. However, they never were adopted by a Jewish family. Furthermore, the home cut off all communication between the boys and their foster family and would not allow the foster family to visit Marcel and his brother. Marcel only found them again in 1998 and honored them at Yad Va Shem.

Marcel and others who lived in that home explained that in the back of the orphanage was a shelter/jail where the Dutch army held German prisoners and NSBers: "How can they [the Jewish community] do such a thing like that? What kind of thinking is behind that? They didn't care very much about us. I'm sure they did not care, because we had a very, very hard education there."

Marcel stayed in the orphanage for eleven years. His surviving relative was a very cold person who did not spend much energy on the boys. Like others I interviewed, Marcel is aware that he and the other orphans were not easy children:

There were rules, but we didn't give much notice to them. We did what we wanted to do. I don't think we were very nice children. But I don't think, on the other hand, that the people in charge of us tried to understand us. So there were always conflicts, and we got hit.

When he was 18, Marcel wanted to emigrate to Israel. "So I think they [the Jewish organizations] said to themselves, 'OK, good riddance! No problem—we'll send them to Israel.' They sent us to Israel, also to an Orthodox kibbutz. After a week there, we ran away." He and a friend asked to be sent to a non-Orthodox kibbutz, a situation that worked out better; indeed, Marcel met his future wife there. Marcel was drafted into the Israeli army shortly thereafter, and during weekends and holidays when soldiers returned to their families, he had nowhere to go, so he slept on park benches in Tel Aviv. He has strong and bitter feelings about the Dutch state abdicating its responsibilities by allowing him to leave Holland as a minor, only to be part of yet another war. Yet the Jewish community, not just the state, was also in charge of Jewish orphans. It is interesting that he does not blame any Jewish organization for this decision—"I was a Dutch citizen of Dutch nationality, and I think the Dutch government should have looked after me." But he also feels that the Jewish community did not do its job in protecting orphans like himself. His reaction to having been in an Orthodox environment is very negative: "I'm very, very anti-Orthodox. In my opinion, it is like a Khomenism."

Marcel has always been fit and ready to defend himself, and later, his family as well. In his youth, he and the other Jewish orphans from his home were all active in wrestling, and Marcel also trained in boxing between the ages of 12 and 18. He was on the Israeli national judo team for years. Currently, he jogs, and at age 61, which is how old he was when I met him, he was still involved in karate. "I'm still fighting on the mat with guys twenty years old—that is not normal." He suspects that this urge is connected to a strong feeling that "the orphans had to know how to fend for themselves, since no one else would do it." Marcel is a gentle man who has been able to create a warm extended family environment. Although he and his brother are trying to recapture some of their parents' bank accounts, no amount of restitution will ever fill the void he feels: "I just want to know who I was and who my parents were. I've searched for it for a long, long time, and nobody can tell me."

Born in 1938 to a working-class family, twins Joop and Salo were the most tragic figures in this group of former hidden children. Like Marcel and others, they went into hiding at age 4, but both still seem to have carried the effects of the trauma wrought by their situation well into middle age. While Joop stated that he was hidden in 16 different places, his brother, Salo, was in about 7. It does not appear that either one had a close connection with an adult during the war years, although Joop's final hiding family remained in some contact with him. It is clear that during their postwar years when they were minors they also lacked a good connection with any one adult. When comparing cases such as Joop's and Salo's with Marcel's above, I found similarities in terms of the age of separation from parents and in terms of living in the cold and hostile institutional environment of the boys' orphanage. Yet there the similarities end. This is not to say that Marcel did not suffer long-term effects from his war experiences but only that their life courses differed considerably in terms of their ability to form relationships and to carry on with families of their own. One important difference is that Marcel was in one hiding place for three years and became close to his hiding mother, whereas neither twin had a strong connection to any of their many hiding parents. Although personality differences and other predispositions also enter in here, it is my sense that Marcel's connectedness with his foster mother allowed him to create a warm and caring family environment later in life.

Salo contacted me after I put a request for interviews in the newsletter of the Amsterdam-based hidden children's organization of the Netherlands when I had just begun this project in 1997. Calling from his workplace in New Jersey to my home in The Hague, he said in his strongly accented English, "No one has ever asked about it [the postwar period]. It was the worst part [crying], not the war, but the orphanages. It's difficult to talk about, it hurts; it's very difficult." I was taken aback by his phone call because he was very upset. At the same time, it was one of the first moments when it was clear that my research had hit a nerve, that I was possibly on the right track. Although we were unable to manage the logistics to meet in spring 2000, when I did my East Coast interviews, we finally met in fall 2001, when I came to Rutgers for a conference.

I conducted Joop's interview in Holland in 1999, and despite the presence of a Dutch translator, it was confusing. However, from his and Salo's interviews and the interview of another friend of theirs from the orphanage, I was able to get the gist of Joop's experience. Because of Salo's fluency in English, his interview was tragically clear.

Both are attractive, white-haired, youthful-looking middle-aged men. Despite their separation by continents and the three years between the two interviews, both dressed similarly, sporting high-quality leather jackets. Both have what appear to be signs of Parkinson's—trembling hands—and both experience pain when they walk more than a short distance. Although neither seemed all that healthy, Joop appeared to have more physical problems.

The twins' father died in the early 1940s, and their mother was killed in Auschwitz. They returned "home" to one surviving aunt. Both reported being left in an unheated house in the winter without food, at the age of 7, to fend for themselves. They recalled this trying postwar situation with resentment, and Salo said that he never had a good relationship with his aunt. "I actually hated her. I didn't like her. But she was mentally sick because she lost her husband and son—they were deported."

Both children were removed, most likely by a Jewish social worker, and placed in the Rudolfsheim Stichting (the Rudolf's Home Foundation), in Hilversum. Like others in their situation, they had no Jewish background and were thrust into an Orthodox setting in which they had to learn, through trial and error, the rules and regulations of Jewish practice. Salo recalls high turnover among the directors of this home, perhaps because they were poorly paid or unqualified to deal with the challenge of orphans. He describes the orphanage as a dreary institution:

There was not a drape or a picture of anything to make it a little warm. It was bare. We slept by age, in a room which, like a hospital, had a table in the middle and a toilet in the corner, and about six beds on each side. They were all green army blankets. It was very disciplined and strict, and each group had a counselor . . . a leidster. *I never met one I liked.*

The role of the leader/counselor clearly was to control the boys and keep them in line; compassion and understanding appear to have been at a minimum.

Salo recalls that the general punishment for wrongdoing, which included not knowing the appropriate Torah portion of the week, was to be locked up alone in a room. "They tried to discipline us, but there was no way of handling us because we didn't listen. If they locked us up, we walked out. If they sent us to bed without food, we would organize because in the cellar there was food, and we would steal it."

Salo cried as he recalled his youth spent in the home—how they could not visit the homes of non-Jewish friends from school because their food was not kosher, how cold and militaristic life was.

And then when we came from school, we had to go to shul. I hated it there. I hated every day of my life in that place. There was nothing there except terrible food. There was never a kind word. It was just one day after the other day.

On Saturdays, they had to walk to the synagogue in town for services, which was also a painful experience for Salo because the boys did not feel welcomed by the families there. Salo did not recall any of the families inviting the children home for a Sabbath meal. The twins were bar mitzvahed at age 13, but the ceremony was irrelevant to them. Said Salo, "I didn't care about it. I never felt comfortable. I never go to shul. I never felt I belonged. . . . There was nothing to look forward to." During our interview, Salo recounted the following painful memory: "I also remember I got sick in that home, and they sent me to a hospital for children [takes deep breath and begins to sob]. Nobody ever came [to visit]." At this point he was sobbing heavily, and I turned off the recorder.

When asked about contact with their aunt, Salo recalled that she used to promise to visit them. "I was sitting all day [begins to cry] by the bus stop, but she never came. This happened many times." Joop, however, recalled that their aunt visited often, and he did not feel the same kind of deprivation in relation to her.

Although the principal of his school felt that Salo should have been sent to a high school, instead he was sent at age 14 to Amsterdam, to work in a knitting mill with other young people. His salary went to the orphanage, and then at age 15, he was sent to a children's home in Amsterdam. Joop was sent to a different school because he had epilepsy. Later, at about age 15, he was sent to yet another home, an institution for mentally disabled children, including those who had epilepsy. From the descriptions of that home given by Joop and Philip (see his story above), another orphan, it sounded like a highly undesirable place where mentally ill young people were simply warehoused. Joop described it as being more like a prison. He stayed there until he was 21 and then worked in a carpet factory, where he eventually became a manager. Like other orphans, he remains bitter that he was not given an education that was appropriate to his abilities. He had wanted to do something more artistic with his hands, but such training was not provided.

Joop and his wife had two children and have a modest lifestyle. Although Joop and Salo have a poor relationship, Joop's relationships to his other family members seem strong. Salo, however, presented a much more disrupted and disconnected family life, seemingly reflecting the damage done in his early life. Although Joop wants more of a relationship with Salo, Salo said, "I feel guilty, but I don't love him. I know he loves me." Years earlier, Salo sent a plane ticket to Joop so that he could come visit, and though he gave him a driver and car, and the keys to his vacation house, clearly he was not available to him emotionally. Joop felt that Salo was being ostentatious and felt very much like the poor brother as he recalled that trip with sadness and resentment. Yet Salo's problems extend beyond his relationship with Joop.

Salo remains resentful that he was not well treated in the orphanage. While acknowledging that he and others were not the easiest of children to manage, he feels strongly that they should have given him an education:

They didn't. They basically washed their hands. You know what that means. And I survived, but look at my life. And I'm not blaming them for anything I did with my life because many things I did myself. But I do blame them for not giving me a foundation. When I walk here with you on the grounds [of Rutger's University], and I see all these kids, they go to university, and maybe I could have come to university. I'm not stupid. They could have sent me to school, invested a few years in me and given me something to fall back on because I have no trade. I'm a zero.

When I gently disagreed with him, he repeated

I'm a zero! What am I? If I apply for a job, what am I? I don't have any papers. No education, no nothing. And this bothered me. I was angry. It was more im-

portant for them to have me every day study Torah. I cannot go to the bank with Torah. Am I right?

I will return to Salo's narrative in the next chapter, where his adult life is discussed.

Josef was one of the children who at age 6 found it an exciting adventure to go into hiding; he can still recall with great detail the car in which he was driven away from his parents into hiding. He was also the child who looked part Asian owing to his almond-shaped eyes and who ended up believing the exotic story he was told to spin, that he was part Indonesian (figures 3 and 4).

In hiding with one family for several years, he felt that they treated him like they treated their own children—they were fair, somewhat cool, and distant and showed little affection, in a Calvinistic manner. Because his foster family had registered him after the war, Josef's great-uncle found him, and Josef reluctantly moved into an uncle's house in The Hague, where he lived with him and his wife and son, who was eight years older than Josef. Josef did not find warmth or understanding there; his uncle was strict, and his aunt was even stricter. From letters that Josef has since seen between his hiding family and his uncle, it was clear that his uncle did not want to have or keep Josef.

Josef recalls going to stay with an aunt and uncle in Amsterdam and receiving psychological testing and therapy. Josef believes that he got this kind of attention because he was a "very difficult" child:

I did what I wanted. I didn't want to go to school, I didn't want to learn. I made difficulties everywhere where it was possible.

When I asked if he disobeyed, he responded,

Oh, yes; oh yes!

Basically, Josef was acting out, typical behavior of hidden children after the war, and no one in his family could handle him or even wanted to try. He went to several different schools and failed one year of schooling. L'Ezrat ha-Yeled and OPK got involved, and he was sent first to Jozeboko at Wijk aan Zee about fifteen miles northwest of Amsterdam, a place that was typically used as a summer camp.[1] It was staffed by older women, some of them clearly survivors. He recalls hating that experience and when I asked why, he gave me an example of what life there was like:

The incident was that children who [were sick and] *would bring up their food . . . were sat down, and they had to eat it again. The lady who made that rule was Hungarian and a camp survivor. Her thing was always, "You don't know how important food is; you can't vomit it up; you can't bring it up. Put it back!"*

Josef wet his bed then, something many children did as a sign of their trauma, and he recalls that many other boys did as well, but none of them were punished for it.[2]

Josef was transferred to a small unit of five children in Doorn, and then to a children's home in Hilversum. All along, he was in touch with his hiding family, and even though he didn't write to them, they stayed in touch with L'Ezrat ha-Yeled to find out about Josef. They visited him, as did his uncle in The Hague, who was also his guardian. A Zionist group in Amsterdam encouraged orphans to go to Israel, and at age 14, in 1950, Josef wanted to join them, but his uncle refused to let him go. The Zionist group contacted his hiding family, however, and they were in favor of Josef's move to Israel. Finally, at age 15, in 1951, Josef got his wish. The idealism in the Youth Aliyah movement was contagious, and he was very excited to go. Once in Israel, he was sent to a children's home, K'var Batya, for one year. Children from many different countries were in that home, and their schooling was in Hebrew; however, they were not taught Hebrew first. A family offered to adopt him, and he declined:

I didn't want it; I'd rather be with children that are like me than being in a family where I'd be the only child.

I asked Josef who cared for him emotionally, and he replied:

Now, actually, when I look at it, nobody. There were not enough people, there was not enough time, there was not really anybody who could look after your emotional well-being. So you were left with your peers.

Josef was unhappy at K'var Batya.

I didn't like the whole atmosphere; I didn't learn anything. The regime was too strict. There was no warmth . . . there was nothing. You got food, you learned, you went to school. I found it boring because I couldn't understand [Hebrew], *so I didn't go to school.*

He did learn a skill, however, from working with a milling machine in metal workshop. Josef ran away to Tel Aviv, to an uncle of one of the other boys in the orphanage, and was discovered and returned. Shortly thereafter, he went to the head of the Youth Aliyah movement and asked to be moved elsewhere, to a children's home in Haifa. At age 16, he moved to K'var Ano Adadit, where he thrived. He feels that they took education seriously there and were also concerned with the children's emotional development. Josef gratefully received personal attention from his group leader, whom he clearly liked. His leader was an intellectual German Jew who had grown children and was a father figure to the boys there. Children at this home felt they could ask the leader questions or go to him with their personal problems, about their past or about puberty, and be heard or get an explanation. K'var Ano Adadit was much more welcoming and nurturing for children than the first home, where children were simply supposed to follow orders.

Because of an error in his records that added three years to his age, Josef, then 17, could only stay at the home for one year. By the time they fixed the bureaucratic error, Josef had already moved on and was living on a kibbutz, working full-time. Because he was made an Israeli citizen when he arrived in Israel, the following year he had to join the army, where he stayed for four years, only two and a half of which were mandatory. Josef liked the army because it felt like a family and because he felt he could have a future in it. Clearly, it provided the kind of structure he needed. Becoming a leader and officer helped bolster his self-esteem and his confidence and made him feel as though he belonged to something.

Earlier, when Josef first arrived in Israel, he drew a lot, as a way to communicate, since he could not speak Hebrew, and as a way to gain the other children's admiration:

In the army they encouraged it, not so much because of my artistic abilities but because of my observational talent. I took a number of courses to develop observational skills and was posted at various border locations, drawing hundreds of observational sketches from early morning until late evening. I loved it. This army experience brought on the idea of art school education. At the time Bezalel was the only art academy, and Jerusalem was cheap. I went to Bezalel with the idea to study jewelry design. However, when I had a tour through the Bezalel building I saw a large room filled with looms and girls.

Josef immediately changed his mind about studying jewelry and chose textiles and design, becoming the second male in Bezalel's history to study in that area. He went on to become an independent craftsman, pursuing his weaving while working for architects. He was then asked to set up an office for an import-export company in Amsterdam. At the age of 28, Josef returned to the Netherlands and worked in the business world. That led him to study industrial design two years later in Germany, and then in England, where he received a master's degree and a doctorate. While in London, Josef met and married a Jewish woman. He wanted to return to Israel, but in the end, they settled with their two children in Holland.

In the Netherlands, Josef taught and did research at the university, headed the design department in the Amsterdam Stedelijk Museum for two years, and worked on an exhibition on designing for disabled people at the Tel Aviv Museum. He and two architect friends set up a design business, from which he has retired. Josef's success clearly reflects how important it can be to receive an appropriate education.

Like Josef, Louis G. was another orphan who was lucky enough to get an education. Louis was 16 at the end of the war. He was one of the few I interviewed who went into hiding as a teenager (age 13); thus, he knew his parents and family and had a strong sense of self before the war. Indeed, he hid intermittently with his parents when he was forced to leave his hiding places, and he has fond memories of hiding together in a small space and playing bridge all day long with his sister and his parents, as recounted earlier. The role played by one's age at hiding is apparent in Louis's case because he speaks of how brave and courageous his parents were to send him away, into hiding. This attitude differs greatly from that of children who were very young when they went into hiding and who often remain critical of their parents and angry about being abandoned.

Shortly after a stay with his parents and sister, Louis went into hiding with a family deeply involved in the Resistance. Louis's foster father wanted to bring Louis's sister into hiding as well, but when he went to their hiding place, he found no one. Louis's family had been found and arrested by a former classmate of Louis's father, taken to Westerbork, and sent to Auschwitz, where they were all killed. His foster family had promised his parents that they would take care of Louis, and indeed, they nursed him through diphtheria in 1944. Unlike many others, Louis feels that his foster family was unusual in their warmth and caring. Yet he was aware that they were Christian and wanted him to be Christian too:

I went to church with them after Liberation. I would do anything to please these people, they were really exceptional in a way. They never saw me as a kid who had to be hidden. [Rather, they saw me as] *a kid that had been torn away from his parents, so there was much more human feeling involved. But I also told them I wouldn't convert because . . . I was a Jew. I had gone through all this mess because I was a Jew. That was absolutely ridiculous to now give up on my Judaism. Besides that, it was my tie with my home, with my family. . . . It was like divorcing my family by giving up Judaism. . . . It was not religious, as a matter of fact, I've lost my belief in God, because I can't believe so many innocent people who wouldn't have hurt a fly could be killed if there was God. . . . The people I was with were very understanding and would never, never have pressured me to convert.*

The Jewish social worker convinced him that the religious difference would grow to be a problem:

[He told me that] *it would always be a painful thing for them that I was a Hebrew. And here they were caring for me and bringing me up as if I was their own child. So I made up my mind that I would go back to a Jewish environment. I talked with the family. . . . And they understood.*

Louis had two surviving aunts and one uncle. His aunt, who had lost her husband, her son, and her brothers and their families, went to court to fight for guardianship of Louis. However, the psychiatrist employed by the OPK advised against it, since his aunt was deeply depressed from her losses. Louis had the choice of going to live with a Jewish family who was not related, but since he did not want to feel obligated to yet another family, he ended up going to a Jewish boys' orphanage (the Joods Jongenstehuis) in Amsterdam. "When I look back on it, it was one of the best things that ever happened to me." Louis felt at home with other boys who were in similar circumstances. (See figure 21.) He realizes he had the advantage of having concerned relatives who visited him:

Otherwise, we were all the same. We had ways to vent our anger; there were fights repeatedly. But then we had kids who had come out of the camp and so those who had been in hiding said, "My gosh, we never were dehumanized like they were," so we felt better already about ourselves.

Although Louis was well aware of the pressure other boys felt about going to work and earning their living, he was one of the only orphans I interviewed who was pushed to do well educationally. He had entered the home and a new school at the age of 17, and it was clear that he was lacking several years of education:

After a few months, the principal, a Jewish man, sat me down and said to me, "Look, you're not gonna make it here. I will arrange for you to get private tutoring, and you will have to work very hard, and you probably could catch up and then come back next September. I will admit you if you promise really to work hard, to do it." And then he said one of the most significant things that he ever could have said, "If your parents were alive, they would be sitting here, and I would be talking to them. But this now is your decision. What are you going to do with your life? I will take care . . . I will talk to the director of the boys' home. I will get the financing. I'll get it all set up, but it's you who has to decide you're gonna do it. I'm not going to let you do it if you're not really going to apply yourself." And I said, "I'll do it." . . . So when you ask, What was your emotional state . . . you know, this man really told me, "Grow up right now!" So I started working very, very hard.

By September, Louis was admitted to his third year of high school.

After the *Exodus 47*, full of Jewish Holocaust survivors, was turned away from Palestine in 1947 and returned to Germany, a friend approached Louis to inquire whether he would volunteer to fight for the new Jewish state. "And I said, 'I'm ready.' It gave me an opportunity to assert my Jewishness, to say I'm gonna fight for the Jewish people." (See figure 22.) Although Louis's uncle wanted him to stay in Holland, offering to train him to work in his store, his foster family encouraged him to go to Israel/Palestine. Louis fought in the Israeli army for a short period and then returned to Holland and finished his third year of high school. He then took a civil servant job to train as an air traffic controller. Although Louis's parents would have expected him to go to university, he felt that as an orphan, he had to become independent. During the Korean War, he had the opportunity to emigrate to the United States, and he did so when he was 21. After entering his third war, and his second as a soldier, he was sent to Germany to work as an interpreter. He enjoyed telling me about how he got even with a few Germans by putting them in jail:

They came to my office. I was an interpreter at the base, and so they came in the office and they yelled at me, and you know, with fists on the desk, they wanted to be paid for damage that was done by GIs [laughs]. I said, "Come with me." Nobody yells at me anymore. I locked them up.

Like all U.S. servicemen, Louis benefited from the GI bill. But because of an injury he sustained in the army in which he lost some fingers, he was entitled to even more benefits and was urged by army colleagues to go to college. He ended up with a degree in economics from Columbia University and did graduate work as well but did not complete his doctorate. He was, however, able to obtain a good job, and he supported his family well. Unlike almost all the orphans I interviewed, Louis was able to acquire an education because one pivotal person had paid attention to him early on and had sought the resources to help him. The question remains, Why didn't other orphans also receive such attention or have access to tutoring? It is also clear that coming to the States and having the GI bill allowed Louis to attain a university education, something he would not have acquired had he remained in the Netherlands, like many of his peers. Had he stayed in Holland, he would have continued as a civil servant doing air traffic control, which is still a more secure and highly skilled position than most orphans attained.

Like the protagonist in *Fugitive Pieces* (Michaels 1996), Louis, a resident of Berkeley, California, thinks often about how his sister's life was ended prematurely. He wonders what her life would have been like and is bothered "by the fact that she never was given the chance, not even to enjoy life in a way": "So that has been with me all the time and I think to be able to live with that and deal with it, you need really a lot of understanding." Louis feels that his wife brought that understanding to their relationship and has helped him deal with his deep grief. As I was writing this book, one of their two grown sons died, deepening Louis's grief to an extent that is difficult to imagine.

CONCLUSIONS

In this chapter I have focused on a small number of orphans who spent time in Jewish orphanages. Their reactions to the orphanages were mixed. On the one hand, quite a few of them found solace in the camaraderie they felt with others like themselves. To some, moving into a children's home was a welcome relief after having been in a problematic family setting. One woman feels that it would have been better for her to have stayed with orphans rather than being sent to kin in Israel. The connections made among these orphans, then, created and reproduced a feeling of family that was stronger and more positive than what many other hidden children were able to create with their actual kin. Many of them are still connected to their friends from this time, relationships that reflect a sense of kinship.

On the other hand, it is also clear that some of the Jewish children's homes were very poorly run. While none of the women mentioned a harsh atmosphere, and some even mentioned the opposite when discussing their time in an orphanage, several males experienced mostly coldness and punishment from the adults during that important period of their lives. Some of the orphanages were run with militaristic order rather than compassion. Surely, many of these orphans were difficult children who acted out; however, those who received some attention, understanding, and affection appear to have done well. But those orphans who were stranded in the children's homes had few options, the only escape being Israel, which meant becoming part of yet another war, this time as an active participant. Sending child survivors of one war to fight in yet another demonstrates that compassion, understanding, and wisdom did not dominate the Jewish community's decisions at that time.

Although the Jewish community in the Netherlands was small and overwhelmed with rebuilding its decimated culture, it clearly failed to provide a nurturing environment for these orphans. It also failed to provide them with the education and skills they needed in order to succeed, which many still resent. Although two or three of these orphans were able to develop some skills and acquire an education, they appear to be the lucky few. Without parents or close relatives, most orphans had no resources or social capital on which to draw. The Jewish community had failed to help create and transmit such social capital to the orphans. Thus, while this group did not fare better or worse emotionally as a group than others, they did struggle considerably to make a living and to create a meaningful life.

Creating Postwar Lives, Creating Collective Memory

FROM THE PERSONAL TO THE POLITICAL

Salo, introduced in the last chapter, admitted that he has a difficult time concentrating; however, that is the least of his problems. Simply put, his life is tragic:

I'm anxious. I cannot concentrate. I can never sit in a place other than in my room. Let's say I go to a restaurant, I have to get out. I never go to the movies. I cannot sit in a movie theater. I'm too restless. Very restless. This is for me very tough what you are doing . . . to sit here. But this is the same as what the Dutch government wants me to answer, "What problems do you have because of your experiences in the war?" How do I know? How am I to say? I don't know. I don't know. I know I fucked up my life, but I don't know, sorry for the language, if that's because of that [the war], or if I would have done that anyway. Who is there to tell me? I know I didn't have a fair shot at life. That I know.

In this chapter I analyze the emotional patterns evident in hidden children's adult lives. A small number of former hidden children in my sample have suffered from major emotional distress, such as serious depression or a mental breakdown, that has thwarted them either temporarily or permanently. Despite having experienced multiple traumas, however, the majority of those I interviewed exemplify the resilience of the human spirit. This is not to suggest that their lives are problem free. And it is certainly not to suggest that Jews and/or Holocaust survivors have a special, different, or superior way of surviving and of being successful (Helmreich 1992). However, most have succeeded in living with the wounds inflicted by the war and all that came after it.

My analysis of the long-term tolls of the war and the postwar period have led me to draw three conclusions. First, no one escaped being seriously affected by the experience of hiding and its aftermath, regardless of whether or not parents returned. Even those who have managed well in their lives still feel deeply affected by the war. Second, as previous chapters have clearly demonstrated, and as this chapter shall further corroborate, having one or even both parents return after the war did *not* guarantee a happier or easier postwar life emotionally. Indeed, in some instances, it appears as though many hidden children with surviving parents had a rockier road emotionally than those without. Guilt, denial, and an unwillingness to open up wounds by sharing their terrible experiences compromised the relationships between surviving parents and their hidden children.

Third, the creation of an identity and of a collective memory forty-five years after the war's end has acted as a kind of social medicine that has provided comfort, while healing many hidden children's wounds. In the early 1990s those who had been hidden children in any European country began to organize, meet, and talk about their pasts. This process turned what was experienced in isolation into a social phenomenon, which helped many former hidden children deal with the long-term effects of hiding. Creating a new identity and a collective memory catalyzed a political process in which hidden children were no longer hidden but felt empowered to make claims on the state.

POSTWAR EMOTIONAL LIVES

Before delving into the specifics of the postwar emotional health of for-mer hidden children, I would first like to look at some basics about their adult lives. The majority of those I interviewed were currently married, still in their first marriage, and had children.[1] Quite a number of former hidden children ended up marrying another hidden child, echoing the postwar pattern in DP camps, where camp survivors married other camp survivors (Rosensaft 2001). In some of these relationships, there seemed to be a strong bond based on a shared past. In others, although that commonality may have drawn the couple together initially, it did not always guarantee a lasting connection.

Two women in my sample had not married, one because of her sexual orientation. There were a small number of widows and one widower in my sample. Of course, there were some divorced people, just as there are in the general population. Fourteen people had been married twice, and many of them had divorced twice as well. Three people had been mar-ried three times and divorced twice; one had married and divorced three times. However, most remained with their first and only spouse, and most had grandchildren by the time of our interview. One woman, Sanne, explained why she did not want to have children:

I had very strong feelings that I couldn't be a good mother after what I had gone through. Proof to me was the way I had felt about my half-brother and half-sister after they were born. . . . I used to get furious. I would get so enraged with them that I'd lock myself in my room—away from them, because I wanted to kill them. (Marks 1993: 98)

Her thoughtful response was unusual in this sample.

Major Depression, Breakdowns, and Suicidal Thoughts

Owing to everything that these survivors have been through, a relatively small minority suffered a major depression or emotional breakdown at some point in their lives. The majority of those who experienced a break-down or something akin to it were able to recover, and they now lead reasonably satisfactory and even fulfilling lives. In this part of the chapter, I will first examine what occurred and when, and whether the person afflicted by these emotional challenges was able to overcome them. Then I will discuss where these survivors stand today in their emotional lives—some are beset by emotional problems with which they cannot cope, and others, the majority, have been able to build a fairly meaningful life.

Of the seventy hidden children I interviewed, fourteen people had suffered from major depression, a nervous breakdown, or suicidal thoughts, or some combination of the three. For some, their depression or breakdown occurred earlier in their lives; for others, it came much later. There is no group I can compare my sample with in order to tell if this 20 percent rate is high, but in light of my respondents' pasts, I was very surprised not to find even more in this category. Specializing in child survivors of the Shoah, psychoanalyst Judith Kestenberg asserts that depression "in middle age is a sign of incomplete mourning and unacknowledged anger. Being anxious, angry and depressed is, in fact, a normal reaction to a context of persecution" (quoted in Fogelman 1993: 299).

Indeed, after I presented my findings in August 2005 at the Jewish Child Survivors of the Holocaust conference, one therapist who is also a former hidden child remarked publicly that it is very possible for some people not even to know they are depressed because of the stigma attached to the condition. In some contexts, such as in Israel, emotional problems are still kept under wraps, compared with in the United States, where many people speak freely about their feelings. Thus, a sociocultural and historical context exists in which hidden children may or may not feel encouraged to voice their feelings and problems, depending on their environment, and some may still be in hiding emotionally.

In each category of postwar familial status, there were at least several individuals who suffered from these afflictions at one point in their lives. There were five among the orphans, three among those with one returning parent, and six among those with two surviving parents; put another way, there were five people among the orphans and nine among the nonorphans. It is very curious that in both absolute and relative terms,

more hidden children with two surviving parents suffered from extremely seri-
ous postwar emotional problems. Many surviving parents were depressed
and never overcame their grief at losing most, if not all, of their families.
Their children were aware of all the whisperings, and they heard their
parents crying. Many of those whose parents returned grew up with
emotionally disturbed parents as role models.[2] Having both parents return and being "lucky" in the eyes of other hidden children, therefore,
was no guarantee of happiness or stability. Those hidden children who
had breakdowns at least had an emotional experience that reflected their
trauma. In fact, after going through a breakdown, they may have had a
better chance of leading a manageable life.[3]

Peter was in hiding between the ages of 3 and 6. His wartime guardian
was a single woman who was a nurse to women who had just given
birth. She was clearly attached to Peter, although she did not give him
any warmth or affection or a sense of security. Even after the war, she in-
serted herself into his life, as though Peter were her son. Like many former hidden children, as an adult Peter buried himself in his work. Although a highly successful teacher-researcher at a professional school, he
experienced anxiety attacks for years. The breaking point came when he
was 40:

*I was doing extremely well in my career, but it's all very much related to my
past, to the war, and you are insecure because there was no security at all when
you were in the sensitive period. And you tried to compensate for it by working
very hard, having success, and then it breaks.*

When I asked him what happened, he said,

*I started to cry, and I didn't understand why. I started to cry, and I couldn't stop
anymore for months and months. It took me a year, I think.*

After returning to work for about a year, Peter broke down again and
then eventually cut back to part-time work to decrease his stress level. Peter is likely to be viewed by those hidden children whose parent(s) died
during the war as lucky, since both his parents returned. That advantage
translated into social capital and allowed him to pursue higher education
and have a comfortable lifestyle. The fact that he had good relationships

with his parents after the war, however, did not translate into emotional health. His breakdowns could have stemmed from having been separated from his parents at an early age and feeling both loss and anger at them for having abandoned him. They could also reflect his repressed anger toward his hiding mother, who never let go. Thus, it is important to understand that even those individuals whose postwar lives may *appear* to have been optimal still bear deep emotional wounds.

Several men experienced the onset of depression when their first grandchild was born. Others began to write their story down for the first time at that point. Marcel, a *moshavnik* (one who lives in a *moshav*, or privatized farm in Israel) who still resents the Jewish community for the treatment of Jewish children in the orphanages, had a breakdown after his first grandchild was born:

As a grandfather, I felt that my parents never enjoyed their children, never got to enjoy their grandchildren. I had to start inquiring about what exactly happened to my parents, because if I don't do it, it will be buried. [If I find out], then what happened to my parents really happened. As long as someone can talk about them to the grandchildren and to the great-grandchildren, then they'll be remembered.

At the age of 57, Marcel started therapy. He also began seeking information about his parents' deaths and his own past. He took early retirement and began to take care of his grandchildren: "I don't want strange people to come and take care of the children. I don't want that. I do it myself. I want that if somebody takes care of them it will be a familiar person who loves them." Without question, Marcel's past as an orphan who felt uncared for was pivotal in shaping how he structured his work and family life to the benefit of his grandchildren. Before his grandchildren's births, he refused to talk about his past when his children inquired. For many such as Marcel, the convergence of their own aging process (and perhaps awareness of mortality) with the lessening of family and economic demands—combined with a specific sociohistorical context in which these survivors were finally acknowledged—had the effect of breaking down many of the walls that had been constructed during the 1940s and after.

Marcel was one of several former hidden children who explicitly told me that he would not have been willing or able to do an interview with me some years earlier. Indeed, many of the interviews I conducted proved to be an important step for those who were finally coming to grips with and integrating their past. It clearly was a major step for one woman who was very anxious to do the interview but seemed so emotionally fragile that I cut it short. Although these interviews were not interventions, they did seem to help these survivors to confront honestly their tumultuous and often sad pasts. Perhaps they worked like therapy at times, or like a friendship in which someone helps the other by simply listening, being interested, and empathizing.

Out of my entire sample, three women had been sexually abused in their teens—one by her Jewish foster father and two by their Jewish step-fathers—and all experienced severe depressions at some point. Indeed, two of these women suffered from decades of depression and anxiety, both common among victims of childhood sexual abuse. Two of the three had suicidal thoughts at different times in their lives. One was institutionalized as a young adult but seems to have dealt with her problems directly and successfully in long-term therapy. A second woman seems to have overcome her depression and attributes her happiness to her grandchildren. The third woman was not helped as much by therapy and still suffers from severe insecurity. She's been married and divorced three times; she feels as though her life has been wasted.

Most of those who had a major depression or breakdown recovered— nine of the fourteen are now doing fine. Five remain challenged by their emotional burdens. In the next section, I elaborate on two categories I have created to reflect the present emotional state of the hidden children I interviewed. These are not diagnostic categories, but they will serve our purpose of trying to understand the long-term effects of war, trauma, and hiding.

Ongoing Emotional Fragility

The first category refers to those who are currently in an ongoing state of what I call "emotional frailty." These former hidden children may have been diagnosed with a particular affliction, but not necessarily. They may suffer from ongoing depression, anxiety, and/or an inability to fully function, resulting in a very limited existence. I believe that some in this category may have been depressed for a long time but have never been diagnosed because they have not sought therapy or have not continued with therapy for any length of time.

A total of nine people are in this category. Five of the fourteen who suffered a major depression or breakdown and were discussed in the previous section have not recovered. They join four others who, while they have not suffered from a major depression or a breakdown, experience long-term emotional fragility and have a seriously limited existence. In terms of postwar family status, two people who had two surviving parents, two who had one surviving parent, and five who were orphaned lead perpetually unhappy and highly limited lives due to emotional constrictions. In this category, there were more orphans (five) than nonorphans (four). Since orphans represent only one-third of my sample, they are somewhat overrepresented in this category.

Among these nine people, two women have clinically diagnosed illnesses and have spent considerable time in mental institutions. Another woman suffered from dissociative disorder and was extremely difficult to interview, talking nonstop about herself and her problems, whether or not the tape recorder was on. The others in this category seem emotionally debilitated and unhappy in ways that continue seriously to hamper their lives.

All four women in this category articulated the feeling that they had ruined their lives, that they were afflicted with insecurity and a lack of confidence and self-esteem. For them, this translated into persistent unhappiness. One woman experienced constant fear and anxiety, despite the fact that both her parents had survived the war. All those who left their hiding places to move home to parents or to other Jewish relatives reported disastrous relationships with their mothers or kin (in one case) after the war. Although three of the four had at least one good connection with hiding parents during the war, this did not mitigate what they described as terrible relationships with their cold and uncaring mothers in their postwar lives. Two who had stepfathers felt that their mothers were unavailable and more interested in their husbands' welfare than in theirs. They basically felt abandoned by their mothers. Although they were told by others that they were "lucky" that their parent had survived, they felt miserable. Additionally, one of those two women had been raped by her stepfather. All these women ended up divorced; some have remarried, but unsuccessfully.

Among those hidden children with ongoing serious emotional problems, the gender breakdown is about even, so gender does not seem crucial in explaining this postwar situation. Most of these survivors hid when they were younger than 5 years old, which makes sense psychologically in terms of separation and trauma but still does not explain why *these* individuals and not others who hid at similarly young ages suffer from these emotional constraints.

Salo, the orphan whose narrative began this chapter, seems unable to connect to anyone—his multiple spouses, his child, his grandchildren, his twin brother. His unhappiness is overwhelming—he sobbed throughout our interview, and it was the only time that I had to turn off the tape recorder repeatedly. Salo married three times, never for love, he claims, and has what he terms a "cordial relationship" with his daughter and grandchildren. He married his first wife, the mother of his daughter, because her mother, a non-Jew, was kind to him and took him in. Through debts incurred from gambling, he was in trouble with "people from the underworld" and fled to the United States when his daughter was a year old. He married his second wife to stay in the States. "So I met this Jewish girl who I told the truth to. I told her, 'The only reason I marry you is to stay in the country, no other reasons. So I want you to know that.' She said, 'You'll learn to love me.' But I never did. I never loved anybody."

After fourteen years of what he calls an "unsuccessful marriage," during which he was "always running—gambling and womanizing," he left her for a Russian woman: "I thought this woman would be my answer to many things. She was like a mother to me, she was talented, she knew how to take care of the house." Twenty-four years later, they are still together, although it has not been a good marriage:

But if she would leave me, it wouldn't bother me. It would only bother me because I would be alone, but it wouldn't bother me because I love her. I don't know what makes me tick. I don't know [in a low voice]. *I'm not such a nice guy. I cannot love people. It's my problem. I am very much alone. I sit in my room all day. I don't hardly communicate with my wife. I sit in my room all day because I'm running away from reality. . . . My wife hates my daughter, and my daughter hates my wife. Don't ask me why, I haven't the faintest idea.*

When I asked about his relationship with his daughter, he responded,

My daughter and I are cordial. I did my best to her and her kids. I did many things, honestly, money, presents, when I had it. But she never really forgave me. My daughter is nice to me. But she will never hug me or kiss me.

A few minutes later, as we wrapped up the interview, he told me that he really had told me very little about his past and that he had left out some things he did not want to talk about. After a long pause during which he took a deep breath and began to cry, in a low voice, he stated:

See, I'm just a name or a number, or another guy you interview in order to get what you want. But for me this is very difficult. Because you have to take inventory, right? Not easy. But that's the way it is. I think we're finished, right? You have enough? OK?

I told him I did have enough, and he replied,

Me too. [Laughs, then says in a low voice] *Me too.*[4]

Salo was not too different from David H., a man who spent the war and many years after it in a Salvation Army home because his mother, a non-Jew, had left him there even after she and her new husband had set up their household. Despite having had a mother, David grew up more like an orphan. In his adult life, he took serious drugs and spent fifteen years traveling the globe, stopping for five years in Israel. He was living in Australia working as a macrobiotic chef when he heard from his brother that his children were looking for him. Because of them, he moved back to the Netherlands. When I asked him about his relationship with his three children, he remarked, "It's not very deep."

DW: Do you feel like a father to them? Do you feel fatherly?

No.

DW: Do they want you to be fatherly?

All of them wanted me to be, but I don't have love. With my youngest son, we are more like friends.

DW: Do you wish you could be a father to them?

I don't feel bad about things. I feel uncomfortable about it because they're sort of disappointed. I also think that what I have never felt with my parents, I just don't have that in myself. And I just can't produce it. It's strange because I just feel like an invalid because I just can't reach this part of myself. And maybe because I never knew my father, I could never develop it.

When asked if he can feel love, he responded,

I feel like I can, but I don't show it. I'm very poor at relationships. My whole life, I feel it deep inside, I feel it but never show it. Because when I was in this home [the Salvation Army orphanage] *everything you showed was turned against you. It's always been like that. I really take care not to show things, still now. To my children, I never show love.*

DW: When you see them, do you hug or kiss them?

They do that.

DW: They do that to you?

Yes.

DW: Can you be affectionate with your granddaughter? [He misunderstood and thought I meant his daughter.]

Especially not to my daughter. Everything is always with women; it's always women that decided for me or shaped me. I'm afraid of women.

Near the end of the interview I asked, "If you could say anything to your mother today, what would it be?"

What I really feel that she did to me is that she always kept me very alert and awake because she was so mean sometimes that I had to be. And that turned into a skill. For that, I'm very grateful to her, very grateful. She always kept me awake because my mother was my greatest enemy; it seems like that. But since I'm older, I know she was in danger and she felt in me a sort of laziness. And she was very aware and very violent; she was violent in speaking, and she kept me awake.

It seems that David's mother and his orphanage experience made him hyperalert to criticism and attacks, and as a result he buried his feelings. He seemed suspicious about real and imagined interactions and very cut off from any emotion. When I asked at the end of the interview if there was anything he hadn't said to his children that he wishes he could say, he answered, "I've told them everything in words, but what I feel is . . . everyone is able to express things, but I don't have the tools." After joining group therapy at the JMW with others like him, David was able to speak about his past, and he feels that a dark cloud has lifted:

I have forgiven my mother and I asked forgiveness from her, and I let my father into my being. I went to Westerbork, and I cried all over the place. I cried my lungs out. I've seen those books with his name and where he went to. And then it was over. I was a new man.

David's and Salo's painful and poignant narratives reflect their dissociation and emptiness, likely the result of having spent years in cold and harsh institutions with no positive connections to an adult. David's relationships with his emotionally imbalanced mother and alcoholic, abusive stepfather were very destructive as well, reproducing the harshness of the children's home and creating an unstable and abusive environment. Salo kept repeating that he was not a nice person, and by the end of his narrative, I found it difficult to convincingly counter him. However, these two men are clearly the victims of circumstances far beyond their control—ideologies, policies, and a war that robbed them of parents, family, and a normal home life. Without any kind of positive template for relationships, both men reproduced in their families the havoc and nonrelatedness they experienced as children and seem to continue to experience.

Since the lack of a connection with an adult might explain some cases of emotional fragility, but not all, I looked for other explanatory factors.

One of the nine people in this category lives in the United States, and eight live in the Netherlands. No one in this category was part of my Israeli sample. What difference might these locales make? First, one might argue that by leaving Holland, the survivors had made a clean break with their past and moved to a country which held no bad memories. Yet, those who emigrated to the United States or to Israel as adults may have had certain emotional predispositions that made them a self-selecting group—that is, they may have been more oriented toward the future than the past. Those who stayed in the Netherlands may find comfort in being in their home country and speaking their native language, but they may also have to confront their past on a daily basis in some way. Does being an immigrant in a foreign land force individuals to have a "stiff upper lip," since they have less of a safety net? Or do those who emigrate tend to be less risk averse? The immigration literature would tend to support the latter argument.[5] What we can't know is whether those who are less risk averse simply have that disposition, while others do not, or whether the wartime experiences of some former hidden children caused them to become more (or less) risk averse.

I sought common patterns among those who experience ongoing emotional frailty and those who had serious emotional upheaval but have since recovered. Most of those whose mother survived had one factor in common—a poor postwar relationship with her. Two men who suffered but recovered from a major depression reported having a good relationship with their mother (and father) after the war. However, they were striking exceptions; one of them went into hiding in his mid-teens, and his prewar relationship to his parents seems to have been very strong.

I want to clarify here that although most of those in my sample whose mother survived the war reported not feeling connected to her afterward, clearly not everyone who experienced this lack of connection suffered from serious emotional afflictions. Thus, although postwar detachment between a mother and her child may be an important factor, it is not sufficient in explaining these more troubling emotional patterns, since it was experienced by many.

The other common pattern I found is that most of those who suffered severe emotional afflictions at some point in their lives went into hiding at a young age, usually 5 or younger. In general, it is thought that age at hiding has been inversely associated with postwar emotional health, meaning that the younger the child was when he or she went into hiding, the more emotional difficulties he or she had after the war. However, since most of the people in my sample went into hiding at a very young age, and most of them did *not* suffer from emotional difficulties, I would say that a younger hiding age is not sufficient to explain who did or did not enjoy a life without severe emotional limitations.

Another interesting pattern emerges. All these orphans were very young when they went into hiding, but again, that is true for the majority of my sample. With two exceptions—the twins who lived in an orphanage during their postwar childhood and adolescence—those who experienced more serious problems did not stay with their hiding family after the war. Almost all were living with relatives in a Jewish family or with a Jewish foster family after the war. Several of the women described their postwar family experiences as awful—one was raped by a Jewish foster father, and two others were in abusive family settings. The woman who was raped and the one living with relatives both preferred the camaraderie of the orphanages.[6]

I was struck that more people who had at some point experienced a major depression or a total breakdown had at least one parent return, yet more orphans were currently leading very constricted lives. Perhaps those who had one or both parents return were able to let go and have a breakdown because they had a sense of at least minimum support, whereas those who were orphaned were forced to fend for themselves. I am not suggesting that any of this was conscious, only that some of those orphaned developed the ability to hobble along, even with emotional problems. However, given the small size of my sample, these findings are clearly suggestive.

In his postwar research on Jewish orphans in the Netherlands, psychiatrist Hans Keilson found that children who had had brutal wartime experiences, such as being in a concentration camp, and who ended up in nurturing postwar environments tended to fare better than those who had had an easier time during the war, most likely spending it in hiding, but a difficult foster situation afterward. Keilson's approach was novel for a psychoanalyst, in that he believed that the personality of someone who has gone through trauma can still be influenced. He also believed that it is important to offer children as good a situation as possible after a traumatizing situation or event so that they can develop into healthy adults. In this book, we have seen that most postwar living situations with biological parents, other kin members, adoptive nonkin families, and orphanages were, on the whole, very problematic and unsatisfactory; however, the majority in my sample have been able to overcome those setbacks. Conversely, we have also seen a situation in which a foster child was loved and cared for during and after the war but still ended up with major ongoing emotional issues. Thus, in the long term, it is difficult to distinguish clearly what combination of factors help to predict who is more likely to face emotional challenges and who is more likely to be able to ride them out.

Tender Resilience

The majority of those I interviewed clearly fall into this second category, those with what I call "tender resilience." They were not suffering from any debilitating emotional problems but were seemingly well-adapted people who bore some scars. My sample consisted of therapists, doctors, scientists, merchants, designers, salespeople, businessmen, a translator, journalists, teachers, and others, ranging from some of the most highly educated people in society to those with only a high school degree, and a few without even that. Although many did not have what could be called an easy life during or after the war, most were able to function as able-bodied members of society, and many of them had very satisfying and meaningful lives.

Most have some ongoing fears or problems (e.g., insomnia, anxiety, claustrophobia) that are chronic or can flare up in certain situations. Most of those who were functional were able to integrate less intrusive fears into their everyday lives, learning to avoid elevators, for example; sitting on an aisle seat, near the exit, at the theater or on a plane; or dressing and acting in a way that would not call attention to themselves. Some of the adults in this large group were more unsettled than others, needing sleeping pills to calm their fears at night. Quite a number of those who would be considered successful in their lives mentioned having low self-esteem, regardless of whether or not their parents returned after the war. And some, as has been shown, managed to function by cutting off their feelings. Indeed, a number of them threw themselves into their work to avoid their feelings.

While some felt settled where they lived, others never put down roots. In New York City, in June 2000, Thea explained,

I still feel very nervous and unsettled. A feeling of not belonging. I definitely feel that I don't belong in this country, but I don't know where I do belong. Going back to Holland is not the same anymore. There are too many places that remind me of people, streets that I do not wish to go into. I don't belong there either.

This feeling of not fully belonging anywhere is typical of survivors and is most likely stronger among camp survivors and those who were expelled from their home countries.

The fact that the vast majority of those I interviewed have ended up with reasonably satisfying marriages, family lives, and work lives (or at least with two of those three), given the dangers, separations, and traumas they experienced, is nothing less than astounding. In his longitudinal study of the life courses of children who grew up during the Great Depression, sociologist Glen Elder found, "To an unexpected degree, these children . . . followed a trajectory of resilience into the middle years of life. They were doing better than expected from the perspective of their social origins" (1999: 320). The same could be said of the majority of hidden children I interviewed—they were doing better than I would have expected, in light of the extraordinary difficulties they experienced early in their lives. How can we explain this?

For this resilient group of adults, as with those who lived through the Great Depression, perhaps it is the "potential maturation value of hardship experiences" that creates or helps to develop emotional strengths that serve individuals well during their adult lives (Macfarlane, cited in Elder 1999: 321). The ways in which the Occupation, the war, and postwar life forced Jewish children to grow up quickly were cruel and, in retrospect, difficult to fathom. Resiliency is perhaps one of the more positive aspects that this past engendered. Yet that supposition suggests a causality that is plausible but does not work in all cases. Most hidden children lived through similar circumstances, but not all did equally well. This might suggest that temperament or disposition is also important, either as an independent or an intervening variable.

Resiliency has become something of a catchall concept, used as a category to describe those who are not dysfunctional. This concept also conjures up sociobiology, since until recently resiliency was seen as an inborn trait. A slew of "how-to" books reflect a more recent view that it can be nurtured and taught (Brody 2005). A more relational approach suggests that resiliency is developed not in isolation but in relation to others. Psychologist Linda Hartling suggests that the sources of resilience and strength in the face of hardship, tragedy, or personal trauma are relationships that foster these traits (2003). She defines resilience as the "ability to connect, reconnect and resist disconnection in response to hardships, adversities, trauma and alienating social/cultural practices" (3–4). Although many of the hidden children in this category maintain a certain degree of emotional distance, they do seem engaged with others in their lives, particularly family members.

While resiliency could very well be an adaptive strategy that hidden children learned through the life-and-death challenges they faced, it is important to underscore that resiliency includes living with one's ghosts. It does not mean that existence is pain free. Indeed, I have called this category "tender resiliency" if only to emphasize that, for most, their pain about the war and/or postwar periods is very present and close to the surface.

Everyone in my sample who had a major depression or breakdown has had therapy, and most—but not all—of those with ongoing emotional frailty have also sought professional help. Likewise, many in the category of "tender resilience" have been in therapy. Those who were treated for short-term problems with anxiety or depression at one point in their lives reported that, depending on the timing of their treatment, the war may not have even come up. Before the 1980s, there was little or no social or cultural recognition of Holocaust survivors and how their particular histories connected with their current problems. For example, a teenage boy with high anxiety was interpreted as having problems because he never had a father figure. He lived with his widowed mother, and his foster father supposedly had been more maternal than "manly." This kind of Freudian analysis took precedence over making any connection with the fact that he had separated from his parents at age 2 and had lived through a war that took his father and many relatives. This awareness of war's effects has increased over time, of course, and there has been broader social and cultural recognition of Holocaust survivors and of the effects of trauma.

SOCIAL EFFECTS OF HIDING

Thus far, I have examined how hidden children have fared in terms of dealing with their pasts and their emotions as individuals. Here I'll turn to the social effects of their pasts—how they deal with others and the outside world. This includes their feelings of distrust toward others in general, and how they interact with their children more specifically. I also include a discussion of occupational callings and political involvement, both reflective of a particular social standpoint.

Emotional Distance

A frequent long-term effect mentioned by many in their interviews is that of emotional distance, the inability to be close to or to trust anyone. This may not be a clinically diagnosed problem, and most of these individuals are highly functional and lead satisfying lives. However, a number of interviewees stated that it was a problem for them.

Psychologist Eva Fogelman (1993: 295, 300) explains that most former hidden children felt abandoned by their parents, who sent them into hiding and sometimes did not survive the war, and then by those foster parents who gave them up when biological parents or other relatives returned. Many in my study later suffered from a fear of abandonment, which led them to keep a distance from or even to push away their loved ones. This behavior affected their intimate relationships with partners, lovers, spouses, and children.

Lore, for example, felt abandoned by her parents when she went into hiding at the age of 5. Though they survived the war and returned to her, she seems never to have trusted them again. In a few cases, though interviewees may not have mentioned emotional distance specifically, I noted that during the interview their affect seemed flat and their manner disconnected and unemotive. I also added to this category a few people who were not on speaking terms with their children, even if they did not state anything about emotional issues.

Fogelman also asserts that although distrust of strangers and of new settings was a useful response among hidden children in danger, such distrust can have long-term negative effects on their intimate and family relationships later in life (1993: 295–96). The ways in which many former hidden children described their involuntary emotional distancing reflect this long history of distrust, once useful, now destructive. Fogelman also found that former hidden children may be replaying their fear of abandonment in later intimate relationships without even realizing that they are repeating a very early experience in their lives.

Sixteen people, or about one-fifth of those I interviewed, clearly had problems being close to others, and my guess is that quite a few more than that have had to deal with this issue. The sixteen broke down somewhat unevenly by gender (two-thirds female and one-third male), which may be due to there being more desire among women for emotional closeness or more demands on them for it. That is, emotional distancing is often viewed as an acceptable part of mainstream masculinity but not of femininity. Among those who were emotionally distant, most went into hiding before the age of 5. I would have expected a higher percentage of those who were orphaned to have had significantly more problems with emotional distancing, but, curiously, this symptom is fairly evenly divided between orphans and those with at least one returning parent.

Most of the respondents who were aware of this problem felt that there was considerable emotional distance between them and their children. Those who were conscious of such distance did not seem able to change their behavior, even if they were aware of it. Some mentioned this issue wistfully, as though they wished they could have done something about it.

One mother told me that when her daughter miscarried, although she felt that she *should* have been upset about it, she felt nothing. She knew that her lack of an emotional reaction was a problem but felt that there was nothing she could do to change her personality. She was not ashamed of or embarrassed by this dynamic, but she did not want her daughter to know about it. Another woman described how she sensed her own coldness and felt she did not do right by her children. She admitted to having felt jealous of her children when they became older than she was when her mother died. Yet, she also stated that her children turned out well despite those issues.

Josef, introduced in the previous chapter, was an orphan who lived in two children's homes in Israel and ended up getting an advanced degree in design. Josef's wife is a lively and warm British woman who is well aware of Josef's need for distance and privacy. She explained that it took Josef a full year after they were together to tell her that he had had a sister and that this sister had been killed. She had only heard about some of the dangerous missions he went on in the Israeli army a short time before we met in 1999. While she emphasized that he was a good father, she also noted that he had been somewhat distant with their children when they had decisions to make. She wished that Josef had let himself play a stronger role in such situations, whereas Josef had not wished to influence his children.

Josef once told his wife something that chilled her—that he can walk away from any situation if need be, with nothing. In other words, he doesn't care about material possessions and can leave them behind and adapt if necessary. While this clearly reflects how he coped with the Occupation, the war, and his postwar situation, it did frighten his wife early in their marriage when they had two young children and the usual tensions that accompany that stage of life. However, Josef views this as a strategy he had to develop, somewhat similar to Jeannette's reaction, which she explained when she stated, "I simply leave when I have to without looking back or making a fuss." While highly adaptive, this trait, which developed in reaction to switching homes and families, likely has had an effect on later interpersonal relationships. However, both Josef and Jeannette are strongly embedded in their family lives with their spouses and their children, and Josef relishes taking care of his baby granddaughter, to whom he speaks Hebrew. Though neither is likely to pick up and move at this point in their lives, psychologically they can fall back on knowing they have that ability, should the need arise.

Many of those who were more distant with their children began to thaw and be less distant when their grandchildren were born. Some adults thought about their own pasts when their children were born, but because of the normal pressures of family life with small children and of earning a living, most did not. My sense is also that they were not able to, at least not yet. There was not a broad enough social context within which to frame and understand their pasts when their children were born. However, by the time their grandchildren were born, two factors converged. One was the natural position of grandparents, who can be more relaxed with grandchildren because their child-rearing responsibilities are over and because often they are retired. The other was more sociohistorical in nature, related to the fact that there was more acknowledgment of Holocaust survivors in general in the 1980s and of hidden children specifically in the 1990s.

Regardless of whether or not their current emotional state was basically stable, almost all those I interviewed had children, and most of them had grandchildren. I wondered how their pasts had affected the ways in which former hidden children interacted with and raised their children.

Parenting a New Generation

Almost everyone I interviewed in all categories felt that their past experiences as hidden children indeed had affected the way they brought up their own children.

Most in my sample told me that their reaction to having children was to be overprotective and fearful that something bad would happen to them. Lore explained: "When I went back to work, I knew that when I came home, I'd find my kids dead. I knew that every time I opened the door, they'd be lying in a pool of blood somewhere. They would have been killed by somebody." The other reaction, though less prominent, was to push children to become independent early on so that if they lost their parent(s), they would be able to function. Lore had trouble sending her children away to summer camp, and her children did not even want to go, but she pushed them anyway:

I don't know why, but I felt this was an important thing to learn. Why I thought that it was important to learn that they needed to be alone, away from me, from my husband, I don't know. Certainly, when I think about it rationally, I wonder why I would want to encourage that, when I have so much difficulty with this [separating].

Several men stated that they had been extremely strict with their children. One father reported that he slapped and spanked his sons to toughen them up, so that they would be able to survive anything. Another father said, "I lost my childhood, and I didn't give them theirs"; he is not on speaking terms with his children (and vice versa, perhaps). One man who stayed with his foster family after the war had had a very strict and punitive foster father. Later in the interview, he stated that he had been too strict with his own son and had used corporal punishment. Once, he hit his son while wearing a ring, leaving visible bruises on him. After that incident, he stopped hitting him. Several women reported that their husbands, also former hidden children, had been extremely strict with their children. Though this approach may be somewhat gendered, a few mothers also pushed their children toward independence, and quite a few fathers felt that they had been overprotective.

Betty remarked that she had strong feelings of sadness and anxiety. She wept as she recalled the day her daughter told her that she sometimes cried for her since she had lost her parents: "I was so sad for her, that she's crying for me! The war is always in the house! Always! And it doesn't go away! We often say that Hitler won the war because we are still in it." For many respondents, however, having children and grandchildren was a sign that ultimately Hitler had *not* won.

I was often touched by descriptions of the close relationships some had with their children, in spite of the fact that they had missed out on that dynamic with their own parents. "Well, that's what parents do," stated Jeannette, in a matter-of-fact manner, when referring to helping one of her daughters move to another city, despite the fact that she had never known her own parents, and her aunt and uncle did not seem to have nurtured her after the war. Thus, some former hidden children were able to overcome never having felt unconditional love and heal that emotional wound by becoming the parents they wished they had had. Yet it must also be said that Jeannette's ability to nurture may stem from her prewar relationship with her parents in her infancy; however, that's something we will never know for sure. Others were not able to bridge that gap and are less connected to their children. There are no clear factors that explain how or why some had close relationships in their own families and why others did not, since both groups (among the orphans) included a range of all the variables I was able to measure.

The final area I will explore in order to ascertain long-term social effects are the occupations and political activism of former hidden children.

Professional and Political Callings

Although my sample spanned the range from those in the service sector to highly trained professionals, two specific occupations attracted a number of those I interviewed. One was sales, reflecting the traditional Jewish prewar occupation, which required a high school education or more. The other was therapy, either psychology or social work. Those in the latter profession often mentioned the link between their work and their past; they felt they were attempting to help others since they themselves had been helped and rescued. One woman in my sample is an art therapist.

Among those in the larger sample, a sense of obligation to help others was often reflected in their occupation, their volunteer work, or their political views. When asked if their experience as hidden children affected their political attitudes, many thought it had made them politically liberal, giving them the desire to help others just as they once had been helped. In terms of their political views about Israel and Palestine, a fair number, but not the majority, felt that their past informed their liberal views about the creation of a Palestinian state.

Two women and one man I interviewed were very active politically and viewed this as a direct reflection of their pasts. Elly, a therapist, went to Bosnia for a few weeks every year for some years to work with those who were traumatized. Ruth W., an artist, went to Bhopal after the Union Carbide gas leakage disaster in 1984 that killed and maimed hundreds of thousands. Along with survivors of that event, she designed and mounted a sculpture of an Indian woman blinded by the gas, carrying her baby, while her other child is pulling on her sari from behind, trying to stay connected with her gasping mother. (See figure 23.) This sculpture was meant to represent the fate of an orphaned girl in Bhopal with whom the artist was acquainted, and it also represented the experience of the artist, whose stepmother had been gassed. (Ruth had been visited by her stepmother while in hiding and had to be pulled away from her when she left; this was the last time they saw each other.) Ruth was the most politically active person I interviewed, very involved in leftist political actions, marches, and events supporting immigrant rights, a Palestinian state, and other causes.

Another progressive, Max A., is a journalist who still publishes in a leftist Dutch newspaper. Recently, I emailed him and explained that I was unable to use some of his photos for the book. His response surprised me:

> Thanks for telling me; it does not bother me too much. I am much more concerned about the way the world is starving the Palestinians because they had the evil courage to vote for Hamas. I think that Israel, the U.S., and now also Europe is making a big mistake. We wanted the Palestinians to have democratic elections. They did so, and now we refuse to accept the results. Of course, it is not nice for us that they voted for Hamas. . . . We want Hamas to recognise Israel, but we should not try to force them to do so, but talk with them and give them something in return. We want them to stop violence, sure. But by isolating them we give them no other choice. It is a very tragic situation. . . . It creates so much human suffering.[7]

I am sure that many, if not most, in my sample would disagree with Max's viewpoint. I have also received emails from a few interviewees that reflect a more conservative perspective on Israel and other Jewish-related topics. Although a number of those I interviewed had liberal views on the topic of a Palestinian state, that was before Hamas was elected. While the question of Israel, for many survivors, seems simple and straightforward, it is actually rather complicated, since it plays into feelings of victimization from the Shoah.

Current immigration to the Netherlands is another topic that has galvanized Dutch citizens. Elly wrote me her thoughts on the matter:

> I felt very frustrated when I wrote a letter to the head of all jewish organisations in the netherlands about the asylum seekers policy of our government. I wanted a jewish standpoint about 26,000 people being put out of our country, being taken away from their homes, put in sort of prisons in order to be send over the border. I thought jews in particular should do something about this, people who were often born here, but were not accepted as refugees, after 8 or 10 years court cases, families being ripped apart, one parent would be send to russia, one to africa, those sort of things, awful. many lord mayors from cities refused to cooperate and many teachers helped students to go into hiding. I thought the jews should do something and speak up, but they could not care less I think. at the end I wrote a letter to a liberal rabbi who sent my letter with signatures of others to the minister. never heard anything about it. was a lot of commotion and it made me literally sick.[8]

In general I think it is fair to surmise that most of those I interviewed are not active politically, and that many in Holland are now concerned about immigrants from Muslim countries, who are perceived as anti-Israel or anti-Semitic.

Several hidden children were active in the Jewish community in Holland or the United States—either holding a board position at a synagogue or working in Jewish organizations. Rob, for example, has become extremely active in major Jewish organizations in the Netherlands and was on the Central Jewish Board when the deliberations about state restitution occurred. Many of these individuals, like Rob, see their political task as working for and perpetuating the Jewish community, of which their parents were a part. This includes taking leading roles in organizations of child survivors of the Holocaust.

CREATING IDENTITY, PRODUCING MEMORY

Thus far this chapter has focused on individuals and the long-term emotional consequences of hiding and living through war. Although so many have suffered considerably from these events on a personal level, it is not sufficient solely to individualize or psychologize the war. Genocide and war are public events with public outcomes, in addition to having important private outcomes for those who lose a home, a parent, or an entire way of life (de Haan 2001; de Swaan 1990). I will now move to another perspective—one that is broader and more public—that encompasses former hidden children as individuals and reflects their trauma but also speaks to and for them as a whole.

"Our Personal Craziness Wasn't Crazy!"

Holocaust survivors were "discovered" in the 1980s, encouraged by commercial films that popularized the Holocaust for broad audiences and younger generations. After decades of keeping silent—because no one wanted to listen—survivors began telling their stories to an interested public. However, hidden children were not part of this wave of recognition, nor did they view themselves as survivors. Indeed, as I've written earlier in this book, they were even admonished by Jewish concentration camp survivors who felt themselves to be the true survivors; after all, some argued, hidden children had slept in beds and had access to food on a daily basis. The hierarchy of suffering was established, and hidden children were at the bottom of it; those who had been on the Kindertransport didn't even have a position in that hierarchy.

Hidden children did not challenge such conceptions because they agreed with them, at least initially. Their own parents had dismissed their war history because of the supposed impossibility of children having memories. Additionally, many parents had admonished their children by reminding them that they, the parents, had suffered more. Schoolmates and other friends seconded these tendencies, as did Dutch society, responding with disbelief and disinterest. These silencings forced hidden children to hide yet again, a skill that by now they had honed.

In the early 1990s, two international conferences changed the lives of most hidden children I interviewed. In 1991 the first international gathering of hidden children took place in New York City. Three hundred people were expected, and sixteen hundred people attended. There was not enough room for all of them. In 1992 a second conference, for those hidden in the Netherlands, took place, this time in Amsterdam. Again, a small number was hoped for, but five hundred people came, a large number for such a small country. Mostly the American-based hidden children I interviewed attended the New York conference, but the majority of my sample—those living in Holland, the United States, and Israel—attended the one in Amsterdam.[9] (See figure 24.)

A minority of former hidden children I interviewed did not attend either conference and have no desire ever to attend any hidden children's event. Although they may have answered my ad or request for an interview, they do not believe that being a hidden child is a relevant or attractive commonality. One called those who go to these gatherings part of a "cult," explaining that he feels that those hidden children who have problems tend to attend the conferences. This person seemed to be very closed off to his emotions in general. One lively woman I interviewed explained that she chooses friends for their personalities, not their backgrounds, and that she had enough friends anyway. "My world isn't the Jewish world," stated Eva, although she has engaged in a discussion group with other war orphans.

Several mentioned that they were afraid to attend the conferences, fearful of revealing their emotions or of having them opened up. Quite a few former hidden children I interviewed explained that they had not wanted to attend the early conferences but ended up going because either a friend or a spouse went and urged them to join. What happened once they got there was usually life altering.

Sanne had been in therapy for ten years yet had never discussed her past as a hidden child. To her the hidden child conference was "a relief." Max A. found it to be "a very emotional experience, very intense," even though he does not identify as a hidden child. Rozette had read Max A.'s report about the New York conference. "For the first time, I felt something. I went twice to Auschwitz without feeling anything; I couldn't feel. I was trying to get connected [to my parents]." When the conference in Amsterdam was announced, she thinks she must have been the first to apply, since she was so full of anticipation. At the conference she was in a group with twenty-one people, all of whom told their stories:

I heard my own story twenty-one times! And there, I really started again, really! I came out of hiding, and I understood a lot more and knew what I should work on. I met Mieke there in the same group—she's my age, two weeks younger.

Indeed, quite a few of those I interviewed met someone at the conference with whom they became good friends.

"It was a revelation," explained Jeannette, who had not wanted to attend the New York conference but went with friends anyway:

It was great. . . . I guess the biggest thing was that I wasn't alone. . . . I realized how important the Dutch aspect was of being hidden because the Polish Jews had such a different experience, and the Belgian Jews had such a different experience because they were in all these homes, so they were all with big groups. . . . The Dutch experience was a much more lonely experience.

For Peter V., the 1992 conference in Amsterdam was "very emotional, very important, a relief": "The big theme was . . . what everybody considered as [our] personal craziness from the war wasn't crazy because everybody had the same thing, so within the group, it's normal [chuckles]."

Riwka felt empowered after the Amsterdam conference; she felt as though she had "surfaced" and that, in some way, that change led to her divorce. Thea told me what a huge impact the New York conference had had on her:

[It] was one of the highlights of my life. You are suddenly around all these people who know, who can feel the way you feel. . . . It's like telling a person how it is to give birth to a child, but until you have one yourself, you don't know what it's like. The same goes for experience in life. . . . [No one else understands what it is like] when you are really afraid for your life, every single day, when every sound means "oh, no, that's the end of it—now I'm going to concentration camp."

Aaron told me he "was known as being quite unemotional." But he found the Amsterdam conference to be very moving:

It was the first time you talk with people who have the same problems, the same feelings, the same estrangement from society because in some respect you have been somebody on the margin of society. You're not like the others. And finding that you're not alone in that, there's an overwhelming feeling.

For him, an "unemotional" person, the conference "opened a lot of feeling." For Rita, the 1992 conference "was marvelous": "It was an unbelievable experience for me." Peter H. found the 1992 conference "very emotional": "I cried a lot. . . . It was not relief; it was more. There I realized that I met many people with exactly the same story. "

Ed did not want to attend the New York conference, despite the fact that his wife, Carla, was one of the organizers. He recounted how he had never opened one of his wife's many books on the Holocaust nor his brother's gift of Jacob Presser's book on the Dutch Jews. He went, despite feeling that it would be a waste of his time. Ed describes how he went as an outsider, although he too had been hidden:

And I'm looking and wondering, "Who the hell comes to this thing? . . ." And as these elevators came up, doors would open, and these gray-haired people would come out. And they'd walk up to the counters . . . they would get these labels to stick on themselves. . . . And then they would gather sometimes in little groups and laugh and talk, and I got kind of curious and I thought, "I wonder what they have on those labels? . . ." So I went to see, and they had the names and they said, "I was hidden in Poland" and another name. "I was hidden in Romania," and "I was hidden in France," and "I was hidden in Holland," and I started to cry [beginning to cry]. *It was as if I had been in hiding all by myself. It's as if I was the only child to have been in hiding, it was very strange, because I knew better, of course, but here they were* [in whispering voice] *all around me, sixteen hundred of them, talking. Standing in the urinal a guy standing next to me says, "So where are you from?"* [laughter amid weeping]. *It was marvelous, marvelous, marvelous. . . . I cried, we cried for three days. . . . I've never let myself completely open up, never, not to anyone. Once damaged like that, you never trust completely. I've heard it a hundred times from hidden children. Not like my son, Dan, who sleeps like this at night* [makes a snoring sound and stretches his arms out]. *We sleep like this* [tucked in tight]. *There's always danger. So maybe I fully opened up? Never, but I managed to be a better person, after my grandson* [was born] *and after the hidden children's conference. I became a pretty decent guy. Before, I was too much turned inside. You can't be good to other people if you have terrible trouble with your own self. . . . These were epiphanies.*

Mieke, who has carried the burdens of hiding with her since the 1940s, despite the fact that her parents returned from the war, described her experience:

When I turned 50, there was the conference . . . here in Amsterdam, of the hidden children. And I went there. If my mother had not been dead by then, I'm not sure I would have had the courage to go. But I went. . . . There were six hundred hidden children like me. And they didn't look hidden. Some of them were successful. And I realized that I didn't have a terrible life and that I was successful in things too. And from there, I met Rozette and we became sisters, with a group. And in that group, we came together once a month for two years or so. That's when I came home.

Ruth J. went to the New York conference but did not like it; she felt that she "could not connect with anyone." She went to a support group in New York but could not cry there either. She feels she has "a real problem with groups": "Just because they had been hidden children, we had nothing in common." However, although she's engaged in artwork that reflects her war experience, she feels that she's not very forthcoming or open emotionally.

After I presented my research findings to participants in the 2005 Jewish Child Survivors of the Holocaust conference, one former hidden child, who is the brother of someone in my study, stated:

This is the only group I've ever been able to join and have a sense of legitimacy [in]. In every other group, I've felt alienated, including the community I live in, the schools I went to, without exception. Without exception, I've never been able to join anything that felt real until this. And I feel here I belong.

I have already discussed competitive suffering between camp survivors and hidden children. Unfortunately, this kind of competition also exists among hidden children, and a few people mentioned how it occurred at these first conferences. Others have described how it manifests in support groups. The most typical occurrence is when someone who was orphaned tells another hidden child who had one or two surviving parents that he or she was "lucky," or when someone with only one surviving parent says the same to someone with two surviving parents. If this book has done nothing else, it has demonstrated that even those whose parents and family survived intact did not have an easy time after the war, and, in fact, many were deeply unhappy. Telling someone that he or she is lucky is a way of silencing them, of placing them lower on the hierarchy of suffering.

Yvonne was attacked by another orphan in a group of hidden children who stated that Yvonne was lucky because she had her aunt. This is the aunt who insisted on raising Yvonne even though she was not fond of children and who was very abusive to her. As Yvonne aptly noted, "There are all these really wounded people begrudging each other as to who had it better." As Mieke and many others told me during interviews, they were constantly told that they were lucky, but in some sense, by denying their right to be unhappy, those who told them this only served to silence them and to increase their unhappiness. This dynamic is what led one woman with surviving parents to tell me that she wished her mother had been gassed—at least then she would have been entitled to her unhappiness. It led another woman who had been orphaned but who had been aware of how difficult it was for others whose parents did return to say that she was glad at some level that her parents did not return.

Yet while it is acceptable to make these kinds of statements about one's own life, problems arise when these sentiments are projected onto someone else. At the Amsterdam conference someone said to Jeannette, who was orphaned by the war and had a difficult postwar life, "I envy you not having your parents back." Jeannette told me, "You know, *that's horrible*. It was because . . . it was so difficult after the war with her parents that she could say that." Indeed, it is a shocking and somewhat outrageous statement to make to someone, especially without knowing what his or her life was like after the war. However, we need to bear in mind that such statements clearly reveal the damaging effects of the war and the level of deprivation felt by many former hidden children still today.

Becoming a Collective

Eva Fogelman (1993) finds that interviews, such as the ones Steven Spielberg is conducting, or talk therapy begin the process of "identity integration," which allows hidden children to integrate their fragmented identities. Indeed, quite a number of hidden children mentioned that my interview with them was their first and that they felt it was an important achievement for them. At the same time, more public venues, such as the conferences and the resultant organizations of hidden children, create a group feeling, which is of great psychological value for healing.

Before attending these conferences and group meetings, many hidden children still carried the stigma of their Jewishness, keeping it buried and hidden. Fogelman found that meeting others who had also hidden their Jewish identity gave each participant the courage to acknowledge that part of his- or herself, thus allowing them to begin to integrate it into their identity. In the large-group meetings, being Jewish was positively reinforced. Thus, as these hidden children were able to meet with others from similar backgrounds, "the fear of being openly Jewish gradually dissipated. . . . [This is the] integration of emotions—from being ashamed to feeling proud" (2002: 3).

The hidden children's groups and organizations catalyzed by the conferences sprouted up all over the world. The general feeling expressed to me about these gatherings was that it was the first time being hidden was shared, and it was the first time that some felt their reactions were "normal." Feelings and reactions that many had attributed to their own quirkiness, or in their words, their "craziness," turned out to be common to this large group. What had been understood as an individual problem became a social phenomenon. To paraphrase Peter V., what was felt as personal craziness no longer seemed crazy, but normal. Hidden children finally "came out," as they quite deliberately call it. They gave themselves a name, and they did so with pride rather than with guilt and fear of castigation from others. They claimed themselves worthy of being called "survivors."

A recent issue of the newsletter *The Hidden Child* commemorated the tenth anniversary of those first conferences. The titles of the autobiographical articles speak for themselves: "For Me, It Became a Rebirth" (Lessing 2002: 5); "The 1991 Gathering: It Changed the Course of My Life" (Lichtman 2002: 8); "Celebrating 10 Years—The End of Isolation" (Hasson 2002: 11); "Finding My Past" (Farkas 2002: 14), and "Coming Out of Hiding" (Stark 2002: 15). With the exception of the first one, all these articles were written by those hidden in countries other than the Netherlands.

This process continues today with the annual International Conference of Jewish Child Survivors of the Holocaust, which has moved the personal into the social and political realms. In doing so, it has created an identity and a collective memory for hidden children. (The 2005 conference theme was "Still Going Strong, 1945–2005.") Not only are there hidden children associations and organizations worldwide, but there also exists the Hidden Child Foundation in New York and its international newsletter, *The Hidden Child*, with a global circulation of 6,500, including libraries and research institutions.[10] Hidden children have joined ranks with other survivors in claiming their rights to restitution. They have become a political force making demands on governments and organizations for recognition and reparations. As mentioned at the end of chapter 3, an organization called Maror represented the Jews seeking reparations. Along with Maror, other groups such as the Roma and those from the former Dutch East Indies also took part in a larger committee—Morele Erkenning (Moral Recognition)—all seeking reparations. Beginning in 2000, the Roma were awarded 30 million euros, those from Indonesia received 250 million euros, and the Jews received 400 million euros. Those Jews who received restitution included German Jews and half-Jews who in the 1930s had fled to Holland, where they became stateless. A certain percentage of the money for Jews went toward Jewish organizations as well as to Jewish communities in Eastern Europe. This issue provoked some rancor during committee meetings, since many survivors felt that the full amount should be distributed to individuals, not parceled off to organizations.

The restitution monies were welcomed by those who do not have much; those who are better off put them toward making a special purchase or taking a vacation. Although many hidden children still bear damaging scars that no amount of money can smooth over, at the same time, this collectivization of identity and memory has been liberating for them. Most hidden children felt a huge burden lifted when the first conferences took place and now feel completely recognized by both state and society.

Yet although many hidden children share this collective identity and memory, this does not mean that they are one big happy family. One group in the Netherlands that evolved from the 1992 Amsterdam conference and became an organization in 1994 is HOK, Het Ondergedoken Kind (the Hidden Child), an association of hidden children that came together for social purposes, especially to celebrate Jewish holidays. Another group that wanted to be more inclusive splintered off from HOK and became JOK, Joodse Oorlogs Kinderen (Jewish War Children); it includes all child survivors more broadly, not only those who were hidden. JOK is more oriented toward lectures and discussions that deal directly with its members' pasts. "We laugh, they cry," the leader of HOK remarked when explaining their differences to me, although I think that there are class and educational differences between these two groups too. There are tensions within these two groups as well as between them, and some infighting has occurred in HOK. After HOK celebrated its tenth anniversary in May 2004, a number of board members resigned, and since then, no new activities have been organized. Although hidden children may have discovered their "brothers and sisters" with whom they share a past that is now uncovered, many of their disagreements spark feuds over issues that do not seem all that major because wounds and old feelings of deprivation are often so close to the surface. Thus, although hidden children may share an identity and collective memory, like siblings, they do not necessarily get along.

CONCLUSIONS

One charming man who gave me a copy of a book he had written about animal reproduction stated, after our interview, "It's true that a day doesn't go by that I don't think about the war." Then, as an afterthought he added, with a smile, "But the same is true about sex!" This delightfully honest duality encapsulates both the tolls taken by the past and the normalcy of life that have intertwined over time in the lives of most hidden children I interviewed. These survivors have suffered multiple emotional traumas from multiple separations and moves; however, the vast majority have been able to live with and alongside their pain.

Up until the 1990s, hidden children's memories of the Occupation, the war, and their postwar lives were packed tightly away with the occasional leak that might have resulted in depression or a breakdown. The timing of the first hidden children's conferences and the ability of hidden children to stake their claims did not occur in a vacuum, but during a particular historical moment when public discourse had shifted and Holocaust survivors were in the limelight (Prager 1998; Gordon 1997). The recent development of a collective identity as hidden children and the recognition of their collective memory have enabled them to stake their rightful position and claims as war victims. Their remembering occurred intersubjectively and interactively in a context that allowed their ghosts to surface in a socially and culturally acceptable manner. Although not a panacea, collectively acknowledging and facing these hauntings has lifted a huge burden for many of them.

Conclusion

HIDING² [HIDING SQUARED]

This book has uncovered the hidden history of hidden children in World War II by revealing their experiences before, during, and especially after hiding. The trajectory of hidden children differs considerably from our image of typical survivors—those who were in concentration camps—in multiple ways. Hidden children were given up by their parents, usually as young children, some as young as a few hours old, often to strangers who delivered them to non-Jewish Dutch families. They were openly or clandestinely hidden anywhere from one night to several years. Most children hid in more than one place, yet quite a few experienced the stability of being in one family for a long period. Their time in hiding was a period of danger when they were forced to adopt new identities that did not reflect their Jewish past and to adapt to the ways of a new family. In some cases, these children formed strong emotional attachments to their hiding families and felt it was the best period in their childhood; in most cases, however, close attachments did not develop. The majority in this study hid in satisfactory circumstances, and a small number were in poor if not abusive settings.

For most of the hidden children I studied, the Occupation and wartime period were manageable, however difficult the challenges. The inverse was true for those in camps, who struggled to survive in sites of disease, death, and extermination. Liberation set camp inmates free, although most were stateless and soon discovered that most if not all of their family had been decimated. Among hidden children, the common refrain was "my war began after the war," marking the beginning of a traumatic time for many, for different reasons. Some were torn from foster parents and returned to a parent or parents they did not recognize, rarely reconnecting. Those orphaned by the war had their own problems, particularly if they moved in with Jewish relatives. Staying with a non-Jewish hiding family seems to have been a somewhat less wrenching experience, and living in an orphanage brought mixed results. As my research has made clear, having both parents survive the war was not a panacea and did not make those children any happier or mentally healthier. *Both the survival of parent(s) and the loss of parent(s) signified the beginning of major problems for the majority of those I interviewed, in different ways and for different reasons.*

After the war many were forced into another kind of hiding as parents made it clear that their children's pasts should remain concealed. Parents were joined by friends, teachers, and schoolmates, none of whom wanted to hear about the children's experiences. They were all in a deep state of cultural denial (Cohen 2001), which for Jewish parents and Dutch society may have been a way to assuage their guilt. Hidden children already had developed the skills of cautiousness and vigilance; they continued to apply these to their postwar lives. However, there was a price to be paid for this repression, since some children acted out, and others carried their pain with them for decades, only to have it come out later in the form of depression or breakdowns. For that reason, one of the few advantages enjoyed by those in orphanages was the ability to talk to and bond with others who had had similar experiences. For the majority of hidden children, however, their memories were denied, as were their experiences. These memories became their secrets, which had difficult and sometimes destructive repercussions.

FAMILY LIVES

The narratives covered all possible postwar family configurations and demonstrate that, for the most part, having two parents or even one parent survive and re-creating family life did not guarantee good relationships or a close, loving atmosphere. Many hidden children were shocked by the appearance of a stranger or two whom they were instructed to call "Mother" or "Father." Leaving home for "home" with these new parents was traumatic for many who were never able to establish or reestablish good relationships with their parents. Indeed, most narratives paint a picture of a loosely connected group of individuals who did not share much support, affection, warmth, or love. To reiterate a crucial point, this is not to place the blame on parents, since they were changed by the war, and the world as they had known it was drastically different after the war. But it does demonstrate that intact postwar families experienced tremendous difficulties that were sometimes as scarring as, if not more so than, the wartime experience itself for the children. My data suggest that for many, the key to their survival during the war—hiding with strangers when they were young enough to forget their pasts—was often pivotal in creating unhappiness in their postwar family lives. In the long run, what had saved them led to problematic and destructive relationships in their postwar families.

After being relatively well-behaved children in the homes of strangers, many hidden children started to act out in different ways. Some felt abandoned by the foster family who had given them up and let them go; we now know that many foster parents were terribly upset in doing so, but the children were usually not aware of this. Others felt tremendous anger at their parents for having abandoned them, as they framed it, often stating that they wished their parents had kept the family together, even knowing that their chances for survival would have been severely compromised. Later, as adults who could rationally understand why their parents had made what must have been a horrendous decision—to give their child to strangers for safekeeping—they still felt their childhood rage as well as the sense of abandonment. Furthermore, after becoming parents and grandparents themselves, many stated that they would never make the same decision, in some sense castigating their parents. Indeed, one grandfather who had been orphaned quit his job so that he could care for his grandchildren when they came home from school, so that strangers did not take care of them.

Several children with widowed mothers who did not remarry seem to have had one of the least bumpy postwar rides. However, children with one surviving parent who entered a reconfigured family, especially one with a stepparent and stepsiblings, confronted another layer of complexity and conflict. The majority of stepparents, often survivors themselves with their own baggage, were abusive in one way or another with these young children. Physical abuse was the most common pattern, and sexual abuse occurred in four cases. Although these are small numbers, they are significant in that they deconstruct particular images of Jewish families as safe havens and are likely indicators that this kind of abuse occurred in other survivor families as well.

There were five possible outcomes for those who were orphaned at the war's end, about one-third of my sample: staying with their foster family, living with relatives, living with an unrelated family, going into an orphanage, or going to Israel. Quite a number of orphans experienced two or even three of these options. My findings suggest that the several who remained with their foster families did quite well, and the others seem to have managed, although their experiences were uneven. Orphans who were taken in by Jewish kin did not fare so well, always feeling as though they were second fiddle, more like stepchildren. Some were abused. Living with relatives perpetuated the feelings many had while in hiding—that they were guests rather than full family members and that they had to watch their behavior. As a whole, moving from the households of foster families to those of kin made the children in this group worse off in that many children were more unhappy in their relatives' homes than they had been in the homes of their non-Jewish foster families. Again, Jewish kin in Holland were also grieving and perhaps were not available emotionally. The two instances of orphans living with an unrelated family demonstrate diametrically opposed outcomes—one girl who lived with her siblings in the home of family friends seems to have done well, while another girl was raped by the Jewish foster father whose family wanted to adopt her.

Children in Jewish orphanages benefited from having each other, creating a new family of sorts and forming ties that remain strong to this day. Some orphanages were strict, cold, and unnurturing institutions, while others had a much looser and kinder environment. The main offense all the orphanages committed was not supplying their charges with the education and skills they needed to create a better life once they left. In the boys' orphanages, the children were not given the nurturing that they needed. Further, those whose parent(s) returned or who lived with relatives had access to more resources and social capital than did the orphans living in institutions, which often led to the possibility of higher education, a more skilled profession, and a more comfortable lifestyle than most orphans were able to have.

However, one of my most unexpected findings is that, in the end, it was better for orphans to remain where they were if things were going well, meaning in a non-Jewish family environment, only because it promised continuity and prevented another rupture in a child's primary relationships. This conclusion is obvious from a commonsense perspective but also controversial in that the OPK has been criticized for being all too eager to keep children in Christian homes rather than placing them in Jewish environments. Most of those I interviewed who stayed with their foster families did find their way to the Jewish community and a Jewish identity later in life, although this may reflect a bias in my sampling. Surely many hidden children did not develop a Jewish identity and remain either Christian-identified or neither Christian nor Jewish. It is quite clear that a number of children with surviving parents would have been better off remaining with their foster families if only for continuity's sake, even though this scenario is unrealistic and problematic for other reasons. The most tragic cases are those in which a foster family wanted to keep the hidden child where she was happily ensconced but a Jewish social worker convinced the foster parents to give up the child so she could be adopted by a Jewish family. A number of those children ended up being warehoused in orphanages. (In her recent book, Elma Verhey [2005] refers to Jewish children in these orphanages as "inmates.")

This is not to say that the decisions of the OPK to keep some children in their Christian foster families are vindicated by these findings. The structure of the commission and the decision-making process were extremely insensitive to the few remaining Dutch Jews and the genocide that had decimated their community. Indeed, all scholarly accounts point to anti-Semitic tendencies in the way that the commission was created, was structured, and made decisions. It is understandable that the rebuilding of a Jewish community would not have been a priority for the average Dutch non-Jew—for some, it was even seen as undesirable. That being said, commission members should have been able to recognize that Jews deserved special and sensitive treatment, and they should have been more interested in understanding the role played by Judaism, Jewishness, and Jewish identity in Holland before the war. Instead, commission members and their deliberations reflect not only insensitivity and ignorance but also smugness, arrogance, and chauvinism, all under- and overscored with anti-Semitism. They did not know what the majority of Dutch Jews were like, and they did not care to know. They felt they knew it all from their own religious background. Unfortunately, the OPK simply reflected the broader postwar attitude and policies of the Dutch state in general, which were neither welcoming nor benevolent toward the surviving remnants of its Jewish population.

One Dutch woman in my study had a poignant and insightful reaction to my presentation of research findings at the 2005 Conference of Jewish Child Survivors of the Holocaust. She had been orphaned but not allowed to stay with her foster family, where she had been very happy. Pointing to another person in the room who was allowed to stay with his foster family but was not happy there, she stated, "He is angry, and I am angry. I mean, everything is wrong. You couldn't do it right—every choice was the wrong choice." The moderator added, "Afterward, people who stayed in the foster family said, 'I should have gone to a Jewish family,' and those who went to a Jewish family said that they should have been left with the foster family. Afterward, there is always pain." I wholeheartedly agree. These were extremely difficult and unprecedented decisions made in a less than professional manner. But even if what we would now consider to be highly qualified professionals were involved, many decisions would still have been the wrong ones simply because of the inevitable trauma of war, death, and separation.

The hiding experiences and the postwar situation left indelible marks on these survivors. Most former hidden children can still easily weep when recounting some aspect of their hiding experience or their family lives after the war. Yet one important finding that has been presented in this book is that despite some very deep wounds that still pain them, most of those I interviewed are resilient and have been able to create or at least patch together a rewarding life. Rather than asserting a black-or-white argument as other scholars have done—that survivors are either psychologically damaged or successful and resilient (Helmreich 1992)—the narratives developed in this book demonstrate that both may be true and that one does not necessarily preclude the other.

Among those who suffer from long-term emotional debilitation, almost all postwar family outcomes are represented. Four children were in institutional settings for many years, and three of them (all male) described harsh, cold, and sometimes sadistic conditions void of any affirmation from adults. These four are clear victims of a war that deprived them of parents and of the help they needed. Yet although surviving parents would have filled that void, we have also noted that even when parents returned, they were usually emotionally disabled and unable to help their children recover. Indeed, two individuals in my study who are emotionally fragile had both parents return. That being said, those who were long-term residents in unnurturing institutions would have had a better chance of receiving some kind of help, perhaps in the form of therapy, or at least more of an education, had their parents survived. Yet although orphans who were institutionalized clearly had less support than others, there are also those orphans who have managed to build careers and strong families of their own. In sum, though orphans had the harshest time in terms of resources and opportunities and perhaps the hardest time emotionally, major emotional problems are found among those from all possible postwar family settings.

SOCIOLOGY MEETS THE HOLOCAUST

What are the implications of this study for sociology? And how can sociology draw on this kind of Holocaust study? First, my findings suggest that these hidden children fully experienced what we now call "postmodern families" shortly after 1945, many decades before the term was coined. Owing to persecution, genocide, and war, children from former proletarian and petit-bourgeois Jewish families found themselves caught in a web of relationships with multiple parents and families for which there were no guiding terms or models. Thus, the complicated forms we now see in blended families were present sixty years ago for these surviving children. Given how little we know about postwar or postgenocidal societies, it is likely that such complex family forms may not be unique under these circumstances. At the very least, the family complexities confronted by hidden children in a postwar context challenge any assumptions of an intact biological nuclear family as a reference point for what they considered to be family.

Second, this study asks some deeper questions about the notion of family. What, in fact, constitutes a family? While the separation of young children from their parents was undoubtedly traumatic for all involved, it was doubly traumatic for children to be reunited with biological parents they no longer knew and to be forced to leave the people they thought were their parents. These reunited families tended not to be very successful, despite the ties of kinship. Similar questions have arisen in contemporary controversies when a biological parent has sought to reclaim a child he or she had given up for adoption, and this study underscores that biological ties do not necessarily a family make. The biological parents in this book were also war survivors and faced overwhelming circumstances, and those factors certainly encumbered postwar family reconnections. Furthermore, we saw that Jewish orphans who went to live with relatives never felt at ease or at home, but felt more like stepchildren, again challenging the emphasis on blood relations above all. In these cases, blood was rarely thicker than water. One situation, in which an orphan and her brother were successfully brought up by their parents' friends, leaves me to wonder if parents' friends rather than relatives might not have been better choices for some orphans since, as the saying goes, one can choose one's friends. In any event, this study clearly demonstrates that some adults can be very competent parents to children to whom they did not give birth.

Third, the fact that children and their biological mothers tended not to reconnect after the war brings up questions about mother-child attachment and bonding, currently the focus of much attention in the United States, where a kind of intensive and anxious mothering has taken hold (Warren 2005). The data suggest, however, that a lack of postwar connection to one's mother was not necessarily a predictor for emotional distress and long-term problems. Many of those same children who did not have a good postwar relationship with their mother connected either with a foster parent or with their biological father. In other words, what matters is a connection with a caring adult, even if he or she is not the biological parent.

Some fathers also had trouble reconnecting with their children after the war. There was perhaps less change in fathers' relationships with their children compared with mothers' relationships because of traditional gender norms, but certainly not in all cases. Some survivors I interviewed never sat on their father's lap again after the war, while others had never done so before the war and may not have noticed much of a shift.

Some of my findings center on definitions of the "best interests of the child." The state has used this concept to justify certain decisions that awarded custody to one party and denied it to another. In addition to being a highly cultural and historically specific notion, this contentious concept is riddled with problems connected to knowledge—that is, who exactly knows what the best interests of the child are, and how do they know it? Today in this country we have seen this concept used in highly political and moralistic ways, such as when lesbians are denied custody of their children. Although the ways in which the OPK was created, structured, and run are reprehensible, it is likely that arguments for keeping children with their Christian foster families were often correct from a certain standpoint. At the same time, we can understand why the Jewish community would have wanted Jewish children to be in Jewish environments. Yet sending children to Jewish orphanages rather than keeping them in loving foster homes, albeit Christian ones, was not a wise decision, in retrospect. Also unwise was the push by Jewish social workers for foster parents to give up their foster child so that she could be placed in a Jewish family, since that did not necessarily occur and children were then placed in orphanages. With the advantage of hindsight, it now seems as if a number of Jewish orphans might have been better off had they been able to stay with their foster family while maintaining a link to other Jews and to Jewish education.

This case study, then, is relevant to contemporary quandaries over custody, foster care, adoption, and family reunification. For example, should a birth parent be awarded custody of a child he or she put up for adoption years earlier who no longer knows this parent? Can white families provide an acceptable environment for African American children in need of a foster home or of adoption, or is it best to keep African American children in African American homes? Clearly, these are extraordinarily difficult questions to which there can be multiple answers from multiple perspectives. However, this book points to some possible problematic outcomes when biology is privileged above all, and when religion or ethnicity is privileged.

The changes in Jewish families delineated here reflect the kinds of disruption that fragment families on a global scale today because of economic needs that lead to transnational migrations (e.g., Filipinas going to the Middle East or East Asia to earn money), state intervention (e.g., apartheid), political conflict (as in Bosnia), ecological disasters (as in Somalia), and genocide (as in Sudan). How can families be reconstituted after such serious disruptions? In Canada, researchers and community workers have begun to address the effects of state interventions that institutionalized indigenous First Nation people. These interventions disrupted communities and interrupted and prevented the cultural transmission of fathering (Ball 2006; Stover and Weinstein 2004). Currently, the state is funding the creation of innovative programs that support fathers in learning parenting. Even though postwar Jewish fathers and mothers may have had comparatively more social capital than First Nation peoples do, they still needed support to help them live with their grief and to parent their children, who were also war survivors.

My research also provides evidence for Jeffrey Prager's arguments that memory is constituted in a social, relational, and interactive manner. We have seen how Nazi policies forced young children to repress their prewar memories and how the broader postwar society (and surviving Jewish parents) encouraged continued repression of their wartime experiences. Hidden children kept their memories private, and individual problems were seen as just that—individual. However, a broader cultural acknowledgment of Jewish Holocaust survivors in the 1980s catalyzed a deep interest in their stories and experiences. Memoirs and oral histories of that period gained momentum as the public and especially the Jewish community wanted to hear more.

Ten years later, in the 1990s, within this broader social context, hidden children began to poke their heads up, feeling that it was not only safe but the right time to "come out" into the sun, to claim their shadows, their hauntings, and their histories as survivors. International conferences and the groups that developed from them became the forums in which former hidden children began to remember and discuss their pasts, reconfirming each other's memories. Individuals began to see the social aspect of their pasts and to feel both connected and held by their new identity as hidden children and by their newly constructed collective memory of hiding. I have also argued that the social aspects of producing an identity and collective memory have been healing for many hidden children. This collective memory has not only helped many hidden children feel "normal," but it has given them the strength of a group identity and enabled them to make political claims. These claims have led to apologies, atonement, and reparations, from the Germans especially, and more recently from the Dutch. In this way, private hauntings have become public ones, and as they were confronted collectively, many ghosts were calmed. However, although Germany has engaged in its memory work and confronted its past at many different levels in a process called *Vergangenheitsbewältigung* (a term referring to working through the atrocities committed by Germans, specifically during World War II), Holland has not taken on its past to a similar extent, and most Dutch people feel themselves to be solely victims of World War II.

JEWISH AND HOLOCAUST STUDIES MEET SOCIOLOGY

One of my major findings that contributes to Jewish Studies is that Jewish families were often troubled, problematic, unwelcoming, and, on rare occasions, the sites of abuse. However, this book also normalizes Jewish families to some extent, since it makes clear that all families, Jewish ones included, are host to a wide range of less than admirable behaviors both in wartime and in peacetime. In a poem entitled, "I Guard the Children," Yehuda Amichai (1924–2000), Israel's leading poet, speculates about parent-child relations during the Shoah:

I ask myself: During the Shoah,
would a son still rebel against his parents, would a father beat
his son behind the barbed wire,
was there a mother-daughter struggle in the huts of annihilation,
a stubborn and rebellious son in the carloads of transport,
a generation gap on the platforms of perdition,
Oedipus in the death chambers?

Chana Kronfeld, professor of Hebrew literature and poetry, asserts that although these questions are not answered, "it is the mere asking that breaks the most fundamental social taboos of discourse about the Shoah, at the same time that it rehumanizes and enlivens the victims." She argues that Amichai honors the victims by speaking psychological truths and not simply idealizing their suffering. And in this process of acknowledging the importance of asking such questions, Amichai undermines another taboo about the Shoah by "invoking intra-Jewish violence and brutality" (Kronfeld 2006: 6).

Indeed, in my research I have uncovered family processes, dynamics, and interactions that are also uncomfortable truths. Yet, as does Amichai's poem, they rehumanize the victims without idealizing them. The fact that they took place during, or because of, the Shoah makes them no less troubling. Many of these family patterns were intensified by the stress of war, the grief of loss, and the helplessness of the survivor, but some of them occur during peacetime as well, just as they do in all families. The point is not to air the dirty laundry of an Old World Jewish hamper but to acknowledge that families, even if they are Jewish, are problematic sites, and sometimes they deeply fail their members.

Asking any family to lead a more normalized life after war, separation, and trauma is a tall order. Jewish families struggled to create and recreate some semblance of normality during and after an extraordinary time. Most families failed to regain their footing, and some crashed and burned. Looking inside these Jewish families goes beyond portraying Jews solely as victims and reflects a perspective that acknowledges their agency. Parents were victims, without a doubt, but they were also actors, and often they used the wrong script.

A second implication for Jewish (and Holocaust) Studies is that the Jewish collective memory of the Holocaust is not homogeneous. Even when they are within the same generation, camp survivors have memories that are very different from those of hidden children. Sharing this collective memory, even within the same generation, does not necessarily unite these individuals as part of one big family. A hierarchy of suffering exists between camp survivors and hidden children and even among hidden children, depending on their postwar family outcome. This kind of competitiveness is silencing and disregarding, and it creates divisions. Furthermore, as I have noted, conflict exists between two different associations for hidden children in Amsterdam, one of which now seems dormant. These examples suggest that collective memory is a varied and fragmented entity within which considerable differences can exist. That which brought hidden children together to create an identity and collective memory is also a source of ongoing conflict.

One of the main premises of this book is that the war did not end in 1945 for those who survived it. Rather, its effects were long-term, and many survivors grapple with them every day. The case of hidden children makes this point in an even more poignant manner, given that wartime was livable for most and even pleasant for some, while their postwar experience was, on the whole, much more difficult. The data present a strong argument against studies or oral histories of the Shoah that end in 1945. Indeed, it is my view that to fully understand the Shoah we need to focus just as intensively on the postwar period as we typically do on wartime so that we can grasp not only the events but the meaning of what transpired afterward. In terms of the politics of memory, I am arguing for an extension of the period that has been typically defined as the Shoah. Hidden children feel that their war began after the war, so for them, the period after the Shoah remains the Shoah. This argument can and should be applied to the study of war and genocide more broadly.

BEYOND ANNE FRANK

The history of the Occupation and of Jews hiding in the Netherlands is not a pretty one. Rather, it is riddled with anti-Semitism, collaboration, rejection, and death. Though this is not unique in Western European history, it is the inverse of how the Dutch are perceived in global popular culture. Anne Frank's story has generated a myth about the Dutch and Dutch society that is not borne out by history. Holland's postwar state ideology of resistance, also the inverse of the historical truth, somehow got tangled up with the Anne Frank story, and together they have become the accepted truth. The postwar actions of the state and the disinterested reactions of Dutch society, though paralleled elsewhere in Europe, with the exception of the OPK, are nonetheless shocking because of perceptions in great part created by the Anne Frank story.

Indeed, this myth continues to be perpetuated, with a focus on those who saved Jews (Klemper 2006). I would argue that we need more focus on the majority of the Dutch population, who ignored their Jewish compatriots. We need to ask why so many Dutch people were witnesses and bystanders rather than actors.

To reiterate an earlier point, by calling the Anne Frank story a myth, I am not concurring with Holocaust revisionists, contesting Anne Frank's existence, her circumstances, or her death. Rather, my point is that her story has been used to spin a fable about how many Jews hid in the Netherlands and, more important, about the benevolence of the Dutch population toward its Jewish population. That she remains an eternal child further fuels the image of innocence and vulnerability protected by good Dutch citizens but ultimately murdered by the bad Germans. Unfortunately, this is not the full story.

Despite the many academic descriptions of and memoirs about genocide, it remains unimaginable to most of us, and impossible to understand. To some extent, this incomprehension, combined with the fact that the Holocaust remains the most visible and publicly acknowledged genocide, continues to rivet our attention on the Shoah. In her essay entitled "The Psychology Behind Being a Hidden Child," Eva Fogelman asserts that

> there is a tendency to want to compare symptoms of members of the group [hidden Jewish children] with those of other traumatized children from, for example, Cambodia and Vietnam or war-torn Lebanon, or of starving children in Africa, or of sexually and physically abused children in our midst. However, the abuse of the hidden children was unique in several ways. . . . They were persecuted merely because they were Jews. (1993: 305)

She then drops any discussion of possible comparisons, having suggested but not really demonstrated that they are not relevant. Such arguments subtly suggest that the Holocaust was worse than other genocides and that it therefore ranks highest on the scale of human suffering.

While I agree that all the comparisons she mentioned may not be relevant, cases such as those involving the children in Bosnia and Rwanda, the stolen generation in Australia, Native American children, and Cambodian children *are* comparable. They seem highly relevant because these children and families were killed or taken from their homes because of who they were—Hutus, Tutsis, Muslims, anti-Communists, Chinese, or Aborigines—not so very different from Jews being persecuted because they were Jews. I would suggest then that we level the genocidal killing fields by not privileging one genocide over another. Of course, that entails first acknowledging the genocides. The Jewish community is quick to express outrage if the Holocaust is denied but has not been quick to acknowledge and act on other genocides until very recently, with Darfur in Sudan.[1]

In *Atonement and Forgiveness,* law professor Roy L. Brooks calls on a "post-Holocaust vision of heightened morality, identification, egalitarianism and restorative justice" as the basis for reparations to African Americans for slavery and segregation (2004: 11). His ideas moved me deeply because he presents a way to apply what we have learned from Jewish victimization in the Shoah to other groups—in this case, to African Americans—in a constructive manner.

Brooks's notion of what I'll call a "post-Holocaust ethic" replaces what has become a self-referential, hierarchical, and competitive framework of suffering with an egalitarian one in which Jewish victimization can be a helpful rather than a displacing model for peoples who have suffered from genocide, kidnapping, war, and slavery. I am not suggesting that we forget the Holocaust, but, instead, that Jewish organizations and individuals cease arguing that Jews are still the top dog in human suffering. This dynamic is parodied in Lore Segal's 1985 novel *Her First American* in a heated conversation between a Jewish refugee and an African American woman:

> Fishgoppel said, "Jews care enough about their children to give them an education."
> Ebony said, "Negroes were lynched if they learned the alphabet."
> "We had pogroms," said Fishgoppel.
> "Slavery," said Ebony.
> "Holocaust!" cried Fishgoppel.

Many Jewish organizations want young people to learn the lessons of the Shoah so that "it never happens again," but they are for the most part referring to another genocide of the Jews never happening again; rarely is it meant to apply to other groups, since the truth is, it has happened again, and it is happening right now. Another Holocaust museum opened in March 2005, this time at Yad Vashem in Israel. It is bigger than any other Holocaust museum in the world. But do we need yet another bigger and better monument that refers solely to the genocide of the Jews?

Israeli author Tom Segev recently noted that the United Nations acknowledged Holocaust Day for the first time in 2006, stating that "the impression is that the status of the Holocaust as a source of moral values is growing continually stronger." While this "globalization of the Holo-

caust" may be positive, he also observes that the Israeli culture of Holocaust commemoration stresses strengthening the state of Israel against its
Arab enemies but "does not equally foster the humanist lessons of the
Holocaust. . . . [It] still tends to close itself off from other groups persecuted by the Nazis and rejects any comparison between the Holocaust
and genocides that have taken place since World War II" (Segev 2006: 1).
In general, this has held true for the American Jewish community as well.

Applying Brooks's post-Holocaust ethic suggests that openness, listening, and generosity may be equally if not more rewarding among
Holocaust survivors who engage in competitive suffering and between
Holocaust survivors and survivors of other genocides. Acknowledging
the pain of others on any level, be it micro-, meso-, or macro-, does not
deny or decrease one's own pain in any manner. If nothing else, I hope
that this book has demonstrated to survivors who are tempted to call
other survivors "lucky" that no one got off easy; no one was lucky in the
end.

Several years ago, an elderly Holocaust survivor spoke to a classroom
about his experience, along with a young woman who had survived the
genocide in Rwanda. I emailed the article and photo from the San Francisco *Jewish Bulletin* to the students in my American Jewish Identities
course because until then, I had never seen a Holocaust survivor share
the stage with anyone but another Shoah survivor. This was a novel and
welcome change. This cooperation and acknowledgment of others' tragedies constitutes a very important first step in a post-Holocaust ethic.

I am heartened to see how American Jewish individuals and organizations finally have united in protest of the genocide in Darfur. I am also
encouraged by this activism because it is focused on a non-European,
nonwhite population, challenging the racism that allowed governments
to stall action against Rwanda during its genocide. Furthermore, those
being targeted are Muslims. Recently, I attended an event at Temple
Emanu-El, a large, well-off synagogue in San Francisco, where individuals spoke briefly in turn about the genocides in Armenia, the Holocaust,
Nanking, Cambodia, Bosnia, Rwanda, and Darfur, in that order. Mira
Shelub, a Polish Jewish survivor who fought as a partisan in the forest,
represented the Holocaust and effectively stated, "I fought for a better to-
morrow, a better day, and a better future. Only through peace can the

horrors of the Holocaust be laid to rest." The Rwandan survivor, Dr. Theogene Rudasingwa, stated, "'Never Again!' can become an empty slogan" and then urged the audience, "Let us make 'Never Again' truly 'Never Again.'"[2]

Sixty-five years after the Shoah, American Jews are finally making the connection between the Holocaust and other genocides: "We know what it means to be victims of those who want to wipe another people off the face of the earth," stated Rabbi Robert Levine, president of the New York Board of Rabbis, to an audience of a hundred and fifty rabbis.[3] "Only two generations ago . . . we looked around and wondered, where was everyone?" (Silverman and Silverman 2006: 17). In July 2004 the American Jewish World Service, an international development organization that funds relief agencies in Darfur, also wanted to seek a political solution. They joined with the U.S. Holocaust Memorial Museum to create the Save Darfur Coalition, an alliance of more than a hundred and sixty secular and religious groups calling for international intervention in Darfur. It is unclear whether it is due to the timing or the circumstances of this genocide, or both; however, clearly the plight of Muslims in Sudan "resonates with Jews in the U.S." (Banerjee 2006: 19), and that is a milestone. One might hope that this alliance and connection with a group of Muslims can extend to other populations such as the Palestinians, in an effort to seek understanding, justice and peace. These are superb examples of the kind of bridging work that needs to be done so that the Jewish community can use its tragedy to reach out to others. Instead of using the Holocaust as the reference point to justify Israeli policies of occupation (Lentin 2000), why not use the Shoah as a reference point to repair, to extend, to bridge?

As much as my research is meant to deepen our understanding of the Shoah, it is also meant to contribute to an understanding of war and genocide more broadly. Applying a post-Holocaust ethic to research means not privileging any one genocide over another and encourages a more comparative effort in studies of the Shoah. This book has entered the domain of postwar Jewish families and uncovered their raw humanity. The task at hand is to acknowledge the humanity of all groups on an equal basis and to attend to the tragedy of all genocides equally.

Notes

1. Throughout the book I use the term *Holland* interchangeably with *the Netherlands*, even though technically *Holland* refers only to the two western provinces in the Netherlands.

2. I use both the terms *Holocaust*, a Greek word denoting a "burnt offering," and *Shoah*, Hebrew for "disaster," interchangeably and with deep dissatisfaction, as both are too passive and too general. The notion that the Nazis offered the Jews as a burnt offering is offensive, while calling what took place a disaster puts it on a par with less significant events, such as hurricanes or financial crashes. However, they are the most commonly used terms we have. At other times, I refer to this period and these acts as *genocide, killing,* and *murder.* I find those terms to be more specific and active, with a clearer designation of perpetrator and victim, although some historians take issue with them (see D. Michman 2003).

3. A small body of literature exists on family formation and the baby boom that occurred in DP (Displaced Persons) camps after the war. See Rosensaft (2001) for a comprehensive bibliography.

4. The term *hidden child* is a curious one because, while it aptly describes the fate of many Jewish children more than sixty years ago, it tends to freeze that period and project it into the twenty-first century. That several contemporary associations and annual conferences of hidden children and of child survivors of the Holocaust exist almost suggests a kind of infantilization of adults whose ages now range from the mid-sixties to the early eighties—hardly children anymore. In fact, most are now grandparents. At the same time, the term and the way it is used by those to whom it is applied is poignant since the memories are still vivid for most. Similarly, when attending a conference of those on the Kindertransport, I noted how those attending referred to themselves as the *Kinder* (children). Thus I use the terms *hidden children* and *former hidden children* interchangeably.

5. Lawrence Graver (1995) vividly demonstrates how in the bitter fight over the U.S. rights to Anne Frank's story, Anne's father Otto "whitewashed" her diary, taking out specific references to her Jewishness or to Judaism, creating a story with a more universal appeal. Indeed, Frank's de-Judaizing of his daughter's diary has clearly contributed to its international success, so much so that young girls all over the world continue to strongly identify with Anne Frank, regardless of their religious backgrounds. More recent controversies have focused on other parts of the diary that were censored, such as Anne's portrayals of her sexuality, her relationship with her mother, and her parents' marriage, suppressing important aspects of family life. Indeed, these particular aspects highlight the question of what is acceptable to portray as family life.

6. Members of Parliament campaigned during the weekend before October 4, 2004, to grant posthumous citizenship to Anne Frank. Rita Verdonk, minister for integration and immigration, said there was no provision in the law to do so. Some historians and keepers of the Anne Frank legacy argued that making her a citizen would not change her place in history and could even denigrate other refugees by depriving them of recognition.

7. Bruno Bettelheim (1979) suggests that had the Frank family devised a plan for escape in case of a raid, some of them might have survived. Their hiding place had one entrance and no other exit. During their months of hiding, they did not attempt to create a plan for escape. Bettelheim is critical of "the universal admiration of their way of coping, or rather of not coping" in light of this shortsightedness (1979: 250). Indeed, most of the hidden children I interviewed knew there was a "plan B" in case of a raid, which on occasion did occur.

1. THE HISTORY AND MEMORY OF HIDDEN CHILDREN

1. Dwork refers to these two types of hiding as "visible" and "invisible" hiding (1991: 81).

2. See D. Berkani's film *Une résistance oubliée: La mosquée de Paris* (A Forgotten Resistance: The Mosque of Paris).

3. Most Jewish children on the Kindertransport were placed in Jewish rather than Gentile homes in England, although it appears that there were often pronounced differences in ethnic backgrounds (German or Austrian children were placed in Eastern European Jewish homes) and in their religious observance (children from observant, kosher households were put in nonkosher Jewish homes). Some lived with relatives. In a number of cases, young girls were exploited and expected to serve as maids by families who could not afford to hire help.

4. Every year, the World Federation of Jewish Child Survivors of the Holocaust holds a conference in a different city in Europe or North America. Child survivors include those who were in hiding, those who were on the Kindertransport, and those who were in concentration camps. Very few children survived the last. I have attended two of these congresses—one in Washington, D.C., in 1998 and one in Amsterdam in 2005, where I gave a talk about my research.

5. In his book *The Seventh Million*, Tom Segev (2000) argues that Holocaust survivors were ignored in Palestine and, later, in Israel as well. State ideology positioned Shoah victims as passive sheep, an image that was then juxtaposed against that of the strong, muscular Zionist who is free from the sickness of living in the Diaspora and will actively fight for his or her country. To be a victim of the Shoah was seen, therefore, as shameful, unless one was involved in active resistance. Indeed, Shoah studies in Israel are dominated by the theme of heroism and resistance (as in the Warsaw Ghetto uprising), whereas they are given quite a different emphasis in the United States. Only recently has this image of Shoah survivors shifted in Israel, allowing individual histories and trauma to be part of a broader collective memory.

6. The U.S. Holocaust Memorial Museum's definition of a survivor is very inclusive, almost to a fault. Under its definition, European Jews who fled Nazism before the war are also considered survivors. Thus, those Jews like my family, who fled Nazi Europe and spent the war out of danger in the United States, would be termed survivors, a categorization that is very problematic.

7. In the literature geared to a popular audience, two main books in English exist: Andre Stein's *Hidden Children: Forgotten Survivors of the Holocaust*

(1993) and Jane Marks's *The Hidden Children: The Secret Survivors of the Holocaust* (1993). The latter book draws from direct narratives of twenty-three people (three of whom I also interviewed) and concludes with two academic chapters, one by former hidden child and sociologist Nechama Tec and the other by psychotherapist Eva Fogelman. These books draw on the experiences of former hidden children from diverse European countries.

8. In the introduction to her short overview of the Jewish community in the postwar Netherlands, Chaya Brasz (1995: 8), historian and executive director of the Institute for Research on Dutch Jewry at the Hebrew University, mentions that Elma Verhey (1991) pointed out to her that it is not coincidental that the first historian who published on the postwar Jewish community in Holland and "especially on the painful issue of the Jewish war orphans" was not a Dutch scholar but an American, Joel Fishman (1973, 1978a). Fishman's articles, she points out, were not translated into Dutch, and they were published outside the Netherlands. Even psychiatrist Hans Keilson (1992), who published a seminal book on trauma among Jewish war orphans, was of German (Jewish) origin, although he became a Dutch citizen.

9. See also historian Bert-Jan Flim's book on the underground organizations that hid and kept in touch with Jewish children (2005).

10. Evers-Emden's book covers a vast array of questions about prewar family life, the circumstances of hiding, and the postwar experience, including questions about socioeconomic class, demographics, and emotional reactions. The questionnaire was multiple choice and close-ended, with room for writing additional reactions. The book discusses each survey question and presents a univariate analysis of the responses in percentages, includes some quotations from additional reactions that were written out, and offers some analysis of the response. The descriptive data and the authors' sample of three hundred complement and supplement my smaller sample and qualitative data.

11. Dr. Hans Keilson was a Jewish refugee from Germany who received his degrees in the Netherlands. His research on Jewish war orphans after World War II for L'Ezrat ha-Yeled became his doctoral thesis at the University of Amsterdam. I am grateful to Dr. Marita Keilson-Lauritz and to Dr. Keilson for their clarifications of my original summary.

Keilson's focus was guided by a hypothesis that a relationship exists between the point in the child's development at which traumatization occurred and the effects of the trauma. For his sample, he selected 10 percent from each age group deemed relevant by its developmental stage (e.g., 0–18 months; 18 months–4 years; 4–6 years; 6–10 years; 10–13 years; and 13–18 years) as related to the "development of the libido," creating a total of 204 cases (1992: 42). The data could not, however, corroborate his second hypothesis, that the "severity of the disturbance corresponds to the severity of the traumatization process" (47).

12. PTSD applies to multiple, if not indeterminable, exogenous influences on an individual's psyche, ranging from historical events such as war to more personal events such as domestic violence. The diagnosis of PTSD was developed within a particular historical context, as a reaction to the returnees from the Vietnam War. It was not so much the actual events of war that disturbed these veterans, since these events had passed, but the *memory* of the events that haunted them. Thus, what was historically called "shell shock" or "war neurosis," particularly after World War I, evolved into PTSD, a disorder that afflicts veterans well beyond the traumatizing event, sometimes resurfacing years after the event occurred (Summerfield 1999). This diagnosis has been accepted by the medical profession and applied to former hidden children in the Netherlands. See Summerfield (1999) for important criticisms of PTSD, particularly of its social construction and of its wholesale and inappropriate export to vastly different cultures.

13. Y. Michal Bodemann's 2005 *A Jewish Family in Germany Today* is a superb study of one family in postwar Germany, although there is little analysis of family dynamics. Bodemann explicitly stated that he did not want to write another Holocaust book, but the effects of the Holocaust on this family are inescapable.

14. Other remembrance environments include the ethnic group, the profession, the workplace, the religious community, the nation, and the state.

15. The centrality of memory and identity in Friedlander's remarkable story reflects Jewish themes but also pivotal issues connected to the hiding experience. Friedlander writes about changing his identity and his name multiple times—he was "Pavel" during his Prague childhood; he then became "Paul" when he was hidden in a Catholic seminary, where he studied, forgot his Jewish identity, and decided to become a priest. After the war he reclaimed his Jewish identity, went to Israel, and became "Shaul" ("Saul" in English).

16. Marita Sturken notes that memories are "created" in tandem with forgetting, since one would be overwhelmed if one remembered everything. Thus, she argues, "forgetting is a necessary component in the construction of memory" (1997: 7).

17. For example, Langer (1991) differentiates between deep memory, anguished memory, humiliated memory, tainted memory, and unheroic memory and delineates the distinctive aspects of each.

18. Prager's 1998 work is a critical approach to the recovered memory movement that recognizes individuals who suddenly uncover scores of memo-

ries of past sexual abuse. He relates a session with a particular patient described as Ms. A. in which she suddenly wonders if she was abused by her father. Prager notes that if there had been no public context for and discourse about sexual abuse, this thought may never have surfaced. He applies this approach to the so-called recovered memory of Binjamin Wilkomirski (1996), who wrote *Fragments,* now a discredited memoir.

19. Prager rejects Freud's ideas about memory, but in different ways. Freud argued that the past plays a persistent role in an individual's unconscious. Prager argues instead that the present, including current interactions with others, rather than solely the past, plays a role in creating a person's memories. Thus, for Freud, memories reside in the isolated individual, whereas for Prager and other sociologists who deal with collective memory, a more socially interactive approach accounts for memory creation.

20. It is clear, however, that not every generation has the same memory of the Holocaust, since most Jews alive today were born after 1945. Marianne Hirsch's concept of "post-memory" is most helpful here. She notes that post-memory "is distinguished from memory by generational distance and from history by deep personal connection" (1997: 22). Thus, the post-memory of the second or third generation differs considerably from the memory of a Holocaust survivor. Also, despite the tremendous educational and ideological attention paid by the Israeli state to transmitting the history of the Holocaust to Israeli children, in great part as a way to justify the establishment and existence of the Jewish state (Zerubavel 1995), at the very least, we are very likely to categorize different types of memories of the Holocaust in Israel by ethnicity and race (Ashkenazic vs. Sephardic, Russian Jews vs. Ethiopian Jews), even if we control for generation.

21. For example, the notion of collective memory as originally conceptualized posits individuals as somewhat mindless, passive recipients and transmitters. Contemporary sociologists acknowledge the agency of social actors and are concerned with how people digest, interpret, reinterpret, and transmit this collective memory rather than presuming its passive acceptance. Additionally, the notion of a collective memory suggests an animate being that takes on "a life of its own" (Olick and Robbins 1998: 111). However, as anthropologist Michael Kenny points out, collectives do not have minds or memories—individuals do (1999: 421). Yet at the same time, individuals need the sociocultural groups and collectivities that make their identities meaningful.

22. Other criticisms focus on how the notion of a collective memory posits a monolithic memory that is similar enough to unite various individual members of a group or a society. A collective memory within one group, however, can be contradictory and disjointed, depending on many factors,

including the socioeconomic status of group members. Additionally, the notion of collective memory does not distinguish between generational differences in memory. For example, those who experienced an event such as a revolution do indeed carry the memory of it with them, but how can the second or third generation have a memory of an event that was over before they were born? Sociologists are more likely to study what is transmitted intergenerationally and how it is transmitted, rather than to presume that the collective memories of the first, second, and third generations are homogeneous. Furthermore, there might be differences in the meaning of this memory depending on the race, ethnicity, class, and gender of the subject; these differences would be crucial points of sociological inquiry.

23. One interview was never finished because the interviewee talked almost incessantly, not letting me ask questions; he was also too busy to reschedule a second meeting, or perhaps he did not want to continue. Another man who responded to one of my published appeals for volunteers turns out to have been in hiding for only a few days when he was discovered and sent to a concentration camp; he was also over 18 when he hid. One woman was half-Jewish and was in a very different situation since she did not have to hide all the time. And one person withdrew after being interviewed, which is discussed in the section entitled "Methodology and the Research Process."

24. One possibility is that more women than men found the idea of an interview more appealing, since, generally speaking, women are more social than men. Another possibility is that more female than male hidden children are still alive. And a final possibility is that these gender proportions reflect more broadly the proportions of males and females who were taken into hiding, since some Resistance activists have suggested that young girls were the easiest to place in hiding. My sense is that some combination of the first and final options explains the higher number of female respondents, although I must state that I was pleased to see how many men readily volunteered when I was first introduced at the hidden children's meeting in Amsterdam.

25. Psychotherapist Dina Wardi (1992) found that in families of survivors there is usually one child who is unconsciously designated to be a "memorial candle" for relatives who did not survive. This child serves as a link to the past, preserving family history and bringing it to bear on the present and future. Although I'm not the child of survivors in the traditional sense, I am very much the bearer of family history, including the pasts of my parents and grandparents, and in that sense, I am very much the memorial candle of my family. Parts of my bookshelf in my study serve as a family museum in miniature, and photos of the deceased surround me as I write.

26. Clinical studies have found long-lasting negative effects on a survivor's emotional state and ability to function (Niederland 1964; Eitinger 1980; Krystal 1968; Dimsdale 1980; Chodoff 1980), while a few studies have focused on the more positive side of survivor adaptation (Hass 1996; White 1988), challenging notions of Jewish passivity and pathology.

2. BEFORE AND DURING THE WAR

1. Ashkenazic Jews come from Western and Eastern Europe, whereas Sephardic Jews originally hail from Spain and Portugal. They speak different languages (Yiddish, Ladino), eat different foods, and observe different customs.

2. Yad Vashem, in Israel, is a global memorial to all Jews killed in the Shoah. All visiting foreign officials to Israel are taken to this site as a very political reminder of the fate of the Jews historically; the state of Israel presents itself as preventing a recurrence by the very fact of its existence.

3. These numbers were on the Yad Vashem website as of May 1, 2006, www.yad-vashem.org.il/righteous/index_righteous.html. It appears that the dynamic of Jewish survivors honoring co-citizens is highly related to cultural factors. For example, although just as many, if not more, Jews were hidden in Belgium as in the Netherlands, far fewer Belgian non-Jews have been nominated and honored at Yad Vashem.

4. I am extremely grateful to my colleague Eric Grodsky, who did these calculations seemingly without effort, something I envy.

5. In early 1996 Claude Lanzmann, best known for his documentary film *Shoah*, visited the Netherlands for the television screening of his film. He chose Holland in light of "the impeccable wartime record of the Dutch toward the Jews" (cited in Gerstenfeld 2001: 8). As recently as 2001, in the *Jewish Travel Guide*, the introduction to the section on the Netherlands remarks that despite the high rate of Jews deported, the "local Dutch population tended to behave sympathetically toward their Jewish neighbors, hiding many" (8). Anne Frank did write about the good people who hid her family; however, there is almost no awareness among those who read her diary that Dutch people betrayed the Frank family, raided their hiding place, arrested them, and ran the trains that sent them to Westerbork and eastward.

6. I am grateful to Dan Michman for pointing this out (personal correspondence, January 30, 2005).

7. Dan Michman's research has focused on the Shoah, with particular attention to the Netherlands. His father is the eminent historian Jozeph Mich-

man, a Dutch Jew who emigrated to Israel, where he taught history, and who has published extensively on the Shoah.

8. At that time, an employed worker in the harbor would have earned about fifteen hundred guilders annually. The study found that 69 percent of the Jewish community in Amsterdam lived on less than a thousand guilders annually, and 50 percent earned less than five hundred guilders annually (Moore 1997: 27).

9. There were 14,895 half-Jews and 5,990 who were considered one-quarter Jewish (Flim 2004).

10. I am indebted to Ido de Haan for pointing out that registration was not a Dutch tradition but was introduced by the French during the Napoleonic occupation. An identity card is still resisted by Dutch citizens (personal correspondence, March 6, 2005).

11. Selma Leydesdorff points out that many of these young men and boys were trained in boxing, a traditional Jewish working-class sport at that time (1993: 354).

12. Moore points out that shifting the meeting point for Jews who received summons from the central train station in Amsterdam may have been done for "cosmetic reasons," to move the site of deportations from a very public space to one that was less central and out of sight (1997: 94).

13. Moore reports that there were 690 Catholic Jews (Jews who converted to Catholicism) in the Netherlands and that 300 were foreign Jews already held in camps. Some of the others were partners in mixed marriages who were subsequently released because of their privileged status. He states that a total of 92 were deported to Auschwitz, about 100 fewer than Michman reported (1997: 128).

14. Dan Michman, personal correspondence, January 30, 2005.

15. Until the 1980s, some of the explanations for why these shocking statistics come from the Netherlands focused on geography. First, Jews attempting to flee Holland to safety had to cross several borders (Belgium and France) in order to reach a third, safe country such as Switzerland. This situation differed from that of Jews in other European countries, which had more borders that directly led to easier escape; for example, getting from France to Switzerland only involves one border crossing. Second, the Dutch landscape did not offer large clusters of unoccupied forests in which Jews could hide long-term, as did countries such as Poland and France. Instead, the Netherlands was a small, densely populated country, making it much more difficult to hide in the woods. However, contemporary scholars have been able to discount those explanations and have focused on more structural state and social aspects (Blom 1989).

3. AFTER THE WAR

1. In his calculations of deportees, Jozeph Michman included about 2,000 Dutch Jews who were deported from France and Belgium (1990: 1055). I left them off the total number, since I am focusing only on what happened in the Netherlands. However, some of these 2,000 Dutch Jews may be represented among the 5,200 survivors. Of the 60,000 Dutch Jews sent to Auschwitz, about 1,000 survived. Thirty-four thousand were sent to Sobibor, and 19 survived. Almost 5,000 were sent to Theresienstadt, and almost 2,000 survived. Out of approximately 1,750 sent to Mauthausen, there was only 1 survivor. About 2,200 Dutch Jews were sent to other camps or to Auschwitz from Belgium and France, where they had fled; perhaps 100 survived, but this is not known for sure (J. Michman 1990: 1055).

2. Thanks go to Carla Lessing for helping me tweak the translation.

3. Ido de Haan points to a case in the 1950s in which it came out that the former mayor of The Hague was involved in the deportation of a Jewish family (2001: 415). A group of law professors signed an open letter opposing the investigation into the case. A committee of his supporters argued on his behalf, even though his story did not pan out. De Haan feels that what matters here is that the public did not see his actions as constituting murder or treason.

4. Ido de Haan points out that the debate about trauma, and the appropriation of the term, began with confrontations between the first and second generations of Jewish victims (personal correspondence, March 6, 2005).

5. The organization is spelled Le Ezrath ha-Jeled in its Dutch transliteration. Here I use the English transliteration of the Hebrew.

6. One example he gave is the correspondence between van der Molen and the Ministry of Justice in reference to the president of the Jewish Coordination Commission's nomination: "From our side there is much objection against this, not only because this man is a Zionist but also very fanatical and . . . definitely feels un-Dutch" (Fishman 1981: 429).

7. From the unpublished translation by Jeannette Ringold.

8. Almost the same number of Jewish children survived in Belgium— between 3,000 and 4,000—but it is not clear how many had been in hiding and then betrayed (Brachfeld 1998: 419). The Belgian Jewish community was much smaller than the Dutch one to start with, but a much smaller percentage of Jews were deported and killed.

9. In France, there was a case similar to the Anneke Beekman affair concerning two brothers (the Finalys), whose parents were murdered. Because they were in a Catholic institution, where they were baptized, it took eight years and a similarly long legal battle to get them back (Sciolino and Horowitz 2005: 6).

4. MEMORIES OF OCCUPATION, WAR, AND HIDING

1. The now-late husband of a woman I interviewed told me that once when driving in Amsterdam, he pointed to an apartment and told his 5-year-old granddaughter that he had hidden there for nine months. Since the term for hiding also means "to dive under," she responded quite logically, "But Opa, how did you hold your breath for that long?"

2. Mirjam does not know, however, if her parents asked her grandmother to join them in hiding and if she had refused to go. Her grandmother and aunt were deported and died in a camp.

3. In 2005 the Resistance Museum in Amsterdam mounted an exhibit entitled *Dag pap, tot morgen: Joodse kinderen gered uit de crèche* (Bye Dad, See You To-morrow: Jewish Children Saved from the Crèche) that displayed photos and stories of children who were rescued from the crèche (Bakker 2005). Of the fifteen individuals whose short stories are in the book, two are in my study, and several more I interviewed were saved from the crèche.

4. Just to demonstrate how careful clandestine hiders sometimes had to be, one subject's mother and baby brother were betrayed when a neighbor, who knew that the occupants did not have a baby, saw diapers hanging to dry in the kitchen.

5. His mother was caught and deported when she was out visiting another son at a later time. She survived the war.

5. WHEN BOTH PARENTS RETURNED

1. This traditional Hebrew blessing of daughters means "May God bless you as Rebekah, Lea, and Sarah."

6. WHEN ONE PARENT RETURNED

1. See the Minnesota Center against Violence and Abuse's extensive bibliog-raphy on "Sexual and Domestic Violence in the Jewish Community." It includes sources on wife beating, marital rape, and child abuse, as well as sexual abuse perpetrated by rabbis. Available at www.mincava.umn .edu/documents/bibs/jewish.

7. ORPHANS LIVING WITH FAMILIES

1. Bloeme was an adult orphan born in Amsterdam to a father who was a di-amond cutter and a mother who was a seamstress. Altogether, Bloeme hid in sixteen different places. She was caught in hiding and sent to the Hol-landse Schouwburg; she was able to escape by going to the children's nurs-

ery. Back in hiding again, she was betrayed and caught in a raid. Bloeme was sent to Westerbork and then to Auschwitz. At Auschwitz, her stay overlapped with that of Anne and Margot Frank; she and Margot had been schoolmates. At Liberation, Bloeme was 18 and alone; her entire family had been murdered. To get a lift back from Maastricht to Amsterdam, she had to use the tiny amount of money given to her by the Dutch government at the border to pay a truck driver. She arrived in Amsterdam with few clothes, owning nothing and having no family to whom she could turn. Bloeme lived with a friend and his family until she married. She pursued her university education after marriage.

2. In the film *Secret Lives,* a Polish Catholic priest who had been hidden by a Polish family expresses a similar sense of feeling different as a child. The priest was only told by his mother about his Jewish past when he was 35 and had been in the priesthood for twelve years.

3. For example, one entire interview was unemotional, a fact that could be interpreted as a reflection of positive experiences. However, after the interview, when I was chatting with the interviewee and his friend, who had joined us at the end, the friend began to elaborate on how troubled the interviewee's sibling continues to be, into middle age. The interviewee told his friend to stop talking, so I could not pursue any questions, but that interjection made it clear that there was a great deal below the surface of my respondent's narrative.

4. Eva's father was a widower with three sons when he married her stepmother, a divorcée. After her father's wife died, his three sons, Eva's halfbrothers, were split up and lived in the houses of their deceased mother's sisters. One of those sisters, a widow before the war, was hiding in the same area as Eva and searched for her. She was about 50 years old at the end of the war, and both her son and daughter were already grown up. Thus, she claimed Eva as the "daughter of my brother-in-law."

5. Literally "it should serve her in good health," a sarcastic expression in Hebrew meaning "if that's what makes her healthy and happy, so be it."

6. Apparently, the husband was an NSB member and told the SS that his wife had a lot of Jews in their house. His wife was sent to Ravensbrück and survived. She divorced her husband and in the late 1970s managed to find Greet.

8. LIFE IN JEWISH ORPHANAGES

1. Jozeboko is short for *Joodse* (Jewish) *Zee* (sea) *en* (and) *Bos* (woods) *Kolonie* (camp).

2. There are mixed reviews of this camp. Jeannette has "wonderful memories of Jozeboko": "This was the first time I realized that my brother and I were *not* the only orphans around. . . . The group solidarity and support were amazing to me." However, her brother's and a male friend's experiences there, like Josef's, were not positive.

9. FROM THE PERSONAL TO THE POLITICAL

1. In general, researchers argue that married people are happier and healthier than those who are single. Although in past comparisons with single people, married men appeared to be much healthier compared to married women, demographer Linda Waite has also made a case for married women's health being better than single women's; however, this result may be more relevant in the U.S. context, where married women often obtain health coverage through their spouses (Waite and Gallagher 2000).

2. I am grateful to Carla Lessing for this insight.

3. I am grateful to Dr. Hilde Burton for pointing this out.

4. This was a devastatingly sad interview, and also a challenging one. At one point, Salo made a somewhat negative and accusatory statement about how *I* had contacted *him* for an interview. However, he was the first person to respond to a blurb I had put in the Dutch hidden children's association newsletter asking for volunteers. In fact, he called me long-distance from the United States to the Netherlands, where I was living, to volunteer. He denied having done that until I was able to convince him that he had contacted me, not the reverse. I am sure that the unpleasantness I experienced during the interview reflects some of what Salo feels most of the time.

5. Again, I'm grateful to Carla Lessing for reading this chapter and asking me a question that led to this analysis, in this particular group, of who emigrated and who stayed.

6. They and a few of the others who were in Jewish families also spoke of the bonds they had formed with other orphans.

7. Max A., personal correspondence, April 14, 2006.

8. Elly, personal correspondence, November 11, 2004.

9. Because of my sampling method, the majority of my interviewees are likely to have attended the conference and at the very least are involved in some kind of group related to the war; most of these groups were established after these initial conferences (see "Methodology and the Research Process," chapter 1).

10. Carla Lessing, personal communication, March 15, 2005.

CONCLUSION

1. Because of its diplomatic and political ties with Turkey, Israel still officially denies the Armenian genocide (Auron 2003).
2. This event took place on April 6, 2006.
3. Unfortunately, these American Jewish efforts are not being replicated in Israel. Two hundred refugees from Darfur reached Israel but were imprisoned and have remained jailed since their arrival. The government does not want to encourage more refugees to come.

Glossary

Comité voor Joodse Vluchtelingen (CJV)	*Dutch.* Committee for Jewish Refugees, established to meet the welfare needs of German Jews who fled to Holland after Hitler came to power, especially after Kristallnacht.
Displaced Persons (DP)	Jews who were stateless after World War II. DP camps were set up in Germany.
Gereformeered	*Dutch.* Literally, "reformed Protestant," Orthodox Protestant, member of the Dutch Orthodox Calvinist Church.
Hachsharah	*Hebrew; spelled Hachsjarah in Dutch.* Zionist youth group that prepared young people for emigration to Israel.
heit	*Frisian Dutch.* Father.
Hollandse Schouwburg	*See* Joodse Schouwburg.

Joods Maatschappelijk   *Dutch.* Jewish Social Welfare Organization. This organi-
Werk (JMW)   zation has all the dossiers on hidden children concerning postwar decisions about where they would live.

Joodse Raad   *Dutch; Judenrat in German.* Jewish Council. Set up by the
Nazis to organize the Jewish community. Its most controversial role was creating lists of Jews to be deported.

Joodse Schouwburg   *Dutch.* Previously the Hollandse Schouwburg. A theater
in Amsterdam that was turned into a specifically Jewish
theater during the German Occupation and then became the intermediary transit point for Jews who were
rounded up for deportation. Children were kept in the
crèche alongside it, and hundreds were smuggled out
by Resistance members.

Kinder   *German.* Children; a term used by those on the Kindertransport to refer to themselves and to others.

Kindertransport   *German.* A program in which Jewish children from Germany and Austria were sent to safety in England in the
1930s to live with British families.

Kristallnacht   *German.* "Night of broken glass," November 9, 1938. A
pogrom during which synagogues all over Germany
were vandalized, burned, and destroyed by the Nazis.
Many German Jews fled to Holland after this event.

L'Ezrat ha-Yeled   *Hebrew; Le Ezrath ha-Jeled in Dutch.* "To the Aid of the
Children." Postwar Jewish organization that helped
child survivors.

Maror   *Hebrew.* Bitter herbs, often horseradish, one of the sym-
bolic foods eaten at the Passover seder to symbolize the
bitterness of slavery in Egypt. Also the name of the
group representing Jews in Holland who sought restitution from the state in the late 1990s.

mem   *Frisian Dutch.* Mother.

Mutti   *German.* Mom or Mommy.

Nationaal-Socialistische Beweging (NSB)	*Dutch.* National Socialist Movement, the largest Nazi party in Holland, established in 1931.
onderduiken	*Dutch.* To "descend" into hiding.
onderduiker	*Dutch.* Someone in hiding.
oom	*Dutch.* Uncle.
opa	*Dutch.* Grandpa.
OPK	*See* Voogdicommissie voor Oorlogspleegkinderen.
razzia	*Dutch, from French.* Raid.
tante	*Dutch.* Aunt.
vader	*Dutch.* Father.
Voogdicommissie voor Oorlogspleegkinderen (OPK)	*Dutch.* Guardian Commission for War Foster Children, set up after the war to deal with mostly Jewish war orphans and other Jewish children who were claimed by parents as well as their hiding family.
Westerbork	*Dutch.* Initially built by the Dutch Jewish community to house German Jewish refugees temporarily but later used by the Nazis as the main transit camp in Holland for Jews who were then deported. Located in a dreary, isolated site in Drenthe near the German border.
Wet Uitkeringen Vervolgingsslachtoffers (WUV)	*Dutch.* Act for Benefits for Victims of Persecution, 1940–1945. A state-run fund for all World War II survivors.
Yad Vashem	*Hebrew.* Holocaust memorial in Israel where Gentiles who helped Jews during the war are honored.
zuilen	*Dutch.* "Pillars" or segments of society that were vertically stratified, for example, Protestants and Catholics.

References

Adorno, Theodor W. 1986. "What Does Coming to Terms with the Past Mean?" In *Bitburg in Moral and Political Perspective,* ed. Geoffrey Hartman. Bloomington: Indiana University Press.

Alexander, Jeffrey C. 2004. "Toward a Theory of Cultural Trauma." In *Cultural Trauma and Collective Identity,* ed. Jeffrey C. Alexander, Ron Eyerman, Bernhard Giesen, Neil J. Smelser, and Piotr Sztompka, 1–30. Berkeley and Los Angeles: University of California Press.

Ardith, Rita. 1999. *Searching for Life: The Grandmothers of the Plaza de Mayo and the Disappeared Children of Argentina.* Berkeley and Los Angeles: University of California Press.

Auron, Yair. 2003. *The Banality of Denial: Israel and the Armenian Genocide.* New York: Transaction Publishers.

Bakhtin, M. M. 1991. *The Dialogic Imagination.* Ed. Michael Holquist. Austin: University of Texas Press.

Bakker, Alex. 2005. *Dag pap, tot morgen: Joodse kinderen gered uit de crèche* (Bye Dad, See You Tomorrow: Jewish Children Saved from the Crèche). Hilversum: Verloren.

Ball, Jessica. 2006. "Beginning the Journey: Indigenous Fathers in Canada Learning Fatherhood." Victoria: Canada School of Child and Youth Care, University of Victoria.

Ballinger, Pamela. 1998. "The Culture of Survivors: Post-Traumatic Stress Disorder and Traumatic Memory." *History and Memory* 10 (1): 99–132.

Banerjee, Neela. 2006. "Muslims' Plight in Sudan Resonates with Jews in U.S." *New York Times*, April 30.

Barnert, Elizabeth. 2006. "Hundreds Are Still Missing in El Salvador." *San Francisco Chronicle*, Op-Ed piece, April 6.

Bauman, Zygmunt. 1989. *Modernity and the Holocaust.* Ithaca, NY: Cornell University Press.

Benner, Patricia, Ethel Roskies, and Richard S. Lazarus. 1980. "Stress and Coping under Extreme Conditions." In *Survivors, Victims, and Perpetrators: Essays on the Nazi Holocaust,* ed. Joel E. Dimsdale, 219–58. Washington, DC: Hemisphere Publishing Company.

Berger, John. 2005. *Here Is Where We Meet.* New York: Pantheon Books.

Berger, Ronald J. 1994. "Remembering the Holocaust: Some Observations on Collective Memories and Survivor Orals/Life Histories." *Sociological Imagination* 31 (2): 117–24.

———. 1995. "Agency, Structure, and Jewish Survival of the Holocaust: A Life History Study." *Sociological Quarterly* 36 (1): 15–36.

Bettelheim, Bruno. 1979. *Surviving and Other Essays.* New York: Knopf.

Biale, David. 1986. *Power and Powerlessness in Jewish History.* New York: Schocken Press.

Blom, J. C. H. 1989. "The Persecution of the Jews in the Netherlands in a Comparative International Perspective." In *Dutch Jewish History: Proceedings of the Fourth Symposium on the History of Jews in the Netherlands,* ed. Jozeph Michman, 2: 273–89. Maastricht: Van Gorcum, Assen.

Blum, Lenore, et al. 1991. "Tellers and Listeners: The Impact of Holocaust Narratives." In *Lessons and Legacies I: The Meaning of the Holocaust in a Changing World,* ed. Peter Hayes, 316–28. Evanston: Northwestern University Press.

Boas, Henriette. 1967. "The Persecution and Destruction of Dutch Jewry, 1940–1945." In *Yad Vashem Studies,* ed. Nathan Eck and Aryeh Leon Kubovy, 6: 359–74. Jerusalem: Yad Vashem.

Bodemann, Y. Michal. 2005. *A Jewish Family in Germany Today: An Intimate Portrait.* Durham, NC: Duke University Press.

Boucher, Herbert. 1997. *Miracle Survival: A Holocaust Memoir.* Berkeley: Judah L. Magnes Museum.

Bowlby, John. 1969. "Attachment and Loss." In *Attachment,* 1: 117–30. New York: Basic Books.

———. 1973. *Separation: Anxiety and Anger.* New York: Basic Books.

Brachfeld, Sylvain. 1998. "Jewish Orphanages in Belgium under the German Occupation." In *Belgium and the Holocaust: Jews, Belgians, Germans*, ed. Dan Michman, 419–31. Jerusalem: Yad Vashem.

Brasz, Chaya. 1995. *Removing the Yellow Badge: The Struggle for a Jewish Community in the Postwar Netherlands, 1944–1955*. Jerusalem: Institute for Research on Dutch Jewry, Hebrew University of Jerusalem.

Bregstein, Philo, and Salvador Bloemgarten. 2004. *Remembering Jewish Amsterdam*. Trans. Wanda Boeke. New York: Holmes and Meier.

Brenner, Rachel Feldhay. 1997. *Writing as Resistance: Four Women Confronting the Holocaust: Edith Stein, Simone Weil, Anne Frank, Etty Hillesum*. University Park: Pennsylvania State University Press.

Brody, Jane E. 2005. "Get a Grip: Set Your Sights above Adversity." *New York Times*, March 1, science section.

Brooks, Roy L. 2004. *Atonement and Forgiveness: A New Model for Black Reparations*. Berkeley and Los Angeles: University of California Press.

Brzuzy, Stephanie, Amber Ault, and Elizabeth A. Segal. 1997. "Conducting Qualitative Interviews with Women Survivors of Trauma." *Affilia* 12 (1): 76–84.

Buckler, Steve. 1996. "Historical Narrative, Identity, and the Holocaust." Special Issue on Identity, Memory, and History. *History of the Human Sciences* 9 (4): 1–20.

Cassidy, Jude. 1999. "The Nature of the Child's Ties." In *Handbook of Attachment: Theory, Research, and Clinical Applications*, ed. Jude Cassidy and Phillip Shaver, 3–20. New York: Guilford Press.

Chodoff, Paul. 1980. "Psychotherapy of the Survivor." In *Survivors, Victims, and Perpetrators: Essays on the Nazi Holocaust*, ed. Joel E. Dimsdale, 205–18. Washington, DC: Hemisphere Publishing Company.

Citroen, Michal. 1999. *U wordt door niemand verwacht: Nederlandse joden na kampen en onderduik*. Utrecht: Het Spectrum.

Clarke, Greg, William Sack, and Brian Goff. 1993. "Three Forms of Stress in Cambodian Adolescent Refugees." *Journal of Abnormal Child Psychology* 21 (1): 65–78.

Climo, Jacob J. 1990. "Transmitting Ethnic Identity through Oral Narratives." *Ethnic Groups* 8: 163–70.

Cohen, Stanley. 2001. *States of Denial: Knowing about Atrocities and Suffering*. London: Polity Press.

de Costa, Denise. 1998. *Anne Frank and Etty Hillesum: Inscribing Spirituality and Sexuality*. New Brunswick, NJ: Rutgers University Press.

Covington, Richard. 2001. "The Recently Renovated Anne Frank House in Amsterdam, Where the Gifted Teenager Hid from the Nazis, Celebrates Her Legacy." *Smithsonian* (October), 71–75.

Croes, Marnix. 2004. "The Netherlands 1942–1945: Survival in Hiding and the Hunt for Hidden Jews." *Netherlands' Journal of Social Sciences* 40 (2): 157–75.

Das, Veena. 1997. "Sufferings, Theodicies, Disciplinary Practices, Appropriations." *International Social Science Journal* 49 (4): 63.

Das, Veena, and Arthur Kleinman. 1997. Introduction to *Violence and Subjectivity,* ed. Veena Das, Arthur Kleinman, Mamphela Ramphele, and Pamela Reynolds, 1–18. Berkeley and Los Angeles: University of California Press.

Delbo, Charlotte. 1995. *Auschwitz and After.* Trans. Rosette C. Lamont. New Haven, CT: Yale University Press.

Dimsdale, Joel E. 1980. "The Coping Behavior of Nazi Concentration Camp Survivors." In *Survivors, Victims, and Perpetrators: Essays on the Nazi Holocaust,* ed. Joel E. Dimsdale, 163–74. Washington, DC: Hemisphere Publishing Company.

"Dispute over Anne Frank." 2004. *New York Times,* October 5.

Doland, Angela. 2005. "Vatican Document Reopens Holocaust Wounds." *San Francisco Chronicle,* January 1.

Domingues, Virginia R. 1993. "Questioning Jews." *Ethnologist* 20 (3): 618–24.

Dratwa, Daniel. 1998. "Genocide and Its Memories: A Preliminary Study of How Belgian Jewry Coped with the Results of the Holocaust." In *Belgium and the Holocaust: Jews, Belgians, Germans,* ed. Dan Michman, 523–55. Jerusalem: Yad Vashem.

Durlacher, Gerhard. 1991. *Stripes in the Sky.* Trans. Susan Massotty. London: Serpent's Tail.

Dwork, Deborah. 1991. *Children with a Star: Jewish Youth in Nazi Europe.* New Haven, CT: Yale University Press.

Eitinger, Leo. 1980. "The Concentration Camp Syndrome and Its Sequelae." In *Survivors, Victims, and Perpetrators: Essays on the Nazi Holocaust,* ed. Joel E. Dimsdale, 127–62. Washington, DC: Hemisphere Publishing Company.

Elder, Glen H., Jr. 1999. *Children of the Great Depression: Social Change in Life Experience.* Boulder: Westview Press.

Enzer, Hyman, and Sandra Solotaroff-Enzer, eds. 2000. *Anne Frank: Reflections on Her Life and Legacy.* Urbana: University of Illinois Press.

Epstein, Helen. 1979. *Children of the Holocaust.* New York: Putnam.

Epstein, Julia, and Lori Hope Lefkovitz. 2001. Introduction to *Shaping Losses: Cultural Memory and the Holocaust,* ed. Julia Epstein and Lori Hope Lefkovitz, 1–12. Urbana: University of Illinois Press.

Evers-Emden, Bloeme. 1994. *Geleende kinderen: Ervaringen van onderduikouders en hun joodse beschermelingen in de jaren 1942 tot 1945* (Borrowed Children: Experiences of War Foster Parents and Their Jewish Charges during the Years 1942 to 1945). Kampen: Uitgeverij Kok.

———. 1996. *Geschonden Bestaan: Gesprekken met vervolgde joden die hun kinderen moesten "Wegdoen"* (A Damaged Existence: Conversations with Persecuted Jews Who Had to "Get Rid Of" Their Children). Kampen: Uitgeverij Kok.

————. 1999. *Je ouders delen* (Sharing your Parents). Kampen: Uitgeverij Kok.

Evers-Emden, Bloeme, and Bert-Jan Flim. 1995. *Ondergedoken geweest: Een afgesloten verleden?* (Hidden during the War: A Closed-Off Past?) Kampen: Uitgeverij Kok.

Eyerman, Ron. 2004. "Cultural Trauma: Slavery and the Formation of African American Identity." In *Cultural Trauma and Collective Identity,* ed. Jeffrey Alexander et al., 60–111. Berkeley and Los Angeles: University of California Press.

Ezrahi, Sidra DeKoven. 1997. "See Under: Memory." *History and Memory* 9 (1/2): 364–75.

Farkas, Eva. 2002. "Finding My Past." *Hidden Child* 11 (2): 14.

Fein, Helen. 1979. *Accounting for Genocide: National Responses and Jewish Victimization during the Holocaust.* New York: Free Press.

Fishman, Joel. 1973. "Jewish War Orphans in the Netherlands: The Guardianship Issue, 1945–1950." *Wiener Library Bulletin* 27 (30/31): 31–36.

————. 1978a. "The Anneke Beekman Affair and the Dutch News Media." *Jewish Social Studies* 25 (1): 3–24.

————. 1978b. "The Reconstruction of the Dutch Jewish Community and Its Implications for the Writings of Contemporary Jewish History." In *American Academy for Jewish Research,* 45: 67–102. Jerusalem: Hebrew University.

————. 1981. "The War Orphan Controversy in the Netherlands: Majority-Minority Relations." In *Dutch Jewish History,* ed. Jozeph Michman, 421–32. Jerusalem: Hebrew University.

————. 1993. "Three Recent Studies of Postwar Jewish Life in the Netherlands." *Studia Rosenthaliana* 27 (1/2): 94–100.

Flim, Bert-Jan. 2001. "Opportunities for Dutch Jews to Hide from the Nazis, 1942–1945." In *Dutch Jews as Perceived by Themselves and Others: Proceedings of the Eighth International Symposium on the History of the Jews in the Netherlands,* ed. Chaya Brasz and Yosef Kaplan, 289–305. Leiden: Brill.

————. 2004. *Encyclopedia of the Righteous among the Nations: The Netherlands,* ed. Jozeph Michman and Bert-Jan Flim, 30–39. Jerusalem: Yad Vashem.

————. 2005. *Saving the Children: History of the Organized Effort to Rescue Jewish Children in the Netherlands, 1942–1945.* Trans. Jeannette K. Ringold. Bethesda, MD: CDL Press.

Fogelman, Eva. 1993. "The Psychology Behind Being a Hidden Child." In Jane Marks, *The Hidden Children: The Secret Survivors of the Holocaust,* 292–307. New York: Ballantine Books.

————. 1994. *Conscience and Courage: Rescuers of Jews during the Holocaust.* London: Doubleday.

————. 2002. "A Tenth-Year Follow-Up to the First International Gathering of the Hidden Child." *Hidden Child* XI (1): 2, 6.

Friedlander, Saul. 1975. *When Memory Comes*. New York: Farrar Straus Giroux.

―――. 1992. Introduction to *Probing the Limits of Representation: Nazism and the "Final Solution,"* ed. Saul Friedlander, 1–21. Cambridge, MA: Harvard University Press.

―――. 1993. *Memory, History, and the Extermination of the Jews of Europe*. Bloomington: Indiana University Press.

van Galen Last, Dick, and Rolf Wolfswinkel. 1996. *Anne Frank and After: Dutch Holocaust Literature in Historical Perspective*. Amsterdam: Amsterdam University Press.

Gans, H. M. 1989. "The Jews in the Netherlands." In *Dutch History: Proceedings of the Fourth Symposium in the History of Jews in the Netherlands*, ed. Jozeph Michman, 2: 387–402. Maastricht: Van Gorcum, Assen.

Gerson, Judith, and Diane L. Wolf, eds. Forthcoming. *Sociology Confronts the Holocaust: Memories, Identities and Diasporas*. Durham, NC: Duke University Press.

Gerstenfeld, Manfred. 2001. "Image and Reality: The Dutch Holocaust Past." *Midstream* 47 (1): 10–20.

Goldberg, Michael. 1995. *Why Should Jews Survive? Looking Past the Holocaust Toward a Jewish Future*. Oxford: Oxford University Press.

Goldenberg, Myrna. 1996. "Lessons Learned from Gentle Heroism: Women's Holocaust Narratives." *Annals of the American Academy of Political and Social Science* 548: 78–93.

Gordon, Avery F. 1997. *Ghostly Matters: Haunting and the Sociological Imagination*. Minneapolis: University of Minnesota Press.

Graver, Lawrence. 1995. *An Obsession with Anne Frank: Meyer Levin and the Diary*. Berkeley and Los Angeles: University of California Press.

Gray, Peter, and Kendrick Oliver. "The Memory of Catastrophe." *History Today* 51 (2): 9–15.

Greenberg, Joel. 1997. "The Babies from Yemen: An Enduring Mystery." *New York Times*, September 2.

Greenfeld, Howard. 1993. *The Hidden Children*. New York: Ticknor and Fields.

Greenspan, Henry. 1998. *On Listening to Holocaust Survivors: Recounting and Life History*. Westport, CT: Praeger.

Gubrium, Jaber F., and James A. Holstein. 1997. *The New Language of Qualitative Method*. New York: Oxford University Press.

Gugerlberger, Georg, and Michael Kearney. 1991. "Voices for the Voiceless: Testimonial Literature in Latin America." *Latin American Perspectives* 70 (18): 3–14.

de Haan, Ido. 1997. *Na de ondergang: De herinnering aan de jodenvervolging in Nederland, 1945–1995* (After the Destruction: The Memory of the Persecution of the Jews in the Netherlands, 1945–1995). The Hague: Sdu Uitgevers.

―――. 1998. "The Construction of a National Trauma: The Memory of the Persecution of the Jews in the Netherlands." *Netherlands' Journal of Social Sciences* 34 (2): 96–217.

———. 2001. "The Postwar Jewish Community and the Memory of the Persecution in the Netherlands." In *Dutch Jews as Perceived by Themselves and Others: Proceedings of the Eighth International Symposium on the History of the Jews in the Netherlands*, ed. Chaya Brasz and Yosef Kaplan, 403–35. Leiden: Brill.

Haidu, Peter. 1992. "The Dialectics of Unspeakability: Language, Silence, and the Narratives of Desubjectification." In *Probing the Limits of Representation*, ed. Saul Friedlander, 277–99. Cambridge, MA: Harvard University Press.

Halbwachs, Maurice. 1992. *On Collective Memory*. Trans. Lewis Coser. Chicago: University of Chicago Press.

Harris, Mark Jonathan, and Deborah Oppenheimer. 2000. *Into the Arms of Strangers: Stories of the Kindertransport*. New York: Bloomsbury Publishing.

Hartling, Linda M. 2003. "Strengthening Resilience in a Risky World: It's All About Relationships." Working Paper 101, presented at the Stone Center, Wellesley Centers for Women, Wellesley College.

Hartman, Geoffrey H. 1994. "Introduction: Darkness Visible." In *Holocaust Remembrance: The Shapes of Memory*, ed. Geoffrey Hartman, 1–22. Oxford: Blackwell Publishing.

———. 1996. *The Longest Shadow: In the Aftermath of the Holocaust*, ed. Geoffrey Hartman. Bloomington: Indiana University Press.

Hass, Aaron. 1990. *In the Shadow of the Holocaust: The Second Generation*. Cambridge: Cambridge University Press.

———. 1996. *The Aftermath: Living with the Holocaust*. Cambridge: Cambridge University Press.

Hasson, Stefa. 2002. "Celebrating 10 Years: The End of Isolation." *Hidden Child* 11 (2): 11.

Helmreich, William B. 1992. *Against All Odds: Holocaust Survivors and the Successful Lives They Made in America*. New York: Simon and Schuster.

Hess, Steven. 1991. "Disproportionate Destruction: The Annihilation of the Jews in the Netherlands, 1940–1945." In *The Netherlands and Nazi Genocide*, ed. G. Jan Colijn and Marcia S. Littell, 63–76. Lewiston, NY: Edwin Mellen Press.

Heuvel, Eric. 2005. *A Family Secret*. The Netherlands: Anne Frank House and Resistance Museum Friesland.

Hilberg, Raoul. 1985. *The Destruction of the European Jews*, vol. 2. New York: Holmes and Meier.

Him, Chanrithy. 2000. *When Broken Glass Floats: Growing Up under the Khmer Rouge, a Memoir*. New York: Norton.

Hirsch, Marianne. 1996. "Past Lives: Postmemories in Exile." *Poetics Today* 17 (4): 659–86.

———. 1997. *Family Frames*. Cambridge, MA: Harvard University Press.

Hirschfeld, Gerhard. 1988. *Nazi Rule and Dutch Collaboration: The Netherlands under German Occupation, 1940–1945*. Trans. Louise Willmot. Oxford: Berg.

Hoffman, Eva. 2004. *After Such Knowledge: Memory, History, and the Legacy of the Holocaust*. New York: Public Affairs.

Holmes, Colin. 1992. "Death's Shadow: Reflections on the Holocaust." *Jewish Journal of Sociology* 34 (1): 43–50.

Hondius, Dienke. 2003. *Return: Holocaust Survivors and Dutch Anti-Semitism*. Trans. David Colmer. Westport, CT: Praeger.

Jacobsen, Ruth. 2001. *Rescued Images: Memories of a Childhood in Hiding*. New York: Mikaya Press.

de Jong, Louis. 1990. *The Netherlands and Nazi Germany*. Cambridge, MA: Harvard University Press.

de Jong, Pieter. 1981. "Responses of the Churches in the Netherlands to the Nazi Occupation." In *Human Responses to the Holocaust: Perpetrators and Victims, Bystanders and Resisters*, ed. Michael D. Ryan, 121–45. New York: Edwin Mellen Press.

Kaplan, Marion. 1998. *Jewish Life in Nazi Germany: Dignity and Despair*. Oxford: Oxford University Press.

Karen, Robert. 1994. *Becoming Attached*. New York: Warner Books.

Kaufman, Debra Renee. 1996. "The Holocaust and Sociological Inquiry: A Feminist Analysis." *Contemporary Jewry* 17: 6–18.

Keilson, Hans, with the collaboration of H. Sarphatie. 1992. *Sequential Traumatization of Children: A Clinical and Statistical Follow-Up Study on the Fate of the Jewish War Orphans in the Netherlands*. Trans. Yvonne Bearne, Hilary Coleman, and Deirdre Winter. Jerusalem: Magnes Press.

Kenny, Michael G. 1999. "A Place for Memory: The Interface between Individual and Collective History." *Comparative Studies in Society and History* 41 (3): 420–38.

Kestenberg, Judith. 1995. *The Diversity of Child Survivors of the Holocaust Children: War and Persecution*, ed. Stiftung für Kinder. Osnabrück, Germany: Secolo Verlag.

———. 1996. "Hidden Children: Early Childhood and Latency." In *The Last Witness: The Child Survivor of the Holocaust*, ed. Judith S. Kestenberg and Ira Brenner, 27–52. Washington, DC: American Psychiatric Press.

Kim, Elizabeth. 2000. *Ten Thousand Sorrows: The Extraordinary Journey of a Korean War Orphan*. New York: Doubleday.

Kleinman, Arthur. 1995. "Pitch, Picture, Power: The Globalization of Local Suffering and the Transformation of Social Experience." *Ethnos* 60 (3–4): 181–91.

Kleinman, Arthur, Veena Das, and Margaret Lock. 1997. "Introduction." In *Social Suffering*, ed. Arthur Kleinman, Veena Das, and Margaret Lock, ix–xxvii. Berkeley and Los Angeles: University of California Press.

Klempner, Mark. 2006. *The Heart Has Reasons: Holocaust Rescuers and Their Stories of Courage*. Cleveland: Pilgrim Press.

Koonz, Claudia. 1987. *Mothers in the Fatherland: Women, the Family, and Nazi Politics.* New York: St. Martin's Press.

Krell, Robert. 2001. "Jewish Child Survivors as Displaced Persons." *Hidden Child* 10 (1): 4.

Kronfeld, Chana. 2006. "The Language of Love and Tea with Roasted Almonds." Paper presented at the Duke University Amichai Symposium, Durham, North Carolina.

Krystal, Henry. 1968. "Patterns of Psychological Damage." In *Massive Psychic Trauma*, ed. Henry Krystal, 212–43. New York: International Universities Press.

Kuper, Simon. 2003. *Ajax, the Dutch, the War: Football in Europe during the Second World War.* London: Orion.

LaCapra, Dominick. 1994. *Representing the Holocaust: History, Theory, Trauma.* Ithaca, NY: Cornell University Press.

———. 2001. *Writing History, Writing Trauma.* Baltimore: Johns Hopkins University Press.

Lagerwey, Mary D. 1996. "Reading Anne Frank and Elie Wiesel: Voice and Gender in Stories of the Holocaust." *Contemporary Jewry* 17: 48–65.

Lagrou, Pieter. 1997. "Victims of Genocide and National Memory: Belgium, France, and the Netherlands, 1945–1965." *Past and Present* 154 (February): 181–222.

Langer, Lawrence. 1988. "The Dilemma of Choice in the Death Camps." In *Echoes from the Holocaust: Philosophical Reflections on a Dark Time*, ed. Alan Rosenberg and Gerald Myers, 118–27. Philadelphia: Temple University Press.

———. 1991. *Holocaust Testimonies: The Ruins of Memory.* New Haven, CT: Yale University Press.

Latina Feminist Group. 2001. *Telling to Live: Latina Feminist Testimonios.* Durham, NC: Duke University Press.

Lentin, Ronit. 2000. *Israel and the Daughters of the Shoah: Reoccupying the Territories of Silence.* New York: Berghahn Books.

Lessing, Ed. 2002. "'For Me, It Became a Rebirth.'" *Hidden Child* 11 (1): 5.

Levi, Primo. 1986. "The Memory of Offense." In *Bitburg in Moral and Political Perspective*, ed. Geoffrey Hartman, 130–37. Bloomington: Indiana University Press.

Leydesdorff, Selma. 1993. "The Mythology of 'Solidarity,' as Shown by the Memory of the February Strike of 1941." In *Dutch Jewish History: Proceedings of the Symposium on the History of the Jews in the Netherlands*, ed. Jozeph Michman, 3: 353–70. Maastricht: Van Gorcum, Assen.

———. 1994. *We Lived with Dignity: The Jewish Proletariat of Amsterdam, 1900–1940.* Trans. Frank Heny. Detroit: Wayne State University Press.

———. 2002. "The Veil of History: The Integration of Jews Reconsidered." In *Dutch Jewry: Its History and Secular Culture (1500–2000)*, ed. Jonathan Israel and Reinier Salverda, 225–38. Leiden: Brill.

Lichtman, René. 2002. "The 1991 Gathering: It Changed the Course of My Life." *Hidden Child* 11 (1): 8.

Lifton, Robert Jay. 1980. "The Concept of the Survivor." In *Survivors, Victims, and Perpetrators: Essays on the Nazi Holocaust*, ed. Joel E. Dimsdale, 113–26. Washington, DC: Hemisphere Publishing Corporation.

Linden, R. Ruth. 1996. "Troubling Categories I Can't Think Without: Reflections on Women in the Holocaust." *Contemporary Jewry* 17: 18–33.

Linenthal, Edward T. 1995. *Preserving Memory: The Struggle to Create America's Holocaust Museum*. New York: Viking.

Luchterhand, Elmer. 1980. "Social Behavior of Concentration Camp Prisoners: Continuities and Discontinuities with Pre- and Postcamp Life." In *Survivors, Victims, and Perpetrators: Essays on the Nazi Holocaust*, ed. Joel E. Dimsdale, 259–83. Washington, DC: Hemisphere Publishing Corporation.

Manne, Robert. 1998. "The Stolen Generation." *Quadrant* 42 (1–2): 53.

Markle, Gerald E., et al. 1992. "From Auschwitz to Americana: Texts of the Holocaust." *Sociological Focus* 25 (3): 179–202.

Marks, Jane. 1993. *The Hidden Children: The Secret Survivors of the Holocaust*. New York: Fawcett Columbine.

Mason, Henry L. 1952. *The Purge of Dutch Quislings: Emergency Justice in the Netherlands*. The Hague: Martinus Nijhoff.

———. 1984. "Testing Human Bonds within Nations: Jews in the Occupied Netherlands." *Political Science Quarterly* 99 (2): 315–43.

Mechanicus, Philip. 1968. *Waiting for Death: A Diary*. Trans. Irene R. Gibbons. London: Calder and Boyars.

Meershoek, Guus. 1998. "The Amsterdam Police and the Persecution of the Jews." In *The Holocaust and History: The Known, the Unknown, the Disputed, and the Reexamined*, ed. Michael Berenbaum and Abraham J. Peck, 284–300. Bloomington: Indiana University Press.

Menchu, Rigoberta. 1984. *I, Rigoberta Menchu*. Trans. Ann Wright. London: Verso Press.

Meyer, Michael A. 1990. *Jewish Identity in the Modern World*. Seattle: University of Washington Press.

Michaels, Anne. 1996. *Fugitive Pieces*. London: Bloomsbury Press.

Michman, Dan. 1978. "Jewish Refugees from Germany in the Netherlands, 1933–1940." PhD diss., Hebrew University.

———. 1981. "Tmurot beyahasam shel haHollanddim layehudim erev haShoah" (Changes in the Attitude of the Dutch to the Jews on the Eve of the Holocaust). In *Mehkarim al toledot yahadut Holland* (Studies on the History of Dutch Jewry), ed. Jozeph Michman, 3: 247–62. Jerusalem: Institute for Research on Dutch Jewry.

————. 1984. "Problems of Religious Life in the Netherlands during the Holocaust." In *Dutch Jewish History: Proceedings of the Symposium on the History of the Jews in the Netherlands*, ed. Jozeph Michman, 1: 379–99. Jerusalem: Institute for Research on Dutch Jewry.

————. 1993. "The Uniqueness of the Joodse Raad in the Western European Context." In *Dutch Jewish History: Proceedings of the Fifth Symposium on the History of the Jews in the Netherlands*, ed. Jozeph Michman, 3: 374–80. Maastricht: Van Gorcum, Assen.

————. 1998. "Research on the Holocaust in Belgium and in General: History and Context." In *Belgium and the Holocaust*, ed. Dan Michman, 3–38. Jerusalem: Yad Vashem.

————. 2001. "The Place of the Holocaust of Dutch Jewry in a Wider Historical Fabric: Approaches of Non-Dutch Historians." In *Dutch Jews as Perceived by Themselves and Others: Proceedings of the Eighth International Symposium on the History of the Jews in the Netherlands*, ed. Chaya Brasz and Yosef Kaplan, 374–91. Leiden: Brill.

————. 2003. *Holocaust Historiography—A Jewish Perspective: Conceptualizations, Terminology, Approaches, and Fundamental Issues.* London: Vallentine-Mitchell.

Michman, Jozeph. 1990. "The Netherlands." In *Encyclopedia of the Holocaust*, ed. Israel Gutman, 3: 1045–57. New York: MacMillan.

————. 2001. "Ideological Historiography." In *Dutch Jews as Perceived by Themselves and Others: Proceedings of the Eighth International Symposium on the History of the Jews in the Netherlands*, ed. Chaya Brasz and Yosef Kaplan, 205–14. Leiden: Brill.

Miller, Judith. 1990. *One, by One, by One: Facing the Holocaust.* New York: Simon and Schuster.

Milton, Sybil, and Ira Nowinski. 1991. *In Fitting Memory: The Art and Politics of Holocaust Memorials.* Detroit: Wayne State University Press.

Minco, Marga. 1991. *Bitter Herbs: Vivid Memories of a Fugitive Jewish Girl in Nazi Occupied Holland.* Trans. Roy Edwards. New York: Penguin.

Modell, John, and Timothy Haggerty. 1991. "The Social Impact of War." *Annual Review of Sociology* 17: 205–24.

Moeller, Robert G. 2001. *War Stories: The Search for a Usable Past in the Federal Republic of Germany.* Berkeley and Los Angeles: University of California Press.

Mollica, Richard, Charles Poole, Linda Sen, Caroline Murray, and Svang Tor. 1997. "Effects of War Trauma on Cambodian Refugee Adolescents' Functional Health and Mental Health Status." *Journal of the American Academy of Child and Adolescent Psychiatry* 36 (8): 1982–2007.

Moore, Bob. 1986. *Refugees from Nazi Germany in the Netherlands, 1933–1945.* Dordrecht: Martinus Nijhoff Publishers.

————. 1997. *Victims and Survivors: The Nazi Persecution of the Jews in the Netherlands, 1940–1945*. London: Arnold.

Muller, Melissa. 1998. *Anne Frank: The Biography*. New York: Metropolitan Books.

Niederland, W. C. 1964. "Psychiatric Disorders among Persecution Victims: A Contribution to the Understanding of Concentration Camp Pathology and Its After-Effects." *Journal of Nervous and Mental Diseases* 139: 458–74.

Nijstad, Jaap, ed. 1990. *Westerbork Drawings: The Life and Work of Leo Kok, 1923–1945*. Hilversum: Onkemhout.

Nora, Pierre, ed. 1992. *Les Lieux de mémoire*. Vol. 7. Paris: Gallimard.

Novick, Peter. 1999. *The Holocaust in American Life*. Boston: Houghton Mifflin.

Oberschall, Anthony. 2000. "Preventing Genocide." *Contemporary Sociology* 29 (1): 1–13.

Ofer, Dalia, and Lenore Weitzman, eds. 1998. *Women in the Holocaust*. New Haven, CT: Yale University Press.

Olick, Jeffrey K., and Joyce Robbins. 1998. "Social Memory Studies: From 'Collective Memory' to the Historical Sociology of Mnemonica Practices." *Annual Review of Sociology* 24: 105–40.

Oren, Laura. 2001. "Righting Child Custody Wrongs: The Children of the 'Disappeared' in Argentina." *Harvard Human Rights Journal* 14 (Spring): 123–95.

Paldiel, Mordecai. 1993. "The Rescue of Jewish Children in Poland and the Netherlands." In *Burning Memory: Times of Testing and Reckoning*, ed. Alice Eckardt, 119–39. New York: Pergamon.

Polak, Jack. 1991. "Response to Miller's *One, by One, by One*." In *The Netherlands and Nazi Genocide*, ed. G. Jan Colijn and Marcia S. Littell, 77–90. Lewiston, NY: Edwin Mellen Press.

Polt, Renata, ed. and trans. 1999. *A Thousand Kisses: A Grandmother's Holocaust Letters*. Tuscaloosa: University of Alabama Press.

Prager, Jeffrey. 1998. *Presenting the Past: Psychoanalysis and the Sociology of Misremembering*. Cambridge, MA: Harvard University Press.

Presser, Jacob. 1988. *Ashes in the Wind: The Destruction of Dutch Jewry*. Trans. Arnold Pomerans. Detroit: Wayne State University Press. (Orig. pub. 1965.)

Read, Peter. 1998. "The Return of the Stolen Generation." *Journal of Australian Studies* 1 (Dec.): 8–24.

Riding, Alan. 2006. "Dutch to Return Art Seized by Nazis." *New York Times*, February 7. Section E, p. 1.

Riesel, Arye. 1998. "Re-education of War-Orphaned Jewish Children and Adolescents in Children's and Youth Homes in Belgium, 1945–1949." In *Belgium and the Holocaust: Jews, Belgians, Germans*, ed. Dan Michman, 438–97. Jerusalem: Yad Vashem.

Ringelheim, Joan. 1985. "Women and the Holocaust: A Reconsideration of Research." *Signs* 10 (4): 741–61.

Rittner, Carol, ed. 1998. *Anne Frank in the World: Essays and Reflections*. New York: M. E. Sharpe.

van der Rol, Ruud, and Rian Verhoeven. 1993. *Anne Frank: Beyond the Diary*. New York: Puffin Books.

Romijn, Peter. 1995. "The Image of Collaboration in Post-War Dutch Society" and "1945: Consequences and Sequels of the Second World War." *Bulletin of the International Committee for the History of the Second World War* 27/28: 311–24.

Rosenfeld, Alvin. 1991. "Popularization and Memory: The Case of Anne Frank." In *Lessons and Legacies: The Meaning of the Holocaust in a Changing World*, ed. Peter Hayes, 243–78. Evanston, IL: Northwestern University Press.

Rosensaft, Menachem, ed. 2001. *Life Reborn: Jewish Displaced Persons, 1945–1951*. Washington, DC: United States Holocaust Memorial Museum.

Rubinoff, Lionel. 1993. "Jewish Identity and the Challenge of Auschwitz." In *Jewish Identity*, ed. David Theo Goldberg and Michael Krausz, 152–70. Philadelphia: Temple University Press.

Saigh, Philip A., John A. Fairbank, and Anastasia E. Yasik. 1998. "War-Related Posttraumatic Stress Disorder among Children and Adolescents." In *Children of Trauma: Stressful Life Events and Their Effects on Children and Adolescents*, ed. Thomas W. Miller, 119–40. Madison: International Universities Press.

Schama, Simon. 1988. *The Embarrassment of Riches: An Interpretation of Dutch Culture in a Golden Age*. London: Collins.

Scheper-Hughes, Nancy, and Carolyn Sargent. 1998. *Small Wars: The Cultural Politics of Childhood*. Berkeley and Los Angeles: University of California Press.

van Schie, A. H. 1984. "Restitution of Economic Rights after 1945." In *Dutch Jewish History: Proceedings of the Symposium on the History of the Jews in the Netherlands*, ed. Jozeph Michman and Tirtsah Levie, 401–20. Jerusalem: Institute for Research on Dutch Jewry.

Sciolino, Elaine, and Jason Horowitz. 2005. "Saving Jewish Children, but at What Cost?" *New York Times*, January 9.

Segev, Tom. 2000. *The Seventh Million: The Israelis and the Holocaust*. New York: Owl Books.

———. 2006. "True Lessons of the Holocaust." *Ha'aretz Weekly*, international edition, April 29.

Sicher, Efraim. 2000. "The Future of the Past: Countermemory and Postmemory in Contemporary American Post-Holocaust Narratives." *History and Memory* 12 (2): 56–91.

Silverman, David J., and Rachel Silverman. 2006. "Many Jewish Groups Take on Darfur Persecution." *J. weekly* (March 17), 17.

Spitzer, Leo. 1998. *Hotel Bolivia: The Culture of Memory in a Refuge from Nazism*. New York: Hill and Wang.

Stark, Henry. 2002. "Coming Out of Hiding." *Hidden Child* 11 (2): 15.

Stein, André. 1993. *Hidden Children: Forgotten Survivors of the Holocaust.* Toronto: Penguin.

Sternbach, Nancy Saporta. 1991. "Re-membering the Dead: Latin American Women's Testimonial Discourse." *Latin American Perspectives* 70 (18): 91–102.

Stier, Oren. 2003. *Committed to Memory.* Amherst: University of Massachusetts Press.

Stover, Eric, and Harvey Weinstein. 2004. *My Neighbor, My Enemy: Justice and Community in the Aftermath of Mass Atrocity.* Cambridge: Cambridge University Press.

Sturken, Marita. 1997. *Tangled Memories: The Vietnam War, the AIDS Epidemic, and the Politics of Remembering.* Berkeley and Los Angeles: University of California Press.

Suleiman, Susan Rubin. 1996. "Monuments in a Foreign Tongue: On Reading Holocaust Memoirs by Emigrants." *Poetics Today* 17 (4): 639–57.

Summerfield, Derek. 1999. "A Critique of Seven Assumptions Behind Psychological Trauma Programmes in War-Affected Areas." *Social Science and Medicine* 48: 1449–62.

de Swaan, Abram. 1990. *The Management of Normality: Critical Essays in Health and Welfare.* London: Routledge.

Tec, Nechama. 1984. *Dry Tears: The Story of a Lost Childhood.* New York: Oxford University Press.

———. 1996. "Women in the Forest." *Contemporary Jewry* 17: 34–47.

———. 2003. *Resilience and Courage: Women, Men, and the Holocaust.* New Haven, CT: Yale University Press.

van Thijn, Ed. 2001. "Memories of a Hidden Child: A Personal Reflection." In *Dutch Jews as Perceived by Themselves and Others: Proceedings of the Eighth International Symposium on the History of the Jews in the Netherlands,* ed. Chaya Brasz and Yosef Kaplan, 265–76. Leiden: Brill.

Ultee, Wout, Frank van Tubergen, and Ruud Luijkx. 2001. "The Unwholesome Theme of Suicide: Forgotten Statistics of Attempted Suicides in Amsterdam and Jewish Suicides in the Netherlands for 1936–1943." In *Dutch Jews as Perceived by Themselves and Others: Proceedings of the Eighth International Symposium on the History of the Jews in the Netherlands,* ed. Chaya Brasz and Yosef Kaplan, 325–53. Leiden: Brill.

Velmans, Edith. 1998. *Edith's Story: A True Story of a Young Girl's Courage and Survival during World War II.* New York: Bantam.

Verhey, Elma. 1991. *Om het joodse kind* (About the Jewish Child). Amsterdam: Nijgh and Van Ditmar.

———. 2001. "Hidden Children in the Netherlands: The War after the War." *Hidden Child* 10 (1): 1, 2, 6, 15. Trans. Jeannette Ringold.

———. 2005. *Kind van de rekening* (Footing the Bill). Amsterdam: De Bezige Bij.

Vital, David. 1991. "After the Catastrophe: Aspects of Contemporary Jewry." In *Lessons and Legacies: The Meaning of the Holocaust in a Changing World*, ed. Peter Hayes, 120–38. Evanston, IL: Northwestern University Press.

Waite, Linda, and Maggie Gallagher. 2000. *The Case for Marriage*. New York: Broadway.

Wardi, Dina. 1992. *Memorial Candles: Children of the Holocaust*. London: Routledge.

Warmbrunn, Werner. 1963. *The Dutch under German Occupation, 1940–1945*. Stanford, CA: Stanford University Press.

Warren, Judith. 2005. *Perfect Madness: Motherhood in the Age of Anxiety*. New York: Riverhead Books.

Wasserstein, Bernard. 1996. *Vanishing Diaspora: The Jews in Europe since 1945*. Cambridge, MA: Harvard University Press.

Weine, Stevan, Daniel F. Becker, Thomas McGlashan, and Dolores Vojvoda. 1995. "Adolescent Survivors of 'Ethnic Cleansing': Observations on the First Year in America." *Journal of the American Academy of Child and Adolescent Psychiatry* 34 (9): 1153–60.

Weiss, Meira. 2001. "The Immigrating Body and the Body Politic: The 'Yemenite Children Affair' and Body Commodification in Israel." *Medical Anthropology Quarterly* 15 (2): 206–22.

Werner, Emmy. 2000. *Through the Eyes of Innocents: Children Witness World War II*. Boulder: Westview Press.

White, Naomi Rosh. 1988. *From Darkness to Light: Surviving the Holocaust*. Melbourne: Collins Dove.

Wieviorka, Annette. 1994. "On Testimony." In *Holocaust Remembrance: The Shapes of Memory*, ed. Geoffrey Hartman, 23–32. Oxford: Blackwell Publishing.

Wilkomirski, Binjamin. 1996. *Fragments: Memories of a Wartime Childhood*. Trans. Carol Brown Janeway. New York: Schocken Books.

Wolf, Diane L. 1992. *Factory Daughters: Gender, Household Dynamics, and Rural Industrialization in Java*. Berkeley and Los Angeles: University of California Press.

———, ed. 1996. *Feminist Dilemmas in Fieldwork*. Boulder: Westview Press.

———. 1997. "Family Secrets: Transnational Struggles among Children of Filipino Immigrants." *Sociological Perspectives* 40: 457–82.

———. 2002. *From Auschwitz to Ithaca: The Transnational Journey of Jake Geldwert*. Bethesda, MD: CDL Press.

Wolman, Ruth E. 1996. *Crossing Over: An Oral History of Refugees from Hitler's Reich*. New York: Twayne Publishers.

Wyman, Mark. 1998. *DPs: Europe's Displaced Persons, 1945–1951*. Ithaca, NY: Cornell University Press.

Yahil, Leni. 1990. *The Holocaust: The Fate of European Jewry, 1932–1945*. Trans. Ina Friedman and Haya Galai. New York: Oxford University Press.

Yerushalmi, Yosef Hayim. 1996. *Zakhor: Jewish History and Jewish Memory.* Seattle: University of Washington Press.

Young, Allan. 1995. *The Harmony of Illusions: Inventing Post-Traumatic Stress Disorder.* Princeton, NJ: Princeton University Press.

Young, James E. 1988. *Writing and Rewriting the Holocaust: Narrative and the Consequences of Interpretation.* Bloomington: Indiana University Press.

————. 1993. *The Texture of Memory: Holocaust Memorials and Meaning.* New Haven, CT: Yale University Press.

————. 1997. "Between History and Memory." *History and Memory* 9 (1/2): 47–58.

————. 2000. *At Memory's Edge.* New Haven, CT: Yale University Press.

van der Zee, Nanda. 1992. "The Recurrent Myth of 'Dutch Heroism' in the Second World War and Anne Frank as a Symbol." In *The Netherlands and Nazi Genocide,* ed. G. Jan. Colijn and Marcia S. Littell, 1–14. Lewiston, NY: Edwin Mellen Press.

Zerubavel, Eviatar. 1996. "Social Memories: Steps to a Sociology of the Past." *Qualitative Sociology* 19 (3): 283–300.

Zerubavel, Yael. 1995. *Recovered Roots: Collective Memory and the Making of Israeli National Tradition.* Chicago: University of Chicago Press.

Zuccotti, Susan. 1996. *The Italians and the Holocaust: Persecution, Rescue, and Survival.* Lincoln: University of Nebraska Press.

Zuckerman, Yitzhak. 1993. *A Surplus of Memory: Chronicle of the Warsaw Ghetto Uprising.* Trans. and ed. Barbara Harshav. Berkeley and Los Angeles: University of California Press.

Index

Text: 10/14 Palatino
Display: Bodoni Book; Univers Condensed
Compositor: Sheridan Books, Inc.
Indexer: Andrew Joron
Printer and binder: Sheridan Books, Inc.